ASIA: LOCAL STUDIES/GLOBAL THEMES

*Jeffrey N. Wasserstrom, Kären Wigen,
and Hue-Tam Ho Tai, Editors*

1. *Bicycle Citizens: The Political World of the Japanese Housewife*
   by Robin M. LeBlanc
2. *The Nanjing Massacre in History and Historiography*
   edited by Joshua A. Fogel
3. *The Country of Memory: Remaking the Past in Late Socialist Vietnam*
   by Hue-Tam Ho Tai
4. *Chinese Femininities/Chinese Masculinities: A Reader*
   edited by Susan Brownell and Jeffrey N. Wasserstrom
5. *Chinese Visions of Family and State, 1915–1953*
   by Susan L. Glosser
6. *An Artistic Exile: A Life of Feng Zikai (1898–1975)*
   by Geremie R. Barmé
7. *Mapping Early Modern Japan: Space, Place, and Culture in the Tokugawa Period, 1603–1868*
   by Marcia Yonemoto
8. *Republican Beijing: The City and Its Histories*
   by Madeleine Yue Dong
9. *Hygienic Modernity: Meanings of Health and Disease in Treaty-Port China*
   by Ruth Rogaski
10. *Marrow of the Nation: A History of Sport and Physical Culture in Republican China*
    by Andrew D. Morris

11. *Vicarious Language: Gender and Linguistic Modernity in Japan*
by Miyako Inoue

12. *Japan in Print: Information and Nation in the Early Modern Period*
by Mary Elizabeth Berry

13. *Millennial Monsters: Japanese Toys and the Global Imagination*
by Anne Allison

14. *After the Massacre: Commemoration and Consolation in Ha My and My Lai*
by Heonik Kwon

15. *Tears from Iron: Cultural Responses to Famine in Nineteenth-Century China*
by Kathryn Edgerton-Tarpley

16. *Speaking to History: The Story of King Goujian in Twentieth-Century China*
by Paul A. Cohen

17. *A Malleable Map: Geographies of Restoration in Central Japan, 1600–1912*
by Kären Wigen

18. *Coming to Terms with the Nation: Ethnic Classification in Modern China*
by Thomas S. Mullaney

19. *Fabricating Consumers: The Sewing Machine in Modern Japan*
by Andrew Gordon

20. *Recreating Japanese Men*
edited by Sabine Frühstück and Anne Walthall

21. *Selling Women: Prostitution, Markets, and the Household in Early Modern Japan*
by Amy Stanley

SELLING WOMEN

Amy Stanley · SELLING WOMEN

Prostitution, Markets, and the Household in Early Modern Japan

FOREWORD BY MATTHEW H. SOMMER

University of California Press

Berkeley   Los Angeles   London

University of California Press, one of the most
distinguished university presses in the United
States, enriches lives around the world by advancing
scholarship in the humanities, social sciences, and
natural sciences. Its activities are supported by the UC
Press Foundation and by philanthropic contributions
from individuals and institutions. For more information,
visit www.ucpress.edu.

University of California Press
Berkeley and Los Angeles, California
University of California Press, Ltd.
London, England

© 2012 by The Regents of the University of California

Library of Congress Cataloging-in-Publication Data

Stanley, Amy, 1978–.
   Selling women : prostitution, markets, and the
household in early modern Japan / Amy Stanley.
      p.   cm. — (Asia: local studies/global themes ; 21)
   Includes bibliographical references and index.
   ISBN 978-0-520-27090-9 (cloth : alk. paper)
   1. Prostitution—Japan—History. 2. Prostitutes—
Japan—Social conditions. 3. Women—Sexual
behavior—Japan—History. 4. Sex—Japan—
History.   I. Title.
   HQ247.A5S73   2012
   306.740952—dc23

                                 2011047050

Manufactured in the United States of America

21 20 19 18 17 16 15 14 13 12
10 9 8 7 6 5 4 3 2 1

In keeping with a commitment to support
environmentally responsible and sustainable printing
practices, UC Press has printed this book on Rolland
Enviro100, a 100% post-consumer fiber paper that is
FSC certified, deinked, processed chlorine-free, and
manufactured with renewable biogas energy. It is
acid-free and EcoLogo certified.

For my parents

CONTENTS

List of Illustrations   ix

Foreword   *Matthew H. Sommer*   xi

Acknowledgments   xvii

A Note on Currency and Prices   xxi

Introduction   1

PART ONE   REGULATION AND THE LOGIC OF THE HOUSEHOLD

1. Adulterous Prostitutes, Pawned Wives, and Purchased Women: Female Bodies as Currency   23

2. Creating "Prostitutes": Benevolence, Profit, and the Construction of a Gendered Order   45

3. Negotiating the Gendered Order: Prostitutes as Daughters, Wives, and Mothers   72

PART TWO   EXPANSION AND THE LOGIC
          OF THE MARKET   103

4. From Household to Market: Child Sellers, "Widows," and Other Shameless People   111

5. Glittering Hair Ornaments and Barren Fields: Prostitution and the Crisis of the Countryside   134

6. Tora and the "Rules of the Pleasure Quarter"   163

Conclusion   189

Notes   199

Bibliography   225

Index   243

ILLUSTRATIONS

FIGURES

1. Torii Kiyotada I, *Shin-Yoshiwara ōmon-guchi* (The Main Gate, New Yoshiwara) *51*
2. Utagawa Hiroshige II, *Nagasaki Maruyama no kei* (View of Maruyama in Nagasaki) *73*
3. Kawahara Keiga, *Ransen nyūkō no zu* (Arrival of a Dutch Ship) *74*
4. Ushibukaya, *Shinkoku Hizen Nagasaki zu*, Nagasaki pocket map *78*
5. Shitomi Momosuke, *Onna isshō michi shirube*, map of a woman's journey through life *82*
6. A nineteenth-century ranking of brothel districts from Kitagawa Morisada's encyclopedia of manners and customs *104*
7. Keisai Eisen, *Fukaya no eki* (Fukaya Station) *135*

MAPS

1. Japan *13*
2. Niigata in the early nineteenth century *112*
3. Highways and major post stations in Musashi and Kōzuke provinces *139*
4. The eastern Inland Sea region *168*

FOREWORD

Amy Stanley's wonderful book demonstrates once again Joan Scott's insight that the analytical perspective of gender changes our understanding of the big picture.[1] Stanley uses women's experience of prostitution to reinterpret two big changes that bookend the early modern period of Japanese history: the Tokugawa shogunate's establishment of a status-based social order, and the commercial boom that would eventually spell that order's doom. In the process, she also revises long-standing Eurocentric assumptions among feminist scholars about the relationship between stigma and female agency in the context of the sex trade.

The standard assumption of past scholarship (to the extent that it has considered women in this context) is that the status system imposed in the seventeenth century was *bad* for women, because it subordinated them to household heads, defined them in terms of normative family roles, and denied them individual autonomy. But in a striking act of revisionism, Amy Stanley poses the question: "bad for women" compared to *what?* She organizes her inquiry around a comparison of the condition of prostitutes under the paternalistic status system with both what had preceded it and what followed its demise. These comparisons highlight how much women actually gained under the Tokugawa order, and how much some *lost* when that regulatory regime broke down under the pressure of market forces.

Key to Stanley's argument is the insight that almost any form of order would have been preferable to the bloody chaos of the Warring States era, during which women had suffered at least as much as men. Ieyasu's great achievement was to end the warfare and impose an order that would secure a very long period of peace and stability—and within the constraints of that order, his regime extended some important protections to women, including even prostitutes.

Previously, women could be treated as liquid assets: they could be exchanged for one another, used to secure loans, and sold for cash indiscriminately. Under the new regime, however, women's status was redefined: no longer the property of men, they were now subjects of the state. This redefinition imposed limits on their commodification and on their abuse by men.

With regard to sex work, the status system distinguished prostitutes from wives: legal prostitution consisted of filial *daughters* being indentured *temporarily* into prostitution in order to help support desperately poor parents.[2] Prostitution was also spatially segregated in special urban enclaves—and both status and spatial boundaries were to be carefully policed. This paradigm of prostitution conformed to and reinforced the normative hierarchies that defined patriarchal order on both micro and macro levels. Within this framework, prostitutes could claim protection from a benevolent, paternalistic state; they might even invoke their filial obligations to parents in order to subvert their contractual obligations to brothel keepers. Moreover, although a household head was free to indenture his daughter into prostitution, he was forbidden to treat his *wife* in this way. In other words, the clear legal distinction between prostitutes and wives (reflecting a prior distinction between a father's legitimate authority over his daughter and a husband's over his wife) granted wives protection from being trafficked or forced into prostitution; it entitled them to remain monogamous within marriage. This may not seem like much, but it was far more legal protection than either sex workers or wives had had before.

The second half of Amy Stanley's book treats the explosive expansion and concomitant deregulation of the sex trade during the late Tokugawa commercial boom. Here, she offers a fundamentally dystopian interpretation of Japan's early modernization. Past scholarship has often celebrated this dynamic phase of commercialization as having a liberating effect on the individual level, by undermining the stultifyingly rigid status order imposed in the seventeenth century and fostering a consumer culture of pleasure and play. But once again, the angle of women's experience in prostitution offers a different view. The old regulatory regime had collapsed, due to the pressure of market demand and the increasing reliance of officials at all levels on the tax revenues and economic stimulus generated by the sale of sexual services. Now, the priority of promoting prosperity outweighed any official interest in enforcing old regulations; and the sex trade became an untrammeled market in which the familial obligations of filial daughters had been supplanted by the profit-driven "teahouse rules" of entrepreneurial brothel keepers backed by proto-yakuza thugs. This new system stripped sex workers of family ties and paternalistic protections, reducing them to commodities pure and simple, to be traded over increasingly long distances. Superannuated samurai were not the only losers in the demise of the old order; most sex workers and many other women lost out too.

It was in this context, in the late Tokugawa, that stigma first emerged as a significant factor. The stigmatization of prostitutes was part of a new discourse that emerged out of widespread anxiety at the threat to patriarchal authority posed by such dramatic economic and social changes.

Stigma is tricky: its sources and consequences both deserve scrutiny. It is easy to disapprove of prostitution, and there are good reasons to do so. But disapproval tends to overlook the fact that, among other things, prostitution is *work:* work that generates income and supports families, that contributes to the GDP. Prostitution may be no one's dream job, but sex workers themselves often report that it is the least bad and certainly the highest paid option realistically available to them. Most women who have engaged in sex work in different parts of the world have done so on a part-time or temporary basis in order to help support their families. In many places, prostitution may occupy a few years prior to marriage during which a young woman can help support her parents and prepare her bridal trousseau (this was certainly one pattern seen in Japan). Under the circumstances, well-intended measures to suppress the trade may actually harm the people whose welfare is their ostensible goal, by depriving them of income or driving them underground, where they become more vulnerable to exploitation and other mistreatment.

In the West, traditional moralists have tended to portray sex workers either as lascivious, avaricious, and diseased criminals who are to be reviled and punished, or as passive, enslaved victims in need of pity and rescue. In a somewhat different vein, some feminists have argued that the stigma attached to female promiscuity is so pervasive and so damning that no woman can be said really to have "chosen" sex work as a way to earn a living; in their view, it is this constraint on female agency that makes sex work wrong. What these critiques of prostitution have in common is a focus on stigma and individual agency: the stigma of sex work is taken for granted, and the question is whether a woman has chosen, or even *can* choose, to do it.

In two respects, Amy Stanley shows, Tokugawa Japan challenges these assumptions. First, female promiscuity in and of itself did not carry the intense stigma found in many other times and places. To be sure, select categories of women were expected to remain chaste or even celibate; but it was not unusual for ordinary commoner women to have more than one sexual partner over a lifetime, and such relationships did not signal moral failure. As long as prostitutes could pose as filial daughters acting on their parents' behalf, there was no problem with their promiscuity. The stigmatization of prostitutes that emerged in the late Tokugawa had a very different focus.

Second, few women (or men, for that matter) in early modern Japan had much choice about where they lived, what work they did, and whether or to whom they would marry. If you were born a peasant, most likely you would die a peasant—as would your children and grandchildren after you. In general, productive and reproductive labor would be deployed by heads of households to achieve collective goals, and the marriages of young people were arranged by elders for purposes other than individual emotional fulfillment. In that context, women's lack of choice in prostitution was unexceptional. Our emphasis on choice and consent reflects our own values, but it seems anachronistic in the historical context of early modern Japan.

In that context, as Stanley makes abundantly clear, prostitutes became targets of opprobrium only when perceived as free agents who *chose* sex work in pursuit of economic gain: it was the specter of woman as autonomous economic agent that provoked fear and loathing. In other words, what was stigmatized then is exactly what feminists might value today. The irony is that very few prostitutes really had any choice in the matter, even when punished for the perception that they did.

Stanley's narrative unfolds both chronologically and spatially, as she traces the changing geography of the sex trade. The rise of commercial agriculture created a mass market for prostitution along transportation routes for sailors and travelers, and for young peasant males with new discretionary income. After the mid-eighteenth century, the expansion of prostitution took place, not in the great cities, but in provincial towns, post stations, and villages. The urban consumer culture extended its tentacles into the countryside. Meanwhile, girls and young women were being trafficked over increasingly long distances, sundering their ties to natal families and communities.

In this environment, a new discourse emerged in which prostitutes embodied all the dangers of the alien market forces and consumerist values that were creeping into small towns and villages and that, according to panicky local patriarchs, threatened traditional modes of authority. Their fear focused on the image of the avaricious prostitute, herself free of family discipline, who would seduce gullible peasant youths away from their duties, inducing them to use their new disposable incomes to declare independence, to buy sex and even wives without deference to parents, customs, or village elders. In other words, even as sex workers lost paternalistic protections and family ties and were subjected to even more extreme forms of commodification than before, they were simultaneously made scapegoats for all the ills of the rapidly expanding market economy. This scapegoating made it even harder for women to claim the status and modest protections they had once enjoyed. In sum, the new economy and the new discourse it fostered both made conditions worse for women in the sex trade.

Stanley's account of prostitution in early modern Japan suggests intriguing parallels with China. During the eighteenth century, in China, too, an older status-based system for regulating prostitution gave way to pervasive market pressures that had rendered it obsolete. Under the old system, prostitution was tolerated as a feature of the debased legal status that attached to certain households, who were not expected (or entitled) to live according to the values associated with free commoner status, notably, female chastity. By law, wives and daughters of free commoner status were expected to remain absolutely chaste, and their extramarital sexual activity was criminal regardless of whether money changed hands. But in the context of debased legal status, prostitution was tolerated, taxed, and even protected: heads of prostitute households would pimp their wives and daughters with impunity. Such households had a stigmatized but accepted place in the social order, and on that basis sex workers and their families could claim official protection against various kinds of abuse. Moreover, there existed a large gray area in which people who had not necessarily inherited the appropriate status labels were nevertheless in practice permitted to engage in sex work.

But during the Yongzheng reign (1723–35), a series of reforms abolished the legal status categories associated with sex work, in effect promoting these households to free commoner status. The assumption was that the people so promoted would no longer engage in sex work or other debased occupations linked to their erstwhile status. What this meant in practice was the criminalization of these people's previously tolerated occupations. Of course, the result of criminalization was not the elimination of prostitution—on the contrary, sex work in its myriad forms would remain a ubiquitous phenomenon that provided vital income for a vast number of urban and rural families. Instead, the result was to drive prostitution underground, stripping sex workers and their families of legal protection, and exposing them to greater exploitation (including extortion by government functionaries).[3]

Amy Stanley's account of the late Tokugawa shows how the unraveling of a status-based regulatory regime in favor of an untrammeled market for sexual services harmed women, especially sex workers. In the Chinese case, the shift was from regulation to prohibition, yet the net result was equally harmful to women's interests. In both cases, a system of legally defined status categories had created a legitimate position for sex workers that entitled them to significant protections; and in both cases, the end of that older system increased these people's vulnerability to victimization.

Stanley's account also calls to mind the paradoxical position of prostitution in Shanghai during the Republican era (1912–49). As in late Tokugawa Japan, prostitution played a vital role in the city's economy: sex workers constituted the single largest cohort of female labor, outnumbering even the spinners in Shanghai's famous cotton mills, who are usually seen as the archetype of Chinese working-class women; and licensed prostitution paid a huge amount of revenue to the Chinese and foreign authorities who shared jurisdiction over the city. At the same time, however, elite discourse and the mass media obsessed over the perils of prostitution: the sinister threat of venereal disease, but also the ways in which the sex trade's prominence at the epicenter of semi-colonialism seemed to embody the crisis of national weakness and compromised sovereignty. As in Japan, Shanghai's sex workers became scapegoats for a host of anxieties and resentments about problems that were not their fault, even as their labor fueled the city's economy and helped finance its administration.[4]

Amy Stanley's sobering reassessment of Tokugawa history offers a perspective on commercialization from the standpoint of women who became commodities, even as they were demonized for supposedly acting as free economic agents. The narrative arc of progress does not slope in the same direction for everyone. No one mourns Japan's ancien régime—and yet, as Stanley shows, the old order treated sex workers with a modest measure of humanity and decency that, once lost, would not be seen again for a very long time.

Matthew H. Sommer
Stanford University

ACKNOWLEDGMENTS

This book began not with a flight to Japan, but with a flight of stairs. They led to Hal Bolitho's office, which was perched on top of the East Asian Languages and Civilizations building at Harvard. During my first visit to that office, when I was a sophomore in college, I told Professor Bolitho that I wanted to study Japanese history. He suggested that I specialize in the Tokugawa period. There were so many archival sources waiting to be discovered, he said, that one could even find people's shopping lists and learn what they were eating for dinner. (Food, I would later find out, was one of his favorite topics.) I took his advice. Over the next nine years—as he advised my undergraduate thesis and, eventually, my dissertation—I climbed that staircase many times. I went to get help with translations, to go over the papers he marked up with his dreaded green pen, and to discuss everything from *bushidō* to beef Wellington. He passed away last year after a long illness. I'll miss his sense of humor and always regret that I never got to send him a copy of this manuscript. I'm sure it would have benefited from a few encounters with that green pen.

Since the day Professor Bolitho convinced me to give Tokugawa history a chance, I have accumulated a number of debts to those who helped me find my way as a scholar. As a graduate student at Harvard, I was fortunate to be able to work with a wonderful cohort of fellow students and faculty members in Japanese history. Andrew Gordon was a generous adviser and mentor, and his thoughtful comments improved my work in countless ways. In the years since he signed off on my dissertation, I find myself relying on his wisdom and kindness more than ever. Dani Botsman asked the questions that inspired this book, and he has turned out to be a good friend, an incisive critic, and my favorite person with whom to debate the finer points of Tokugawa and Meiji history. Also during my time in Cambridge, seminars with Helen Hardacre, Edwin Cranston, and Mikael Adolpshon broadened my horizons, and wonderful friends and colleagues, including Marjan Boogert, Fabian Drixler, Rusty Gates, Izumi Nakayama, Emer O'Dwyer, Eiko Maruko Siniawer, Jun Uchida, and Noell Wilson made graduate school interesting and (dare I say it?) fun.

This book would not have been possible without the guidance and support of Japanese scholars. Yabuta Yutaka at Kansai University encouraged my interest in this subject, shared his vast knowledge of Tokugawa women's history, and even accompanied me to archives in Saitama and Hiroshima. I owe him a great debt. I am also grateful to Fukaya Katsumi for sponsoring my research and providing me an academic home at Waseda University. Sone Hiromi, a groundbreaking scholar in this field, shared her work and pointed me toward the archive in Yutaka-chō, where the archivist, Kataoka Satoshi, was extremely generous with his time and resources. Tsukada Takashi helped me interpret some of my documents, and Watanabe Kenji welcomed me to his seminar at Rikkyō University. Mega Atsuko, Shiba Keiko, Ōguchi Yūjirō, Nagano Hiroko, and others provided a sense of intellectual community in women's and gender history. My patient tutor, Wakui Yukiko, taught me to read *kuzushiji* and helped me decipher the archival sources that became the basis for the last chapter. Murayama Kōtarō, another wonderful teacher, continues to be a great friend, and he can explain just about anything in the field of Japanese history. Along with Kinoshita Haruka, Morimoto Ikuko, and other members of the Celery and Fukaya *zemi*, he has offered valuable advice, encouragement, and companionship over the past several years.

I am also grateful to many fellow historians of Japan who have made this an exciting and supportive field in which to work. Kären Wigen, who believed in this book from the beginning, offered insight and advice at several crucial junctures. There were many days when an encouraging e-mail from her was the only thing that kept me from quitting. Anne Walthall and David Howell read my dissertation and provided perceptive comments that helped me reenvision it as a book. Sarah Thal introduced me to the archives in Kotohira, and fellow graduate students David Eason and Mike Wert shared their perspectives on early modern history.

At Northwestern, faculty members in the History Department created a congenial and stimulating environment in which to conduct my research. I could not have asked for a better senior colleague than Laura Hein, whose insight shaped my argument and helped me come to a better understanding of my own work. Melissa Macauley also read the entire manuscript and offered excellent suggestions. Sarah Maza's comments greatly improved the book's introduction, Ed Muir helped with the big picture, Kate Masur lent books and advice, and Peter Carroll shared the view from China. At several points in the writing process, I benefitted from the support of the department chair, Peter Hayes. Conversations with colleagues too numerous to name here brightened my days and improved my work, while fellow members of the East Asian Research Seminar, especially Phyllis Lyons, Sarah Frasier, Laura Miller, and Jim Huffman, helped me refine my ideas.

During my research, I received financial support from the Japan Foundation, the Reischauer Institute, the Whiting Foundation, the Japanese Ministry of Education, Culture, Sports, Science, and Technology, and the Weinberg College of Arts and Sciences at Northwestern University. Librarians and archivists at the Saitama Prefectural Archive, the Kotohiragū Library, the Saitama Prefectural Library, the Niigata Prefectural Library, the Niigata City Library, the Niigata City History Museum, the Yutaka-chō Archive, and the Nagasaki Museum of History and Culture were unfailingly kind and helpful. Closer to home, Harriett Lightman and Qunying Li at Northwestern University Library made sure I had everything I needed to complete this book. The staff in the Interlibrary Loan department also deserves special commendation for dealing with all my complicated requests with good cheer.

I have been very lucky to work with the fantastic team at University of California Press. My editor, Reed Malcolm, and series editors, Kären Wigen, Jeffrey Wasserstrom, and Hue-Tam Ho Tai, shepherded this manuscript through the publication process. Two anonymous reviewers offered thoughtful criticism and advice. Stacy Eisenstark, Hannah Love, and Rachel Berchten answered my endless questions and kept the production schedule on track. Peter Dreyer was a careful and tactful copy editor, and Alexander Trotter did a great job with the index. Don Pirius of dpmaps.com deserves special thanks for the beautiful maps that appear in these pages.

I am indebted to my friends and family for all kinds of emotional and logistical support. During the years I spent working on this book, Masayuki, Naoko, Takuya, Saki and Kano Amagai provided me with dinners, cell phones, apartments, space heaters, birthday cards, and—most important—a Japanese family. My sister and best friend, Kate Stanley, put up with "thesis girl" in all her annoying variations and kept me up-to-date on the world outside Tokugawa Japan. My parents, John and Barbara Stanley, nurtured me in countless ways and inspired me with their lifelong dedication to teaching and learning. I cannot begin to thank my husband, Brad Zakarin, whose quick wit filled my life with laughter and whose love made everything seem possible.

Finally, to my son, Sam: Thank you for the hugs, pats on the back, and loud, smacking kisses. I needed them.

A NOTE ON CURRENCY AND PRICES

In the Tokugawa period, gold, silver, and copper were independent units of currency. Exchange rates fluctuated, and the value of copper was particularly volatile. But as a rule, one gold *ryō* bought about six silver *ryō* (sixty *monme*) or 4,000 copper *mon*. Rates hovered in this vicinity until the late 1850s, when foreign speculation drove up the value of gold in relation to silver and provoked a currency crisis.

Regional variations also complicated the picture. Traditionally, merchants in eastern Japan (including Edo and its hinterland) preferred gold currency, while those in the west (including Kyoto, Osaka, and the Inland Sea region) tended to use silver. Moreover, certain periods—the mid-nineteenth century in particular—saw rapid inflation. One gold *ryō* in 1860 bought far less than it would have in 1700, and by 1866 it bought less still.

These are the denominations of gold, silver, and copper currency and some estimations of value that are relevant to the subject of this book:

Gold: One *ryō* equals four *bu* equals sixteen *shu*

Silver: One *kan* equals 100 *ryō* equals 1,000 *monme*

Copper: One *kanmon* equals 1,000 *mon*

In general, gold and silver *ryō* were used for major expenses such as rent. This was also the currency used in contracts for indentured service. *Mon* was pocket money.

In early nineteenth-century Edo, a piece of relatively low-quality sushi cost eight *mon* and a bowl of soba cost about sixteen *mon*. During the same period, one night with a post-station or port-town prostitute in Kansai or along the Japan Sea coast averaged between 300 and 500 *mon*. In the vicinity of Edo, post-station proprietors sometimes charged as much as one *bu*, which was considered exorbitant.

INTRODUCTION

The early modern prostitute is an iconic figure in Japanese history. Like the medieval samurai and the late twentieth-century salaryman, she personifies her era. In movies, television dramas, historical fiction, and academic scholarship, she symbolizes both the economic and cultural dynamism of the shogunate's great cities and the subjugation of women during a period of intense social repression. Among her contemporaries, she occupied a similarly ambiguous, and equally prominent, place in the popular imagination. During the Tokugawa period (1600–1868), an immense volume of cultural production surrounded the sex trade, making the imagined pleasures of the brothel accessible to a broad audience. Frustrated men and curious women could indulge their fantasies with woodblock prints depicting high-class prostitutes (*yūjo*), guides to urban "pleasure quarters" (*yūkaku*), and brochures that explained the finer points of whorehouse etiquette. Or they could lose themselves in the realm of fiction, where *yūjo* appeared as the tragic heroines of short stories and kabuki plays.

This proliferation of seductive imagery obscured a less palatable reality. Prostitution was not only a social institution that allowed men to enjoy sexual and aesthetic entertainment; it was also a business that relied on the labor of poor young women. In this regard, its economic impact was enormous. Since prostitution did not create a tangible product, there are no bales of rice, reels of silk, bags of salt, or bolts of cotton cloth to enumerate as evidence of its scope. Instead, its influence must be measured in its geographical reach and in the number of women it employed.

Unfortunately, counting prostitutes has proved to be a nearly impossible task for historians, even those who work on periods for which modern statistical data are available.[1] In the case of Tokugawa Japan, the difficulty is magnified. There was no comprehensive, countrywide census, and population records from various jurisdictions are fragmentary. Moreover, brothel keepers wishing to elude regulation or evade taxes often lied about how many prostitutes they employed. Still, rough estimates suggest that many young women in urban areas were involved in selling sex. The shogun's capital of Edo (later renamed Tokyo) had roughly one million residents in the mid-nineteenth century, approximately 60 percent of whom were commoners. Population registers from the middle of the 1840s counted seven thousand *yūjo* in Yoshiwara and about a thousand "serving girls" (*meshimori onna*) in post stations on the city's outskirts, yielding a total of around eight thousand officially recognized prostitutes. But this number did not take into account brothel workers in dozens of other entertainment districts, nor did it include geisha, streetwalkers, and those who sold sex part-time. Adding these women and allowing for post-station innkeepers' tendency to undercount yields a conservative estimate of somewhere between ten and fifteen thousand.[2] Meanwhile, elsewhere in the archipelago, several tens of thousands of prostitutes worked in designated areas in shogunal cities and castle towns, in the lively neighborhoods surrounding pilgrimage sites, at post stations strung along rural highways, and in countless ports dotting the coastline. Some were *yūjo* and serving girls indentured to brothels and inns, while others were itinerant peasants who sold sex when they could not find other work.

These women were not marginal figures, and they did not labor in an underground segment of the economy. The sex trade was ubiquitous and deeply embedded in everyday life. By the end of the Tokugawa period, it is unlikely that there were many adults on the archipelago, whether they were male or female, rich or poor, urban or rural, who had never encountered a woman who worked, had worked, or would someday work in the sex trade. Even fewer would have been unaware of the substantial profits prostitutes generated for their employers or ignorant of their contributions to government coffers. Prostitution was an obvious source of wealth and revenue, and like other major enterprises, it reshaped the demographic profiles of the cities and towns where it flourished. It also altered patterns of social life, shifting the balance of power within families and straining relationships between neighbors. The young women who supplied labor to this endeavor, colloquially called "selling women" (*baijo* or *baita*), were not only hailed as icons of sophistication and coveted as objects of desire; they were also recognized as economic actors whose work transformed communities across Japan.

Their vast business is the subject of this book, which considers how prostitution shaped the relationship between the household, the state, and the emerging market economy in early modern Japan. The following chapters explain how the sex trade achieved its formidable influence and examine the destabilizing consequences of its expansion. They also address the many ways in which prostitution became the focus of contention over the place of women within their families, communities, and the realm at large. The exchange of sex for payment was a unique economic endeavor in that it raised questions, not only about the appropriate relationship between the state and commercial development, but also about the permissibility of treating female bodies as objects of exchange. Thus the astonishing growth of the sex trade prompted people from all walks of life to attempt to demarcate boundaries between the household and the marketplace and to define the limits of women's autonomy in both spheres. As the business of selling women expanded across the archipelago, it left an indelible mark on the landscape, changing relationships between men and women, prostitutes and wives, parents and children, farmers and townspeople, and rulers and subjects.

PROSTITUTION, CHOICE, AND MORALITY

The mention of prostitution in early modern Japan conjures up images of an exotic Far East where innocent women were sold into servitude and compelled to cater to men's erotic desires. This characterization of Japan has a long history in the United States. The Congregational minister, author, and educator William Elliot Griffis, who first traveled to the archipelago in 1870, included a discussion about prostitution in his popular book *The Mikado's Empire* (1876), which established him as America's foremost expert on Japan. In an uncharacteristically critical passage, he lamented that "the Japanese maiden, as pure as the purest Christian virgin, will at the command of her father enter the brothel tomorrow, and prostitute herself for life."[3] He intended this statement to illustrate the extreme subjugation of Japanese women, which, he believed, only the introduction of Christianity could remedy. But his account of submissive virgins forced into brothels had another, perhaps unforeseen, consequence: it presented Japan as a place of sexual possibilities scarcely imagined in the United States. Two images of the archipelago—one disturbingly barbaric and the other beguilingly erotic—are intertwined in his account of Japanese women's suffering, mutually enhancing a sense of Japan's distance from the straight-laced, presumably enlightened West.

Similar Orientalist stereotypes of the Japanese sex trade still loom large in the American popular imagination, most recently fueling the success of Arthur

Golden's novel *Memoirs of a Geisha* (1997).[4] These discourses about prostitution, which emphasize women's oppression and their submission, "otherize" the Japanese past. But if we dismiss Tokugawa Japan as unfathomably backward and distant, we might also miss what the examination of prostitution in this era has to contribute to debates about sex work in other times and places. Among them is a contentious question that has long preoccupied feminist theorists and historians: can labor in the sex industry be interpreted as an exercise of agency by women making rational economic decisions, or is the stigma attached to the profession so overwhelming that the "choice" to sell sex can never be freely made?[5]

The former position—that prostitution is an exercise of agency—assumes that women can choose to work in the sex trade for their own benefit. The latter—that degradation cannot be freely "chosen"—assumes that the stigma attached to female promiscuity is universal. Neither premise applies to Tokugawa Japan. First, Japanese women in that era almost never made autonomous decisions to exchange sex for payment. As the following chapters discuss, most prostitutes were indentured to brothels as children or young teenagers. Since their salaries were paid to their parents in advance, unless they received small gifts or tips from clients, they never saw the proceeds from their long years of labor. For this reason, the practice of indenturing a woman to a brothel was literally called "body-selling" (*miuri*), reflecting the prostitute's lack of volition. At the same time, female promiscuity was not heavily stigmatized. Commoners, who accounted for over 90 percent of the population, did not automatically associate promiscuity with moral failing, shame, or humiliation. Although Confucian-influenced texts emphasizing the importance of female chastity circulated widely by the middle of the eighteenth century, these teachings had to contend with a heterogeneous collection of religious beliefs and practices surrounding sex. Many of these regarded heterosexual intercourse as polluting, but they did not universally condemn sex outside of wedlock.[6] Rather, the location and timing of intercourse (or, in the case of supposedly celibate monks and nuns, the religious status of participants) marked certain sex acts as transgressive. Thus prostitution might be frowned upon if it took place near a sacred site or served as a temptation to monks, but the idea that one woman might have multiple partners, or that she might have intercourse outside of wedlock, was not inherently problematic.

Among townspeople and peasants, it was not unusual for a woman to have more than one sexual partner over the course of a lifetime. Tokugawa-era commoners cohabitated before formalizing their marriages, divorced relatively frequently, and accepted widow remarriage as a matter of course. Adultery, defined as sex between a married woman and a man who was not her husband, was widely understood to be immoral, but only because an unfaithful wife had undermined her spouse's authority in the household and disturbed the social order within her community, not because she had pursued sexual relationships with multiple men.[7] These mores were not consistent across class boundaries, and they changed over time: by the middle of the eighteenth century, the daughter of a prosperous peasant family would certainly have been expected to refrain from premarital sex. But chastity never became a universal standard of sexual morality by which all women were judged and prostitutes were found wanting.

This was not the case elsewhere in East Asia, where commoners drew moral distinctions between prostitutes and other women. In Chŏson Korea, legal prostitution was restricted to a hereditary class of entertainers called *kisaeng*, who often became the concubines of wealthy men. Art and literature celebrated them as romantic heroines, but their sexual availability marked them as the moral inferiors of both elite and commoner women, who aspired to Confucian ideals celebrating abstinence outside of marriage.[8] These mores inspired a more judgmental attitude toward the open display of promiscuity. Korean ambassadors who visited Tokugawa Japan were appalled at the number of brothels lining the shogun's highways, regarding them as proof of Japanese licentiousness.[9]

In Qing China, too, Confucian norms inspired the legal and social marginalization of promiscuous women. As in Chŏson Korea, literati celebrated high-class prostitutes' beauty and lauded their artistic accomplishments. Few condemned courtesans for their occupation; rather, they expressed sympathy for poor girls whose parents had "cast them into the mire." Yet their stories often portrayed courtesans as tragic heroines who aspired to sexual fidelity even when it was impossible, thus cementing the ideal that "ordinary" women should value chastity.[10] Japanese literature employed similar tropes, particularly in plays for kabuki and puppet theater, but the Qing legal context was quite different from the Tokugawa. In the early eighteenth century, the Yongzheng emperor outlawed prostitution, making the point that all his female subjects, regardless of their status or economic situation, should be monogamous within marriage and otherwise chaste. Thereafter, prostitutes and their customers were punished for "illicit sexual intercourse," and pimps were subject to stiff penalties for abetting it.[11] Attitudes among non-elite, illiterate people are more difficult to discern, but evidence from criminal case records suggests that even peasant wives and widows often had a stake in promoting or appearing to promote the chastity ideal.[12]

Because female promiscuity has been condemned in so many historical and cultural contexts, it is tempting to assume that the defining fact of prostitution is that it involves sex with multiple partners and that prostitutes are reviled because they are sexually undisciplined. Following this logic, many studies position the history of the sex trade within the history of sexuality and the body.[13] But prostitution is also a business—an explosive combination of sex and money—and Tokugawa-era Japanese were usually far more concerned about the latter than the former. To them, the salient fact about prostitution was not that it involved female promiscuity but that it required the exchange of cash. For this reason, they did not often insult licentious or adulterous women by calling them "whores," although writers of popular fiction suggested that promiscuous women might want to engage in prostitution in order to indulge in their favorite activity. In general, unless a woman (or, more likely, her pimp or brothel keeper) received payment for her services, it made no sense to call her a prostitute.

Like Tokugawa-era commentators, I focus on prostitution not as a stigmatized sexual practice, but as an economic endeavor with moral implications that changed over time. The expansion of the sex trade occurred in tandem with the emergence of a market economy, a trend that began in the cities of Osaka and Kyoto at the turn of the eighteenth century and spread to the countryside by the beginning of the 1800s. In this context, when people—usually samurai officials and elite male commoners—debated the issue of "selling women" and their trade, they were weighing the cultural differences between rural and urban Japan, or addressing the problem of why some regions developed rapidly while others were left behind, or considering whether authorities should prioritize protecting their subjects over encouraging development. To men schooled in Confucian ethics, which defined a good government as one that promoted agriculture, discouraged overconsumption, and ensured at least a basic level of subsistence to all its subjects, these were weighty moral issues.

Undergirding these debates was a common concern about the integrity of the patriarchal family in the face of economic change. By the end of the eighteenth century, the expansion of commercial agriculture and the proliferation of cottage industries had forced commoners and samurai alike to grapple with the phenomenon of women participating in profit-making enterprises outside the household. This development seemed to hold out the promise of economic and social autonomy for wives and daughters who had formerly been subordinate to male household heads. In particular, the idea that women might voluntarily choose to work as prostitutes, even though this was only a perception and almost never a reality, was unsettling, because it suggested that they might deploy their sexuality for profit rather than in service to the household. Taken to its extreme, this portended a future in which all women might become autonomous economic actors, concerned more for their own financial prospects than the well-being of their parents, husbands, or children.

As in other national contexts, the perception of a moral "problem" with prostitution coincided with the identification of a problem with women in general. However, in early modern Japan, this sense of crisis was associated with the impending triumph of individual choice over obligation, rather than with the breakdown of bodily discipline and rationality. This meant that women did not decide to sell sex in spite of the stigma associated with promiscuity. Rather, anxiety surrounding female agency actually *created* the negative value judgment attached to the act of exchanging sex for payment. It was only when prostitutes were suspected of choosing and personally benefiting from their profession that they became targets of opprobrium.

Since prostitutes were almost always indentured servants, who had not chosen their occupation and who worked on behalf of their parents, it is ironic that elite men came to perceive them as representatives of women's economic and social emancipation from the household. But it was their visibility, not the reality of their situation, that made prostitutes useful symbols. They appeared along roadsides, adorned in colorful clothes and calling out in loud voices. They were, quite literally, women outside the household. Moreover, their dress and comportment ensured that they did not blend in with local populations of women, particularly in rural areas. As their numbers increased, it was easy for samurai officials and village headmen to single them out and contrast them with virtuous wives and daughters. The paradoxical result was that the same women who would have been praised in seventeenth-century cities as paragons of filial piety were maligned in the nineteenth-century countryside as selfish opportunists.

This rhetorical shift illuminates how Tokugawa-era elites viewed themselves and their society. For men, prostitutes' bodies promised gratification. Among different constituencies—clients, magistrates, brothel keepers, parents, and village headmen—they aroused fantasies, not only of erotic fulfillment, but also of making money, reinvigorating neighborhoods, reviving failing domestic economies, or saving villages. By patronizing prostitutes, extending them legal protections, employing them in brothels, or using their indenture money to support families, men were able to become or imagine themselves as generous patrons, benevolent governors, prominent businessmen, and the patriarchs of stable, intact households.[14] But by the late eighteenth century, prostitutes began to provoke nightmares about the decaying countryside, the failing state, and the crumbling family. They held up a mirror that turned those benevolent governors into despots, generous patrons into irresponsible hedonists, patriarchs into immoral child sellers, and businessmen into parasites. Discomfited by this reflection, men blamed women for showing them what they preferred not to see. The sex trade's size and scope had made it obvious that the wealthy oppressed the poor, men preyed upon women, parents exploited their children, and rulers either enabled or helplessly observed this process. The moral crisis attending prostitution was, on a broader scale, the crisis of a society grappling with the unsettling ramifications of an economic transformation.

THE SEX TRADE AND TOKUGAWA HISTORY

The sex trade so pervaded Tokugawa society that its history can also be read as a history of social and economic change in early modern Japan. At the same time, it can challenge the standard narrative by forcing us to view it from the unaccustomed perspective of the poor young women who worked in prostitution. The crude outlines of the familiar story are as follows. After over a century of constant warfare, the Tokugawa shogunate succeeded in pacifying the archipelago in the first years of the seventeenth century. In order to mobilize resources and ensure its own military preparedness, the new regime began to sort and categorize the population. Following some precedents that had been established by commoners themselves, as they organized to protect their interests amid the warfare of the sixteenth century, governors assigned households to various status groups (samurai, outcasts, peasants, townspeople, etc.), with designated places of residence and obligations to the state. For example, samurai in castle towns were delegated responsibility for governing and defending the realm, peasants in villages were burdened with providing tax revenue to their warrior overlords, and outcasts in designated hamlets were required to undertake stigmatizing tasks such as executing criminals (these developments are treated in more detail in chapter 1).[15]

This framework created the social and political stability necessary for economic growth, which is examined in greater depth in the prologue to Part II of this book. By the end of the 1600s, as samurai exchanged tax rice for cash and luxury goods at central markets, urban centers such as Osaka, Kyoto, and Edo were thriving. In the following century, rural areas began to develop, albeit unevenly, as cultivators started to orient production toward the market. By the turn of the nineteenth century, peasants in most regions had embraced commercial agriculture, and provincial towns were booming. Samurai who lived on fixed stipends, which were usually paid in rice, suffered as its price fell and demand for processed and manufactured goods increased. The relative poverty of the ruling class, along with an increasingly obvious mismatch between commoners' assigned occupations (typically as rice cultivators) and their actual livelihoods (as sake brewers, moneylenders, etc.), threatened the logic of the status order. The shogunate's inability to cope with economic change contributed to its weakness and eventual collapse in 1868, the proximate cause of which was a rebellion by samurai who opposed the regime's handling of incursions by Western powers.

The story related in the following pages adds a new dimension to this narrative. First, it calls attention to how, in Joan Scott's words, "politics constructs gender and gender constructs politics."[16] As the first chapters of this book argue, the Tokugawa system of rule, which took shape over the middle decades of the seventeenth century, transformed women from property held by their household heads into female subjects of the state. This point is sometimes lost in the growing body of work on the status system, which focuses on how male heads of household were divided into occupational groups.[17] But when young women are placed at the center of this narrative of political change, it becomes clear that the status order was also a gendered order, because the construction of status would not have been possible without the initial work of constituting households and establishing gendered divisions of power within them. While the early Tokugawa rulers claimed to make a polity in the image of the patriarchal household, they also remade patriarchal households in the idealized image of the polity. The legal innovations of the mid-seventeenth century created miniature realms of benevolent patriarchs and dutiful dependents in order to mirror a larger realm of benevolent governors and dutiful subjects. Many feminist historians have pointed out that this logic, which equated wifely loyalty to political submission, limited women's autonomy: laws subordinated women to male heads of household and established harsh penalties for adultery, which was analogous to treason.[18] But there was another element to this shift. Since patriarchs, like rulers, were supposed to wield benign authority rather than despotic power, the Tokugawa state also limited men's control over women's bodies. From the mid-seventeenth century onward, the state, not the individual patriarch, would determine whether a woman was eligible to be sold or rented out for sex.

The shogunate's laws divided women into groups of wives and prostitutes. Neither category allowed for sexual or social autonomy: wives owed fealty to their husbands and prostitutes were bound to their employers. However, both groups could claim certain protections from the state. Wives were entitled to monogamy, and no longer needed to fear being bought or sold. Prostitutes, on the other hand, had a legal status that was premised on their role as dutiful daughters who worked to support their parents. By invoking this status, they could ask officials for protection from abusive brothel keepers and unscrupulous traders. These opportunities were limited, since this strategy of appeal required the presence and cooperation of parents who would support their daughters' claims to filial piety. Nevertheless, this possibility of resistance meant that prostitutes did not experience the new political order solely as a form of oppression; in some circumstances, it could be a source of security.

This delicate balance of subjugation, obligation, and protection was destroyed by economic developments that transformed the realm, and in particular the countryside, during the late eighteenth century. Recent scholarship has argued that the market economy threatened to break the strictures of the established political, social, and even spatial orders.[19] In the second half of this book, I contend that a gendered notion of order was also destroyed. The rapid growth of the sex trade, the result of a sharp increase in demand on the part of newly prosperous commoners, threatened the hierarchies of age and gender that undergirded the realm and bound communities together. Ultimately, many elite commoners and samurai officials came to believe that prostitution was destroying households and destabilizing the realm. In their view, the sex trade reduced sexual relations to financial transactions, supplanting marital bonds with market relations. It tore women from their home provinces and transported them across the archipelago, turning daughters and subjects into commodities. And it gave increasing numbers of unmarried women the opportunity to appear in public wearing bright clothing and gold hair ornaments, making the prospect of life outside the household look perversely alluring to girls from "good" families. But despite these misgivings, traditional elites found themselves powerless to curb the expansion of the sex trade, which was an increasingly vital segment of the rural economy. Poor peasants who indentured their daughters used the proceeds to make tax payments, levies on brothels supported the administration of post stations and port towns, and prostitution attracted travelers and pilgrims to jurisdictions that depended on their patronage.

This could be construed as part of a liberating trend, one in which tired standards of official morality and hierarchical means of political organization were undermined by the emergence of the market economy. Some who celebrate the cultural dynamism of the Tokugawa period argue that commoners used their newly acquired discretionary income to participate in a "culture of play," which included patronizing brothels, in order to escape to a separate realm in which the shogunate's exhortations to diligence and frugality were rendered meaningless. Women who imitated the style of famous prostitutes, like men who indulged in the sensual delights of the "pleasure quarter," were forming relationships based on their shared participation in recreational activities and common aesthetic tastes rather than their positions within a fixed status hierarchy. Thus the non-everyday space of the "floating world" (*ukiyo*) offered an oblique, yet effective, way of protesting an oppressive social and political order.[20] But apart from a very privileged few, the women who worked in brothels and bathhouses were suffering, not playing, and their floating world was not a place of shared pleasure or radical aesthetic experimentation.[21] Most had little reason to celebrate the expansion of their business or to admire the ways in which their clients' pursuit of gratification undermined the dictates of prudish authorities.

Rather, as the sex trade began to elude official control, prostitutes became products circulating within a market rather than subjects with fixed places in an orderly realm, and it became more difficult for them to rely on their standing within the status system to demand benevolence and protection. Some were indeed liberated by the proliferation of opportunities to work in prostitution, which allowed them to escape impoverished families, migrate to more prosperous areas, and pursue social mobility. But more were left behind. They were separated from parents and communities that might have offered protection, victimized by rapacious brothel keepers, and denied the support of local officials who were more interested in proprietors' profits than young women's welfare. This, too, was the product of a freewheeling popular culture in which everything was for sale, and the legacy of an era in which patterns of consumption, rather than status-bound relationships, were beginning to determine individuals' places in the world.

GEOGRAPHY AND ORGANIZATION

The Tokugawa-era sex trade, like other businesses, adhered to a particular geography. This principle operated not only within cities, where peripheral areas might be designated "pleasure quarters," but also across the archipelago in its entirety. Large urban centers typically featured a diverse array of sexual services, established to cater to sophisticated upper-class men as well as down-and-out manual laborers. Smaller clusters of brothels tended to spring up in male-dominated areas, such as mining towns, and in places where travelers and sailors congregated, such as port cities and pilgrimage sites. In some cases, particularly in maritime cities, the demography of these areas shifted so that among permanent residents, women actually outnumbered men; the "extra" women were prostitutes catering to a transient male population. Meanwhile, small villages typically did not have the population density necessary to support a thriving sex trade. A widow might establish a small operation catering to her neighbors, but that was usually the extent of the business.

Employment patterns in prostitution also followed their own spatial logic, which usually reflected local variations in the cost of female labor. City proprietors recruited from nearby neighborhoods, taking advantage of a large pool of lower-class townspeople willing to indenture their daughters to brothels. But in provincial towns situated along transportation routes, procurers tended to seek out even cheaper sources of labor in impoverished regions served by the same roads and waterways. Along the post roads of northeastern Japan, for example, brothels typically employed women from Echigo province. Recruiters who focused on this area timed their visits to coincide with seasons when local peasants were most desperate: the early spring, when food stores were running low, and the late summer, when tax payments were due. They led unsophisticated peasant girls over the mountain passes to work in provincial brothels, where customers would not protest if their companions for the night spoke with country accents. Over time, these recruitment patterns were reinforced by the familiarity of procurers with certain regions and villages, and groups of women in the same post station would hail from the same county in Echigo.

As this book traces the shifting geography of early modern Japan's sex trade, each chapter alights in a different region of the archipelago, beginning in the northern wilderness in 1600 and ending along well-trodden Inland Sea pilgrimage routes at the close of the era (see map 1). This method of organization asks the reader to keep track of movements across space as well as changes over time. Yet I believe this structure has an important advantage over the single-city studies that have been typical of histories of prostitution in other times and places. First of all, as noted above, labor arrangements and working conditions in the sex trade varied depending on the particulars of a town's economy and its position in relation to roads, temples, mines, and harbors. Moreover, a region's position as a supplier of women to work in brothels or as a center of demand for sexual services often determined local residents' attitudes toward prostitution and prostitutes. Differences in jurisdiction could also have profound consequences for women working in the sex trade: if a woman wished to protest her mistreatment at the hands of a brothel keeper, she was probably better off appealing to a samurai magistrate who took the idea of benevolent rule seriously than a local merchant serving as town elder who was more interested in promoting area businesses.

The structure of this book is also intended to reveal how change over time entailed change over space. In the early Tokugawa period, brothels were an urban phenomenon. Although small-scale businesses might have operated in provincial towns and ports, the sex trade did not begin to thrive in these areas until the middle

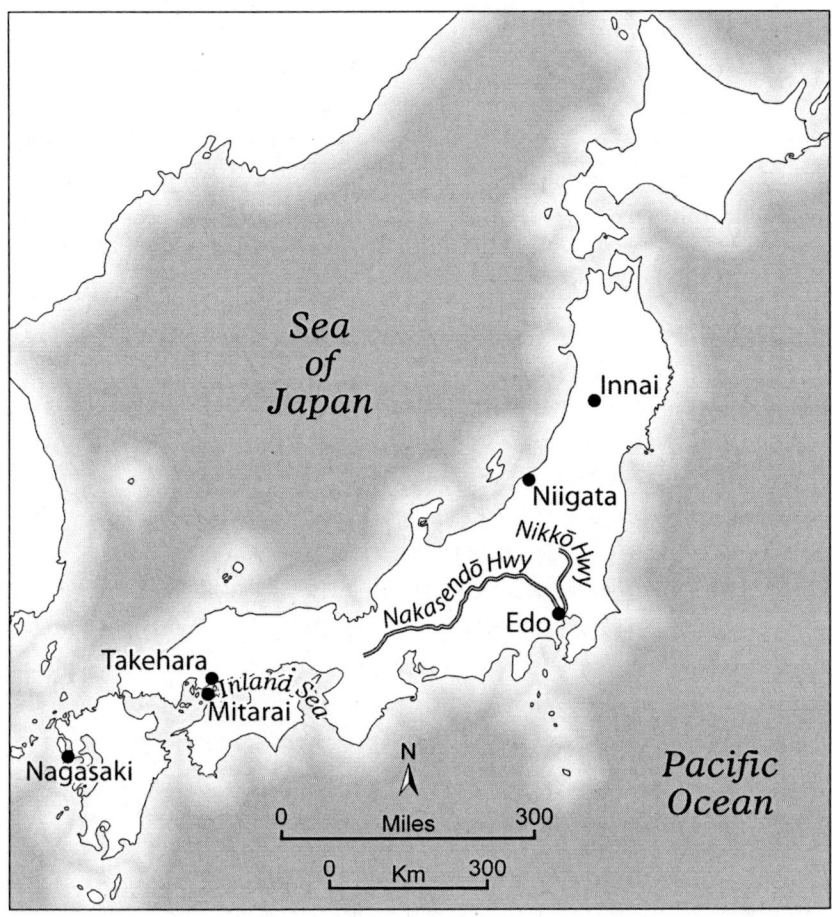

MAP 1.
Japan, highlighting sites mentioned in text.

of the era. The rise of commercial agriculture, in particular, created a market for prostitution by sending travelers and sailors along improved transportation routes and granting peasants the discretionary income necessary to purchase sex. Thus after the mid-eighteenth century, most of the expansion of the sex trade occurred, not in great cities, but in the provincial towns surveyed in the final chapters. These geographical shifts created social tension as local commoners and administrators were forced to confront the fact that the consumer culture of the cities had taken root in their villages and small towns. They were more likely than their counterparts in urban areas to worry that traditional modes of authority would be disrupted by the growth of prostitution.

Nevertheless, there was some contingency involved in my choice of historical sites. Assuming that there was no "typical" castle town, port town, or pilgrimage site, I looked for places that illuminated important legal developments or economic trends rather than those that could bear the impossible burden of representativeness. Generous Japanese scholars led me to some of my locations. Sone Hiromi told me that there was a cache of documents relating to prostitution in the small town of Yutaka-chō in the Inland Sea; Watanabe Kenji introduced me to Umezu Masakage's diary and Innai Ginzan; and Usami Misako's work inspired me to look at post stations in general and the northern Kantō in particular. Nagasaki and Edo, both major shogunal cities, might seem to be the most obvious locales for study, but I chose them last, realizing that I needed to establish how the shogunate's gendered order was established and manipulated in administrative centers. Happily, since the dynamics of the sex trade varied between sites, the sources left behind in these locations also diverged, revealing different aspects of women's lives and separate problems involved in regulating prostitution. In Nagasaki, for example, the shogunate's surveillance of prostitutes who served foreign clients produced a criminal case record that provided intriguing details about indentured women's day-to-day concerns. In Edo, the documentary record was silent on these issues, but it provided many more examples of how brothel keepers navigated their relationship with the shogunate. Records from villages in Musashi and Kōzuke provinces, on the other hand, contained a wealth of information on how local residents perceived the prostitutes who worked in their midst. In moving from place to place, I hope I was able to capture the various social and political consequences of the sex trade's expansion.

In all the locations visited in these chapters, Tokugawa-era Japanese used an astonishing variety of names to refer to women who sold sex as an occupation. Terms employed in popular discourse expressed playful ideas about prostitutes' activities (e.g., a *yotaka* (night hawk) was a streetwalker who pounced on men after dark) or indicated gradations of rank (in Yoshiwara, a *tayū* ranked higher than an *oiran*). In the shogun's and domains' laws, various words for women who sold sex were intended to express differences in legal status. In the shogunate's documents, a prostitute within the sanctioned "pleasure quarter" was always a *yūjo* and an unrecognized prostitute was always a *baijo*. In other contexts, however, these categories disintegrated. Domain authorities and local officials referred to *yūjo* in all kinds of neighborhoods, whether or not the shogunate would have considered the women legal, reflecting the fact that the legality or illegality of prostitution was often defined locally.²² At the same time, townsmen began to call government-sanctioned *yūjo* as well as illegal "clandestine prostitutes" (*kakushi baijo*) by the same slang term, *baita,* which is best translated as "whore."²³ Other terminology reflected the porous boundary between prostitutes and "ordinary" women. In Inland Sea port towns, women named in brothel registers were often called "servant girls" (*gejo*), and in the town surrounding the temple-shrine complex at Konpira, prostitutes were variously referred to as "tea-steeping girls" (*chatate onna*) and "drink-pouring girls" (*shakutori onna*). In Niigata, women who sold sex were often dubbed "widows" (*goke*), while the shogunate called prostitutes who worked in its territory but outside designated "pleasure quarters" "meal-serving girls" (*meshimori onna*, hereafter referred to as "serving girls") and "laundry girls" (*sentaku onna*).²⁴ Without contextual knowledge from other sources, it would be difficult to discern that these women sold sex at all.

This proliferation of names raises the problem of linguistic categorization—can all these women be considered part of the same group of "prostitutes"? My answer is yes. Although their working conditions, places of residence, and relationships to legal authority differed, they shared an occupation: they exchanged sexual services for cash payment, in order to generate profits for a brothel or to support themselves or their families. And in fact, as the following chapters make clear, selling sex was not the only thing they had in common.²⁵ Although an exclusive urban *yūjo* might have insisted that she bore no resemblance to a post-station serving girl, the terms of their indenture contracts were nearly identical. In addition, as chapter 4 points out, prostitutes who worked in different places and were called by different names were sometimes the same women, encountered earlier or later in their careers. Nevertheless, women's employment arrangements and experiences of labor in the sex trade varied as they moved across the archipelago, and their rulers' and neighbors' judgments of their behavior changed over time and space. While the language I use to refer to women who exchanged sex for payment is consistent, the organization of this book is intended to highlight these spatial and temporal transformations in what it meant to be a prostitute in early modern Japan.

Some readers may wonder why I have left out an entire category of prostitutes: men. As other scholars have demonstrated, male prostitution flourished in Tokugawa Japan, catering to both men and, to a lesser extent, women.²⁶ But female and male prostitution were not the same business; in fact, they were not even symmetrical businesses. The female sex trade was dominated by brothel prostitution, which by the middle of the nineteenth century was a huge, independent, and well-integrated industry that spanned the archipelago. In contrast, the male sex trade tended to be closely associated with and dependent on the theater world—men's sexual services were sold in theater district "teahouses" (*kagemajaya*) or by roving bands of "actors." Perhaps for this reason, the richest Tokugawa-era sources on male prostitution tend to come from the realm of literature (short stories, guides to sexual pleasure, etc.) published in large cities. Male prostitution is almost never mentioned in the records of official business from the small towns and villages discussed in this book (with the important exception of Konpira, which was known for its theater). Finally, the businesses of male and female prostitution followed different trajectories. By the nineteenth century, contemporary commentators all agreed that male prostitution, even "male-male love" in general, had declined.[27] But as the following chapters make clear, female prostitution expanded.

The issues of male and female prostitution also occupied different spheres within an elite discourse on social problems. The shogunate considered the two varieties of the sex trade to be distinct juridical subjects. Male prostitution was never recognized and regulated, nor was it subject to the same scheme of punishments accorded to clandestine female prostitution. To a certain extent, samurai authorities considered both male and female prostitution to be threatening for the same reasons: they promoted profligacy and could incite violence among patrons competing for the same person's favors. But in general, as Gregory Pflugfelder notes, "unsanctioned forms of male-female sexuality provoked greater anxiety among shogunal officials than male-male."[28] This was equally true among elite commoners. Village headmen lamented that their sons spent their money consorting with female prostitutes and their daughters imitated the style of "women in service," but they did not express any opinion whatsoever on male prostitution. This may be because male prostitutes were far less visible in rural areas. But it may also be linked to men and women's different places within the household. Male prostitutes were not perceived to be in competition with local youths as marriage partners; young men and women would never buy out boys, bring them home to the villages, and start families. In fact, the most common analogy that linked male prostitution and familial relationships was not to marriage, but to the bond between an older brother and a younger brother, which suggests that any discussion that connected male prostitution to the fate of the household would have proceeded along different lines.

Part 1 of this book, "Regulation and the Logic of the Household," concentrates on the first two centuries of Tokugawa rule (with occasional forays into the 1800s). It opens in Innai Ginzan, a city that sprang from the wilderness in the early seventeenth century, before the shogunate was able to enforce its prohibitions on the indiscriminate sale of people. This chapter describes the traffic in daughters, wives, maidservants, and other household dependents that emerged from wartime chaos and survived into the first decades of the early modern era. Motivated by the exigencies of domain finance, Innai's magistrate allowed women to be alienated as property, used as currency, or held as collateral—whatever would serve the domain's interests in collecting taxes or enabling men to raise capital. But married women who petitioned the magistrate's office to contest the extent of their husbands' power over their bodies argued that there should be clear distinctions between wives and prostitutes, asserting that the former deserved special protection under the law. Their vision of their place in the realm was never confirmed by the domain administration, but it presaged legal reforms that would later reshape the traffic in people and establish divisions between women who could be sold or lent out for sex and other women.

The next two chapters concentrate on major shogunal cities in order to establish how the Tokugawa legal order functioned at its zenith, separating prostitutes from other women but granting them a platform to appeal for benevolence. Chapter 2 examines the halting process through which samurai officials and brothel keepers in the capital, Edo, reshaped the sex trade. Shogunal authorities, who were concerned that brothels might provide safe haven for rebels and destroy households by trafficking in girls from "good families," cooperated with brothel keepers to create an approach to regulation that addressed both the supply and demand for sexual services. This system enforced new ideas about the place of women in the realm. They were no longer treated as property that could be traded indiscriminately; instead, they were regarded as female subjects whose labor supported their households. Chapter 3 moves to Nagasaki and explores how women and their families navigated this regulatory regime by conforming to cultural scripts that cast them as protective parents and dutiful children. Because the role of filial daughter was consistent with the shogunate's conception of ideal feminine behavior, magistrates found it difficult to reject prostitutes' claims to be acting on behalf of their parents or parents' assertions that they were protecting their daughters. By emphasizing these roles and relationships, prostitutes occasionally were able to resist the brothel keepers' authority, form their own families, or leave the sex trade.

The second section, "Expansion and the Logic of the Market," focuses on provincial ports, pilgrimage sites, and post stations in the late eighteenth and nineteenth centuries, describing the expansion of the sex trade to new areas and examining the social consequences of that shift. As markets for both sexual services and the women who provided them extended across political boundaries, authorities who depended on prostitution to bring prosperity to their own jurisdictions were both unwilling and unable to exert control. Consequently, increasing numbers of poor women caught up in this trade were displaced and dispersed across the archipelago. While brothel keepers and relatively small numbers of independent prostitutes welcomed the opportunities afforded by weakened regulation and an increase in demand for their services, elite commoners and samurai officials were alarmed by these developments. To anxious officials, the noticeable increase in peasants indenturing their daughters to brothels suggested that market forces were tearing households apart and threatening the foundations of the state. Wealthy peasants, too, expressed their apprehension that the availability of commercial sex would overturn the hierarchical relationships that structured communal life in the villages. Meanwhile, the realities of work in prostitution changed as recruitment patterns shifted and powerful men began to view prostitutes as scheming women rather than dutiful daughters.

Chapter 4 concentrates on the port city of Niigata in Echigo province. While Niigata was famous for the variety of sexual entertainments it offered to sailors, the region as a whole was notorious as the supplier of women to brothels throughout the archipelago. The samurai authorities who administered the area—initially retainers of Nagaoka domain and later shogunal appointees—were forced to address both sides of the rapidly expanding and diversifying sex trade, which brought prosperity to their most important city but preyed upon poor women in the countryside. Unable to sacrifice their interest in promoting commerce in Niigata, which was one of the only bright spots in a bleak economic landscape, officials pursued policies that supported the growth of prostitution. But as they abandoned the cause of regulation, they realized that their promotion of a business that treated their female subjects as "famous products" (*meibutsu*) undermined their claim to benevolent government. Faced with the unsettling realities of peasant families selling their children and unmarried women supporting themselves through prostitution, these elite men assigned blame to the women and families who supplied labor to the sex trade. The filial daughters who appeared in earlier official rhetoric were replaced by "shameless women" who relentlessly pursued their own material interests, and prostitutes became symbols of how market relations threatened to supplant the hierarchical ties that structured the household and the state.

The next two chapters examine how commoners—elite peasants and brothel keepers—reacted to the expansion of the sex trade. Along the post roads of the Kantō region, the growing business of providing sexual services to both travelers and local youths attracted large numbers of poor women from the Japan Sea coast who expected to spend a few years working in brothels before leaving to marry peasants from nearby villages. But the incursion of prostitution into the countryside inspired large-scale protests by peasant elites, who argued that prostitutes who had come to the area from other regions were corrupting their wives and daughters and threatening their way of life. Ultimately, prostitutes found that the failure of regulation also meant that the official justification for their existence had been eroded, leaving them vulnerable to criticism and marginalization. The final chapter, set among the port towns and pilgrimage sites of the Inland Sea, follows the story of a teenage prostitute named Tora who was caught up in an extended conflict between her parents and her master. The clashing narratives introduced by the parties to this dispute revealed two conflicting visions of the sex trade. While Tora's parents clung to an older paradigm that pitted caring parents and filial daughters against voracious brothel keepers, the proprietor and his allies presented a new understanding of a business that was guided by the profit-driven "rules of teahouses" and immune to the moral claims of the family. Their explanation of events, which ultimately won out, portrayed Tora as a self-interested schemer rather than a passive victim. Their presentation of this case, which was rooted in their desire to protect their economic interest in Tora's body, paralleled trends in cities and villages throughout the archipelago, as men related prostitution to the threat of female autonomy and castigated prostitutes for their selfishness.

Along with Tora, the dozens of women introduced in these chapters include Kokane, a married prostitute who ran away from her husband; Tama, an apprentice *yūjo* who became involved in a Chinese smuggling operation at her mother's request; and Hatsu, a serving girl who petitioned the authorities to be released from her contract. Though literacy training was part of a high-class *yūjo*'s education, the majority of these women did not fit within that category, and only one of them—Hatsu—wrote about her life. Most prostitutes' stories were recorded by men, who wrote the diaries (*nikki*), criminal registers (*hankachō*), petitions (*gansho* or *sojō*), and accounts of official business (*goyōdome*) that form the basis of this study. As Gail Hershatter points out in her study of prostitution in Shanghai, it is impossible to recover prostitutes' voices through these mediated accounts, as much as one might wish to piece together a coherent story about what they "really" thought of their work.[29] Nevertheless, these fragmentary and incomplete descriptions of women's experiences are essential to this project, which aims to treat them not merely as subjects of discourse or objects of scrutiny, but as major players in an industry that sustained families and communities, filled samurai officials' coffers, contributed to the emergence of regional and national markets, and ultimately transformed early modern Japan.

PART ONE · REGULATION AND THE LOGIC OF THE HOUSEHOLD

CHAPTER ONE • **Adulterous Prostitutes, Pawned Wives, and Purchased Women**
Female Bodies as Currency

Kokane ran away with a man named Sōdayū in 1614, leaving behind her husband and her home in the remote mining town of Innai Ginzan in Akita domain.[1] She was taking her life in her hands. It was illegal for a married woman to leave town without her husband's permission, and it was also extremely dangerous. Although the major military engagements of the Sengoku, or Warring States, era had come to an end, this corner of the archipelago was far from peaceful. Even the newly appointed lord of the domain (*daimyō*), Satake Yoshinobu (1570–1633), a fearsome warrior in his own right, found it difficult to impose order. While he ensconced himself in the fortified castle town of Kubota, the area along the domain's southern border remained ungoverned. Bandits hid out in the mountains, ready to ambush those who dared to traverse their territory.[2] For a woman, even one accompanied by a male companion, the journey over the steep and thickly forested terrain would have been perilous.

Kokane must have had a good reason for breaking the law and risking her life. The record of her disappearance offers an explanation for her reckless escape attempt: her husband, Tahei, had been hiring her out as a prostitute (*keisei*). There is very little information offered about her accomplice Sōdayū, who could have been her lover, a procurer who promised her a job in another city, or a guide she paid to lead her through the mountains. In any case, it made little difference to Akita domain officials. Regardless of the circumstances, the couple had committed a serious crime by absconding. Since the domain had a financial interest in retaining Innai's population of laborers, who extracted silver for the government's coffers, officials imposed the death penalty on those who left the mine without special permission.³ Some absconders were able to argue their way into more lenient punishments, but Sōdayū had compounded his offense by stealing another man's wife. Clearly, he deserved the harshest possible sanction.

Because Sōdayū's crime was so straightforward (and so egregious), domain officials knew exactly what to do with him when they apprehended the couple in the mountains east of the mine: they beheaded him on the spot. But they could not reach an immediate decision in Kokane's case, which was unprecedented in Akita domain's short history. What was the appropriate punishment for a married prostitute who ran away with another man? At a loss, they gave her Sōdayū's head and sent her back to the settlement at Innai.

The decision about Kokane's fate was left to the domain's general mine magistrate (*sō yama bugyō*), Umezu Masakage (1581–1633). In a terse account of his deliberations, sketched out in a few sentences in his diary, he stated that Kokane deserved the same punishment as Sōdayū. But then he seemed to reconsider. In the next line, he mentioned that her husband, Tahei, had invested a large sum of money in her. By juxtaposing these concerns, he suggested the contours of his dilemma: he could not execute Kokane without unfairly depriving her husband of his property, but he could not pardon a married woman who had absconded with another man. Because she was simultaneously a wife and a prostitute, a person and a possession, the magistrate puzzled over the correct response to her transgression. Stolen property would be returned, but an adulteress, particularly one who had compounded her crime by absconding, might deserve to be executed.

While he struggled with the implications of Kokane's multiple identities, Masakage never condemned Tahei for sending his wife out to work as a prostitute. In Kokane's situation, the categories of "wife" and "prostitute" had come into conflict, but only because she had absconded without her husband's permission and forced the magistrate to make a decision about her punishment. The idea that the roles of "wife" and "prostitute" were *inherently* contradictory, that a woman whose sexual body was available to multiple men belonged in a fundamentally different category from a woman whose sexual body was available only to her husband, did not enter into his deliberations. From Masakage's perspective, his task was not to disaggregate two mutually exclusive categories of women, but to decide on a penalty that was appropriate for someone who belonged within both at once.

In the end, Masakage ordered an unusual, and rather spectacular, punishment: he forced Kokane to parade around the mine holding Sōdayū's head. Apparently, the magistrate believed that the sight of a woman carrying a severed head (which was by then a few days old) would serve as a disincentive to others who might be tempted to commit similar crimes.[4] After she had completed this humiliating task, he returned her to Tahei. This compromise reconciled Masakage's desire to punish Kokane with his unwillingness to deprive her husband of his property. Yet it did nothing to settle the larger question about her legal status. She remained both a wife and a prostitute.

AN UNSETTLED AGE

Masakage's dilemma might have seemed irrelevant only a few decades earlier, before the Tokugawa peace had granted samurai administrators like him the luxury of considering the appropriate penalty for a married runaway prostitute. During the constant strife of the Sengoku era (1467–1568), warlords had considered themselves to be lawgivers, and they understood that the security of their domains depended on managing conflict within the ranks of fighting men.[5] However, they were far more concerned with ensuring military preparedness than dictating the terms on which common people related to one another. As long as peasants continued to bring in the harvest and pay their taxes, they were usually permitted to fend for themselves. But in the late sixteenth century, the hegemon Toyotomi Hideyoshi (1537–98) broke with precedent by pursuing a radically ambitious agenda of social reform. Through conquest as well as legislation, he worked to implement his vision of a realm that did not yet exist: a federation of peaceful domains in which warrior magistrates would administer a docile and productive population from their headquarters in castle towns. He forced samurai to abandon the countryside and compelled peasants to relinquish their weapons. By promulgating a series of edicts outlawing violent quarrels among commoners (*kenka chōji rei*), he signaled his intention to extend his rule to all levels of society, from the warriors guarding newly fortified castles to the peasants toiling in carefully surveyed fields.[6]

Hideyoshi died before his vision could be fully realized. But his successors, the Tokugawa shoguns, presided over an initially tenuous and ultimately lasting peace, which gave them the opportunity to extend his project of creating order out of wartime chaos. Tokugawa Ieyasu (1543–1616) and his heirs worked to bolster their authority through a series of policies meant to stabilize and control both the samurai and commoner populations. This task was complicated because the shogunal household directly administered less than a third of the territory in the Japanese archipelago; the rest was parceled out among over two hundred and fifty daimyō. Hideyoshi had allowed them to remain largely autonomous as long as they recognized his preeminence, and the early Tokugawa shoguns elected to continue this strategy. They relocated certain domainal lords whom they considered untrustworthy, but they permitted the daimyō to collect and retain their own tax revenue and to promulgate and enforce their own laws (within certain limits). However, the Tokugawa imposed a strict requirement during the reign of the third shogun, Iemitsu (1604–51): daimyō were obliged to leave their wives and heirs as hostages in Edo and to spend one out of every two years there attending on the shogun. This policy of "alternate attendance" (*sankin kōtai*) ultimately acted as a form of taxation, straining the daimyō's finances and siphoning money into the new capital.[7]

Early Tokugawa policies also imposed obligations on ordinary people. In the first decades of the seventeenth century, the shogunate formalized a system of organizing society in which each household was assigned a status (*mibun*) and placed within a social unit, which John Hall memorably called a "container."[8] These containers—households (*ie*) of samurai or nobles, villages (*mura*) of peasants, city wards (*chō*) of townsmen, sects (*shū*) of Buddhist clergy, and so on—had originated in self-governing communities that took shape amid the violence and uncertainty of the Sengoku period. They were given legal force by the Tokugawa shogunate, which assigned each a distinct responsibility to the state. A household's position in one of these containers determined its place of residence along with its tax burden and corvée labor obligations, and it also established its members' legal standing relative to those who belonged in other containers—a samurai, for example, was considered superior to a peasant, who ranked higher than an outcast. Ideally, every household was headed by a man, and his dependents would take on his status designation.[9]

Eventually, the effects of this project of social reform were felt in villages, port cities, and castle towns all over Japan. But this process took time, and in the first decades of the new era, the status system had not yet been institutionalized across the archipelago. Demarcations of status had no bearing on social life in Innai, where the major divisions were not between samurai, peasants, and townspeople, but between the wealthy prospectors (*yamashi*) who controlled mining operations and the masses of manual laborers and petty shopkeepers. This type of variation was typical of the unsettled early seventeenth century. Elsewhere along the Japan Sea coast, even Hideyoshi's land surveys were not implemented until the middle of the century, and historians have estimated that the iconic Tokugawa village took several decades to develop.[10] Although Innai was isolated deep in the mountains, it was like many other places in that the social order was still quite fluid and administrators were just beginning to assess how best to pacify an unruly population.

According to legend, the settlement at Innai was founded when four masterless samurai (*rōnin*) who had fought on the losing side of the battle of Sekigahara discovered silver in the mountains of Akita and asked the daimyō for permission to begin mining. Eager to exploit this new source of revenue, in 1608, the domain appointed silver mine magistrates (*ginzan bugyō*) to oversee the unruly prospectors. Under their watch, the mine proved to be extraordinarily productive, yielding about five thousand *kan* of silver per year at its peak. The proceeds were forwarded to the castle town of Kubota, where they were used to finance Yoshinobu's fledgling administration.[11]

As the mine grew, Innai's population increased dramatically, reaching seven or eight thousand in only a few years.[12] A later account dismissed the immigrants to the mine as "lonely people who had suffered in the war and chaos of recent years, along with hicks and bumpkins who only yesterday were covered in mud."[13] But in reality, the settlers were a much more diverse and sophisticated group. Skilled miners arrived from Chūgoku, where mining technology was the most advanced, and refiners and metalworkers streamed in from the great cities of Kansai, where the demand for their craft had been highest. Prosperous merchants and down-and-out samurai from all over the realm came as speculators, lured by the promise of easy money during the silver boom, and soon they were trailed by administrators eager to tax their discoveries. Only the unskilled laborers, the men who hauled rocks and dug holes, were local people. Aside from these workers, some of them farmers who worked in the mines during the agricultural off-season, very few of the newcomers arrived with their wives and families. They were unattached young men, just like those who built castle towns during the same period.[14]

Demographically unstable, Innai also faced problems unique to its function and location. Mountain bandits often raided the mine and then fled over the border to Yamagata domain, where it was nearly impossible to apprehend them.[15] Criminals from within the settlement also terrorized local residents, and samurai administrators resorted to violence to pacify their dominion. Herman Ooms's description of the Tokugawa state as a "regime of conquest" aptly characterizes the situation in Innai, where the powerful wielded weapons to mark and subjugate the populace.[16] A mid-seventeenth-century chronicle of the town's history says of these tumultuous early years: "Day after day, the fights and arguments never ceased, and there was no respite from violent, injurious thefts and robberies. Officials carefully examined the harshness of fines, and they designated a place for beheadings, crucifixions, and burning people alive. They piled up mountains of skeletons, and red waves ran over the grasses and trees."[17]

Once their supremacy was established, however tenuously, warriors sought to discover the productive capacity of their conquered lands. As Ooms has written, "power needed knowledge rather than the sword to carry on."[18] Innai was not a rice-producing area, so cadastral surveys were fairly unimportant, but the daimyō Yoshinobu pursued other types of information about the mining town. He needed to measure the *kan* of silver produced from the mine, tally the tax revenue produced by various levies on the townspeople, and count the population. He selected his trusted retainer, Umezu Masakage, to take charge of these tasks. Along with his older brother Noritada, Masakage had begun his career as a lowly masterless samurai. When the highly educated and cultivated Noritada gained a position as Yoshinobu's tea server, Masakage joined him in the daimyō's service. He cemented his place as one of the lord's closest advisers by assassinating a treasonous domain elder (*karō*), and eventually he distinguished himself as an able administrator with a certain amount of technical expertise in the area of mining. When the daimyō appointed him to the post of mine magistrate in 1612, he could be certain that he had chosen a man who would govern with brutal efficiency.[19]

Masakage lived up to his lord's expectations. Realizing that Innai's primary function was to provide income for the domain, he dedicated himself to ensuring that the business of silver mining functioned smoothly. His style of administration reflected this priority: he wielded violence to punish thieves and extort tax payments, but he did not bother to issue many ordinances about where the townspeople could live and what they could wear. Economic productivity concerned him far more than any abstract idea of order. In contrast, officials in political centers—Edo first and foremost among them—focused on their jurisdictions' military preparedness, which depended on a high degree of social organization. Their cities housed thousands of samurai, who needed to be fed, clothed, and disciplined. In order to prevent violent infighting and ensure adequate provisioning of these standing armies, castle town administrators worked to construct and secure a hierarchical order that could withstand challenges from unruly warriors and townspeople. Meanwhile, Masakage was free to make his judgments on a case-by-case basis, never losing sight of his ultimate goal: extracting revenue.

This did not mean that Innai was an outlier, or that Masakage's methods were atypical of his time. Although the early seventeenth century is often regarded as the age of the castle town in Japan, it was also an age of mines. In fact, the two types of settlement were inextricably connected, since mines produced revenue that supported the erection of castles and the building of barracks: unprecedented construction depended on unprecedented resource extraction. In Akita domain, Kubota's ability to function as the domain's capital depended on economic support from Innai, just as Innai's ability to function as a mine depended on administrative support from Kubota. In that sense, both cities—the remarkably orderly castle town and the unusually chaotic mining town—were equally representative (and unrepresentative) of their historical moment. They existed on opposite ends of a spectrum of approaches to urban administration, in which officials weighted their priorities either toward ensuring social stability or guaranteeing economic productivity.

In each type of place, this balance of priorities determined the type of records magistrates left behind. Those in castle towns left a legacy of exhortations, evidence of their drive to control and regulate urban spaces and the people who lived in them.[20] As the next chapter will show, these edicts evoked the kind of society the shogunate wished to create, in which people belonged in "containers." Ultimately, this paradigm would prevail across the archipelago. But during his years in Akita domain's administration, Masakage produced a different kind of documentary record. He left behind a personal diary, in which he wrote of his daily struggles to collect taxes and settle violent disputes, and a register of crimes and punishments, in which he made note of the harsh penalties he imposed on men and women who disrupted the functioning of the mine. His writings had no coherent ideological agenda; they did not set out any grand principles for organizing society. Instead, they represented a series of practical responses to the difficulties of managing a conflict-ridden, violent, and deeply divided community.

From his appointment as mine magistrate in 1612 until his death in 1633, Masakage wrote about his deliberations on hundreds of cases involving men and women from all walks of life and all but two of Japan's sixty-eight provinces. Prominent merchants as well as itinerant laborers petitioned his office to solve problems ranging from petty theft to murder, or they were called before the magistrate after committing crimes or failing to pay their taxes. Dozens of these cases concerned women. Most were the objects of custody or property disputes between men, but some were apprehended as criminals and a few were petitioners themselves. By hearing their testimony and settling their suits, Masakage addressed the question of what, if anything, in the new era distinguished a woman from a possession, a wife from a prostitute, or marriage from human trafficking.

WIVES FOR SALE AND DAUGHTERS IN HOCK

Innai's robust traffic in wives, daughter, prostitutes, and maidservants was shaped by the Tokugawa peace, but it also had medieval precedents. In the centuries preceding the battle of Sekigahara, there had been little distinction between familial authority and ownership: a household's hereditary servants (*fudai genin*) could be purchased, sold, and deeded in wills.[21] Occasionally, they were even used as pawns to settle blood disputes. When a member of a warrior's household committed murder, the victim's relatives often demanded revenge. In order to placate them, the perpetrator's family could respond by dispatching a hereditary servant as a surrogate (*geshunin*) whose life would be sacrificed in place of the murderer's. This strategy was costly, but it had the advantage of preventing a feud that could last for generations.[22]

A household head's wives and children occupied a different social stratum from hereditary servants, but in certain situations they too were counted among a household's possessions. During the Kamakura period (1185–1333), women were permitted to inherit, possess, and amass property. They could keep their own lands separate from their husbands' holdings, and they exercised authority over their own hereditary servants. But the shogunate's law codes considered women's bodies to be part of their husbands' or fathers' estates, treating violent crimes against women as violations of their household heads' property rights. For example, a man who raped a married woman owed compensation not to her but to her husband; the logic was that the rapist had damaged another man's possession. For this reason, Hitomi Tonomura has described the Kamakura period as one in which women could "both *have* and *be* property."[23]

In subsequent centuries, the development of a commercial sex trade contributed to the emergence of a wider market in female bodies. Janet Goodwin has shown that until the fourteenth century, there was no clear distinction between women who made a living selling sex and those who did not. In part, this was because the early medieval economy was in a state of transition: many types of services were still being exchanged for barter goods, and there was no meaningful difference between a gift from a lover and a payment from a client. Relatively permissive sexual norms added to the confusion. It was not unusual for women to have sex with several partners or to enter temporary relationships that entailed some degree of compensation. At the same time, professional providers of sexual services, *asobi* and *kugutsu*, were not easily categorized as prostitutes, because they were also highly trained entertainers.[24] As was typical of the Kamakura period, *asobi*'s labor arrangements did not distinguish between kinship and ownership. While many who entered the profession were the biological or adopted daughters of senior women, other so-called daughters were purchased outright.[25]

By the late medieval period, however, patterns of work in the sex trade had changed. In 1500, lists of prostitutes referred to women who sold sex as their sole occupation, such as the "madame stander" (*tachigimi*) and the "madame person of a narrow alley" (*zushigimi*). These designations reflected the increasingly urban and commercial nature of the business. Sex had become a commodity sold to commoners in city streets and alleys, as well as to aristocrats stationed at court or traveling through the countryside. While groups of sexual entertainers had once been led by women overseeing "families" of "daughters," more and more prostitutes came under the control of male pimps, who confiscated their earnings. In urban areas, at least, there was an increasingly clear distinction between prostitutes, who offered sex to a variety of men in return for payment, and other women, who contributed sexual and domestic labor to their households.[26]

But in other areas, the civil wars of the sixteenth century rendered such finely grained social distinctions meaningless. Girls and women from warrior families were torn from their households when conquerors seized their vanquished enemies' female relatives. Some were held as hostages and eventually ransomed, while others were taken as wives and concubines. Meanwhile, rampaging armies destroyed villages, creating a vulnerable population of war widows and dislocated peasants willing to sell their sons and daughters in return for food.[27] In the midst of this chaos, European traders, who first arrived in Japan in the mid-sixteenth century, began purchasing Japanese slaves and transporting them overseas. In this international slave trade, as in domestic trafficking, sex and ownership were closely related. Officials at the Vatican professed their horror that Portuguese merchants were acquiring Japanese slave girls for sinful purposes.[28]

Meanwhile, Japanese traffickers were conducting their own overseas trade. During Hideyoshi's two invasions of Korea in the 1590s, they bought or seized as many as 60,000 people and sent them to Japan as slaves. A Japanese Buddhist priest who witnessed the second Korean campaign described their work: "Among the many kinds of merchants who have come over from Japan are traders in human beings, who follow in the train of the troops and buy up men and women, young and old alike. Having tied these people together with ropes about the neck, they drive them along before them; those who can no longer walk are made to run with prods or blows of the stick from behind."[29] The fate of these slaves is difficult to trace, but it is likely that many of the women were marketed as prostitutes or concubines.

Although Hideyoshi was indifferent to the plight of Korean slaves transported to Japan, he was alarmed at reports of Japanese peasants being sold and sent overseas.

The spectacle of foreign traders in Kyushu hauling away men and women in chains made a mockery of the peace he was trying to establish, and the export of peasants imperiled his revenue stream by depriving the countryside of agricultural laborers. Domestic trafficking was also a problem, since it allowed rival daimyō to poach one another's workers. Moreover, the domestic and international trades were related: Portuguese argued that they could not prevent their merchants from buying slaves as long as Japanese traders were offering them for sale. Frustrated, Hideyoshi wrote to the Jesuit vice-provincial in 1587 complaining about the "Portuguese, Siamese, and Cambodians" who bought Japanese slaves. He demanded, rather quixotically, that all his countrymen be set free and returned to their homeland. Days later, he promulgated an ordinance forbidding both domestic trafficking and the sale and export of Japanese people. This was the first of many proclamations outlawing the practice of "buying and selling people" (*jinshin baibai*).[30]

Despite these injunctions, the domestic traffic in people, particularly women, was still thriving during the fragile peace of the early seventeenth century. As men flooded into newly established cities and castle towns to work as warriors, artisans, or menial laborers, they created an intense demand for female bodies to serve their sexual needs. Traffickers seeking to supply this new market found that their activities were barely restricted. As long as the male productive population was not disrupted, daimyō were reluctant to penalize men who traded women among themselves. The resulting feminization of human trafficking left traces in the documentary record. Maki Hidemasa's examination of seventeenth-century slavery contracts reveals that almost all the slaves mentioned in these agreements were women. Meanwhile, Daniel Botsman points out that enslavement (*yakko* or *nuhikei*) was a penalty reserved for female offenders until it was abolished in the mid-eighteenth century.[31]

In Innai, human trafficking was also gendered female, although perhaps not as starkly as in other areas. Men as well as women worked in the mine as unfree menial laborers. Many were former peasants who had been forced off their land after defaulting on loans. Sometimes their labor arrangements resembled debt peonage, while in other cases they had been sold to prospectors or foremen (*kanako*) who employed them as porters (*horiko*) or miners (*daiku*).[32] However, the mine magistrate's diary indicates that women were bought, sold, and traded more frequently than men. This pattern might have been attributable to the skewed sex ratio in the mining town—there were many male laborers, all of whom demanded women to serve their needs at various times—but it also reflected the magistrate's assumption that female bodies should circulate, while male workers stayed in place. Masakage procured women as part of his job: just as he traveled to markets to buy horses and hawks for the lord of the domain, he also went on errands to purchase "bought women" (*baijo*) to serve as maids in Kubota castle, securing a lifetime of their labor with a single payment.[33] But Masakage never bought adult men, who were more valuable to the domain as miners, prospectors, and taxpayers. Masakage's conception of men as essential laborers was reflected in his survey of the mine's productive population: he counted adult men, but excluded women along with children, old people, and monks.[34]

Masakage treated male heads of household as autonomous social actors, capable of fulfilling responsibilities to the domain, but he viewed their wives and children as assets that could be liquidated if the need arose. When townsmen defaulted on their taxes, he frequently commanded them to sell all their belongings—including family members as well as inanimate objects such as clothing and furniture—to compensate the domain. In one case, Masakage refused a petition for debt forgiveness, arguing that the townsmen involved would have enough money to pay their outstanding tax balances if they sold their wives and children.[35] When debtors refused to liquidate their wives and children, Masakage seized them; in his estimation, the financial needs of the domain overrode the household head's authority to make decisions about the fate of his dependents. In 1612, Masakage recorded that the master of an establishment called the Kyō-no-shio-ya owed several *kan* in outstanding taxes. Like many men in Innai, Kyō-no-shio-ya had multiple business interests: in addition to working as a prospector in charge of a mineshaft, he was also running a brothel.[36] But he had fallen on hard times, so he left the mine and returned to his birthplace of Kyoto, ostensibly to raise money to pay his debt. Masakage predicted that he would never be able to compel the prospector to return, so he drew up a list of his assets and decided to hold his residence, his wife and child, and his five maidservants as collateral on unpaid taxes.[37] When Kyō-no-shio-ya failed to deliver the money, Masakage sold the maidservants and sent word to the prospector's in-laws informing them that their daughter had been detained in Innai. He held her for the next six years, until her relatives finally arrived to pay ransom.[38]

Innai's townsmen also treated their wives' bodies as assets, exchanging them for money and using them to settle debts. Sometimes Masakage employed the terms "buy" (*kau*), "sell" (*uru*), and "pawn" (*shichi ni ireru*) for these transactions, implying that ownership of the women had been transferred. At other points, he referred to women being "employed" (*yatoi ni oru*), which suggested that they were indentured for discrete periods of time. In either case, these arrangements allowed husbands to capitalize on their marital relationships to raise money in the short term. For example, in 1612, Masakage reported that a hairdresser named Sakuzō had "employed" his wife Osen in order to finance a trip to his home province.[39] In another case, Masakage reported that a man had pawned his wife to raise money for his indebted father-in-law.[40]

Because female bodies were commonly understood as assets, moneylenders could claim them as payment on loans. During Masakage's first year in the mine, a man pawned a woman named Yaya, who died shortly after she was delivered into the pawnbroker's custody. Convinced he had been cheated, the pawnbroker demanded compensation in the form of Yaya's former master's wife. The aggrieved husband complained to the mine administration, but Masakage ruled that he owed the pawnbroker a debt. If he could not come up with cash, he would have to relinquish his wife.[41]

Wives who were put up for sale did not always stoically endure these transactions. Some gave voice to their objections by complaining to the magistrate's office. In 1614, Masakage heard from a woman who objected to her husband's plan to sell her. The man, Sanzaemon, maintained that he wanted to sell his wife because she was a wicked person who told him lies (*warera ni mujitsu to mōshikake, iroiro futodokijin*). Moreover, she had taken up with another man while he was away. She countered that she thought he had abandoned her. After all, he had pawned her for two hundred *monme* and disappeared. She claimed that her husband had invalidated their marriage by pawning her and leaving. Therefore, he no longer had the right to sell her, and since she had finished her term of service, she should be free. Frustrated with their bickering, the magistrate ordered them to settle their dispute without official intervention.[42] Practically, this meant that Sanzaemon won the case; it is difficult to imagine how his wife might have continued to resist his demands.

Other women simply absconded, which was extremely dangerous. The fate of one woman who tried to resist her husband's authority is a poignant example. She ran away from the mine in 1612, only a few days before her husband was supposed to turn her over to a man who had loaned him money. Soon afterward, a miner found her corpse: she had been stabbed to death by a man who had promised to help her escape. The hardhearted magistrate made no comment on her demise, but, in a typically practical judgment, he told the miner who discovered her body that he would be permitted to keep her clothes.[43]

In at least one case, a woman turned to her relatives for help resisting the terms of her sale. (This option was not available to the majority of the mine's women, who were immigrants living far from their natal families.) In 1631, Masakage recorded a dispute relating to an unnamed eleven-year-old girl who had been sold to

Myōemon, a man of unspecified occupation, who also owned nine other women. The girl had escaped his custody, and after a search lasting several years, he found her living with her sister, who was married to a carpenter named Jūemon. The couple hid the girl among relatives in their native village and refused to return her to Myōemon. When he filed suit with the mine administration, Masakage ordered Jūemon to return the girl; if he did not comply, Masakage warned, he would seize Jūemon's wife and send her in her sister's place. The threat had its intended effect, and the girl was returned to Myōemon.[44]

Masakage's judgment in this case, which came very late in his tenure, was in line with a policy that had remained consistent over his two decades in Innai. He always confirmed the authority of a man to sell, pawn, or "employ" his wife, daughter, or maidservant without her consent, and he invariably protected the buyer's right to retain custody of the woman he had purchased. Motivated by the exigencies of domain finance, he allowed women to be alienated as property, used as currency, or held as collateral—whatever would serve the domain's interests in collecting taxes or enabling men to raise capital. According to the mine magistrate, any woman's body could be considered a possession, and her marital status did not confer legal protection from being confiscated or sold. In other words, the monetary value attached to her body was more important than her social role as a wife, sister, or daughter.

SELLING SEX AND ENTERTAINMENT

The same factors that fueled Innai's traffic in women also contributed to the emergence of a thriving sex trade. Brothel keepers and prostitutes, like prospectors and metal workers, were attracted to this remote corner of the archipelago by economic opportunity. In 1608, at the peak of the silver boom, the first prostitutes (*keisei*) migrated to Innai from Kyoto.[45] According to the chronicle of Innai's early history, their arrival represented the merger of the sophistication of the old capital and the new money of the mining town. Rivers of blood ran through the crime-ridden streets of Innai, but when the *keisei* and *shirabyōshi* arrived, "the sounds of their koto, shamisen, taiko, flutes, and drums sounded constantly throughout the narrow streets and alleys of the various wards of the town. It was exactly the sensation of hearing the music of an unseen heaven."[46] These women were veteran brothel employees, accustomed to life in a much larger city, but others were newcomers to the trade. Many were country girls whose families had disintegrated amid the violence of the late sixteenth century. "If there were ten of them," the chronicle asserted, "they might have been from ten different provinces. In wartime, invaders had snatched them from domains that had lost battles, and they were sold from place to place."[47]

Prostitutes and their employers were welcome in Innai, because domain officials were eager to attract people to the mine by any means necessary. Thousands of laborers were needed to extract silver for the domain's coffers, and any increase in population meant that the domain also generated more revenue from its monopolies on the townspeople's daily necessities, particularly lead (which was necessary to refine silver) and rice.[48] Realizing that the availability of entertainment was one of the town's selling points, the domain allowed prostitution, kabuki performances, and sumo bouts in Innai, while prohibiting these activities in Kubota.[49] When the shogunate's precedents contradicted the goal of promoting popular entertainment in Innai and other mining towns, the magistrates ignored them. In 1616, Masakage wrote that although kabuki had been forbidden in Suruga and Edo, he saw no reason to take similar steps in Akita's mines.[50]

He also refused to restrict prostitution. Masakage treated the business of commodified sex just as he treated the business of selling sake, tatami mats, or mushrooms. The year Masakage arrived in the mine, he noted the existence of a "prostitutes' ward" (*keiseichō*), among wards specializing in miso, straw matting, fish, vegetables, and pots.[51] But the homogeneity of these wards did not survive for long, and even the prostitutes' ward soon succumbed to competition from other areas. Masakage made no effort to halt this process. Occasionally, brothel keepers from other areas within his jurisdiction appeared in the diary as taxpayers and petitioners, and their residence outside the prostitutes' ward passed without comment.[52] The magistrate made only one statement limiting the area where prostitutes could solicit: he decreed that they should not enter the mine, presumably because they would distract miners from their work. But this rule did not apply only to prostitutes; it also extended to religious proselytizers and beggars (*kojiki*).[53] The principle behind this ruling was that vagrants should not be able to interfere with mining, not that prostitution in particular should be confined to a certain area.

Although he did not tell brothels where they could operate, Masakage was quite concerned with whether or not brothel keepers were paying the appropriate levies (*yaku*). In the absence of a clearly defined status system that linked occupational identities, places of residence, and responsibilities to the state, the levies played a role in organizing the mine's population and delineating residents' obligations to the domain.[54] Sake sellers paid a sake levy (*sake yaku*), noodle shops paid a noodle levy (*menrui yaku*), bath houses paid a bath levy (*furo yaku*), and every brothel in the mining town, whether in the courtesans' ward or outside it, paid a prostitute levy (*keisei yaku*), a flat tax on each prostitute who worked in the establishment.[55] The brothels' payments totaled twenty-two *kan* annually during the first years after the mine's establishment. This was not the most lucrative levy in Innai (that distinction belonged to the *iriyaku* tax on goods entering the mine), but it exceeded the taxes on tobacco, noodles, and sake.[56]

Ultimately, Masakage's policies were oriented toward protecting this revenue rather than regulating prostitution. The nature of the brothels' business—exchanging sex for payment—was beside the point. Years later, when the brothels attempted to evade the prostitute levy by calling themselves "laundries," Masakage outsmarted them by raising a "laundry levy" equal to the tax on prostitutes. The question of whether the laundry girls were washing clothes or selling sex was irrelevant. What mattered was whether their employers were fulfilling their financial obligations to the domain.[57]

This position echoed the magistrate's policy on human trafficking, which disregarded women's identities, occupational or otherwise, in order to treat their bodies as a form of currency. Masakage respected the brothel keepers' property rights when, like other townsmen, they bought, sold, or pawned their female employees. Since some proprietors also involved themselves in other business ventures in addition to the sex trade, these bodies could be an important source of financing. In 1612, Masakage reported that a speculator named Sukebei had used a prostitute named Yaya as collateral for a loan of six hundred *monme*, which he used to buy a mineshaft.[58]

Like Innai's wives, prostitutes resisted their masters' efforts to treat them as property. One such woman, Jūzō, caused the magistrate so much trouble that he wrote several diary entries despairing of her behavior. Jūzō's master, the proprietor of the Innai branch of a large Fushimi brothel called Nagasaki-ya, had died suddenly, leaving behind four prostitutes—Jūzō, Nagasaki, Hyōzaemon, and Kokane (possibly the same Kokane who ran away with Sōdayū two years later). A few months after her master's death, Jūzō came to Masakage's office and informed him that she wished to return to her home in Kansai. Like many of the mine's women, she had no relatives or acquaintances in Innai, and she argued that she could no longer support herself. Masakage was troubled by her request, and he ordered her to remain in the mine for several more months. If her master's relatives came to claim her, he explained, they would be justifiably upset to learn that she had left the mine.[59] Moreover, he cited a practical concern that revealed his conception of women's limitations: "It would be preposterous," he opined, "for a young woman to go wandering off to unknown places."[60]

After Masakage refused to let Jūzō leave, her colleagues warned him that she was desperately unhappy and might run away. A few weeks later, an enforcer affiliated with the brothels informed Masakage that another prostitute had reported seeing Jūzō leaving the area carrying her extra clothes. When officials questioned Jūzō, she explained that she wanted to pawn these items in order to cover her living expenses. Unfortunately, no one in Innai wanted to buy them, so she had to borrow money from a Yokobori brothel keeper instead. Masakage chastised her because it was forbidden to pawn anything outside of a licensed pawnshop, but he also had other grounds for disapproval: Jūzō claimed that she had been her late master's wife (*nyōbō*), he wrote, but she had actually been his prostitute. The implication was that since she had not been a wife, she did not have the authority to inherit or alienate his property.[61] However, Jūzō ignored this inconvenient distinction and continued to behave as if she were his heir. Ten days after she was scolded for pawning her clothing, she appeared at the mine administrators' office along with Hisaji, a former employee of the brothel, to discuss plans for selling the prostitute Nagasaki to an interested buyer from the mine. Again, Masakage refused, insisting that the brothel's property must remain intact.[62]

A few weeks later, Masakage received a report that Jūzō and Hisaji had left the mine.[63] He sent deputies to look for them in the nearby towns of Kaneyama, Chineko, and Kanazawa, but they all returned empty-handed. Frustrated by his experience with Jūzō, Masakage gave up on the idea of waiting to hear from the Fushimi branch of the brothel and declared that the three remaining women should also be dispersed to other proprietors in the neighborhood, who could sell the women and keep the proceeds.[64] He did not consider the women's preferences.

Masakage's experience with Jūzō must have confirmed his impression that women could not be trusted if they were not left in the care of male guardians. But it also raised some new questions. By acting as if she were her master's widow, Jūzō had revealed an inconsistency in Masakage's policy toward the mine's women. The magistrate's remarks on Jūzō's case suggest that wives possessed some rights not accorded to prostitutes: namely, a deceased man's widow could dispose of his property, while his prostitute could not. However, because Masakage usually considered both wives and prostitutes to be the head of household's assets, he had blurred whatever lines may have separated these two groups. In a bid to claim authority over her late master's household, Jūzō had cleverly exploited the ambiguity in her position, forcing the magistrate to address an uncomfortable question: If both wives and purchased women could be bought, sold, pawned, and sent into service, then what was the difference between ownership and marriage?

ADULTEROUS PROSTITUTES
AND FAITHFUL WIVES

Masakage was forced to confront the issue of women's conflicting roles and identities when he considered women's sexual relationships outside of marriage. He did not employ a specific term for "adultery," but his judgments make it clear that a wife was obligated to be sexually faithful to her husband, whom he deemed her "original man" (*moto no otoko*), as opposed to a lover, who was an "in-between man" (*maotoko*).[65] The penalty for infidelity depended on the specific circumstances of the crime. In one instance, Masakage ruled that an unfaithful wife whose lover had committed ritual suicide (*seppuku*) should be paraded around the streets of the mine holding her lover's head.[66] This was a comparatively light punishment. If an act of adultery was combined with some other crime, however, the penalty was more severe. On two occasions, adulterous women who had conspired to murder their husbands were sentenced to death. The first was stripped naked, led around the mine, put out on display, and then beheaded. The second was burned alive.[67] Conversely, in two instances, men who killed their adulterous wives and their lovers were judged innocent. Apparently, the husbands' anger was considered justifiable given the gravity of their wives' offense.[68]

Masakage made linguistic distinctions between marital relationships and master-servant relationships—he called a woman's employer her "master" (*shujin*) and her husband her "original man"—but in practice, there seems to have been little distinction between the privileges accorded to a husband and those of a master. A husband had the exclusive right to use his wife's body for pleasure, profit, or reproduction, and his wife was obligated to be sexually faithful. But as the penalties imposed on absconding maidservants made clear, a man who employed a woman as a servant was also permitted to profit from her labor and control her sexual behavior, and other men were not allowed to infringe on his prerogatives. In 1612, for example, Masakage apprehended a man named Shichiuemon who had run off with another man's maidservant and punished him by cutting off his nose, one ear, and a finger. The maidservant, meanwhile, was stripped naked and paraded around the mine.[69] The following year, a maidservant named Nene was punished after her plan to elope with her lover went terribly wrong. When she arrived at her lover's residence, he was away laboring in the mine. But another man, Hisaroku, was hiding inside. Hisaroku and Nene lay together (*dakine itasu*), and the following morning she fled to the mountains. From the context—Hisaroku's "hiding" and Nene's intention to marry a different man—it seems likely that their encounter was not consensual. But in his deliberations on the case, the mine magistrate did not address the issue of consent; instead, he repeated the familiar phrase "her master has invested a great deal of money in her" and used this as a justification to spare Nene the death penalty. He decided that Hisaroku should be beheaded, but Nene should be paraded around the mine and returned to her master.[70] Nene attempted to escape again a few days later, but she was betrayed by two men hoping to collect prize money for her return. When she was delivered into Masakage's custody, he issued the same verdict, again reasoning, "her master has invested a great deal of money in her."[71]

Because the bonds of marriage and the requirements of service were so similar, a woman who was married to one man and employed by another had divided loyalties. This led to an obvious question: was a married woman who had been sold to another man still married? Women involved in these ambiguous situations formulated their own answers to the question of whether or not they were married, and they had their own ideas about which men were (or were not) entitled to sexual relationships with them. Some invoked their married status in order to fend off their masters' advances. The hairdresser Sakuzō's wife Osen, who was "employed" for a period of five months to finance her husband's journey home, complained to Masakage when the middleman in her husband's deal tried to claim her as a wife after her term of service expired. She argued that she was still married; she could not be expected to have sex with anyone other than her husband. Luckily, her husband had realized that it was necessary to stipulate that he expected her to remain monogamous, even though he had left her in the custody of another man. He specified in her employment agreement that if he failed to return to the mine by the time her term expired, she must wait until the end of the year before taking up with another man (*otoko wo sezu sōrōte, warera wo tōnenchū machi sōrae*). Masakage considered this contract enforceable and ruled that she could wait for her husband's return.[72]

In another instance, a married woman who had been sent into service with another man argued the opposite: rather than insisting that she was still married, she claimed that her marriage was invalid. After her master died, she refused to return to her husband on the grounds that her period of service had negated her marriage. Like Sakuzō's wife, she believed that marriage constituted an *entitlement* to fidelity, not only an obligation. To her, the fact that her husband had handed her over to another man had negated his marital claim: marriage and service were incompatible. But her husband went to Masakage's office to lodge a complaint, and Masakage, who never approved of leaving women without male guardians, compelled her to return to her husband.[73] This echoed his decision in the case of Sanzaemon's "wicked" wife, whose unsuccessful appeal had been based on a similar argument. She had insisted that her husband had invalidated their marriage when he pawned her and left, so she was free to take up with whomever she liked.

In these instances, married women claimed protections that they did not possess (at least not in Masakage's estimation). They thought that they should be able to refuse to have sex with men other than their husbands. They also believed that a man who sold or pawned his wife relinquished any further claim on her body. Where did they get this idea? Since practically all the mine's women were immigrants from other areas, they may have come from places where a different legal regime prevailed. Those who had arrived in the mine from cities like Kyoto, where monogamous wives and promiscuous prostitutes were more clearly differentiated, might have expected that this would be the case in Innai as well. They would not necessarily have known that the mine magistrate saw female commoners' bodies primarily in terms of their monetary value and cared little for such distinctions.

Appealing to the magistrate was not the only way in which women challenged a conception of marriage that allowed their husbands to use their bodies for profit. Like pawned wives, married prostitutes occasionally took matters into their own hands. Kokane, whose escape with Sōdayū opened this chapter, performed her act of resistance by running away. In 1626, toward the end of Masakage's tenure, the wife of a man named Kōhei chose an even more drastic course of action: she conspired with her lover to poison her husband. While investigating this incident, Masakage discovered that she took lovers with her husband's knowledge and consent. In fact, "she made a living in the same way as prostitutes [do]" (*keisei nado no gotoku yo o watari sōrō*). Masakage did not indicate that Kōhei had forced her to have sex with other men, but it seems safe to assume that she would not have conspired to kill him if she had been happy with their arrangement. As in the case of the maidservant Nene and her brief encounter with the "hiding" Hisaroku, the probable element of coercion in this relationship either escaped Masakage's notice or was treated as irrelevant to his deliberation.

Kōhei's wife's case was similar to Kokane's in that it required Masakage to decide whether a married prostitute could be guilty of adultery, and it posed a similar dilemma: he could not declare her innocent without invalidating her marriage or exempting her from the rule that married women should not commit adultery. But he could not judge her guilty when it was clear that she took lovers with her husband's permission, since doing so would constrain Kōhei's ability to use her body for profit. Masakage paused to consider that her profession might be a mitigating circumstance in her crime, but in the end he decided that the more relevant issue was the conspiracy to commit murder. "Not only did she take a lover," he concluded, "she also asked him to kill her husband, and this is a serious offense." Although she had not succeeded in her attempt on her husband's life, Masakage sentenced her to death.[74]

Masakage's vocabulary distinguished between purchased women, prostitutes, wives, daughters, and maidservants, but his judgments placed them in a uniform mass of "women," all of whom were available for purchase and eligible for sale. When he commanded a man to relinquish his wife to compensate for defaulting on a loan, falling behind on his taxes, or harboring a runaway maidservant, he made the point that all women—even those who were married—were assets that could be liquidated and exchanged at will. In this regard, women's familial roles and relationships were hindrances, because they created emotional and social ties that fixed women in place and prevented them from circulating within the mine's economy. From Masakage's perspective, women were best understood as units of value, differentiated only by the amount that men would pay to access their bodies.

But Innai's women perceived their situation differently. If their complaints to the magistrate are any indication, they thought of themselves in terms of their relationships with their husbands and families. Viewed from their perspective, it is easy to understand how a clearer distinction between categories of women might have been highly desirable. Legal boundaries between marriage and prostitution might have protected married women from being sold or forced to have sex with other men, although this protection for some would have come at the expense of the minority who remained in the sex trade. Unfortunately for married women, however, this distinction was not forthcoming. The mine magistrate was more concerned with maximizing revenue than sorting people into groups, and when he was confronted with the question posed at the beginning of this chapter—"What separated a woman from a possession, a wife from a prostitute, or marriage from trafficking?"—his answers never moved beyond "nothing at all." Since Masakage would not institute a legal distinction between prostitutes and wives, and Innai's men did not perceive any inherent difference between these categories that would make it socially unacceptable to send one's wife into prostitution, the mining town's women were constantly vulnerable to being forced into prostitution or otherwise alienated as property.

In the early seventeenth century, many Japanese women shared their fate. Innai was a distinctive setting in which many of the problems of trafficking were magnified by the aftershocks of war and the instability of the local economy, but it was not the only area where men were selling their wives to brothels, seizing daughters from neighbors who owed them money, and trading family members for cash. As Shimojū Kiyoshi has demonstrated, peasants in Yonezawa domain were selling their wives and children to meet their tax obligations as late as 1642.[75] The shogunate's repeated injunctions against "buying and selling people," which are detailed in the next chapter, suggest that this was an issue throughout the realm.

If women faced a common predicament, however, they did not encounter a uniform legal regime or a stable set of social norms. As the Innai petitioners' squabbles made clear, there was no commonly accepted definition of marriage, no universal understanding of the obligations of household heads, and no standard set of rules defining whether a woman was a wife, a prostitute, or both at once. Amid this uncertainty, Masakage's judgments in the mining town formed one possible set of solutions to the common problems of imposing order and generating revenue.

In the decades after Masakage's tenure, as the Tokugawa shogunate began to standardize approaches to administration, this range of possibilities narrowed. By the middle of the seventeenth century, wives and prostitutes were assigned to distinct legal categories and the traffic in pawned wives and "bought women" was prohibited. Masakage's decisions, which reduced female bodies to assets and allowed men to buy and sell them indiscriminately, never acquired the force of precedent. In fact, his judgments would have seemed foreign to later samurai administrators, who became accustomed to thinking of women (and children, for that matter) as members of households that belonged within fixed status categories. In that sense, his carefully recorded decisions amounted to a dead end in legal history.

But this dead end is useful for thinking about subsequent developments. Recently, feminist scholars have contested the interpretation of the Tokugawa period as a low point in women's history by emphasizing women's ability to travel, attend schools, engage in cultural activities, or wield informal power within the household.[76] But few are willing to defend the Tokugawa legal system, which distinguished between women on the basis of their sexual relationships with men, subordinated them to male household heads, and excluded them from formal political power. If women exercised authority or enjoyed any sort of freedom, they are understood to have done so in spite of Tokugawa law. Yet women's experiences in Innai represent the danger of classifying the comparatively regimented nature of the Tokugawa order as an unambiguously negative development for women. The realistic alternative to the status system was much closer to the situation in Innai than it was to any sort of liberal ideal, and Innai's women certainly did not thrive under the authority of a magistrate who did not implement the shogunate's vision of social order.

Masakage considered all female bodies to be equal, but they were also interchangeable, not only with each other, but with currency and other types of property. This form of equality held no advantages for women. For them, almost any type of legal intervention from the center would have been an improvement.

The Tokugawa shogunate's institution of status categories for prostitutes, which is the subject of the next chapter, should be understood in this context. When the magistrates implemented laws defining prostitutes in opposition to wives, they were not simply institutionalizing a preexisting social practice. Out of many, conflicting ideas and practices, they were creating a new order, one that made subjects out of possessions and ultimately transformed and diversified the roles of women throughout the realm.

Yet one of the patterns established in Innai would survive this transformation, repeating itself again and again as early modern authorities contended with the development of an increasingly commercial sex trade in cities and towns across the archipelago: samurai officials both encouraged and profited from the sale of sex. In Innai, Masakage allowed prostitution because levies on brothels filled the domain's coffers and the flourishing entertainment district attracted new male laborers and consumers to the mine. At the same time, he benefitted from the traffic in women, since permitting men to buy and sell their female dependents allowed them to access capital to open mineshafts and pay their taxes. In subsequent decades, the specific economic incentives for allowing or encouraging the sale of sex would change, but they would still be powerful. The bottom line was that prostitution was profitable for brothel keepers and samurai authorities alike.

CHAPTER TWO · Creating "Prostitutes"
Benevolence, Profit, and the Construction of a Gendered Order

In 1612, an Edo brothel keeper named Jin'emon submitted a petition to the Tokugawa shogunate asking the new government to recognize his business and grant him a plot of land where he and his colleagues could ply their trade. He framed his argument carefully. When his associates had petitioned the shogunate to be acknowledged as a guild in 1605, the magistrates had responded that they saw no reason to extend special privileges to brothel keepers. This time Jin'emon wanted to be certain that his request would be considered, so he appealed to the shogunate's interest in preserving social and political order. First, he took stock of the situation in the growing castle town, which had a rapidly increasing and predominantly male population. This had created an intense demand for sexual services, which the brothel keepers were eager to provide. But an unregulated sex trade could cause a number of problems, which Jin'emon made sure to elaborate in detail: young girls from "good" families could be kidnapped and sold to brothels, samurai could plot rebellions in courtesans' private apartments, and merchants' apprentices could squander their wages carousing with women. After emphasizing the perils of leaving this burgeoning market unregulated, Jin'emon proposed a solution: if the shogunate would grant him a plot of land and a monopoly on the sex trade, he would guarantee that these dangers would be contained. As a show of good faith, brothel keepers would confine their operations to the newly created "pleasure quarter," where they would record the comings and goings of customers and report on suspicious activities.[1]

Jin'emon's request was not without precedent. In 1589, two masterless samurai (*rōnin*) had submitted a similar proposal to Hideyoshi, who controlled the emperor's capital of Kyoto, and he had awarded them an advantageously positioned parcel of land in the center of town.[2] Jin'emon, who hoped for a similar settlement in Edo, waited five long years for a response. Finally, in 1617, the government granted his request but gave him an inconvenient and marshy plot on the outskirts of the city, making clear that the gift was contingent on Jin'emon's offer to limit the disorder associated with prostitution. The shogunate stipulated that the brothel keepers must abide by sumptuary regulations, monitor clients' behavior, and forbid their women to work outside the district.[3]

With this agreement in hand, the brothel keepers began clearing the marsh to create a new quarter, appropriately named Yoshiwara, or "Reed Plain" (later the characters were amended to read "Fortunate Plain"). They plotted out a simple design of four streets, and carpenters worked quickly to erect brothels and teahouses.[4] They also built thick plaster walls and a shallow moat to surround the district. There would be only one way into Yoshiwara, the Great Gate, and it would be guarded at all times so that the brothel keepers could fulfill their promise to supervise the movements of their customers. Just outside this entrance, the shogunate erected a sign confirming the Yoshiwara proprietors' monopoly on the sex trade and stating the rules for those entering the quarter: only doctors were allowed to enter on horses, carts, or palanquins, and no one was permitted to carry a spear or long sword past the gate.[5] After a year of hasty construction, the quarter opened for business in 1618.

Yoshiwara's establishment was important because it marked the invention of a new kind of urban space in Edo; but, equally significantly, it also represented the creation of a new category of women, "prostitutes" (*yūjo*), who would be separated from the rest of the city's female population by the gates and walls of the quarter. Through the collaborative efforts of magistrates seeking stability and brothel keepers pursuing profit, women were divided into subsets based on new understandings of their sexual availability and confined within clear legal and physical boundaries.

This was only one of the ways that the Tokugawa settlement was creating a more orderly and predictable world out of what had been (and in many places continued to be) a brutal, conflict-ridden realm. The shogunate made hierarchy into a virtue, insisting that a social order based on this principle was both morally justifiable and necessary for preserving the peace. The shogun legitimated his rule by invoking the Buddhist ideal of "compassion" (*jihi*) and, eventually, the Neo-Confucian concept of "benevolent government" (*jinsei*). Like many of the daimyō, he positioned himself as a "benevolent ruler" (*jinkun*) devoted to the well-being of his subjects.[6] The model of the patriarchal family was crucial to this ideological formation, which envisioned commoners as dependents in need of paternalistic officials' guidance and protection. Like the ideal relationship between father and children or husband and wife, the relationship between governor and governed was mutually responsible as well as unequal: although subjects owed fealty and tax revenue to their ruler, they were also entitled to a basic level of subsistence, and they could expect to be shielded from abuse and exploitation.[7]

But the analogy was precarious because, as chapter 1 has argued, the household did not have a stable legal or social meaning that applied across the realm. In Innai, the domain-appointed magistrate interpreted marriage among commoners as a form of bondage, in which a man could dispose of his wife's body in any way he wished and she had no recourse. Needless to say, this was not an ideal representation of benevolent government. It was also an unstable foundation on which to build a polity. The constant exchange of women generated conflict, and it was not always clear to whom pawned wives and married prostitutes owed their allegiance. If the shogunate wished to formalize the status system, which assigned households to occupational identities, places of residence, and responsibilities to the state, it would also have to define the household and determine the roles of its members. The type of ambiguity permissible in Innai, where it was not always possible to distinguish a man's wife from his maidservant or prostitute, could no longer be tolerated.

As the shogunate extended its authority over the course of the seventeenth century, it politicized and standardized the household. Laws established the normative expectation that a husband and father should be the household's head, and although later practice made room for women to act in this capacity in certain cases, the state precluded women from wielding legal authority over their husbands or fathers.[8] At the same time, the shogunate also applied its ideal of benevolent government to the most vulnerable members of the population: women and children. They could no longer be regarded as commodities to be bought, sold, and traded indiscriminately. Instead, they would be transformed into subjects and granted places within households and status groups. This new formation was patriarchal, in that it "confirmed the legal powers of a husband/father over his wife, children, and other dependents," and it was also paternalistic, in that it conferred a degree of protection on those who accepted its strictures.[9]

In Edo, magistrates reshaped the sex trade to accord with this gendered order, transforming a frenzy of buying and selling into what they perceived as a moral economy. The system they created prohibited husbands and fathers from abusing their authority by selling their dependents outright or forcing their wives to have sex with other men. At the same time, it protected the patriarchal household in several respects: it prevented married women and the daughters of "good" families from being kidnapped and trafficked, allowed poor families to survive by leveraging their daughters' labor, and ensured that women deployed their sexuality for the purpose of their households' survival and not for personal gain. This system was not only an ideologically driven construct. As Jin'emon's example indicates, it was shaped by the profit motives of brothel keepers and designed to work with, not against, economic growth. By the middle of the period, as proprietors worked diligently to expand the scope of their business, magistrates allowed prostitution to thrive in areas where they desired to revitalize the local economy, reap increased tax revenues, or provide employment opportunities for lower-class commoners. Long after the decline of Yoshiwara's monopoly, the alliance of "benevolent" governors and profit-seeking brothel keepers would survive, shaping the conditions in which sex with women designated as "prostitutes" could be exchanged for payment.

STRATEGIES OF REGULATION: THE "PLEASURE QUARTER" AND THE CONTRACT SYSTEM

THE "PLEASURE QUARTER"

The idea of a designated "pleasure quarter" had been the invention of enterprising brothel keepers, but the new government soon realized the benefits of this arrangement, which mitigated the sex trade's potential to disrupt social and political order. During the precarious decades after the battle of Sekigahara, the shogunate was always alert to the possibility of rebellion, particularly in the capital, and officials worried that men plotting to overthrow the government could find safe haven in the city's brothels. Indeed, *rōnin*, who had reason to be disgruntled with the political order, were closely associated with the business of prostitution. The first headmen of the licensed quarters in Kyoto and Osaka had been *rōnin*, and during the first few years of the district's existence there were reports of masterless samurai living and meeting in Yoshiwara.[10] Jin'emon's offer to provide surveillance helped ensure security, which would have been impossible to maintain if brothels had been scattered around the city. Moreover, shogunal officials recognized that an enclosed brothel district could help achieve another goal: containing disruptive manifestations of what Gregory Pflugfelder has called "perisexual" behavior, referring to the multitude of social activities and practices that surrounded sex acts.[11] In a city dominated by male warriors, public appearances of highly attractive, available women could incite riots; when actresses held open-air performances in Edo and Kyoto during the first years of the seventeenth century, gangs of armed men came to blows.[12] The rule that all customers had to abandon their weapons at Yoshiwara's Great Gate aimed to prevent similar problems in the quarter by ensuring that fights between patrons would not escalate into armed confrontations. In Yoshiwara, samurai could indulge in commodified sex, ideally in moderation, and the brothel keepers would report any suspicious behavior.

By confining the sex trade to a designated space, the shogunate also hoped to suppress an underground traffic in women run by unscrupulous traders who kidnapped girls and sold them to brothels. Later records reveal that this was not entirely effective. *Oshioki saikyochō*, an early eighteenth-century compilation of punishments and precedents, lists several cases in which missing young women were found after their relatives searched Yoshiwara. As Tsukada Takashi points out, these incidents exposed the dark underside of a space ostensibly dedicated to pleasure. The parents of missing girls saw Yoshiwara as a place of danger and imprisonment, rather than as a separate world offering freedom and fulfillment.[13] Yet limiting prostitution to one district served a purpose for concerned parents and paternalistic magistrates alike. Because the "pleasure quarter" existed, they knew where to begin searching for female victims of abduction.

In the decades following Yoshiwara's establishment, the shogunate's concern for social and political stability continued to shape its policies toward the sex trade. The last holdouts resisting Jin'emon's monopoly, brothel keepers from Sumichō, were relocated to Yoshiwara in 1626. Meanwhile, the shogunate repeatedly issued proclamations forbidding women's theatrical performances and prostitution outside the district. In 1640, in a bid to prevent suspicious characters from hiding out in brothels, the magistrates decreed that all Yoshiwara establishments must close before nightfall. During the same year, the shogunate strengthened its regulation of the sex trade in its other two great cities, moving Kyoto's brothels from Yanagichō to the more remote location of Shimabara and forbidding prostitution outside the newly created Shinmachi district in Osaka. The Edo magistrates also tightened their restrictions on Yoshiwara's prostitutes. In previous decades they had been allowed to come and go from the quarter as long as they did not sell sex on their outings, but in 1641, the shogunate barred them from passing through the Great Gate without special permission.[14]

The shogunate's strategy of isolating and containing brothels and prostitutes reached its apotheosis in 1656, when the Edo magistrates ordered the Yoshiwara proprietors to relocate. As the city expanded, the original site, which had been on the outskirts of a much smaller settlement, had become far too central for the magistrates' comfort. They offered a choice of new locations, none of which was particularly desirable. The brothel keepers settled on a plot near the Sensōji temple. As a show of good faith, the shogunate compensated the proprietors for their moving expenses and eased restrictions on nighttime operations. Magistrates also closed down a number of bathhouses, which had been providing sexual services to bathers, as an indication that they would not tolerate infringements of Yoshiwara's monopoly on prostitution.[15]

Like its predecessor, the new district, formally called New Yoshiwara (Shin-Yoshiwara), was home to gaudily dressed prostitutes, child attendants (*kamuro*), and various other types of entertainers. But it operated according to the same principles as other neighborhoods. Although the quarter was exempted from firefighting as a condition of its relocation, it was responsible for fulfilling other obligations (*yaku*) to the shogunate, and these duties cemented its place in the political system. In addition to containing unruly and possibly violent expressions of male sexuality, the secure space of the new district became a site for punishing women. In some cases, it was used as a last resort to confine female criminals who had escaped from their legally mandated guardians. For example, when a woman sentenced to serve as a slave in a warrior household ran away from her new master in 1668, she was condemned to servitude in Yoshiwara.[16] Women who committed sexual transgressions, particularly those that fell just short of the legal definition of adultery (ordinarily a capital offense), could also be sent to serve in the sanctioned quarter's brothels. For a short time during the early eighteenth century, this was a matter of policy across the realm. In 1722, the magistrate in Nagasaki appealed to Edo for advice on how to handle a case in which a disobedient daughter ran off with her lover and refused to return home. Officials in Edo told the magistrate to send her to Nagasaki's brothel district, and she was handed over to that neighborhood's proprietors with the instructions that they were to use her as a prostitute.[17] Although the shogunate developed new punishments for sexual misbehavior in subsequent decades, culminating in the standardized penalties laid out in the One Hundred Articles (*Kujikata osadamegaki hyakkajō*) in 1742, remnants of this earlier policy remained as late as 1740, when the shogunate decided that a lifetime of confinement in Yoshiwara was the appropriate punishment for a married woman who divorced, reconciled with her husband without invalidating the divorce, and then had sex with another man.[18]

FIGURE 1.
Torii Kiyotada I, *Shin-Yoshiwara ōmon-guchi* (The Main Gate, New Yoshiwara). Woodblock print, 43.3 × 64 cm (c. 1740s). *Yūjo*, child attendants, customers, and various entertainers gather on the main street just inside the Great Gate of Shin-Yoshiwara. Photograph © 2011 Museum of Fine Arts, Boston.

Toward the end of the Tokugawa period, Yoshiwara was assigned another official duty. In addition to reporting on suspicious customers and violent disputes in the quarter, the headman was required to inform the shogunal elders (*rōjū*) whenever he heard of strange or mysterious events. Since many of the rumors he reported were sexual in nature, aspects of this intelligence-gathering mission were consistent with Yoshiwara's original responsibility for containing and managing unruly sexual behavior. In 1852, for example, the headman recounted the case of a married woman in Azabu who was arrested when she turned out to be a man in disguise. The next year, he reported that a father in Yoshiwara had petitioned the city magistrates to invalidate his adopted daughter's marriage on the grounds that her husband had never once engaged in sexual intercourse with her. It turned out that the groom preferred to have sex with men and had married a woman for the sake of appearances. In another memorandum, the headman related the story of a sake shop owner's daughter who was released from her term of employment as a maid at a girls' calligraphy school when she suddenly grew a penis and testicles. But these accounts of gender disorder were accompanied by reports of fox possession and other supernatural occurrences. The headman's expanded responsibility for reporting on strange events of all varieties reflected a new understanding that the quarter could be politically useful as "a space of rumors" (*uwasa kūkan*) as well as a place for sex.[19]

As a policy, then, the institution of the "pleasure quarter" was fairly flexible, allowing the magistrates to receive various surveillance and containment services to suit a changing set of priorities. Its physical manifestation, however, was unchanging: it consisted of the four walls and Great Gate containing Yoshiwara, which stood on the outskirts of Edo for all to see. This visible marker was the most readily identifiable, and frequently imitated, aspect of the shogunate's approach to the sex trade. Over the course of the Tokugawa period, not only shogunal cities such as Kyoto, Osaka, and Nagasaki, but also daimyō-controlled cities such as Fukuoka, Kanazawa, and Shimonoseki developed their own walled-in quarters.[20] Occasionally the style was even replicated in provincial towns. The fictional travelers in Jippensha Ikku's classic *Shanks' Mare* (*Tōkaidōchū hizakurige*) remarked that the entertainment district in Fuchū, a post station on the Tōkaidō Highway, looked just like Yoshiwara.[21]

This proliferation of unusual spaces hidden behind walls allowed writers and artists to experiment with the idea of the "pleasure quarter" as a separate world. Books called *sharebon* gave voice to the Yoshiwara's denizens, such as the *tsū*, a consummate sophisticate who dedicated himself to the pursuit of pleasure, and artists drew fanciful maps of the quarter, which served as inverted versions of the political realm. Marcia Yonemoto describes how one such map maker represented the district as a fanciful country called Geppon, the Land of the Rising Moon (rather than Nippon, the Land of the Rising Sun), in which the values and practices of mainstream society were turned upside down. By celebrating the frivolous culture of the brothel district, writers and artists obliquely criticized the shogunate, which regaled its subjects with exhortations toward sobriety, modesty, and productivity.[22] Paradoxically, spaces that the shogunate had developed and reinforced for political reasons were perceived as subverting the administration's most cherished ideals.[23]

The idea of the "pleasure quarter" as a fantastic space was excellent publicity for brothel keepers, who needed to entice customers to make the journey to the outer edge of the city. But from the perspective of those who lived in the quarter, the neighborhood was an everyday space that functioned according to the same hierarchical principles that structured life in other areas. Like every ward in Edo, Yoshiwara was governed by a headman and elders (*toshiyori*). Social relations among the district's several thousand residents were organized much as they were in the rest of the city, ordered by unequal relationships between landlords and renters and masters and servants.[24] The exotic trappings of Yoshiwara—the prostitutes' affected language (*arinsu kotoba*), their elaborate processions through the streets of the quarter, and their observation of complicated brothel etiquette—simply camouflaged this more mundane reality.

Nevertheless, the physical barrier formed by the walls of Yoshiwara made it possible to imagine the space inside the quarter as an inversion of the city outside, and it also invited men to categorize women in diametrically opposed groups: those inside the quarter were prostitutes, while those outside were wives, mothers, and daughters.[25] Seeking to profit from married men's restlessness, sex trade proprietors encouraged this idea of the brothel as an escape from and counterpart to the household. As William Lindsey argues, some of the quarter's elaborate rituals gently parodied the rites of the marriage ceremony in order to "co-opt its normative meaning, turn it on its head, and drain all notions of fertility from relations between a courtesan and client."[26] From shogunal officials' perspective, the walls around Yoshiwara facilitated surveillance and helped promote their goals of social and political order. But for many of the shogunate's male subjects, the walls began to serve a different purpose: they separated fantasy from reality, pleasure from reproduction, and prostitutes from wives.

THE CONTRACT SYSTEM

While the shogunate used the institution of the "pleasure quarter" to control the market for sexual services, it used new policies on indentured servitude to stabilize the market for female bodies. In 1616, following Hideyoshi's precedents, the shogunate promulgated its first law forbidding the practice of buying and selling people.[27] In an ordinance the following year, aspects of which were reissued periodically during the first decades of the century, the shogunate elaborated on this policy, mandating the death penalty for traffickers who kidnapped and traded people. It also punished the middlemen who purchased and then resold people, as well as those who operated inns where traffickers came to do business. "Long terms of service" were also forbidden, though the precise meaning of "long" was left unclear. In the following decades, the shogunate set the limit at ten years, and longer contracts, terms of indefinite length, and "eternal terms of service" (*eidai hōkō*) were all declared illegal.[28]

These new laws were meant to apply all over the realm, but initially they were enforced unevenly. As chapter 1 demonstrates, Akita domain authorities allowed commoners to buy and sell women well into the third decade of the seventeenth century. In the shogunate's own cities, however, reform had come much earlier. In 1612, four years before the shogunate issued its first general decree forbidding human trafficking, its deputy in Kyoto (*Kyōto shoshidai*) established rules for that city's brothel district that punished kidnapping with the death penalty and obligated brothel keepers to ensure that prostitutes had been sold into service with their relatives' consent. The deputy's office also stipulated that the brothels must be able to supply written contracts designating the prostitutes' length of service and terms of compensation.[29]

These restrictions on trafficking were part of the early Tokugawa project of state-building, a process that sought to link individuals to the polity through the institution of the patriarchal household. According to the shogunate's legal manuals as well as its newly instituted population registers, the household was the building block of the state; it was how the shogunate conceived of and kept track of its population, and it was the mechanism through which people were sorted into status "containers." On a more abstract level, the household functioned as a realm in miniature. As Nagano Hiroko has argued, many of the shogunate's and domains'. policies toward women served to reinforce a central metaphor that equated the wife's loyalty to her husband or the daughter's obedience to her parents with the subject's submission to his ruler. For this reason, Tokugawa law addressed women as members of households rather than as individuals, and time and again the shogunate's judgments upheld the husband and father's authority over his female relatives.[30] Yet in order for this legal and ideological system to function smoothly, the patriarch could not wield complete or arbitrary power over his dependents. Not only would this disturb the shogunate's philosophy of benevolent government by legitimizing abuse and coercion, it might also interfere with the shogunate's authority by allowing intermediaries to make decisions that were not in the state's best interest: if a husband allowed his wife to commit adultery, for example, this would undermine the metaphor linking wives to subjects by permitting the equivalent of treason.[31] The shogunate had an interest in supporting the household head, but not at the expense of the state.

Regulations on trafficking furthered this agenda by bolstering the head of household's authority while limiting his despotic tendencies. Although the patriarch was deprived of the ability to "buy and sell" his dependents, his dominion over them was confirmed in one crucial respect: the law determined that only a woman's legal guardian (*hitonushi*), ordinarily her male head of household, could sign her indenture contract and receive compensation for her term of service as a prostitute. This confirmed his exclusive authority to profit from his dependents' labor in the sex trade. His female relatives could not sign their own contracts and collect their own salaries, and unrelated men could not pose as guardians and interfere with his prerogative. This second principle was violated fairly often, as unscrupulous procurers assumed false identities in order to receive contract money from brothel keepers. One fictional example can be found in the kabuki play *Taiheiki shiroishi banashi* (*The Tale of Shiroishi and the Taihei Chronicles*), in which the heroine crosses paths with a venal procurer who tries to pose as her uncle in order to indenture her to an establishment in Yoshiwara.[32] When such cases came to the Edo magistrates' attention, they treated them seriously, imposing the death penalty on go-betweens trading in illegally procured women.[33]

While the rules about guardianship confirmed the head of household's authority to reap the proceeds of his dependents' labor, other laws subjected his power to important limitations. First, a household head could not indenture a woman to a brothel if her biological parents objected. In other words, if an adoptive father, stepfather, or affinal uncle attempted to send a woman into service as a prostitute, the woman's biological mother or father could protest that the contract was invalid. This was permitted even if the biological parent had relinquished custody. In 1684, for example, the Edo magistrates heard the complaint of a woman named Haru, who had allowed a townsman named Ken'emon to adopt her young daughter, Fuku. Over the years, Haru had visited her daughter regularly, but one day she arrived at Ken'emon's residence to find Fuku missing. Ken'emon told Haru that he had sent the girl into service, but he refused to divulge the name or location of her new employer. When the magistrates investigated, they found that Ken'emon had indentured Fuku to a Yoshiwara brothel. They invalidated the agreement, imprisoned Ken'emon, and returned the girl to Haru's custody.[34] Stepfathers were also penalized when they committed similar violations. In one such instance, a mother objected that her new husband had promised to indenture her daughter as a maidservant, but instead committed her to work as a prostitute. The stepfather was duly punished, and the girl was returned to her blood relatives.[35]

The shogunate also recognized and enforced private contracts that prevented household heads from sending their adopted daughters to work in brothels. By the late Tokugawa period, standard adoption contracts explicitly prohibited this practice.[36] Agreements to take in abandoned children, which were subject to official approval, contained the same caveat.[37] The existence of these contracts suggests that many biological parents perceived a categorical difference between prostitution and other types of work, such as domestic service, and that they desired to protect their daughters from a particularly hazardous or degrading form of labor. (However, as chapter 3 makes clear, not all members of the urban lower classes shared this opinion.) At the same time, the shogunate's willingness to uphold these agreements and to hear lawsuits related to this issue indicates that officials granted a special status to the presumably potent bond between biological parents and their children, which closely resembled their idealized conception of the ties between ruler and subject. Even a household head, who wielded ultimate authority over his dependents in so many other respects, could not be permitted to interfere with a biological parent's "natural" desire to protect his child.

The new laws on trafficking also limited the household head's power in another important respect: they prevented him from profiting from his wife's sexual labor. In several cases recorded in *Oshioki saikyochō*, husbands were imprisoned after indenturing their wives to brothels (and remarkably, if the wife had consented, she was also held responsible for the crime and punished).[38] In addition, husbands were penalized if they allowed their wives to serve as other men's concubines.[39] Both these practices violated the same new principle: a married woman was both obligated and entitled to remain monogamous. There was only one exception, established by the shogunate's One Hundred Articles in 1742, which declared that a man could allow his wife to work in prostitution if he was compelled by extreme poverty and she consented.[40] This was a last resort, however, and it is significant that the woman's consent was deemed necessary: this indicated that regardless of the circumstances, wives could not be forced to engage in extramarital sex. This was a dramatic shift away from the situation in the early seventeenth century, when in some parts of the realm, a husband could sell or rent his wife as a prostitute even if she objected.

Although these legal innovations restricted the pool of women eligible to work as prostitutes, Yoshiwara brothel keepers were able to manipulate the contract system to serve their interests. They ensured that prostitutes' labor agreements were far more coercive and restrictive than those for other servants. Extant indenture contracts from Yoshiwara are particularly difficult to find, probably because they were destroyed by the many fires that ravaged the quarter in the mid nineteenth century. But the conditions of labor in Edo's brothels can be inferred from those in the shogunate's other sanctioned "pleasure quarters," such as Kyoto's Shimabara and Osaka's Shinmachi. An agreement indenturing a teenager to a Kansai brothel in 1803 read:

Our biological daughter Hisa is at present nineteen years old. From the sixth month of the year of the boar until the sixth month of the year of the dragon—a period of exactly five years—she will be indentured for twenty-five *ryō* in gold. According to the terms of this contract, we will receive the sum total of this money [in advance] and then send her to you to serve as a *yūjo*. These terms are clear and definite.

She does not belong to the Christian faith, which has been prohibited by the shogunate. Rather, her family has belonged to the Jōdo sect for many generations, and a document confirming her temple affiliation has been attached to this contract.

If she incurs expenses at any time, we will pay them. Naturally, if she absconds with your property or escapes, we will certainly return the money that you lent us at the beginning of her term, even though she has [already] been [working as] an indentured servant. Of course, we will also compensate you for the items she has stolen. In addition, if she takes an unauthorized leave from service, she will not be able to claim [any items she has taken with her as] a loan. If at any time during her period of indenture she does not fulfill the terms of service, then you may do as you wish: if she incurs expenses you may return her to us, or you may send her into a similar type of service elsewhere. In that case, you may indenture her for as much money as you wish, and you will receive the sum of that money. If at the end of her period of indenture she has taken money or has outstanding debts, then we will settle the matter according to the established protocol and return her to you.

If she dies, whether she expires of illness or dies suddenly or accidentally, after investigating the matter you may bury her body wherever you wish. We will not say one word of complaint. Even if we are informed of this circumstance after the fact, we certainly will not express any hostility.

If someone pays to buy her out of service, you may demand an extra fee (*reikin*) as a token of gratitude. You may release her to anyone from anywhere, and as long as it is not for another term of service, he may have custody of her in perpetuity. Whatever his livelihood may be, we certainly will not complain.

After she has satisfactorily completed her term of service, if the signatories to this contract [i.e., her parents and guarantors] have died or moved someplace where they cannot be located, she may be indentured as a maid or used as a servant, or she may consent to be married—you may make whatever plans you wish and we will not raise the slightest objection. Moreover, during her term of service, we guarantee that you will not be troubled by anyone who comes forward claiming to be her husband, her previous master, or anyone else [who might invalidate the contract]. In addition, if there is any other problem or incident, we will come from any distance to settle the matter, and it will not cause you any difficulty.

So, for posterity, this is a contract for indentured service as a *yūjo*.⁴¹

The agreement was signed first by Hisa's father Kyūzō, a townsman from Osaka, and then by her mother Tsuya, a guarantor, a go-between, and finally Hisa herself.⁴²

The first part of this contract established that Hisa was Kyūzō's biological daughter. Such confirmation was crucial to the brothel keeper: if Hisa was not actually Kyūzō's daughter, another party might come forward later and claim to be her legitimate guardian. In that case, the contract could be declared invalid and the brothel keeper would be forced to take a loss. Hisa's new master wanted to avoid this problem, which is why the end of the contract also guaranteed that no one else would come forward with a prior claim. The other basic terms of the contract were stated in the first paragraph: Hisa would serve for five years in return for twenty-five *ryō*, a considerable sum of money for a poor Osaka townsman. Generally, a woman like Hisa, who was already sexually mature at the age of nineteen, would be worth more than a younger girl who was not yet ready to see customers (customarily, the age of majority was fifteen). A child could be used as a servant, but this was less profitable than employing an older woman who could be put to work seeing clients immediately.⁴³

There were several significant differences between this contract and that of a maidservant. First, a maidservant's contract would not contain the clause guaranteeing that no one with a prior claim would come forward to contest the indenture. Second, a servant's parents or guarantors would receive only part of her indenture money upfront, and she would receive the rest in intervals or upon completion of her term.⁴⁴ The prostitute's contract, in contrast, provided for all the money to be paid to her guardian at the time of indenture and did not contain any mention of the employee receiving compensation.⁴⁵ Third, a maidservant's contract would not contain clauses providing for sudden death or the possibility of a suitor buying out the contract. Finally, in a prostitute's contract, the master reserved the right to transfer the indentured woman to another employer.⁴⁶

While the first of these unique provisions suggested that indentures for prostitution were more likely to be contested than those for other types of work, the second and fourth blurred the line between involuntary servitude and indentured labor. In particular, the provision for transfer between brothels, a practice called *sumikae*, allowed the brothel keeper to engage in human trafficking. When a master sold one of his women to a different brothel, he was acting as her new guardian, and he possessed the legal authority to dispose of her labor. The wishes of her original guardian, in this case her father, were not relevant. The brothel keeper could draw up a new contract with different terms, which allowed him to profit from the arrangement by indenturing her for more money than he had paid her father. This could lead to a situation in which a woman ended up with a term of service that exceeded the ten-year limit set by the shogunate. For example, if she had served her first master for four years and her new contract provided for a term of eight years, she would end up serving twelve years in total. This was illegal, and when the magistrates heard about these situations, they punished the brothel keepers.[47] However, contracts contained intimidating language prohibiting the indentured woman or her parents from issuing even "one word of complaint" about the practice.

While brothel keepers manipulated contractual language in order to elude the ten-year limit on service, they were much more willing to comply with the law forbidding men from indenturing their wives into prostitution, which was compatible with their own interest in separating marriage from trafficking. For example, when the Yoshiwara *yūjo* Usugumo II was bought out of service in 1700, her future husband signed a statement that included the following clause: "Hereafter, I shall not let her work as a courtesan, which is prohibited by the law; nor would I let her work at a teahouse, inn, or any other questionable establishment. If I were found violating such rules, I would be content to submit to punishment by the authorities."[48] This provision protected Usugumo, but it also protected the brothel keeper. If there were no conditions attached to marriage agreements, any client with sufficient resources could redeem a prostitute through marriage and then sell her to a competing establishment. In this case, as in so many others, the interests of the shogunate and the brothel keeper dovetailed: both were invested in maintaining the distinction between marrying a woman and purchasing her with the intent to turn a profit, the shogunate on the grounds that chaste wives should be protected and the brothel keeper on the grounds that such rules were good for business.

CHALLENGES AND READJUSTMENTS: FROM MONOPOLY TO STATUS

SHIFTS IN POLICY

The shogunate's initial strategy of regulation through containment was continually challenged by a growing population of "clandestine prostitutes" (*kakushi baijo*) who worked outside Yoshiwara. Some were streetwalkers who solicited along riverbanks or went out on boats to meet customers. Common people called them "whores" (*baita*), and fiction writers portrayed them as pitiful, degraded creatures. Ihara Saikaku's *The Life of an Amorous Woman (Kōshoku ichidai onna)* depicts a group of elderly streetwalkers who charge only ten *monme* per encounter. They return home at the end of the evening exhausted and disheveled, only to hand their pimps 50 percent of the proceeds.[49] Women who worked in these circumstances belonged to the most vulnerable segments of urban society: they were the daughters and wives of socially marginal men, or they were former brothel workers who had been cast out after they became too ill to see clients. In many cases, they were employed by gangsters, gamblers, amateur sumo wrestlers, criminals, and other underworld figures seeking to earn some quick cash. Other women sold sex at the behest of their male relatives. For example, in 1728, the Edo city magistrates interrogated a tenant from Fukagawa who admitted that since he was having trouble making a living, he lent his wife to a boat captain, who had her service his passengers every night. He claimed that she had consented, but the magistrates found his story incredible and sentenced him to banishment.[50] The labor arrangements in these cases did not rely on the contract system, and if there had been contracts involved, the shogunate would not have considered them enforceable.

Other outfits employing clandestine prostitutes were large-scale operations that purported to have contracted their employees for purposes other than selling sex. The chronicle *Keichō kenbunroku* (Things Seen and Heard in the Keichō Era) reported that as early as 1614, four years before the Yoshiwara brothels opened for business, there were bathhouses in every ward of the city where twenty or thirty "seductive" women would scrub men's bodies and rinse their hair.[51] By the middle of the seventeenth century, Yoshiwara proprietors began to complain that the bathhouses were hurting their business, particularly since they were allowed to operate at night, while the quarter's brothels were still limited to daytime hours. After sundown, the bathhouses took over many of the brothels' functions; they even held drinking parties where their employees played the *shamisen* to entertain guests. To make matters worse, the bathing girls (*yuna*) were cheaper than *yūjo*, and the bathhouses, which operated in each ward, were far more conveniently located than Yoshiwara.[52]

During the seventeenth century, the Yoshiwara proprietors, fearing for their monopoly, often petitioned the magistrates asking them to eradicate prostitution outside the sanctioned quarter. Officials usually responded by encouraging or compelling clandestine prostitutes and their employers to relocate to Yoshiwara. In the aftermath of the Meireki fire in 1657, for example, officials closed 200 bathhouses and apprehended 600 bathing girls. Some of the bathhouse proprietors subsequently moved their businesses and their women to Yoshiwara, and the quarter's monopoly was restored.[53] The shogunate pursued the same strategy when dealing with streetwalkers. A precedent from the seventeenth century mandated that if women apprehended for clandestine prostitution had consented to sell their bodies, they should be punished in the same way as those who had committed other types of sexual indiscretions: they would be enslaved or sent to work in Yoshiwara.[54] Eventually, the penalty was standardized, and in 1742, the One Hundred Articles stated that all women apprehended for clandestine prostitution should be sentenced to three years' service in the "pleasure quarter."

But the magistrates' strategy of enforcement actually changed dramatically in the eighteenth century. "Inns" (*hatagoya*) and "teahouses" (*chaya*) selling sex emerged in several areas of the city, usually near post stations and religious institutions. The approach to Nezu shrine, the district surrounding Eitaiji temple in Fukagawa, the neighborhood near Yanaka's Kannōji temple, the approach to Ekōin temple in Honjo, and the four post stations leading out of Edo (Itabashi, Senju, Shinagawa, and Naitō Shinjuku), among other areas, became known as "hill places" (*okabasho*) where men could buy sex. By the end of the period, commentators alleged that there were over twenty-seven of these areas in Edo, excluding the post stations and including four neighborhoods dedicated to male prostitution.[55] In many of these locales, shogunal officials had an interest in promoting the sex trade. The temple and shrine magistrates (*jisha bugyō*), who administered territory surrounding religious institutions, deliberately ignored prostitution within their jurisdiction because brothels masquerading as teahouses attracted pilgrims who financially supported temples and shrines. In fact, during the late Tokugawa period, it was not unusual to find Yoshiwara brothel keepers temporarily setting up shop in the precincts of Sensōji temple, presumably with the magistrates' tacit approval.[56] Road magistrates (*dōchū bugyō*) were equally willing to promote prostitution because it brought revenue to post stations, which were vital components of the shogunate's transportation system. In 1718, in order to augment the post stations' finances, they allowed each inn to employ two "serving girls" who were actually prostitutes. In 1771, the shogunate relaxed this restriction for stations near Edo, which were particularly cash-strapped, allowing Shinagawa 500 and Itabashi and Senju 150 serving girls each.[57]

This policy was not unique to Edo. In Osaka, shogunal magistrates were even more explicit about promoting prostitution in areas where they thought it would benefit economic development. Osaka had a designated "pleasure quarter,"

Shinmachi, which was modeled after the Shimabara district in Kyoto, and proclamations stated that Shinmachi *yūjo* were the city's only legal prostitutes. Yet bathhouses and teahouses in other areas soon began to offer sexual services, and their neighborhoods were popularly termed "islands" (*shima*), much like the "hill places" of Edo. Unlike their counterparts in the capital, however, the Osaka city magistrates formally recognized these districts and issued legislation limiting the numbers of women proprietors could employ. They also played a more active role in creating such neighborhoods. When a series of riparian works along the Yodo River created new landfills at the turn of the eighteenth century, the authorities encouraged teahouses, brothels, and bathhouses to begin operations there, reasoning that they would jump-start economic development in formerly uninhabited zones.[58] It is possible that Edo-based magistrates had learned from these successful measures in Osaka and then applied the same policies to the neighborhoods in their own city where they hoped to stimulate growth. For the sake of propriety, however, they did not formally acknowledge the *okabasho* in the heart of the capital, even though they sanctioned the serving girls in the post stations leading out of the city.

Unlike streetwalkers and even bathhouse girls, who were scattered around the city and were not clearly distinguishable from other townswomen, the post-station serving girls and *okabasho* teahouse girls had distinct characteristics that made it possible to incorporate them into the status system. Post-station prostitutes had a clearly defined place of residence (the post station), answered to a legally recognized chain of authority (the innkeeper, the post station officials, and then the road magistrates), and in their own way contributed to their employers' responsibility to the state by bringing revenue to the stations. They adhered to sumptuary regulations and were assigned a consistent designation in legal documents, where they were always referred to as *meshimori onna*. Teahouse girls' claim to a coherent status was more tenuous, but they did tend to reside in specific locations (around temples and shrines), they answered to legally recognized authorities (the teahouse master, occasionally the temples and shrines themselves, and ultimately the temple and shrine magistrates), and they fulfilled a responsibility to the state by supporting religious institutions.

The *okabasho* prostitutes and post-station serving girls also worked according to patterns that supported the gendered political order. They were held to indenture contracts nearly identical to those of the prostitutes in Yoshiwara, in which each was signed into service by a guardian (usually a parent) and had a term of no more than ten years.[59] While the conditions of these agreements were restrictive for the women involved, they were acceptable to the shogunate. They did not jeopardize the institution of the patriarchal household because they precluded the possibility that women could sell sex to support an independent livelihood. Since they provided for limited, rather than eternal, terms of service, they also conformed to the limits the shogunate had placed on "buying and selling people." In contrast, the labor patterns of streetwalkers, who did not work under contract and were often pimped by their own husbands, were extremely problematic. As victims of disease and coercion, their presence on the streets of the city could highlight problems of poverty, moral degradation, and abuse of power. *Okabasho* and post-station prostitutes, whose suffering was less visible, did not present the same challenge to the ideal of benevolent government.

Like Yoshiwara *yūjo*, teahouse girls and serving girls were daughters working on behalf of their families, not wives forced to commit adultery or single women supporting themselves. As girls who sacrificed their chastity to benefit their parents, they fulfilled the shogunate's conception of the appropriate place of women in the realm. While the magistrates' promotion of prostitution in the post stations and *okabasho* compromised the original policy of regulation through containment, then, it did not undermine a broader notion of order, which envisioned prostitutes as female subjects who deserved a certain degree of protection, but who were confined to subordinate positions within their own households and the polity at large. By encouraging the growth of the sex trade within these limits, the magistrates could reconcile their pursuit of prosperity with the maintenance of patriarchal authority.

TARGETED ENFORCEMENT

As the shogunate adjusted its policies to take advantage of opportunities to profit from prostitution outside the "pleasure quarter," the status distinctions dividing prostitutes from other women were decoupled from the moribund idea that all legal prostitutes belonged in a specific location. Ironically, Yoshiwara brothel keepers contributed to this shift (and the ensuing loss of their monopoly) through their selective enforcement of the laws on clandestine prostitution. In 1664, when the containment strategy was at its height, the Yoshiwara brothel keepers were granted the privilege of patrolling the city and apprehending illegal prostitutes.[60] On the surface, the shogunate's delegation of such duties to Yoshiwara was perfectly logical: the quarter's proprietors had an interest in preserving their monopoly, and they also benefited from the arrests, since the apprehended women would provide free labor when they served out their terms of punishment in Yoshiwara. But the Yoshiwara brothel keepers had other interests as well, and some of them were oriented toward protecting or even perpetuating prostitution outside the quarter. As Tsukada

Takashi and Yoshida Nobuyuki have demonstrated, the Yoshiwara proprietors had much in common with their colleagues elsewhere in Edo. Even in the seventeenth century, when they worked to limit clandestine prostitution, the very methods they used revealed the extent of their ties to illegal operations. For example, in 1668, a mission to apprehend brothel keepers in the neighborhood of Tsukiji-chayamachi was compromised because the offenders were alerted ahead of time. To find out who had betrayed their plans, the Yoshiwara headmen gathered thirty of their procurers (*zegen*) and compelled them each to relinquish the contracts of twenty clandestine prostitutes. This demonstrated that the procurers were ultimately responsible to the Yoshiwara proprietors, but it also revealed that the sanctioned district's brothels and the illegal establishments relied on the same networks to recruit women.[61]

Brothels inside and outside the quarter were also connected by informers (*meakashi*) employed by the shogunate. These men were usually recruited from the ranks of former (or current) criminals and deputized to report on illegal activity.[62] Yoshiwara's proprietors had strong connections to the informers and frequently used them to relay information about the locations of illegal brothels. At the same time, the informers themselves were often the proprietors of such establishments.[63] As with the procurers, the Yoshiwara brothel keepers were dependent on their own competition, and they had no motive to punish the men with whom they did business. In the seventeenth century, many of the Yoshiwara's informers, procurers, and go-betweens were residents of Asakusa Tamachi, a neighborhood just outside the gates of the quarter. As a result, when the Yoshiwara brothel keepers went out to apprehend illegal prostitutes, they tended to spare the residents of this ward, even though the neighborhood was well known for its brothels. The shogunate followed the association's lead, and when it charged Asakusa Tamachi proprietors with abetting clandestine prostitution, it assigned them comparatively light punishments.[64]

During the second half of the Tokugawa period, the geographical extent of the Yoshiwara brothel keepers' connections expanded and ties between their district and the most prominent *okabasho* became even more pronounced. Fires in Yoshiwara forced brothel keepers to temporarily relocate eighteen times between 1768 and 1866, and in each case the proprietors requested to be moved to places that were already notorious *okabasho*, including neighborhoods in Fukagawa, Honjo, and Asakusa. Presumably these areas were appealing because prostitution was already established and there was a built-in clientele.[65] In some cases, the brothel keepers inside and outside Yoshiwara were literally the same people. When the Naitō Shinjuku post station was reopened in 1771 after a decades-long shutdown, many proprietors moved there from Yoshiwara, leading observers to comment that the customs in both areas were nearly identical.[66]

The shogunate inadvertently strengthened connections between the *okabasho* and Yoshiwara when it cracked down on clandestine prostitution during the Tenpō Reforms in 1842. This was one of the few occasions when the shogunate insisted on reviving the confinement model of regulation, in this case due to political pressure to rectify manners and morals in the midst of an unprecedented economic crisis. (Notably, at least one of the city magistrates opposed such measures, insisting that curbing conspicuous consumption, relocating playhouses, and shutting down entertainment districts hurt the city's economy and did not qualify as "benevolent government.")[67] When the reforms were implemented, the *okabasho* proprietors were forced to abandon their profession or relocate to Yoshiwara. Those who chose the latter option formed lasting relationships with their new neighbors. In 1866, some of the former Fukagawa proprietors, who had spent nearly two decades in Yoshiwara, petitioned the shogunate to be permitted to move back to their old neighborhood. Rather than objecting on the grounds of their monopoly, the Yoshiwara brothel keepers' association supported the petition, reasoning that there was more than enough business to go around.[68] By the end of the Tokugawa period, then, the Yoshiwara proprietors had ceased viewing the *okabasho* as a threat. Instead, they had begun looking for allies in their bid to extend their business beyond the gates of their quarter.

As maintaining the location-based monopoly became less important to both magistrates and brothel keepers, the boundary between legal and illegal prostitution came to be demarcated, not by the walls of the "pleasure quarter," but by the economic institution of the contract. The clandestine prostitutes mentioned in the shogunate's *Oshioki reiruishū* (Collection of Punishments and Precedents), which was compiled periodically throughout the second half of the period, were usually not indentured laborers from post-station or *okabasho* brothels, which were protected by their associations with Yoshiwara proprietors and informers as well as shogunate-supported religious institutions and post stations. Instead, they were women who were not working under contract: wives pimped by their husbands or streetwalkers affiliated with gangsters. Two townsmen's wives, Masa and Shun, both convicted for clandestine prostitution and acquitted for adultery after they left their husbands for clients, were among these unfortunate women.[69] Another, Mine, was apprehended in 1790 for selling her body while working as a waitress in her husband's pub and sentenced to three years in Yoshiwara.[70] Of course, the women targeted for punishment accounted for only a tiny proportion of the clandestine prostitutes working the streets of Edo. Still, it is significant that in the absence of an anomalous political situation such as the Tenpō Reforms, this was the type of infraction that attracted the authorities' (limited) attention, while the large brothels in the *okabasho* were allowed to thrive.

In that sense, the *okabasho* and Yoshiwara were integral parts of the same system and not fierce competitors. Through their connections, embodied by procurers and informants, they worked together to corner the market in women by strengthening the contract system and diverting enforcement to the marginal operators who threatened the shared foundations of their business. Although this strategy subverted the distinction between prostitutes inside and outside the "pleasure quarter," it reinforced the commonality between indentured prostitutes in both locations and their difference from other townswomen. Proprietors supported the contract system for economic reasons—because it was profitable for individual brothel keepers and because it allowed them to form networks, exchange employees, and expand their business. At the same time, because the women involved were always daughters working to support their family members, usually fathers or older brothers, proprietors' adherence to this model preserved households and confirmed the ideal of patriarchal order. This may have been an unintended consequence of the brothel keepers' attempts to promote and protect their business, but it was likely a welcome outcome for most of them. After all, if proprietors were helping young girls support their families, then their occupation could be justified. By pursuing their own economic interests, they might even be perceived as advancing the cause of benevolence.

THE GEISHA PROBLEM

The magistrates' and brothel keepers' efforts to police the sex trade overlooked a significant number of women who sold sexual services as a secondary occupation. These cases could be difficult to investigate; it was much easier to find and apprehend streetwalkers than it was to locate and arrest women who made spontaneous or sporadic decisions to exchange sex for payment. The shogunate recognized this problem, and the city magistrates decided in the 1730s that waitresses and dancers who were called to teahouses to serve as entertainers would not be regarded as clandestine prostitutes if they entered into private agreements with customers who were willing to pay them for sex.[71] But the magnitude of this type of activity increased dramatically during the mid eighteenth century when artistically accomplished young women began to imitate the style of male entertainers called geisha, who played music and made conversation at parties in Yoshiwara. These newly minted female geisha, who entertained at private gatherings throughout the city, started a craze by parading around Edo in men's short jackets (*haori*). Soon they became more popular than their models.[72] These women often crossed the blurry line between prostitution and performance. To avoid the appearance of competing with brothel keepers' employees, Yoshiwara geisha insisted that they did not sell sex.[73] But they were the exception. Geisha working in the Fukagawa *okabasho*, as well as smaller districts such as Yotsuya and Ryōgoku, were eager to pursue any means necessary to make a living, and they were notorious for having sex with clients.[74]

As the profession of female "geisha" became more established, geisha house proprietors, like the *okabasho* brothel keepers before them, modeled their employment arrangements after the contract system for indentured labor in prostitution. Geisha contracts contained the same clauses as prostitutes' contracts: a girl's master had the right to transfer her at any time, her biological parents were liable if she committed suicide, and the sum of her indenture money was paid to her guardian at the time of indenture.[75] This system forged connections between geisha house operators and brothel proprietors, and some geisha's contracts bluntly stated that their employers could transfer them to brothels.[76] Since they were closely aligned with established businesses, women recruited and employed in this manner posed little threat to brothel keepers elsewhere in the city. Moreover, the magistrates could rest assured that an indentured geisha, like a legally recognized prostitute, was a daughter working to support her parents.

During the early nineteenth century, however, ordinary townsmen began to take advantage of this new occupational category, which allowed them to profit from the sale of sexual services without technically breaking the law. If they hired out their daughters to entertain at banquets, they could call them geisha and earn revenue from their labor without signing contracts or relinquishing their parental rights. Conversely, they could use adoption as a strategy to acquire unrelated girls as "geisha," whom they would then send out to work as prostitutes. In 1848, one of the shogunate's secret inspectors (*onmitsu mawari*) complained to his superiors in the city magistrates' office:

Since the Bunsei era [1818–30], there have been regulations about female geisha in town. In some instances, families hire out their daughters as geisha as a last resort, because a parent or older brother is ill and unable to make a living. But these cases are exceptional; mostly, people hire out [their daughters as] geisha for no legitimate reason, or they hire out indentured women [*kakae onna*] as geisha. There have been proclamations against this, but somehow enforcement has become lax. People have changed what they call their indentured women; they use the pretext that their charges are adopted daughters. But in reality they are employing as many as two or three women and hiring them out as geisha. These women are not quite clandestine prostitutes, but [there is some resemblance]: their adoptive parents will make arrangements between a customer and his favorite girl, and for a fee of a few *ryō* in gold, they will agree to give her leave for a few months, during which time she will become his kept concubine [*ishō*]. Therefore, her parents have granted her permission to engage in illicit sexual relations [*mittsū*], which is even more perverse than clandestine prostitution [*kakushi baijo yori mo wake chigai sōrō*].[77]

The inspector's commentary highlights the problem of trafficking in the guise of adoption. Although he accepted that some biological parents would send their daughters to work as geisha "as a last resort," he recoiled at the idea of adoptive parents pimping their "daughters" to make a profit. He condemned them for promoting what he described as "illicit sex," using the shogunate's preferred term for adultery and other relationships that threatened a husband or father's authority to control his female relatives' sexuality. Obviously, the inspector thought it appropriate for a father (even an adoptive father) to attempt to *limit* his daughter's sexual relationships rather than encourage them. By sending their adopted daughters out to work as geisha when it was not necessary to ensure their households' survival, so-called "parents" were making a mockery of their prescribed role.

The inspector was also alarmed by the increasing popularity of women who worked as geisha on their own initiative. He reported that their primary occupation was teaching singing and shamisen lessons, but they supplemented their income by going out to entertain on boats and at teahouses and occasionally engaging in illicit sex with their customers. In his estimation this was not quite the same as straightforward clandestine prostitution, since they typically "assumed a cold and distant attitude" and only sold sex when they had trouble making ends meet. He did not judge this behavior harshly, probably because he was convinced that it was motivated by desperation and not lasciviousness or desire for profit. But he concluded that these geisha's activities would eventually become mixed up with clandestine prostitution and lead to a decline in general morality. At the end of his report, he listed 163 women between the ages of fifteen and thirty-five who were known to be working as geisha. Some were described as indentured women belonging to an establishment such as a teahouse, but many more were listed as townsmen's daughters.[78]

Soon after the city magistrates received this report, they issued a new ruling meant to ease the confusion: if necessary to alleviate extreme poverty, each townsman's household would be permitted to send one daughter to work as a geisha.[79] In theory, the new rule would limit the informal geisha business to situations the inspector deemed acceptable—those in which a family experienced hardship and sacrificed a daughter as a last resort. It made no allowance for geisha who worked on their own initiative, deploying their sexuality for their own profit rather than for the sake of their households' survival. This compromise echoed the clause in the One Hundred Articles stating that husbands were allowed to send their wives out as prostitutes, but only if the latter had consented and extreme poverty made it absolutely necessary. It upheld a principle that had become fundamental to the functioning of the contract system and the shogunate's conception of gendered order: women were permitted to exchange sexual services for payment only if they were supporting their families and all other money-making strategies had failed.

From the establishment of the Yoshiwara "pleasure quarter" in the early seventeenth century to the official sanction of the Fukagawa *okabasho* in the mid-nineteenth century, city magistrates and brothel keepers worked together to create a strategy of regulation that could encourage economic growth and generate profits, while also maintaining order. From the shogunate's perspective, the meaning of order changed over time. Initially, it meant containing unruly male perisexual activity and eliminating the possibility of rebellion. But over the course of the eighteenth century, it came to encompass a broader and different range of priorities, including maintaining the financial stability of religious institutions and post stations and protecting the integrity of poor townsmen's households. If building brothels outside temples, in post stations, or on reclaimed lands enlivened those areas' economies, or if allowing poor families to send daughters to work as geisha saved them from ruin, then promoting the expansion of the sex trade could be interpreted as a strategy toward social order and a form of benevolence. Moreover, the success of these establishments directly or indirectly contributed to the government's coffers. By the end of the Tokugawa period, Edo magistrates had decided that unruly male sexual or perisexual behavior was a small price to pay for these benefits.

Meanwhile, brothel keepers found ways to make their economic goals compatible with the shogunate's changing priorities. Initially, Yoshiwara proprietors offered to contain unruly perisexual behavior and report on suspicious activity in return for a monopoly. Later, as the shogunate began to promote prostitution as a strategy for revitalizing urban neighborhoods and supporting religious institutions and post stations, they were quick to take advantage of the opportunity to do business outside the "pleasure quarter." Although the walls surrounding the Yoshiwara appeared rigid and unyielding, they were not reliable symbols of the strategy of regulation in Edo, which was subject to constant renegotiation. By the end of the period, the destruction of Yoshiwara's monopoly on the sex trade was considered acceptable, and even desirable, by proprietors and magistrates alike.

Yet both groups continued to insist on the integrity of the contract system for indentured service in prostitution, which had become the primary means of distinguishing between prostitutes and other women. The magistrates did so because it allowed them to maintain patriarchal order: contracts ensured that women in the sex trade were working on behalf of their families and not to support an independent livelihood outside the household. Meanwhile, brothel keepers favored this system because it allowed them to exploit women's labor while also creating a network that connected them to proprietors in various areas of the city. For the same reasons, both groups had a stake in eliminating prostitution of or by women who were not held to indenture contracts. If husbands were allowed to pimp their wives or women were able to support themselves through streetwalking, then the magistrates had sanctioned behavior that visibly challenged their commitment to benevolence and unsettled the metaphor linking the household and the realm. Brothel keepers inside and outside Yoshiwara also had a stake in limiting this type of activity, which threatened their monopoly on the lucrative business of selling sex. Thus both the contract system and the enforcement of the statutes on clandestine prostitution limited legal work in the sex trade to cases in which a filial daughter was indentured for a "short" term of service by a desperate parent.

In the nineteenth century, this arrangement was challenged by townsmen who sent their daughters to work as geisha and allowed, or even encouraged, them to sell sex. This negated the distinction between townswomen and prostitutes, threatened the brothel keepers' monopoly on the sex trade, and upended the ideal of the household by turning the benevolent patriarch into a pimp. The magistrates' response to this test of their regulatory strategy revealed just how far they were willing to compromise. When they relented and allowed townsmen to rent out their daughters as geisha in cases of extreme economic hardship, they sanctioned behavior that undermined the contract system, albeit on a limited basis. But they would not abandon the ideal of the prostitute as a filial daughter (rather than an adulterous wife or free agent). Ultimately, this was the most important way that prostitution supported the gendered political order. As long as the women involved labored on behalf of their parents, and ideally their fathers, work in prostitution reinforced patriarchal authority in the household and the realm.

Outside the shogunate's legal compilations, the conception of the prostitute as a devoted daughter took on a life of its own. It figured in *Yūjo daigaku* (The Greater Learning for Prostitutes), a mocking take on a popular didactic text for women, which featured an illustration of a daughter's departure for the brothel captioned with the character *kō* (filial piety). A similar scene appeared in the popular play *Chūshingura* (A Treasury of Loyal Retainers), which portrayed a teenage girl who entered service in Kyoto's Shimabara in order to support her impoverished parents.[80] By evoking this cultural trope, playwrights and other artists probably meant to inspire feelings of sympathy for the women they depicted, and their renderings likely moved audiences of samurai, upper-class townsmen, and prosperous peasants to tears. But to families who were living out the stories prescribed in legal manuals and dramatized onstage, the officially approved narrative of reluctant parents and dutiful daughters could have other uses. Their interactions with brothel keepers and the state are the subject of the next chapter.

CHAPTER THREE · Negotiating the Gendered Order

Prostitutes as Daughters, Wives, and Mothers

Prostitutes in the southern port city of Nagasaki, like their counterparts in the shogun's capital of Edo, were often immortalized in colorful woodblock prints and paintings. Sometimes they closely resembled Yoshiwara *yūjo*, wearing elaborate robes, spiky gold hair ornaments, and high wooden clogs. But while Yoshiwara's women are usually depicted gazing into mirrors, posing with parasols, or playing with their pets, Nagasaki's prostitutes are shown engaging in a broader (and, for their time, more unusual) array of activities: looking through telescopes, playing pool, and watching for tall ships in the harbor. Others look more like townsmen's wives, in relatively plain robes and with modest hairstyles, but they have unusual companions, such as exotic Siamese cats and redheaded babies.[1]

These images highlight Nagasaki *yūjo*'s most distinctive characteristic: their close association with foreign men. Like *yūjo* in Yoshiwara, Nagasaki's legal prostitutes were indentured to brothels located in an enclosed district, the renowned "pleasure quarter" of Maruyama. But unlike *yūjo* in the capital, the majority left their neighborhood frequently for appointments with Dutch and Chinese traders. Some even lived with foreign men for years at a time. These relationships were intriguing to Japanese observers, most of whom had never encountered anyone from outside the archipelago. Visitors to Nagasaki filled the pages of their travel diaries with salacious details about the city's prostitutes. For example, the boisterous Owari merchant Hishiya Heishichi, who visited Maruyama in 1811, wrote that he enjoyed hearing prostitutes discuss the sexual predilections of their Chinese clients.[2] These

FIGURE 2.
Utagawa Hiroshige II, *Nagasaki Maruyama no kei* (View of Maruyama in Nagasaki), from the series *Shokoku meisho hyakkei* (One Hundred Famous Views in the Various Provinces), woodblock print, vertical *ōban* (1859). A Maruyama *yūjo* looks through a telescope at passing ships in Nagasaki harbor. Photograph © 2011 Museum of Fine Arts, Boston.

FIGURE 3.
Kawahara Keiga, *Ransen nyūkō no zu* (Arrival of a Dutch Ship), from *Rankan emaki* (Scroll of the Dutch Factory). Color on paper, 35.5 × 22.5 cm (mid-nineteenth century). Two Dutchmen survey Nagasaki harbor from Dejima, attended by two *yūjo* and an Indonesian servant. The women wear relatively sober clothing and modest hairstyles. One carries a red-haired baby, presumably her Dutch companion's child. Nagasaki Museum of History and Culture.

accounts, like most contemporary scholarship, positioned Nagasaki's prostitutes as intermediaries between their own relatively closed society and a more cosmopolitan realm just beyond the reach of ordinary Japanese men and women.[3]

This emphasis on *yūjo* as cultural or sexual mediators privileged the foreign over the familiar and the exotic over the mundane, often obscuring the bonds that linked women to their natal families and native communities. Yet these ties were central to *yūjo*'s everyday lives. In her work on colonial Nairobi, Luise White has observed that "the work of prostitutes was family labor." This, she argues, was not an unusual circumstance. In contexts as diverse as Victorian York, turn-of-the-century Kansas, and mid-twentieth-century Bengal, "prostitutes were not the victims of weak families; they were the victims of strong ones."[4] This was equally true of Nagasaki's *yūjo:* their indenture money supported their parents, and while they were in service, they often continued to find ways to provide financial assistance to their relations. Through their links to their natal families, *yūjo* were enmeshed in social and economic networks that extended far beyond their individual encounters with traders. They connected the "pleasure quarter" to city neighborhoods even as they bridged the distance between Japan and the outside world.

The shogunate, which was interested in maintaining control over economic and social contacts between Japanese and foreigners, kept a careful watch on Nagasaki's *yūjo*. This heightened surveillance had unintended consequences. In addition to exposing illegal dealings between city residents and Dutch and Chinese traders, it also revealed the enduring ties between *yūjo* and their families. As Miyamoto Yukiko has demonstrated, cases involving prostitutes' parents appeared regularly in the Nagasaki criminal register (*hankachō*).[5] References to *yūjo*'s families also crowd the pages of the Yoriai ward record, a series of reports authored by the brothel keepers in charge of one of the two districts comprising the Maruyama quarter. These accounts of women who ran smuggling rings for their brothers, brought home imported silk for their mothers to sew, or left their children for their parents to raise demonstrate how prostitutes encountered the law both as indentured women belonging to the status group *yūjo* and as women belonging to their natal households. In their capacity as daughters, wives, and mothers, Maruyama's prostitutes were certainly liminal figures, but not only in the way that printmakers and diarists imagined. Their work linked their own families' domestic economies to the shogunate's larger vision of a moral economy in which daughters worked to benefit protective parents, just as subjects worked to serve benevolent rulers.

Contrary to what Tokugawa officials might have imagined when they positioned rulers as analogous to parents, the interests of the family and the realm did not always align perfectly. Magistrates were appalled to find that parents might put their daughters in harm's way for profit's sake rather than to ensure their households' survival, and they were conflicted when women claimed that they had broken the law out of a sense of filial duty. Yet when commoners' values and practices intersected with official expectations, women and their families could exploit these overlapping ideas about fealty and obligation to resist abuse and exploitation. By giving prostitutes a place in the gendered order of the status system, the shogunate had also granted them a platform from which they could argue for official consideration.

This observation about the uses of status is by now a familiar argument in the historiography of Tokugawa Japan. Several scholars have described how the male heads of peasant households stressed their roles as cultivators, so-called honorable peasants (*onbyakushō*), when they petitioned the authorities for tax relief. Often they succeeded by appealing to the domainal or shogunal magistrates' benevolence and their sense of obligation toward their perceived inferiors.[6] But women were forced to take a slightly different approach to this type of negotiation. As Anne Walthall has shown, peasant women involved themselves in written appeals only in exceptional cases when they had to speak for absent husbands or fathers.[7] Unlike "peasant," the status category *yūjo* applied only to women who were not heads of households; but *yūjo*, like peasant women, rarely made written appeals to magistrates. Instead, they leveraged their position by taking direct action (absconding, for example) and waiting for their cases to be decided, or by relying on their parents to speak for them.

These strategies capitalized on the tension created by a political order that both literally and metaphorically linked patriarchal households to the state. As chapter 2 has explained, the shogunate reconciled its economic interest in promoting the sex trade with its political interest in preserving households by restricting legal prostitution to situations in which an unmarried woman labored to support her parents. If a woman was a *yūjo*, then by definition she was under contract to a brothel and working on behalf of her family. This gave her a positive role to play relative to patriarchal authority writ both large (as a prostitute whose labor contributed to the realm's prosperity) and small (as a daughter whose sacrifice saved her father's household). But when the two roles conflicted, a woman's identity as a prostitute could never quite subsume her identity as a daughter. While *yūjo* were technically members of brothel keepers' households, they were defined by their service to their natal families. And as even brothel keepers recognized, the bond between parent and child was more politically potent than the contract linking master to servant. As a result, prostitutes' obligations to their employers could always be subverted by their duties to their parents.[8] This proved useful for prostitutes and their families when they hoped to nullify contracts and create paths toward marriage and motherhood. Whether they were appealing to begrudging brothel keepers or benevolent magistrates, conforming to cultural scripts that required dutiful (passive) daughters and protective parents enabled some *yūjo* to carve out lives beyond the "pleasure quarter."

BETWEEN FOREIGN AND FAMILIAR

By the dawn of the Tokugawa period, the area surrounding Nagasaki had already been established as a center of Japan's foreign trade. In the late sixteenth century,

European and Chinese ships dropped their anchors at the nearby island port of Hirado, where the Dutch East India Company eventually established a trading post in 1609. While stationed at Hirado, foreigners often formed sexual relationships with local women. Sometimes these liaisons were temporary: if a sailor found himself stranded in port during the typhoon season, he could strike a deal with an unmarried girl's parents and purchase her companionship for a period of weeks or months. After a few summers engaged in this type of work, a girl could acquire enough money to complete her trousseau, at which point she would marry and retire from the business of selling sex.[9] In other instances, traders stationed for longer periods took women as concubines or entered into marriage agreements. The diversity of options available to foreign residents resulted in some unorthodox arrangements. The Dutch trader Cornelis van Nijenroode, appointed chief factor of the Dutch trading post in 1623, carried on simultaneous affairs with two Japanese women and had a daughter with each.[10] Zheng Zhilong, a Hokkien trader who did business with the Dutch East India Company, established a more conventional family. He married a local woman and made their son, Zheng Chenggong (better known in English as Coxinga), heir to his piratical empire.[11] The Englishman William Adams, who entered the service of the first shogun, Tokugawa Ieyasu, split the difference: he married a Honshu post-station headman's daughter but also kept a concubine in Hirado.[12]

The Hirado trade came to an abrupt end in 1640, when the shogunate, anxious about the spread of Christianity and eager to appropriate the local daimyō's share of foreign commerce, removed the traders from the island and razed their storehouses. This inaugurated a period of "maritime prohibition" (*kaikin*), in which foreign contact with Japan was limited and the shogun's subjects were forbidden to travel outside the realm.[13] The Dutch, the only Europeans allowed to continue their trade with Japan, were moved to the artificial island of Dejima, which had been built to house Portuguese traders before they were expelled from the country. Surrounded by high walls and heavily guarded, the island was extremely cramped. It contained only two streets, a warehouse, and a few shabby buildings, which one despondent occupant later derided as "goat pens."[14] Dejima's residents (hereafter referred to as Dutchmen, although the group also included other Europeans employed by the Dutch East India Company, as well as Indonesian and African slaves and servants) were seldom permitted to leave their miserable outpost and not allowed to associate with the Japanese population. Ordinarily, Nagasaki townsmen were prohibited from entering the enclosure; the only exceptions were various officials, guards, translators, the traders' servants, and the peddlers who came

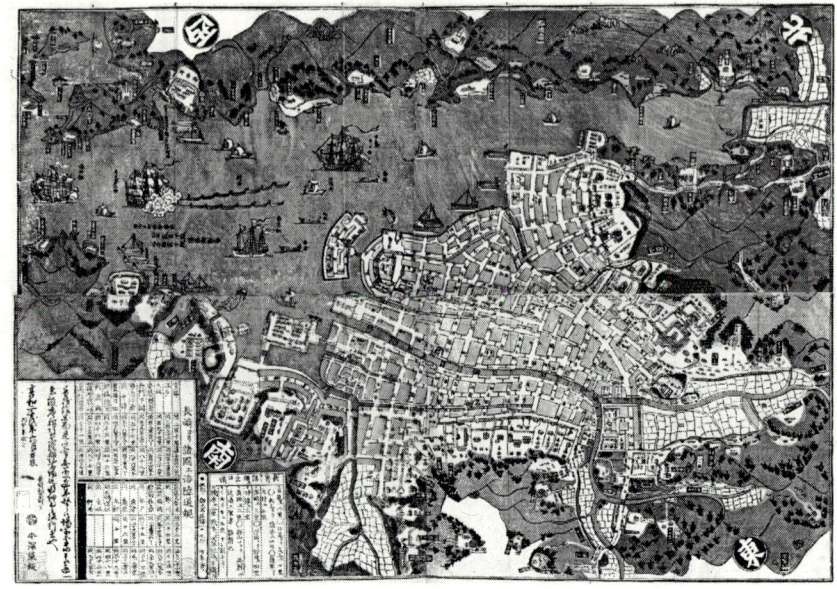

FIGURE 4.
Ushibukaya, *Shinkoku Hizen Nagasaki zu* (New Edition of Nagasaki in Hizen), pocket map of Nagasaki, 61 × 86 cm (1846). Dejima is the fan-shaped island in the center of the map. The Chinese quarter appears in the bottom left quadrant, just above where the two text boxes meet. Yoriai and Maruyama are immediately to the right of the Chinese quarter. Courtesy of the C. V. Starr East Asian Library, University of California, Berkeley.

periodically to hawk their wares. Barred from bringing their wives and children to Japan, the few dozen stranded men usually had only one another for company.

Initially, Japanese women were not allowed to set foot on Dejima, which meant that foreign traders who resided there had no opportunity for heterosexual intercourse. This marked a drastic change from their situation on Hirado. But the shogunate proved surprisingly sympathetic to this aspect of their predicament, and at some point during the decade after Dejima's establishment officials proposed a compromise: the city's brothel keepers, who had been relocated in 1642 to a newly constructed "pleasure quarter" encompassing the adjacent wards of Maruyama and Yoriai, would be allowed to send certain *yūjo* to service foreigners on Dejima.[15] In the meantime, other women would still be barred from the island. To the traders' amazement, the shogunate confirmed this policy by erecting a sign at the entrance to their quarter: "Women other than prostitutes are forbidden to enter."[16]

Beginning in 1688, Chinese traders stationed in Nagasaki found themselves in a similar situation. Previously they had been allowed to reside in various neighborhoods of the city, but a series of smuggling incidents convinced the shogunate's Nagasaki magistrates that it was necessary to segregate the Chinese population. The newly constructed Chinese ward (*tōjin yashiki*), which was much larger than Dejima, included several warehouses, residences, and temples. During periods of prosperity, it housed several thousand people. Like their Dutch counterparts, the Chinese were subject to restrictions: their quarter was guarded (though not as closely as Dejima), Japanese visitors required special permission to enter, and Chinese residents were forbidden to leave without a permit. Japanese townswomen were entirely excluded from the district. Decades later, the Nagasaki magistrate contended that the Chinese traders' isolation was related to fears that they would molest Japanese women: "Because the Chinese are extremely ill-mannered [*fusahō*], they had illicit sex [*mittsū*] with people's wives and daughters [when they were allowed to live in the city], and we hear that their conduct led to all sorts of wickedness. Therefore, we believe that they cannot be placed in regular inns."[17]

This restriction meant that the Chinese, like the Dutch, were forbidden to consort with "ordinary" Japanese women. Instead, they received visits from *yūjo* and their child attendants. At first, prostitutes were not allowed to spend more than one night in the Chinese ward, but this prohibition was not strenuously enforced—if a *yūjo* took one symbolic step outside the gate, she could return immediately. Finally, the constant comings and goings of prostitutes began to annoy the guards, and women were permitted to stay for five days at a stretch. In subsequent decades, restrictions were loosened to the point where a high-ranking Chinese trader could purchase an indentured prostitute and have her live with him for several years.[18] A similar settlement was reached on Dejima: women's stays, initially limited to three days, could be renewed indefinitely, so that a Dutch trader could enjoy the company of a prostitute for as long as he continued paying his bills, provided that she consented to the arrangement.[19]

Since the shogunate was committed to keeping foreigners in enclosed spaces, the prostitutes who served them had to be allowed (and even encouraged) to move around the city. In contrast to the situation in Edo, where *yūjo* were forbidden to leave Yoshiwara after 1640, Nagasaki's *yūjo* left Maruyama and Yoriai on a regular basis. Women who traveled to the Chinese ward were popularly termed *karayuki* (going to the Chinese), while prostitutes who served the Dutch were known as *orandayuki* (going to the Dutch). Both groups could serve Japanese clients, but *karayuki* were not allowed to enter Dejima and *orandayuki* were forbidden to set foot in the Chinese ward. The Nagasaki magistrates worried that if prostitutes were permitted to visit both neighborhoods, they might carry messages or currency between the Dutch and Chinese. Apart from these two distinct categories, a smaller, more exclusive group of prostitutes was known as the *nihonyuki* (going to the Japanese). They tended to be the highest ranking and most artistically accomplished women in the district. They were a small minority, however; in the 1670s, only ten of the district's 766 *yūjo* were reserved solely for Japanese clients.[20]

Karayuki and *orandayuki* had financial incentives to cultivate relationships with foreigners, one of which was that they offered lucrative opportunities to engage in smuggling. Nagasaki merchants were permitted to acquire foreign goods at auctions run through the government-sanctioned Nagasaki Accounting House (*Nagasaki kaisho*), but the tariffs were quite high, at least 35 percent.[21] Thus townspeople were eager to make their own, independent contacts with Dutch and particularly Chinese businessmen, and they often paid *yūjo* to carry messages and currency back and forth to residents of the foreign enclosures. Women also dabbled in petty smuggling for their own benefit, hoping to sell their wares on the black market. They hid small items in their voluminous robes and wound lengths of imported silk under their wide sashes. In one memorable instance, the guards stopped an attendant who had buried a ginseng root in her elaborate coiffure.[22] This strategy was risky, however: *yūjo* suspected of smuggling were referred to the Nagasaki magistrate, and if judged guilty they were permanently banned from both the Chinese ward and Dejima. They probably also received harsh punishments at the hands of their employers, who would have resented the impact of such sanctions on their business.

Luckily, there were easier ways to profit. When prostitutes became involved in long-term relationships with foreign traders, they were often rewarded with valuable gifts. For example, during the years 1754–55, the Yoriai brothel keepers recorded that the *yūjo* Asazuma's Dutch lover gave her six tortoiseshell combs, two koto picks, two bolts of *kaiki* cloth, one *tan* of calico, a *katabira* (an outer garment worn during the summer), one *tan* of red *chijimi* cloth, five more tortoiseshell hair ornaments, and one more *tan* of calico.[23] Other women received gifts of coveted white sugar from Indonesian plantations. The shogunate, always concerned about smuggling, established strict rules for disposing of these items, and women were obligated to report them to the Japanese officials on Dejima or at the Chinese ward.

However, the magistrates also ruled that brothel keepers could not confiscate these gifts: they belonged to the *yūjo* who had received them.[24]

Although *yūjo* were subject to unique restrictions and allowed rare opportunities, their parents and neighbors probably regarded them as ordinary girls in their late teens and early twenties. Like their peers, they were engaged in the increasingly common practice of working outside the household. By the late seventeenth century, urban women labored for wages in the nascent textile industry and worked as maidservants in samurai or wealthy townsmen's houses. These opportunities were mediated by class: poor girls served as drudges, while more fortunate women who had received some training in dancing and shamisen could find less taxing positions as companions and entertainers.[25] In the eighteenth century, this pattern of work outside the household spread to the countryside. Prosperous peasants' daughters competed to serve as maids in a daimyō or shogun's harem, positions that paid nominal wages but actually functioned as a type of finishing school. Through constant contact with their social betters, these girls honed their artistic sensibilities and refined their manners before retiring to marry suitable young men. Farther down the social scale, the daughters of poor and middling commoners were sent out to work as domestic servants, weavers, or agricultural laborers, which allowed them to support their families while learning valuable skills. These women, too, would eventually marry, though perhaps later in life than their more upwardly mobile counterparts, and they might also find themselves returning to work outside the household after marriage.[26]

For girls without the resources to find good positions in prosperous households, or for those whose impoverished families demanded an advance on their wages, prostitution could fill the same space in the lifecycle. Print culture often depicted work in the sex trade as a bridge between childhood and marriage or as a precursor to other occupations. According to an illustrated guide for girls published in 1756 under the title *Onna isshō michi shirube* (A Woman's Map through Life), women might spend time traveling the Road of Maid Service or living in "Pleasure Quarter" Province before they reached their desired destination, a long and happy marriage (see figure 5). Board games marketed to women also portrayed prostitution as a temporary "stop" along the way to matrimony: players could land on a square representing a term of service in the sex trade, then proceed to another profession with the next role of the dice.[27] Meanwhile, as Yokota Fuyuhiko points out, by the late seventeenth century, published lists of occupations for women catalogued employment in the sex trade alongside other forms of work, suggesting that the boundary between "ordinary" labor and prostitution was permeable.[28]

FIGURE 5.
Shitomi Momosuke, *Onna isshō michi shirube* (1756). From *Chizu de yomu Edo jidai*, ed. Yamashita Kazumasa, 211. Map of a woman's journey through life. A girl starts out at Conception Mountain in the bottom right corner and then passes Doll Shrine and the Field of Needlework en route to the crossroads in the center. If she is unlucky enough to be sent down the path of service in prostitution, she will pass by Ten Year Hill (symbolizing the years of her indenture), then wait at Child Attendant Pine or Apprentice Geisha Beach in order to board a Shaimsen Boat to Pleasure Quarter Province in the bottom left corner. From there, she can board a Redemption Boat to Concubine Hall in the upper left.

Yokota argues that this association between prostitution and market labor was the source of great anxiety to middle- and upper-class patriarchs who had begun to send their daughters to work. But the idea that prostitution was but one of a spectrum of labor opportunities for young women would have made sense to lower-class Nagasaki townsmen. Like their predecessors in sixteenth-century Hirado, they had few qualms about allowing their unmarried daughters to earn money by selling sex to foreign men. By the eighteenth century, they had even devised a system that would enable them to profit from their daughters' sexual labor without giving up custody. Parents would pay brothel keepers a significant fee in return for their daughters' affiliation as "part-time" (*shikiri*) or "nominal" (*nazuke*) *yūjo* who continued to live at home but were sent out to see customers on Dejima and in the Chinese ward when the brothels could not cover all their appointments.[29] These part-time prostitutes were never isolated from their communities, and neither their place of residence nor their official status distinguished them from other townswomen. Nagasaki townsmen and brothel keepers profited from this situation, but the magistrates objected: the system disregarded the status distinctions that separated prostitutes from townswomen and prevented the latter from consorting with foreigners. In 1751, officials apprehended 120 part-time *yūjo* who had been residing on Chinese ships in the harbor and punished them with the standard penalty for clandestine prostitution, three years of uncompensated labor in the "pleasure quarter."[30]

Though apparently short-lived, the existence of this part-time system, which was completely at odds with the shogunate's approach to regulating the sex trade, suggests that townsmen perceived little utility in status distinctions separating prostitutes from other women. Even those who could afford to retain custody of their daughters were willing to allow them to work in the sex trade and attend on foreign clients. While outsiders may have fixated on the Nagasaki *yūjo*'s difference, particularly their intimate access to mysterious places and people, to lower-class townspeople the *yūjo* were familiar figures: they were their own sisters, daughters, and neighbors.

FILIAL TIES

Nagasaki townspeople's familial relationships bridged the distance between the "pleasure quarter" and the rest of the city, as well as the status differences between prostitutes and other women. Indentured *yūjo* in Maruyama and Yoriai remained both emotionally and geographically close to their parents, who almost always resided in other wards of Nagasaki.[31] Since prostitutes were allowed to leave the quarter, they could visit home fairly frequently, and parents were involved in even the most mundane aspects of their daughters' daily lives. Girls caught up in smuggling investigations testified that they often returned home to drop off laundry or sewing. In an 1849 incident, a *kamuro* named Tama was detained at the gate of the Chinese ward when a guard found over seven *ryō* wrapped in a handkerchief and sewn into the collar of her robe. It turned out that Tama's widowed mother, Mune, had been approached by a stranger who asked for a favor: he needed a courier to deliver a package to a Chinese trader. Mune accepted the wrapped parcel (along with three *shu* for her trouble) and brought it home, where a few days earlier Tama had visited to drop off her laundry. Mune sewed the packet of coins into the collar of one of her daughter's freshly laundered robes. When Tama returned to retrieve her things, Mune dressed her in the robe and instructed her to deliver the package.[32] In another case a *yūjo* apprehended for smuggling Chinese silk admitted that she had given the material to her mother, who was making it into a kimono.[33]

To some extent, the relationships between Nagasaki *yūjo* and townspeople may have been unique to that city, in which prostitutes were permitted to leave Maruyama to walk to appointments with foreign clients. On the other hand, it is also possible that the higher level of surveillance in Nagasaki exposed activities that otherwise would have left no trace in the documentary record. Edo's *yūjo* were forbidden to leave Yoshiwara, and a few even resorted to arson in order to create an excuse to meet relatives or lovers elsewhere in the city.[34] But many, perhaps even the majority, of the capital's prostitutes did not reside in an enclosed district, and the Edo natives among them may have traversed the city and visited their families or former neighbors. In Hakata, another city with a walled-in brothel quarter, magistrates appointed by Fukuoka domain were suspicious when brothel keepers filed several reports in a row indicating that their women had "escaped," and they warned the proprietors to take more responsibility for tracking prostitutes' movements.[35] It is quite possible that Hakata *yūjo*, who like their counterparts in Nagasaki tended to be natives of the surrounding city, were leaving to visit their families. However, the domain did not keep track of their activities to the same extent, and records from the brothel district are not extant.

In Nagasaki, as elsewhere, brothel keepers allowed and even encouraged relationships between *yūjo* and their families, in part because parental concern could be a valuable resource. If a proprietor could rely on a prostitute's parents to nurse her through periods of illness, he would not need to waste money paying for the room, board, and medical care of an unprofitable employee. The Yoriai brothel keepers' association's guidelines for treating indisposed employees, implemented in 1812, indicated that it was routine practice to temporarily transfer sick women to the custody of their parents.[36] A few decades later, when prostitutes were forbidden to leave the quarter during the Tenpō Reforms, brothel keepers sent the Nagasaki magistrates several petitions asking permission for ailing women to return home to convalesce.[37]

Proprietors also made allowances for indentured prostitutes who wished to discharge a variety of emotional and spiritual obligations, such as caring for ill family members, attending funeral services, and visiting graves. In 1752, a *yūjo* reported that a Chinese trader seeking to make contact with a Japanese townsman had requested that she deliver a message the next time she left her quarter to visit the graveyard.³⁸ Apparently, it was common knowledge—even in the Chinese ward—that a *yūjo* could be granted a short leave to pay her respects to departed relatives. Brothel keepers also tolerated prostitutes' visits home to care for ill family members, provided that they were not absent for too long. The proprietors' 1812 regulations included instructions for women who went home to nurse their parents, and contracts could designate a specific amount of time off for that purpose.³⁹

The brothel keepers did not make these concessions solely out of sympathy for their employees. They could not easily reject prostitutes' claims to be filial, because doing so would contradict one of the cultural tropes justifying work in the sex trade and underpinning the brothels' legal status. The idea that prostitutes were dutiful daughters supporting their parents cast brothel proprietors in a positive role as the saviors of poor families. It also resonated with shogunal officials, who promoted the ideal of filial piety (*kō*) as the most important virtue commoners could uphold, reasoning that the propagation of patriarchal households was necessary for the stability of the realm. As Sugano Noriko points out, according to this reasoning, a daughter's devotion to her parents was "both a public and a private good."⁴⁰

This ideal of filiality took precedence over the bond between master and servant. The shogunate's *Kankoku kōgiroku* (Official Records of Filial Piety), which detailed the good deeds of meritorious subjects across the realm, lauded those who were loyal to masters, but individual cases made clear that devotion to one's parents was more important. For example, an indentured maidservant named Koya was celebrated for leaving service early to care for her ailing father. She worked diligently to repay her indenture money, and the master who complained that she could not leave without compensating him was cast as the villain. The account noted that other peasants thought his demand "outrageous" (*kaiki*) and supported Koya.⁴¹ In accordance with these values, the Nagasaki city magistrates looked kindly on *yūjo* who bent the rules of service to pay their respects to their families, particularly if they had not broken any laws in the process. Conversely, officials could not be expected to sympathize with proprietors who forbade their employees to take medicine to ailing parents or visit their grandparents' graves.

In this context, playing the dutiful daughter conferred certain advantages. Like the rural women Walthall describes, who "appropriated the conventions of the devoted wife" when they petitioned the authorities for clemency in the wake of peasant rebellions, prostitutes facing official punishment capitalized on conventional expectations of feminine behavior in order to argue for leniency.[42] Often they presented themselves as caregivers. In 1765, a *yūjo* named Hanazato disappeared from a Yoriai brothel, then returned a month later, claiming that she had gone to visit sick relatives in a nearby village. She apologized for her absence and explained that she was forced to leave on short notice and had no time to inform the appropriate officials. The ward elders may or may not have believed her story, but they petitioned the magistrate for a pardon so that she could continue to work.[43] In another series of cases, a crackdown on illegal border crossings in 1791 and 1792 resulted in the detention of three prostitutes, all of whom claimed that they were on the way to visit ill grandparents in other domains.[44] The brothel keepers had reason to believe that these stories were not true—in similar cases, proprietors noted in their own records that the women in question had actually run away to escape debts[45]—but they petitioned the magistrate for pardons, which were granted. Afterwards, they probably administered their own, private punishments. According to rumor, at least one brothel disciplined women who had attempted to escape by confining them to a dark room for days at a time.[46] But this possibility was not mentioned in the official record, which presented an appealing narrative about dutiful granddaughters, benevolent magistrates, and compassionate masters.

Occasionally, *yūjo* and their families were able to take advantage of these tropes in order to resist the demands of abusive employers. In one instance, a *yūjo* named Wakamatsu fled to her father's house after a nasty beating at the hands of the brothel's supervisor (*yarite*). Initially, her master did not notice anything amiss. Since Wakamatsu went to visit her father fairly often, the proprietor assumed she would return in due time. When she failed to materialize, he began to make inquiries with Maruyama ward elders. They notified the magistrate, who launched an investigation and apprehended Wakamatsu's father. After hearing his explanation, however, the magistrate decided that the brothel keeper was at fault for allowing his supervisor to administer such a violent punishment. Wakamatsu was returned to her father's custody, and her master was warned to show more restraint in the future.[47] In this case, the magistrate determined that the parent's interest in protecting his daughter from harm superseded his obligation to the brothel. This decision nullified a contract, but it bolstered the ideal of benign patriarchal authority by rewarding a father who claimed to act out of concern for his child's welfare.

Precisely because the magistrates tended to be sympathetic in these situations, asserting a desire to protect a child's welfare was a convenient excuse for guardians who had mixed motives for retaking custody. One such ambiguous case was referred to the Nagasaki magistrates in 1753, after an eleven-year-old girl named Take ran away from Yoriai's Aburaya. She had been indentured for a term of fourteen years (four as an attendant, and then ten as a *yūjo*) at the extremely low price of sixty *monme* in silver. After the proprietress beat her severely, however, Take found it difficult to continue working. She consulted with her uncle, who told her that if she came home, she would have to enter service elsewhere; apparently, he was unable or unwilling to support her otherwise. Ultimately, Take decided to take her chances. Her uncle changed her name to Fuyu and sent her to work as a maid-servant in Kurume domain for a much better price: three hundred silver *monme*. The proprietress petitioned the Nagasaki magistrate for an investigation, but failed to mention that her beatings had triggered the girl's disappearance. In this case, the decision found fault with all three parties. Take was returned to Yoriai ward and forced to work without recompense for three years. Her uncle was held in jail for five months and compelled to return all the money he had received for her contracts. Finally, the proprietress was scolded for lying to investigators and ordered to home confinement for three days.[48] In this case, the magistrate must have concluded that Take's uncle's primary motivation was not to protect his niece but to turn a profit. This did not align with their view of an appropriate familial relationship, in which a parent or guardian cared for and protected his child.

Brothel proprietors suspected that parents often complained of abuse in order to conceal their real objective, which was to release their daughters from their contracts. When the Yoriai brothel keepers' association sent the magistrates a list of "things that are detrimental to business" in 1850, among their complaints was the following observation:

> When a woman runs home to her parents, they start saying all kinds of troublesome things about how it would be cruel to return her or how she will die if she returns to the brothel. When we try to negotiate, they sometimes gather a group of "assistants" [*sukedan no mono*] who pretend that she has thrown herself in the well. They will make up all kinds of shocking stories. The truth is that none of it is the *yūjo*'s idea at all [*mattaku yūjo no kokoro yori itashi sōrō gi ni kore naku*]. It is extremely problematic.[49]

The allegation that so-called "assistants" were faking women's deaths suggests that parents called on others in the community (likely unsavory elements) to help them press their cases. At the same time, the brothel keepers' assertion that *yūjo* were not involved in these machinations was designed both to defend proprietors from allegations of abuse and to raise doubts about the parents' motivations. The suggestion that parents did not look out for their daughters' interests made a direct appeal to the magistrates' normative assumptions about appropriate relationships between parents and children, arguing that parents, not brothel keepers, were perverting social norms.

As the proprietors were well aware, parents looked out for their own interests as well as their daughters', and their desire for financial gain could eclipse their concern for their children's welfare. On the other hand, daughters were obligated to support their parents, which was exactly why so many were indentured to brothels in the first place: their families needed the money. This dynamic of obligation and dependency could easily devolve into exploitation, and it could survive the *yūjo*'s transition from household to brothel. The magistrates' findings sometimes indicated that family members pressured indentured prostitutes to engage in smuggling so that they could continue to profit from their work. In 1756, the Nagasaki magistrates punished a *yūjo* after one of her older brother's associates confessed that she had been the intermediary in their smuggling network.[50] Other incidents suggested that the impulse toward filial piety could lead prostitutes to break the law (or, at least, that women were quick to claim this as a motivation). In one poignant case, a *yūjo* named Mikawa testified that she had turned to the black market after a servant informed her that her mother was ill. She pawned her clothing and accessories and used the money to buy medicine. But she had not yet paid for her newest hair ornament, and she started smuggling to settle the debt.[51]

For both the magistrates and brothel proprietors, filial piety was a double-edged sword. It provided a moral justification for work in the sex trade, but it could also legitimize resistance to the demands of brothel keepers or serve as an excuse for breaking the law. William Lindsey points out that the predominant "value models" governing women's sexuality aimed to limit this subversive potential by encouraging *yūjo* to transfer their loyalty from their parents to their employers.[52] If this modeling had been successful, then prostitutes' responsibilities as daughters could not have induced them to defy their masters or engage in illegal activities. To the extent that this was not the case, these value models may have been more successful in reassuring anxious men than in shaping women's behavior. From the perspective of lower-class townspeople and their daughters, entering service in a brothel was best understood not as a transition from one household to another—as the logic of the status system and didactic texts might suggest—but as a new way of serving the same household. Moreover, since the magistrates looked kindly on *yūjo*'s claims to be dutiful daughters, and brothel keepers relied on the ideal of filial sacrifice to legitimize their employment practices, this understanding had some appeal to members of these groups as well. Nagasaki *yūjo* worked as prostitutes, but they would always be daughters first.

FROM PROSTITUTION TO MARRIAGE AND MOTHERHOOD

Most townswomen would marry by their mid-to-late twenties, but *yūjo* faced some significant barriers to matrimony: they could not legally contract marriage, they were obligated to reside in enclosed districts, and they were unable to form any monogamous attachment that interfered with their masters' business. Couples who were frustrated in their desire for marriage and monogamy sometimes resorted to violence. In a typical "love-suicide" (*shinjū*, or in legal parlance, *aitaijini*), the male partner would slit his lover's throat before stabbing himself. When this maneuver was successful, it could be impossible to distinguish a love-suicide from an ordinary murder-suicide, so couples left notes documenting their intentions or bound themselves together to symbolize their attachment. Female survivors of thwarted attempts often testified that they had agreed to die because they "wanted to be husband and wife."[53] Forming a suicide pact was not the only way for a *yūjo* to prove her sincerity, however; in less lethal displays of devotion, also called *shinjū*, women would mutilate themselves to express their desire for monogamy. Typically, they would remove their fingernails and send them to their lovers.[54]

Occasionally, Nagasaki prostitutes and their Japanese partners were driven to similar measures. These cases were exceptional, however; only two love-suicides appear in the criminal record amid dozens of references to *yūjo* involved in smuggling rings or running away from brothels.[55] Love-suicides were dramatic and visible, often celebrated on the stage and in popular fiction, and they created the impression that *yūjo* viewed marriage as a goal that could only be realized in death. In reality, however, most prostitutes who survived their terms of service married. Work in the sex trade did not necessarily limit their opportunities to meet potential husbands, since lower-class townsmen attached no value judgment to prostitution and were sympathetic to local girls from impoverished families. Engelbert Kaempfer (1651–1716), a German physician who resided on Dejima in the 1690s, commented: "If [Nagasaki] prostitutes marry honest people, they pass as honest women among the commoners, since they are not responsible for their profession and furthermore have been well educated."[56] In 1843, a local official described this as a regional phenomenon: "Here, unlike in other places, most of the prostitutes come from this city or other nearby villages, so prostitutes and customers know each other's backgrounds. Customers are aware that the women have only been sold into service because they are poor, and they inevitably end up falling deeply in love."[57]

Actually, this was the case throughout the realm. The contract to let a Yoshiwara *yūjo* out of service for marriage, mentioned in chapter 2, was replicated many times over in provincial cities and towns (some of which are featured in the following chapters). In these cases, lasting relationships were initiated in brothels, and ultimately *yūjo* became wives and clients became husbands. Of course, *yūjo*'s contractual debts presented a major financial obstacle for the lower-class townsmen who were prostitutes' most obvious partners. But even this barrier could be overcome, especially if the woman in question was able to enlist her parents' support. There is some evidence that this was a normative expectation. The *yūjo* heroine of Chikamatsu's play *Hara-kiri of a Woman at Nagamachi* (*Nagamachi onna harakiri*), chastises her stepfather for trying to block her marriage so that he can indenture her again: "All the courtesans I know say / That their parents cherish them / and spare no trouble on their behalf. / 'Your contract is almost up. / Find yourself a successful man / and make plans for the future, / so we can see you settled!' That's what every parent says!"[58] This attitude could be a source of great frustration to brothel proprietors seeking to maximize their investments. In their "list of things detrimental to business," they complained: "When it comes to light that a *yūjo*'s parents are involved in secret dealings with one of her customers, then she begins to pine for him and will absolutely refuse to break off their relationship. Finally, after the parents and the suitor come to an agreement, she will likely stop working in the middle of her term of service. This ends up being a loss for the brothel keeper and a problem for the business."[59]

Typically, these incidents escaped officials' notice because they were settled privately. However, one such case is entered in the Yoriai ward record because the proprietress involved insisted on petitioning the magistrate.[60] The conflict erupted in 1765 after a *yūjo* named Hatsuura tried to break her contract with Yoriai's Chikugoya. The brothel had taken custody of Hatsuura thirteen years earlier, when she was only seven years old. In a memorandum addressed to the Yoriai ward elders, the Chikugoya proprietress commented that when families sold their daughters so young, they were usually in dire straits. But over the years, they sometimes forgot about their earlier desperation and began to make unreasonable demands. According to the proprietress, Hatsuura's family fit this profile. When Hatsuura suffered from illness in the spring of her twentieth year, the proprietress sent her home to convalesce, and her mother insisted that the brothel pay for several doctor's visits. The proprietress complied, but when Hatsuura finally recovered and returned to the brothel, she began to act insane (*ranshin*). Her unpredictable behavior puzzled the proprietress, who could find nothing physically wrong with her. Around the same time, in a seemingly unrelated development, the brothel received a request from the parents of a young townsman, Ichitarō, who was Hatsuura's regular customer and resided in the same ward as her mother. Ichitarō's parents asked the brothel to prevent their son from seeing Hatsuura, and the proprietress was happy to comply, noting that he rarely paid his bills. Meanwhile, Hatsuura began to behave even more erratically. In desperation, the proprietress contacted Hatsuura's mother, who suggested that her daughter's behavior would improve if the brothel allowed her to see Ichitarō. When the proprietress reluctantly agreed, Hatsuura recovered immediately.

The proprietress thought the matter was settled, but a few weeks later, Hatsuura ran home to her mother and refused to return. After a period of unsuccessful negotiations, the proprietress went to see them. Suspecting that Ichitarō was somehow involved in her employee's obstinacy, she tried to explain that the girl would be foolish to attach herself to a client. "When his hot blood cools," she warned, "you could end up divorced and back in service." But Hatsuura's mother refused to listen, and in the meantime Ichitarō continued to press his suit. Eventually, Hatsuura and Ichitarō began to live together as a married couple; one of the proprietress' employees reported that he had seen them sleeping together in Hatsuura's mother's house. The proprietress was livid, but she indicated that situations like Hatsuura's were not unusual, just undocumented: "Since most brothel keepers are men," she complained, "when things like this happen they are afraid that the world [*seken*] will hear about it, so they avoid petitioning the authorities and instead just discreetly let the matter lie [*yamiyami to sono mama nite sashioki sōrō*]." (This would explain why so few of these cases were recorded in the ward record or the criminal register, even though they merited inclusion on the list of "things detrimental to business.") But the proprietress was determined to bring her complaint to the authorities' attention. "As long as this type of harmful situation is allowed to occur," she pointed out, "unscrupulous people will continue to take indentured women out of service in a disorderly fashion." She asked the brothel keepers' association to support her attempt to force Ichitarō to return her employee or at least pay to release her from service. The following year, her suit reached the magistrate, who ordered it resolved through private settlement. Eventually, the parties involved agreed that Hatsuura would return to the brothel temporarily, but the remaining six years on her contract would be halved and her outstanding loans would be forgiven.[61]

By employing various strategies to challenge the brothel proprietress's legal authority, from faking illness to refusing to work, Hatsuura and her mother had subtly undermined the laws placing prostitutes in a different status "container" from other commoner women. On the other hand, these strategies worked beautifully with the logic of a political order based on the patriarchal household. Although Hatsuura did not have a father, her mother was able to smooth her daughter's path to marriage by relying on her authority as a parent, which was so central to the functioning of the household and the state that it could never be completely effaced by the rules of status or the provisions of indenture contracts. This forced the proprietress to come up with her own competing logic: at one point, she argued that she had raised the girl from the age of seven and deserved more consideration as a surrogate mother. In other words, she tried to use the idea of filial piety to justify her own claim to Hatsuura's loyalty.[62] But Hatsuura and her mother obviously disagreed, and this argument did nothing to convince the magistrate to hear the proprietress's case. Moreover, since the proprietress was a woman who was not a head of household (she was separated from her husband, and her young son was nominally in charge of the brothel), her ability to argue her case was limited. At one point, members of Hatsuura's faction brought negotiations to a halt when they insisted on speaking to the proprietress's husband, who wanted nothing to do with his wife or her dispute.

The proprietress's separation from her husband, like Hatsuura's relationship with Ichitarō, exposed the gaps that could open between the legal definition of a household and its social reality. The proprietress's husband had left the brothel to his son and moved to another ward; clearly, he and his wife were divorced in all but name. But the townspeople representing Hatsuura believed that they could drag him into this episode of legal contention, since he still retained some nominal authority over his wife and the operation of his former business. Meanwhile, Hatsuura and Ichitarō were not legally married—officially, she was still a *yūjo*—but when they began sleeping under the same roof, they rendered the proprietress's legal claim socially meaningless. When they began to act as husband and wife, they were married in the eyes of their neighbors.

As Hatsuura's case suggests, prostitution and marriage were not mutually exclusive conditions; they could be sequential and even overlapping stages in the same woman's life cycle. Nowhere was this more apparent than in the long-term arrangements between *yūjo* and their foreign partners. Technically, legal marriage was impossible for these couples for two reasons: *yūjo* could not contract valid marriages while they were in service, and Japanese women were forbidden to marry foreigners. Monogamy and cohabitation, however, were attainable goals. Since these were the most important features of townswomen's marriages in any case, *yūjo* who resided for long periods of time with foreign partners might have thought of themselves as married women. Certainly, both Chinese and European traders expected the women they hired for sexual services to perform wifely roles. The Dutch chief factor G. F. Meijlan (1785–1831), for example, praised Japanese prostitutes for their fidelity and emphasized their domestic responsibilities, such as preparing tea for lonely traders during the long, cold nights on Dejima.[63] His compatriots later suggested that he underscored the similarity between prostitutes and wives in order to excuse the fact that the residents of Dejima violated Christian morality by paying for extramarital sex and shocked many of their contemporaries' sensibilities by having intercourse with nonwhite women.[64] But Chinese traders, who lacked these inhibitions, also expected their partners to behave as if they were wives. This was illustrated to dramatic effect in an 1821 incident involving a *yūjo* named Miyukino. She had been living with a Chinese trader for several months before he suddenly fell ill and died. After she returned to her Maruyama brothel, she heard rumors that a group of his countrymen had threatened to rape her if she ever set foot in their district again. They alleged that she deserved this treatment because she had refused to nurse her partner during his illness. In their opinion, Miyukino's client had paid for companionship and domesticity as well as specific sex acts, and they wanted to punish her for destroying the illusion that she cared about his well-being. Eventually, the brothel keeper had to arrange for her parents and the traders' representatives to negotiate a settlement.[65] In another case, a Yoriai brothel keeper resorted to an elaborate string of lies to prevent Chinese traders from finding out that one of the prostitutes formerly assigned to the Chinese ward had left in order to marry a Japanese man. He said he feared the consequences if her former partner found out about her new arrangement.[66]

Nagasaki townspeople regarded unions between *yūjo* and foreign traders as legitimate, even when the law did not recognize them. The German physician Phillip Franz von Siebold (1796–1866) and his partner Sonogi (1807–69) were local celebrities. Sonogi, whose original name was Kusumoto Taki, was indentured to the Yoriai brothel Hikitaya, but she resided with Siebold for six years until he was deported on suspicion of espionage. Subsequently, Sonogi remarried a Japanese man, and her daughter by Siebold, Oine, became famous as Japan's first female physician. In later years, some Nagasaki residents claimed that Kusumoto Taki had never really worked as a prostitute at all—her parents had changed her official status so that she could marry Siebold, who had fallen in love with her while he was out visiting patients in the city.[67]

Regardless of its veracity, this story points to an important implication of the shogunate's policy: in order to "marry" a foreigner, a woman had to be a prostitute. This situation became problematic when *yūjo*'s terms ended and they wished to continue their "marriages." In 1786, the Yoriai brothel keepers asked the shogunate if there was any circumstance in which a *yūjo* could reside in the Chinese ward after her term of service ended. The magistrates replied that there was no such circumstance, but the woman in question could have her term extended. In response, the brothel keepers inquired about the maximum acceptable age for a *yūjo*, and officials confirmed that there was no limit.[68] This created a loophole that women occasionally exploited. Decades later, the Yoriai record mentioned a thirty-six-year-old prostitute who had been living with her partner in the Chinese ward for a dozen years.[69]

Yūjo sometimes found that their residence in the foreign enclosures complicated their relationships with their families elsewhere in the city. This was not necessarily because parents disapproved of "marriages" to foreigners, but because they were unable to engage in the social rituals that formed and sustained bonds between households and across generations. In 1852, a townswoman named Hide explained that her attempt to smuggle money into the Chinese ward was actually an innocent, although misguided, effort to acknowledge her daughter's union with a Chinese trader. Hide had asked another *yūjo* to take a gift of three *ryō* to her daughter Chimoto's partner. Apparently, he had been sending Hide small presents such as incense sticks, and she wished to express her gratitude. She testified that she had considered giving him some sort of Japanese-made object as a souvenir, but she knew that such items were difficult to smuggle into the Chinese ward. Eventually, she decided to give him money so that he could buy something from one of the Japanese peddlers who visited his district. Although other parties confirmed this story, Hide's explanation did not satisfy the magistrate, who banished her from the city.[70] If Hide's daughter's partner had been a Japanese townsman, there would have been nothing unusual about sending him a gift; in fact, it would have been a necessary and expected gesture. Only her daughter's involvement with a Chinese trader prevented Hide from participating in an otherwise normal social interaction.

Childbirth was equally complicated. Like Yoshiwara *yūjo*, whose masters usually forbid them to have children, Nagasaki's indentured prostitutes probably used contraception to control their fertility and abortion to terminate pregnancies.[71] But a few births were entered in the Yoriai ward record every year, suggesting that Nagasaki *yūjo* bore children more often than their counterparts in Edo. Miyamoto argues that this marked an important difference between Yoshiwara and Maruyama: while Edo *yūjo* were regarded as objects or playthings, their counterparts in Nagasaki were viewed as human beings and acknowledged (if not valued) as mothers.[72] In fact, allowing *yūjo* to deliver safely was both a diplomatic and financial strategy on the part of the shogunate. Children of Japanese women and Dutch traders were considered Japanese subjects, and when they were boys, their fathers often paid to arrange political appointments for them.[73] Every time a prostitute conceived a foreigner's child, brothel keepers were required to send reports to the magistrate's office noting the *yūjo*'s name and brothel affiliation, as well as the father's name and nationality. When she gave birth, they noted the sex of the baby, the place of birth, and the name of the child's guardian.[74] This level of surveillance, combined with the fact that many *yūjo* who became pregnant resided in the enclosures and not in brothels, allowed women to bring their pregnancies to term without interference from their masters.

Moreover, pregnant *yūjo* could count on assistance from their families. Their foreign partners paid child support, and their parents stepped in to raise their children. Reports in the Yoriai ward record indicated that prostitutes usually left the quarter to give birth in their natal households and then awarded custody to their parents, who looked after their grandchildren while their daughters continued to work.[75] Of the eleven births reported between 1821 and 1829, six babies were placed in the custody of their mothers' relatives and four others were stillbirths (or, at least, that is how they were recorded in the register). In the one remaining case, guardianship of the child was not recorded.[76] On occasion, grandparents took custody of multiple children. In 1738, the Yoriai proprietors reported that the *yūjo* Ryōzan had three children with a Chinese trader. One had died, but the other two, who were aged fifteen and sixteen, remained in her parents' household.[77] Prostitutes could also raise their children in brothels, but this seems to have been a last resort, reserved for when grandparents were unable to fulfill their responsibilities. The *yūjo* Hanaginu brought her five-year-old son to live with her in Yoriai because he was sickly and her mother could not care for him. When he recovered a year later, however, he returned to live with his grandmother.[78]

This child-raising arrangement indicates that *yūjo* found it difficult to raise children while they were in service. But it is also evidence of the strength and endurance of prostitutes' emotional ties to their parents. In 1757, the *yūjo* Wakaura returned to her father's house to give birth, after failing to inform the brothel keeper that she was pregnant. Instead, when she asked for time off, she pleaded illness and exhaustion. It seems that she had been concealing her condition because the baby's father, a Dutch trader, wanted to bring his child home to Holland. Like other desperate *yūjo*, Wakaura turned to her parents, who insisted that they would not relinquish their granddaughter unless they received a direct order from the magistrate. The brothel keeper, utterly perplexed by the Dutchman's demands and Wakaura's parents' obstinacy, appealed to the magistrate for instructions on how to proceed. Displaying little knowledge of the shogunate's precedents, which had forbidden half-Japanese children from leaving the country, the magistrate declared that the consent of both parents would be necessary to remove the child from Japan, and the baby stayed with her grandparents.[79] Since they had tried to prevent the Dutchman from discovering his child's existence, their actions would be impossible to explain if they were only concerned for the financial support that he might provide for their daughter and her child.

On rare occasions, prostitutes reared their children in a more "conventional" setting: a two-parent household in one of the foreign enclosures.[80] Sonogi raised Oine while living with her partner Siebold in their private residence, and a few years later, Yoriai brothel keepers reported that another prostitute and her infant were staying on Dejima. These *yūjo* were often the consorts of high-status men, and since women of a certain social standing were not expected to breast-feed, they required wet nurses to attend to their babies.[81] This was complicated, however, because Japanese women other than prostitutes were not allowed to enter the foreign enclosures. In these instances, the problem was resolved when the mothers were granted permission to employ wet nurses who nominally changed their status designations to become *yūjo*.[82] Like the thirty-six-year-old prostitute living with her partner in the Chinese ward, these women secured the brothel keepers' and the magistrates' permission to appropriate the conventions of the status system to fit their needs. Rather than petitioning for exceptions to the shogunate's rules, they temporarily became *yūjo* for purposes that had nothing to do with selling sex. Since women who worked as wet nurses already had their own children, their service as *yūjo* overlapped with motherhood and possibly marriage. Their existence is one more example of how the category of "prostitute" could be enlarged to accommodate multiple relationships and identities.

For women who changed their names and places of residence to work in Nagasaki's sex trade, entering service in a brothel was not a radical break from the past. Nor did it preclude a future. While working as prostitutes, *yūjo* maintained familial relationships, and they also occasionally forged new ties through marriage and motherhood. In the eyes of officialdom, indentured service as a *yūjo* marked a transition from one status "container" to another, entailing distinct legal privileges and restrictions. Meanwhile, in the popular imagination, Nagasaki prostitutes were certainly marked by their difference, both from other women and from their counterparts in other cities. But from the perspective of many Nagasaki townspeople, *yūjo* were familiar—in both senses of the word.

Prostitutes' familial bonds always contained threads of exploitation. After all, parents had sold their daughters into prostitution and continued to depend on their earning potential, to the point where some parents pressured their daughters to participate in illegal activities. The same mother who sent her daughter to work in a brothel might also welcome her home to drop off her laundry, and then use her as an intermediary in a smuggling ring. Yet when they faced unyielding employers and angry magistrates, parents and daughters tended to emphasize their affective ties and mutual obligations, conforming to cultural scripts that demanded protective parents and dutiful daughters. This is noteworthy, because it indicates that enduring bonds between *yūjo* and parents were expected and often honored. Shogunal officials did not assume that a woman's status as a *yūjo* superseded other categories of identity based on her familial relationships. In fact, as the examples of "married" *yūjo* and their unconventional families demonstrate, status could be manipulated in the service of other roles. Women were *yūjo* in order to be responsible daughters, wives, mothers, or wet nurses, and sometimes they were not even expected to work as prostitutes.

This manipulation of the shogunate's status order did not entail a rejection of its conception of gendered order. In fact, this idea was essential to prostitutes' modest efforts to create opportunities for self-determination, since the magistrates never relinquished their expectation that the sex trade should sustain individual households and affirm the ideal of benevolent patriarchy. According to this vision, parents indentured their daughters to brothels out of desperation, while women worked as prostitutes out of a sense of obligation to their families; brothel keepers served the community by providing employment opportunities for poor young women and sexual outlets for Japanese men and foreigners; and compassionate magistrates protected all their subjects. This was not necessarily the case: some parents indentured their daughters out of a desire for profit, some prostitutes probably entered service willingly in order to wear fine robes or receive gifts, and some brothel keepers cheated parents and abused their employees. Moreover, magistrates protected some (high-status male) subjects at the expense of exploited young women. Nonetheless, this was a powerful, and useful, framework. This set of norms motivated runaway *yūjo* to claim that they were visiting ill relatives rather than escaping debts, and it inspired parents to argue that concern for their daughters' welfare, rather than the pursuit of profit, led them to retake custody of runaway girls. The magistrates expected women to obey, submit, and sacrifice, and *yūjo* who conformed to these expectations (or at least appeared to) found that they were entitled to a modicum of protection.

Meanwhile, those who subverted these norms were punished. In 1819, the Yoriai brothel keepers complained that the city's geisha—in this case, women who worked outside their district—were "selfish" (*wagamama*). Not only did they violate both the law and conventional ideas of propriety by selling their bodies willingly, as independent contractors rather than employees of brothels, they also refused to contribute their agreed-upon allotment to public works projects. Although the magistrates must have appreciated the geisha's donations to city coffers, even if they were smaller than expected, they promptly accepted the brothel keepers' petitions and limited the geisha's activities.[83] There was no room for "selfish" women in the city's legal sex trade.

In Nagasaki, the shogunate's strategy of regulation survived until the end of the period, just as it had in Edo. In both cities, officials continued to distinguish between legal and clandestine prostitution, protecting both the integrity of the patriarchal household and the brothel keepers' business by restricting "selfish" women's opportunities to profit from the sale of their own sexual services. At the same time, they regarded the daughters who worked on their parents' behalf, not as criminals or deviants, but as appropriately self-sacrificing female subjects, who had a claim to official benevolence. If this was meager consolation for women who were forced to spend years of their lives in an occupation that they had not chosen, which made them vulnerable to physical abuse and venereal diseases, then at least it was better than the most likely alternative: being despised for a fate that was beyond their control and being denied the chance to complain of mistreatment. The shogunate's strategy of regulation closed off possibilities for women who might have engaged in prostitution in order to support themselves rather than their families, but it preserved others. Because legal prostitutes had not chosen their profession, in this view, they could not be blamed for it; because they conformed to feminine ideals, they could not be stigmatized. Particularly in areas such as Nagasaki, where girls indentured to brothels were never far from their families or isolated from their communities, this understanding of the value of prostitutes—as responsible members of households as well as female bodies to be used for the purpose of profit or pleasure—provided a framework within which they could passively resist brothel keepers' authority, form their own families, or leave prostitution.

But this logic of regulation—in which prostitutes were able to ask for consideration as dutiful daughters and loyal subjects—did not apply everywhere. In order for prostitutes to take advantage of their entitlement to protection, there had to be a representative, whether a parent or a potential husband or a ward elder, available to speak on the woman's behalf. Nagasaki *yūjo* were uncommonly fortunate in this respect. As the following chapters will discuss, by the late eighteenth century recruiting patterns were carrying women farther and farther from home, and many could not access this type of support. Meanwhile, Nagasaki's labor market for prostitution continued to be fairly closed, probably because the city magistrates were worried about the security ramifications if brothels employed "unknown" women from faraway places. Moreover, Nagasaki *yūjo* were legal prostitutes in an area where magistrates managed the sex trade, which ensured that samurai officials would hear their appeals. This had become relatively unusual by the end of the eighteenth century, as the sex trade expanded throughout the provinces, taking root in smaller towns where commoner officials were in charge of day-to-day administration.

At the center of the Tokugawa polity, in cities like Nagasaki and Edo, magistrates would always insist that the sex trade should function in ways that supported individual households and a broader ideal of paternalistic authority. This did not mean that there was no change over time. In Edo, the definition of order was flexible: as chapter 2 has argued, by the middle of the eighteenth century, it had expanded from its original focus on the integrity of households and the defense of the shogunate to include the solvency of post stations and the survival of poor urban families. In Nagasaki, where officials concentrated on managing foreign affairs and controlling smuggling, the shogunate's policy toward prostitution was relatively consistent. But by the beginning of the nineteenth century, magistrates were sanctioning geisha outside Maruyama in return for monetary contributions to building funds. In both cities, then, officials had begun to prioritize economic development. But prosperity was not only an end in itself; it was a means of maintaining the infrastructure of rule, whether it consisted of bridges, post stations, or households. In that sense, promotion of the sex trade was entirely compatible with the maintenance of the gendered order.

But by the beginning of the nineteenth century, many samurai and elite commoners had come to believe the opposite: they insisted that prostitution destroyed households and threatened the hierarchical relationships that structured the realm. This shift was barely apparent in places like Nagasaki and Edo, although hints of it surfaced in complaints about "selfish" geisha and greedy parents who seemed too willing to sanction their daughters' illicit affairs. The story of how the sex trade began to be understood as a danger to the political and social order unfolded in provincial towns and villages, areas where officials proved more willing to abdicate responsibility for regulating the sex trade. These places form the setting for the next section, which considers how a regulatory regime based on the logic of households, a construction that understood prostitutes as filial daughters and dutiful subjects, was overcome by the logic of the market.

PART TWO · EXPANSION AND
THE LOGIC OF
THE MARKET

In 1678, Fujimoto Kizan's *Shikidō Ōkagami* (The Great Mirror of Love) offered what was intended to be a complete list of Japan's "pleasure districts" (*yūri*) ranked in order from number one (Kyoto's Shimabara) to twenty-five (Satsuma's Tamachi).[1] Over a hundred and fifty years later, Kitagawa Morisada included a reproduction of a similar ranking in his encyclopedic account of late Tokugawa manners and customs. This version took the form of a *banzuke*, which was typically used to publicize sumo wrestlers' standing in a tournament. This time, Edo's Yoshiwara took the number one spot, and Shimabara was tied with Osaka's Shinmachi for number two. But the most striking difference was in the remainder of the list. Whereas in 1678, only twenty-five neighborhoods merited ranking, Morisada's *banzuke* included 206. Many of the new entries were entertainment districts located in the great cities: Edo's Shinagawa, for example, occupied a prominent place on the *banzuke*, although it had not appeared in Fujimoto Kizan's list. But a significant number were provincial towns: pilgrimage sites such as Konpira in Shikoku's Sanuki province, ports such as Itako in Mito domain, and post stations such as Kanagawa along the Tōkaidō Highway.

To some degree, the *banzuke* reflected a more liberal attitude toward what counted as a "pleasure district." But the number of places where men could purchase sex had also increased dramatically over the years. The proliferation of these sites, and the increase in the population of women who worked in them, did not go unnoticed by contemporary commentators. In 1816, Buyō Inshi, pseudonymous author of an impassioned tract decrying the collapse of social order, argued that the skyrocketing popularity of prostitution was evidence of a general decline in public morality. In Hideyoshi's era, he pointed out, there had been only two hundred and thirty prostitutes in Kyoto, but by the early nineteenth century,

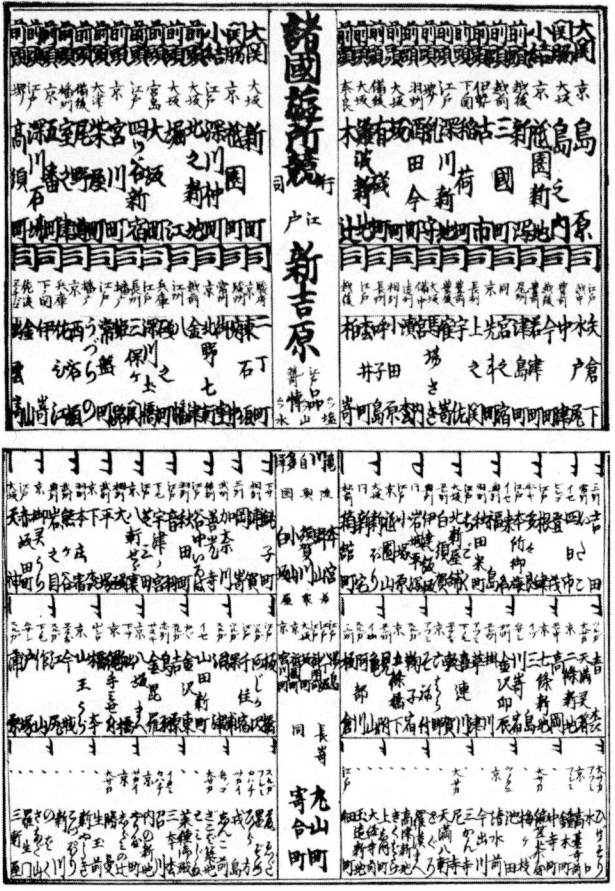

FIGURE 6.
Shokoku yūsho kurabe (A Ranking of Pleasure Districts in the Various Provinces). Reproduced in Kitagawa Morisada, *Morisada mankō* (Morisada's Sketches). A ranking of brothel districts included in Kitagawa Morisada's encyclopedia of manners and customs. Shin-Yoshiwara appears in large print as the "champion" at the center of the chart. Nagasaki's Maruyama and Yoriai are coupled at the bottom center. Niigata (chapter 4) appears in the top row on the right. Kumagaya (chapter 5) is in the third row on the left side, but it is likely that Fukaya is intended. Onomichi and Muro (chapter 6) are on the left side of the top row, while Konpira is on the right side of the fourth row. Kitagawa copied this from another source and noted that he did not agree with all the rankings. Reproduction from Kitagawa Morisada, *Morisada mankō zuhan shūsei*, ed. Takahashi Masao.

there were as many as twenty thousand. He counted an additional ten thousand *yūjo* in Osaka's "pleasure quarters," three or four thousand in Yoshiwara, and thousands more clandestine prostitutes scattered throughout the city of Edo. To this total he added nearly four thousand city geisha. Moreover, he estimated that in the provinces, which had seen the rise of entertainment districts in ports, harbors, and post stations, more than a hundred thousand women worked as prostitutes. According to his reckoning, this was the sector of the business that had seen the most growth.[2]

The sex trade's expansion into the provinces, like the growth of the service economy in general, was a consequence of the market revolution that transformed small towns and villages all over Japan during the mid-to-late eighteenth century. In predominantly rice-growing regions, wealthy peasants moved into sake or soy sauce brewing and money lending, amassing more land at the expense of their indebted neighbors. Meanwhile, in areas where there was easy access to roads and waterways, or where large-scale commercial agriculture was difficult, rural families turned to manufacturing, producing finished or semi-finished items to sell to distant markets.[3] Both patterns of development put cash in the hands of provincial commoners, bringing a wider array of cultural offerings within their reach. Historians have described how newly empowered peasants purchased books, learned poetry, and sponsored noh and kabuki performances, activities formerly limited to upper-class merchants and samurai.[4] But men in the countryside were also eager to spend their money on the pleasures of the flesh. When offered the opportunity, they patronized prostitutes at least as enthusiastically as they perused the latest publications from Edo and Osaka.

While peasants' increased purchasing power accounted for part of the spike in demand that fueled the growth of the provincial sex trade, another important factor was the emergence of a culture of travel. As road conditions improved and sailing technology evolved throughout the late seventeenth and early eighteenth centuries, men and women from all walks of life began to travel more frequently. Many of these people were involved in trade: they led the packhorse trains and piloted the cargo vessels that brought raw materials to manufacturers in the countryside and finished items to consumers in emerging markets across the archipelago. Others were migrant laborers who walked to newly developed rural towns to find work. By the early nineteenth century, a significant number were recreational travelers on pilgrimages and sightseeing expeditions.[5] Their peregrinations fueled the development of a travel industry that was also in large part a sex industry, since travelers were eager to spend time and money in the company of prostitutes. They purchased sexual access to local women for the same reasons that they collected amulets and ingested local delicacies: all these activities were ways of encountering and creating memories of unfamiliar places.[6] Those who lived in areas frequented by travelers were quick to capitalize on this demand, and they made sure to offer prostitution along with food and lodging.

As demand for sexual services grew, brothels' recruitment networks began to expand. They tended to move women from relatively poor regions, where the cost of labor was low, to the more prosperous areas where travelers were numerous and local residents had discretionary income to spend on entertainment. Often this entailed transporting women across the political boundaries that carved the realm into domains. In a study of protoindustrial development, Kären Wigen has argued, "commercial ventures followed their own spatial logic, which was not that of the Tokugawa feudal settlement; economic regions coexisted with political regions, but did not conform to them."[7] Ultimately, this was as true of the sex trade as it was of commerce in paper products, textiles, or lacquer bowls.

However, because it involved the movement of people rather than objects (or, more accurately, because it moved people *as if* they were objects), the sex trade's disregard for jurisdictional distinctions posed unique problems for provincial samurai officials. Not only did they have to deal with the complexity of controlling an industry whose operations constantly extended beyond their reach, they also had to grapple with the political implications of a business that treated women as commodities rather than as female members of households rooted in specific towns and villages. In other words, it was not only space that brothel keepers perceived differently from their rulers; it was also the female half of the population.

Meanwhile, the samurai authorities who might have reasserted their laws regarding women's place in the realm were preoccupied with their own economic problems, which became more acute over the course of the eighteenth and nineteenth centuries. Traditionally, Tokugawa Japan's rulers had relied on land taxes, assessed and paid in bales of rice, as their primary source of revenue (other forms of payment included lumber, dried sea goods (seaweed and very small fish used as fertilizer), fish, and, by the nineteenth century, cash). Since daimyō and their retainers could not live on rice alone, they converted these payments into hard currency. But as rice production rose sharply over the seventeenth and eighteenth centuries, the crop's cash value declined and administrators were unable to increase tax rates enough to compensate. To make matters worse, samurai were spending more of their income purchasing the processed goods that had become daily necessities, and many domainal administrations found themselves in debt to urban merchants who offered tempting lines of credit, often using projected tax revenue as collateral. To escape this cycle of indebtedness, officials began to seek alternate sources of income. With varying degrees of success, they turned their attention to the possibilities presented by the growth of commerce. In some domains, officials sponsored monopolies and nurtured nascent industries such as papermaking or cloth weaving, hoping that peasants' and townsmen's commercial endeavors would ultimately contribute to the "prosperity of the country." More heavy-handed administrators levied forced loans on successful peasants and townspeople, appropriating profits that they had no effective means of taxing.[8]

Because they found themselves perpetually short of cash, samurai authorities were unable to separate their interest in promoting prosperity from their desire to impose their vision of social order. If the shogunal magistrates in charge of post stations and the domain authorities responsible for provincial ports, pilgrimage sites, and market towns did not ensure the vitality of their jurisdictions, they had no hope of funding their administrations. Moreover, they realized that promoting prosperity in general—regardless of its effect on tax revenue—could be a strategy toward ensuring social stability, because the poor were less likely to riot in times of plenty. In that sense, it was counterproductive to attempt to impose order by cracking down on so-called vices such as prostitution; doing so risked inhibiting commerce, breeding poverty, and initiating a cycle of unrest. As Part I has argued, shogunal magistrates in political centers followed the same logic, which was why they ultimately decided to sanction prostitution outside designated "pleasure quarters." But in provincial towns, many of which were dependent on the discretionary spending of sailors, pilgrims, and other travelers, the incentives to promote the sex trade were even stronger. Unlike their counterparts in the great cities, who always stopped short of tolerating forms of prostitution that seemed to undermine the patriarchal household, officials in many of these areas abandoned regulation entirely. Some permitted women to sell sex to support an independent livelihood, while others stood aside as brothels enticed peasant boys to squander their families' wealth in the pursuit of sexual gratification. They also relinquished control over the labor market, allowing proprietors to extend their recruiting networks across domainal boundaries and looking the other way as peasant families sent daughter after daughter to brothels in distant provinces.

These decisions to turn away from regulation were usually made in a piecemeal fashion, as improvised responses to local conditions. But in the aggregate, their impact was staggering, because they allowed the sex trade to expand rapidly in response to increased demand. This trend had varied social consequences. Credit-starved families in less-developed regions learned to survive by sending "extra" daughters to brothels, and entire communities began to specialize in women, who became "famous products" (*meibutsu*) of their region, akin to sake, buckwheat noodles, ceramic dishes, or paper umbrellas in other areas. Commoners who lived in port towns and pilgrimage sites tended to welcome the influx of these young women, because they recognized that prostitution attracted travelers and contributed to local prosperity. They became accustomed to living in a "floating world" in which men and women did not seem to be rooted to locations or households, but drifted through communities on their way to other destinations, often relying on work in the service economy rather than productive labor. But in more settled agricultural villages, the encroachment of the sex trade became a disturbing example of how economic change was transforming social relations, as local young men deserted the fields and frittered away their cash wages carousing in brothels.

As more peasants indentured their daughters to brothels, more husbands squandered their assets visiting prostitutes, more widows sold sex in the streets, and more women were classified and categorized as "products," these social changes inspired a new kind of moral panic associated with prostitution. While residents of cities like Edo and Osaka could understand the proliferation of city entertainment districts as a continuation of long-standing trends or as welcome evidence of urban vitality, those in the countryside perceived prostitution's expansion as a sudden and shocking change. To many, commoners and samurai alike, it seemed that the hierarchical, mutually responsible relationships that constituted the family, bound communities together, and undergirded the polity would not survive the expansion of a business that turned sex into a financial transaction and made women into objects of exchange. Prostitution, like the growth of the market economy in general, began to provoke the fear that all human relationships would come to be mediated by the exchange of cash rather than being ordered by bonds of fealty and obligation.

Samurai and wealthy peasants had the most to lose if generational and gender-based hierarchies collapsed: the former worried that the disintegration of the household presaged the dissolution of the realm, while the latter feared that they would not be able to maintain their power within their own communities. Prostitutes, who worked outside the household in a business that symbolized the worst excesses of commercialization, were obvious scapegoats. When they were still imagined solely to be dutiful daughters, they had been understood as epitomizing the ideals of feminine sacrifice, submission, and obedience. But elite men had begun to believe that the brothel and the household were diametrically opposed and irreconcilable institutions, and they could not imagine that prostitutes belonged within both realms at once. In their minds, women who worked in the sex trade were no longer paragons of filial devotion; instead, they began to represent the negatively inflected market values of self-interest, acquisitiveness, and, in particular, autonomy. This mode of thought isolated prostitutes from the protective structures of the household and the village community, turning them into stigmatized outsiders.

Throughout, the vast majority of prostitutes were still young indentured women working on behalf of their families. For some, the new discourse on prostitution was less important than their altered material conditions. They were able to disregard the samurai who called them "shameless" and the village headmen who portrayed them as selfish because the possibilities presented by the expansion of the market were more important than the changed perceptions of their work. In the absence of regulation, they could take advantage of rare chances to work for themselves or more common opportunities to migrate to more prosperous regions. But for others, the new discourse on the meaning of prostitution had unwelcome consequences. When elite men no longer perceived them as exemplars of feminine virtue, prostitutes found it more difficult to engage the narrative strategies that had enabled them to access official protection. Moreover, the new perception that prostitutes acted autonomously was not usually borne out by women's experiences. In most cases, it remained a dangerous idea, one that isolated prostitutes from their communities and closed off the avenues through which they might have sought support.

CHAPTER FOUR · **From Household to Market**
Child Sellers, "Widows," and Other Shameless People

The agronomist, strategist, and economist Satō Nobuhiro (1769–1850) remarked in 1829 that prostitutes were a "famous product" (*meibutsu*) of the northeastern province of Echigo.¹ He followed this pronouncement with a brief discussion of the thousands of women who had left the region to work in brothels throughout the archipelago. Like Satsuma sugar, Chōshū salt, and other "famous products," Echigo women were renowned for qualities said to be unique to their place of origin. According to lore, they were fair-skinned beauties, as pale and luminous as the snow that blanketed their region for much of the winter. In the province's most prosperous city, the port of Niigata, male visitors could test this theory in a variety of venues. In Furumachi, a district in the center of town, sumptuous brothels welcomed well-heeled clients. On Teramachi, an inland avenue lined with shrines and temples along one side, women called *ukimi* amused guests at private parties. At the outer edges of the city, on Bishamonjima, an outcropping in the Shinano River; Kumagaya kōji, a northern fishermen's district; and Dapon kōji, a coastal area named for the *dapon* sound of anchors dropping in the water, sailors patronized inexpensive teahouses and brothels. Meanwhile, on the banks of the river, women known as "river sellers" (or "gourd sellers," *kawauri*) offered their services to passersby. And throughout the city of roughly 30,000, hundreds of freelance prostitutes called "widows" (*goke*) sold sex, companionship, and entertainment to male callers.

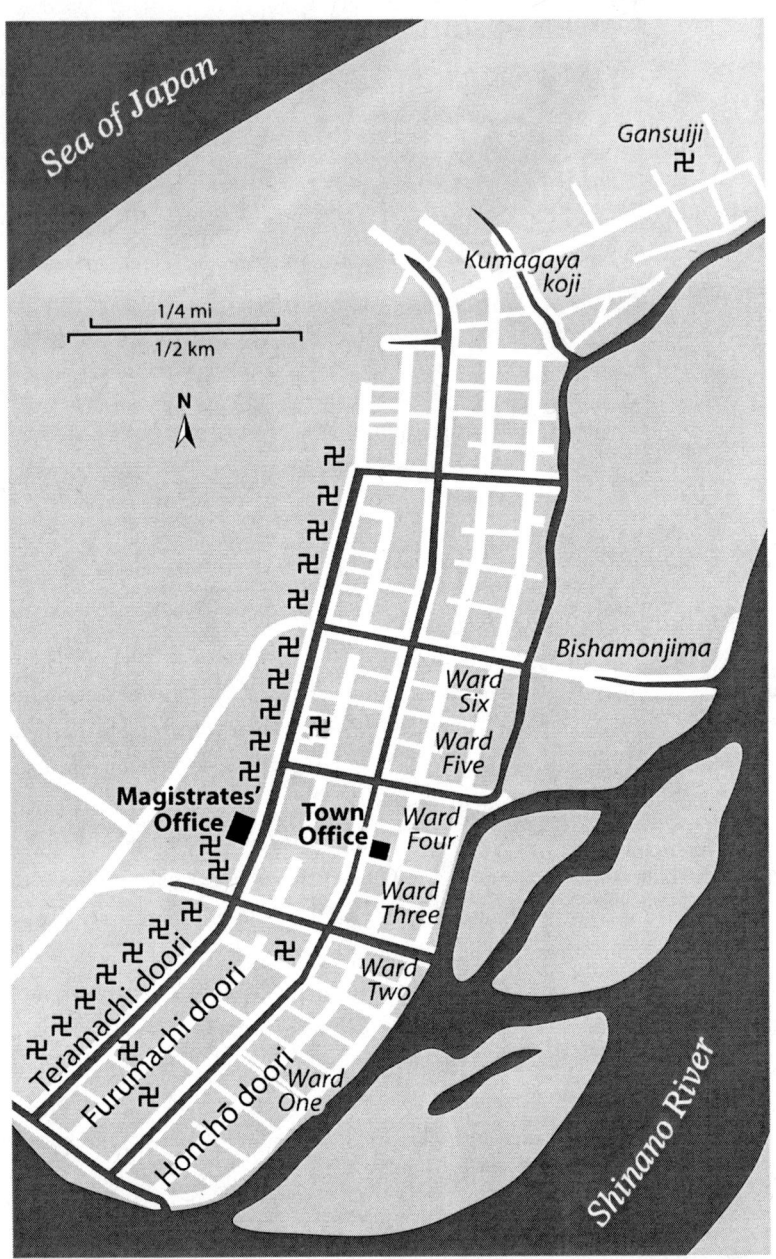

MAP 2.
Niigata in the early nineteenth century; adapted from Niigata-shi hensan kinseishi bukai, ed., *Niigata shishi tsūshi hen*, vol. 2: *Kinsei ge* (1997). The reverse swastikas mark the locations of temples.

These "famous products" of Echigo—both those who remained in Niigata and those who left the region to work in other provinces—had proliferated in response to a heightened demand for sexual services, stimulated by a number of social and economic developments in the mid-eighteenth century. These included the rise of commercial agriculture, which supplied a broad population of commoners with the discretionary income necessary to purchase sex; the improvement of sailing technology and sea transportation routes, which contributed to an increase in sailors eager to visit prostitutes in port cities; and the emergence of a culture of travel among ordinary peasants and townspeople, which fueled tourism-related business, including prostitution. Although these factors affected cities and towns across the archipelago, they had a disproportionate impact on Niigata and its hinterland, much of which was administered by Nagaoka domain. Chronically indebted and unable to raise taxes on their impoverished cultivators, Nagaoka authorities could not halt the exodus of peasant women who left the region to work in brothels. At the same time, they were unwilling to impose restrictions on the sex trade in Niigata: taxes on maritime commerce were their most reliable source of income, and any policy that discouraged sailors from dropping anchor at port imperiled this revenue stream. This combination of economic constraints and incentives ensured that prostitution in Nagaoka was not ordered by the logic of households, which mandated that the only women permitted to work in the business were filial daughters whose labor supported desperately poor parents. Instead, officials "ignored" the region's sex trade, yielding to the logic of the market, in which prostitutes were variously "products" and entrepreneurs.

Between the mid-eighteenth and the mid-nineteenth centuries, Nagaoka's flourishing market for sexual services evolved into an economic necessity for the domain. But at the same time, the Niigata area's reputation for supplying women to distant brothels and passing sailors became a political liability for the region's samurai administrators, who were concerned for their image in the realm. Hamstrung by their own financial interests, they could only watch as local families exchanged their daughters for cash and unmarried women treated their own bodies as marketable commodities. As long as the sex trade was relatively small-scale, these instances could be dismissed as regrettable, but ultimately necessary, survival strategies for a tiny minority of suffering families. But the business had expanded to the point where even outsiders were touting the domain's female subjects as "products." This put officials in the awkward position of justifying their lenient policy toward the sex trade. How could benevolent rulers allow so many of their cultivators to sell their children and permit so many unmarried women to sell sex in the streets? Good governors were supposed to shield their subjects from harm and teach them to value familial relationships over the pursuit of profit. But as more and more of Echigo's women became "products," rather than wives or daughters, it seemed that the boundaries between the household and the marketplace were collapsing, leaving a government based on an analogy between familial authority and political authority on unstable ground.

NAGAOKA DOMAIN AND THE TRAFFIC IN WOMEN

THE PROBLEM OF DAUGHTER SELLING

Niigata was Nagaoka's most important possession, a famously prosperous city in a notoriously impoverished region. Although it was surrounded by "snow country," where bitter cold curtailed the growing season, the port was favorably situated at the mouth of the Shinano River and in the middle of the coastal shipping route between Hokkaido and the Inland Sea. When the domestic sea trade accelerated during the late seventeenth century, Niigata became a major destination for ships transporting tax rice from northeastern domains to the central market in Osaka. This meant that the city's fortunes depended on the quality of the rice harvest and the changing conditions of the harbor, which at one point in the early eighteenth century became too shallow for massive rice ships. But by the early nineteenth century, the port's economy gradually stabilized as smaller boats carrying a greater variety of products —including Hokkaido marine goods and manufactured items such as cotton cloth—began to account for a larger proportion of commerce. Traffic became more consistent, and in most years well over two thousand vessels anchored at Niigata.[2]

Echigo was home to many warriors, but Niigata was not a samurai town. There was no castle, and the magistrates' office was a lonely outpost for men of the warrior class. The city was sustained by the commoners who did the daily work of buying, selling, and transporting the rice, sesame seed, fertilizer, salt, dried fish, and bolts of cloth that came through the port. By the early nineteenth century, they also did a brisk, and illegal, business in sugar, Chinese medicines, and red ink smuggled in from distant Ryūkyū.[3] The thriving sea trade attracted migrants from nearby villages who rented rooms in the crowded quarters along the coast and found employment as laborers on the docks. Along with their more affluent neighbors, they flocked to plays, sumo bouts, and raucous festivals.[4]

At the town office (*machi kaisho*) in the city center, town elders (*kendan* and *chōrō*) were responsible for ensuring that land tax revenue, licensing fees, and loans extracted from Niigata's townspeople reached domain authorities.[5] This became an increasingly complicated task during the middle of the period, as the chronically indebted Nagaoka domain attempted to squeeze more and more revenue from the port's residents. The administration had already fallen victim to the same inflationary pressures constraining government finances across the archipelago when a series of fires, floods, and famines in the mid-eighteenth century drained its coffers.[6] Officials attempted to remedy the situation by levying forced loans on Niigata's townspeople. Unfortunately for the city's merchants, who bitterly resented the impositions, this did not begin to solve the problem. By the nineteenth century, the domain regularly borrowed tens of thousands of *ryō* at a time from its wealthiest residents, many of whom were based in Niigata.[7]

Outside the port city, the domain's holdings were impoverished. Echigo rice was renowned throughout Japan, but snow-country cultivators could produce only one harvest per year, and inconsistent weather patterns meant that the yield was never dependable. To make matters worse, they struggled under an unusually high tax burden. Because their overlords were desperate for revenue, Nagaoka's peasants paid more in cash per *koku* of assessed production than their counterparts in nearby villages administered by the shogunate or Takada domain. This did not escape their notice, and they complained of inefficiency and corruption throughout the domain's government.[8]

The region was also burdened by overpopulation. In the late eighteenth century, intellectuals from other areas often praised Echigo peasants for eschewing infanticide even when they were on the brink of starvation. Most assumed that this was attributable to the influence of Jōdo Shinshū, the locally dominant sect of Buddhism, which imposed an especially strict taboo on taking life. The truth was darker and more complicated. Fabian Drixler's work on the demography of Hokuriku (the northeastern region of which Echigo was a part) confirms that families there were slightly larger than average. But his interpretation suggests that this was not because they abstained from infanticide. Rather, they seem to have resorted to it less often than their contemporaries in other areas of northern Japan because they were so adept at finding employment for their "extra" children, who left their destitute villages to become migrant laborers in other regions.[9]

Echigo's daughters, in particular, were in high demand in other provinces. Throughout the seventeenth century, criminals from the neighboring Aizu domain smuggled "Echigo women" out of their home province and sold them as maidservants and agricultural workers. In 1645, one such trafficker was apprehended and crucified after his victim complained that he had deceived her parents by offering to serve as the go-between for an advantageous marriage in Aizu. Instead, he had sold her into an eternal term of service as a maid (*eidai gejo*).[10] Officials were distressed by such reports, and they felt a duty to protect their subjects, whom they viewed as ignorant and easily misled. In 1730, the Niigata city magistrates forbade the townspeople to send their female relatives into service in other domains, warning that the employment brokers who visited the city often took advantage of recruits.[11]

But by the late eighteenth century, the dream of a good marriage in another province was becoming a reality for more Echigo women. In many villages in the neighboring Kantō region, female infanticide and out-migration had skewed sex ratios so far that peasant men could not marry. Headmen visited Echigo to find potential wives for desperate villagers, and some daimyō instituted policies designed to attract marriageable women to their domains.[12] Even contracts for work in domestic service could become matchmaking endeavors. One recruiter who trolled the area around Niigata seeking women to work in the Kantō provinces of Hitachi and Shimōsa kept a ledger in which he recorded his recruits' marital status along with their experience with farm labor and needlework. According to his records, the vast majority indicated that they were open to the possibility of marriage if they met suitable partners in Kantō.[13]

These brides and domestic servants were joined on their journey to Kantō by a growing number of women who were heading to post stations to work as prostitutes. The "push" factor fueling this migration was a combination of heightened economic insecurity and a new "household consciousness" among poor peasants. As Yabuta Yutaka argues, while small-scale cultivators were increasingly attuned to the social mores of their wealthier neighbors, they also found it more and more difficult to uphold the ideal of the cohesive household. Lower-class peasant families, which had begun to depend on the cash proceeds from wage labor or work in cottage industries to pay mortgages, buy fertilizer, and purchase foodstuffs, were intensely vulnerable to economic downturns. Without credit, they could not provide for their own subsistence. In the worst-case scenario, entire families of "broken peasants" (*tsubure hyakushō*) had to disperse and relocate to find work. This was an undesirable outcome for local village leaders, who relied on these families' contributions to pay taxes, and it was socially disastrous for the "broken peasants" themselves, because they and their peers had begun to perceive the failure of a household as a moral calamity. The fear of meeting this fate, along with a chronic need for credit, drove poor peasants' daughters into prostitution, which was much more lucrative than other types of work and had the advantage of offering upfront cash payments.[14]

At the same time, demand for women to work in prostitution increased dramatically over the course of the late eighteenth century. As chapter 5 discusses in more detail, struggling post stations along the shogun's highways were hiring more and more "serving girls" in a bid to attract paying customers. Most sent their procurers on recruiting missions to Echigo, where labor was relatively cheap. Women from the region were working in brothels all over northern and eastern Japan, including the provinces of Shinano, Kai, Kōzuke, Shimotsuke, Musashi, Mutsu, and Hitachi, in the 1820s, according to a regional encyclopedia, *Echigo yashi* (Echigo Field Journal).[15] Population registers from post stations along the Nakasendō, the inland highway linking Edo to Kyoto, tell a similar story, indicating that more prostitutes came from Echigo than anywhere else in the realm.[16] Stations along the Nikkō Highway also recruited heavily from the region. In 1822, shogunal officials raided Kasukabe station in Musashi province and apprehended twenty-one "extra" serving girls. Of those, eighteen were from Echigo, mostly from the county that included Niigata. The 1862 population registers from Suzumenomiya station in Shimotsuke reveal a similar pattern: forty-three of fifty-three serving girls were natives of Echigo, and all but seven were from the villages surrounding Niigata.[17]

This recruitment pattern did some damage to Echigo's image. As Drixler has argued, when commentators in other areas of eastern Japan struggled with their own provinces' reputations for infanticide, they assuaged their hurt regional pride by pointing out that selling babies was almost as bad (and in some cases worse) than murdering them. Murata Ryūmin, an intellectual from Mito domain in the Kantō region, mocked Echigo families for breeding as if they were raising prize animals for auction: "People raise children like dogs and cats, and if they have a fine fur, they sell them in the spring of their sixth or seventh year. To raise prostitutes and thereby support one's own livelihood . . . is as inhuman as eating one's own children."[18] The dyspeptic social critic Buyō Inshi agreed. He condemned the procurers who descended on remote villages in Echigo, Etchū, and Dewa to take advantage of desperate peasants. But he also had little sympathy for parents who "sold their beloved children to strange, faraway provinces" and condemned them to "hell on earth." In earlier eras, he explained, people had been ashamed to sell their children, and others in their villages would point fingers at them and gossip behind their backs. But in his own time, they had no such compunctions. They thought only of their own profit, and as a result more and more girls were being sold.[19]

This type of commentary, which proliferated during the 1790s, had frightening implications for Nagaoka officials. Whether the domain's daughters were pushed into prostitution by their parents' economic desperation or their immoral desire to profit, their rulers could reasonably be blamed. Either Nagaoka had failed to ensure an adequate standard of living for its cultivators, or its officials had neglected to provide an appropriate level of moral instruction. Imamura Yodoshichi, who served as Niigata city magistrate between 1791 and 1801, grappled with this problem in a treatise called *Shinbo Jōwa* (Frank Conversations from the Port of Niigata).[20] Following a popular convention at the time, he structured his work as a conversation between several learned men, each of whom held forth with his own erudite discussion of the administrative issues facing the port city. Their debate about daughter selling, entitled *Kugai no hōkō* (Service in the World of Suffering), picked up the threads of the discourse criticizing Echigo parents and wove them into a very different argument, which ultimately absolved Nagaoka's rulers of responsibility.

The first discussant, a pompous older man whose speech seemed to mimic the moralizing tone of Echigo's critics, addressed the plight of many of Nagaoka's daughters:

> The fate of the prostitute [*tawareme*] is loathsome and wretched. She sells her own body, exposing the shame that a woman should conceal from all except the one man she has married. Day and night, she swallows her pride and exposes this shame, and she tells lies she does not believe to melt men's hearts. . . . Not only this, [but] she cannot sleep at night while others rest, and she is far from her parents and siblings. Or perhaps in the case of her parents' death anniversaries and funerals, even though it is the death anniversary of a family member, she cannot fulfill her desire to prepare the ritual foods or attend the mourning service. . . . To be unable to live out the short life she has been allotted, to turn her back on her innate human dignity and plunge into the abyss of prostitution—it is not an overstatement to say that this is a truly bitter and tragic situation.[21]

This discussant echoed (or perhaps anticipated, depending on precisely when Imamura composed this piece) commentators such as Satō Nobuhiro and Murata Ryūmin, who idealized the family and exalted the "natural" bonds between parent and child. His reasoning explicitly refuted the claim by other samurai administrators that legal prostitution fulfilled the feminine ideals of obedience and sacrifice. According to his logic, filial piety was *not* a legitimate justification for work in prostitution; rather, as service in the sex trade prevented a woman from meeting her filial obligations and severed the ties between parent and child, it was a perversion of Confucian values and a deviation from the "way of humanity" (*jindō*).

This assessment was likely motivated by the new reality of work in the sex trade. As the business of prostitution expanded and the scope of recruitment widened, it became more common for women to go to work in faraway cities and towns, where they could not be expected to keep in close contact with their families. Perhaps if Echigo's sex trade had more closely resembled Nagasaki's, and indentured prostitutes had been able to visit their parents on a regular basis, Echigo's peasants would have received a kinder appraisal from critics such as Buyō Inshi and his fictional counterpart. By shipping their daughters off to distant markets in exchange for payment, however, snow-country parents seemed to be treating their children as commodities rather than family members. To elite men invested in maintaining the political symbolism of the household, this was disturbing evidence of how the crass values of the marketplace had corrupted that protected sphere.

As Imamura's "frank conversation" continued, a less emotional interlocutor agreed that child selling was an evil custom. He admitted that for many families, it was the only chance to escape from grinding poverty, but insisted that this was not always the case. Rather, many of the girls who went to work in brothels were motivated by base greed, and they were encouraged in their ambitions by morally bankrupt parents and neighbors. These misguided peasant girls jumped at the chance to wear fine clothes and gold and silver hair ornaments. Since they lived in villages where people did not pity them for their fate, they were utterly unashamed of their scandalous conduct.[22] This discussant framed work in the sex trade as a reckless exercise in self-gratification. While the first speaker had criticized parents while clinging to the older vision of women as innocent victims who had been "plunged into an abyss of suffering," the second countered this argument by asserting that women were enthusiastic participants in their own degradation.

By juxtaposing these two views, the magistrate expressed his ambivalence about women who worked in prostitution. But there was no such ambiguity in his portrait of their parents. Both speakers agreed that peasants who sold their daughters were not victims who had been oppressed by high tax burdens or led astray by corrupt officials. Rather, they had chosen their fate, either because they were stupid and inherently immoral or because they selfishly aspired to a level of material comfort that was inappropriate to their station. The latter explanation of parents' motives was popular among Confucian-influenced intellectuals who lamented the disintegration of peasant households. The anonymous author of an anti-infanticide tract argued, "People love luxury and so they hate their children and do not want to raise them, or they think [children] will make more work for them, or they think [children] will bring no benefit to them."[23] In China, educated men made similar arguments. In the mid-nineteenth century, a poet who had served as a minor official in the Qing bureaucracy lamented the bitter fate of rural girls put up for sale to Shanghai brothels: "How their parents love cash more than their young ones! / With chilling calculation they cast delicate daughters into the mire."[24] All three authors expressed their fear that market relations were supplanting familial bonds, a trend they attributed to many individual failures of morality and attempted to solve through criticism and exhortation.

But this was a much larger problem, related to uneven patterns of economic development that made it possible for poor peasants in regions such as Echigo to become aware of and aspire to a rising standard of living, even as they had more and more difficulty keeping up with their wealthier neighbors. As Imamura likely recognized, Nagaoka domain could do little to alter the inexorable logic of supply and demand. Echigo was a poor province with too many mouths to feed, and traffickers offered desperate families good money for children, particularly nubile daughters. In its straitened financial condition, Nagaoka could not offer these peasants incentives to behave differently. In fact, the domain had a direct interest in encouraging daughter selling, since the indenture money paid to prostitutes' parents was often converted into tax payments that filled the daimyō's coffers. As long as the domain was unable to settle its own accounts, officials would stand by as demographic and market forces conspired to pull young women from their villages and send them to brothels in distant cities and towns. In that sense, the rulers of Nagaoka were as morally compromised as the peasants they criticized: the struggle to adjust to a changing economy had corrupted the relationship between governors and governed, just as it had broken the bonds between parents and children. But samurai officials, unlike poor peasants, could claim the moral high ground by virtue of their social position. For Imamura's characters, blaming a degraded culture and irresponsible individual choices for young women's misery was a way to avoid addressing how market forces could strain the logic of a paternalistic, "benevolent" government.

"IGNORING" PROSTITUTION

Nagaoka officials expressed their disapproval when the domain's women went to work in brothels in other provinces, but they were unwilling to restrict prostitution within their own most prosperous city. This was not because they had a philosophical objection to cracking down on activities they regarded as vices: they had flatly prohibited the sex trade in the castle town of Nagaoka, which was home to most of the domain's warriors.[25] But in 1756, when the shogunate asked them about their stance toward prostitution in Niigata, they answered with this cryptic statement: "It is not prohibited, but it is not allowed either [*chōji tsukamatsuri sōrō gi mo gozanaku, sashiyurushi sōrō gi mo gozanaku sōrō*]."²⁶

This odd pronouncement was actually an accurate description of the domain's policy, which some of the city's elite brothel keepers found frustrating. Proprietors in Nakamichi, who ran upper-class establishments and called their women *yūjo*, were convinced that they deserved recognition from the domain. They also insisted that they should have a monopoly on the business of selling sex. In 1730, they had petitioned the city magistrates to curtail the business of their chief competitors: the *ukimi* who worked on Teramachi. The complaint stated that the *ukimi* wore fancy clothes, played the shamisen, and usurped the status of *yūjo* [*yūjo no kaku ni shoji tsukamatsuri*]. But Nagaoka officials were evasive. The magistrates urged the *ukimi* to dress more modestly but did not forbid their activities: visiting teahouses, playing the shamisen, and trading sexual services for payment.²⁷ This judgment made clear that no group or area of town could claim an exclusive right to employ prostitutes or engage in prostitution.

In their proclamations to the townspeople, Nagaoka officials never explained why they refused to issue laws confining brothels to certain areas. But magistrate Imamura's *Shinbo Jōwa* (Frank Conversations) suggests that they regarded their tolerance of the sex trade as benevolent and likely to create prosperity. In a chapter devoted to the issue of prostitution in Niigata, a young gentleman speculates that brothels are allowed to operate as a diversion for hard-working townsmen. He is quickly corrected by an older and wiser man, who explains that the sex trade is inherently evil, and the authorities have no wish to promote immorality by allowing brothels to tempt townsmen into forgetting their responsibilities to their households. The domain tolerates prostitution, however, as a form of economic stimulus—brothels are a necessary amenity for visiting sailors and merchants, who might otherwise bypass Niigata and head to more welcoming harbors, devastating the port's economy and ruining its inhabitants.²⁸

Imamura's public statements acknowledged that there was a delicate balance between promoting prosperity and sanctioning disorder. In 1795, he issued a proclamation observing that the expansion of the sex trade led to the deterioration of manners and customs (*fūzoku*).²⁹ These encompassed a set of orderly behaviors that the ruling class thought appropriate for commoners: diligence, thrift, sobriety, and humility. Ideally, they would be manifested in the clothing of the city's residents and the architecture of their houses. As David Howell has explained, "exteriority was at least as important to the maintenance of good rule as was the internalization of the ruling ideology."[30] According to this logic, a wise magistrate could not allow ostentatious brothels to stand alongside townsmen's dwellings, nor could he permit gaudily dressed prostitutes to parade through the streets. In keeping with this understanding of his role, Imamura observed that prostitutes (*baijo*) had moved into neighborhoods where they were not permitted, and he urged influential commoners in those areas to stop their operations. He also complained that townspeople were bringing prostitutes and other poor women to inns to cater to travelers. He declared this practice a disgrace (*hazukashime*) and instructed innkeepers to put an end to it.[31] But he did not impose any penalty for clandestine prostitution, and there is no evidence that his edict was enforced.

By the early nineteenth century, it was clear that years of neglect had limited the domain's options: the city's sex trade had developed so haphazardly that any attempt to limit its scope would risk paralyzing an important sector of the economy. Thus domain-appointed magistrates and their commoner underlings rejected even the most benign regulatory schemes. For example, in 1829, a group of five townsmen in Teramachi suggested that the prostitutes (*baijo*), geisha, and hookers (*shiromono*) in their neighborhood raise their prices and submit a portion of their profits to provide rice to the poor in case of famine. In addition, they proposed that prostitutes should pay the domain a licensing fee (*myōgakin*), which would be used to rent a space to build a storehouse for the rice. But the elders in the town office dismissed this proposal, explaining their reasoning in a memorandum addressed to the city magistrates. They acknowledged that prostitution could attract "evil types" (*akutō*), thus contributing to social disorder. But they saw no way around this problem. They argued that any form of regulation would be tantamount to limiting prostitution, even if this was not the stated intention of the policy. Moreover, even the mildest form of taxation would unfairly penalize the prostitutes' masters, who were only trying to earn a living during a time of hardship. If the sex trade faltered as a result, the effect on the entire city's economy would be catastrophic: the business was too firmly entrenched in too many neighborhoods (over 70 percent, according to their estimate). Such a calamity, they added, would surely result in lost tax revenue for the domain. The city magistrates agreed and rejected the initial proposal.[32]

The ultimate effect of this policy, in which the domain refused to limit Niigata's sex trade, was to negate the legal distinction between prostitutes and other women. Since officials would not impose penalties for clandestine prostitution, a variety of women—even those who were not under contract to brothels—were able to support themselves through work in the sex trade. The most prominent among them were the so-called "widows," who first gained fame sometime in the early nineteenth century. These were not dutiful daughters whose labor supported their parents, but older women who worked for themselves. *Echigo yashi* described them as "prostitutes who have finished their terms of service to brothels and have been let go, but have no husbands and live alone selling their bodies."[33] Some must have been veterans of Niigata brothels, but others had worked in faraway provinces. In 1830, an Edo-based *jōruri* performer who called himself Fujiwara Morohide recorded an encounter with a Niigata *goke* who was around thirty years old (which would have been quite elderly for a brothel prostitute). He was shocked when she recognized him and called him by his former stage name, Shigetayū. She explained that she had previously worked at a brothel in the Fukagawa district of Edo, one of his old haunts. Deeply flattered, he concluded his diary entry for that night: "I thought that these *hachi goke* would be widows who know nothing of the world, but I was gravely mistaken. They come from all over."[34]

The *jōruri* performer should not have been so surprised that the "widow" he met in Niigata was an experienced professional. By the nineteenth century, the word "widow" had become a standard euphemism for single women who supported an independent livelihood by selling sex. This nomenclature, which was particularly popular in port towns, likely originated with the fishermen's wives who turned to prostitution after their husbands were lost at sea. In the Amakusa region of Kyushu, for example, merchants involved in the dried sea goods industry compensated their employees' widows by offering them jobs in the sex trade.[35] As one *senryū* joked:

> the widow's hole
> no time for tears
> to dry
> only her busy beaver
> is washed
> before her next customer.[36]

Although prostitutes who called themselves *goke* were not always widows, the appellation was appropriate in a symbolic sense, because it carried connotations of lustiness, sexual expertise, and availability. Like their counterparts in Qing China, Tokugawa officials idealized widow chastity. Some of the women celebrated in the shogunate's *Kankoku kōgiroku* (Official Records of Filial Piety) were those who remained in their marital households, refused to remarry, and worked tirelessly to support their in-laws and children after their husbands had died.³⁷ But this type of behavior was noted and rewarded precisely because it was unusual: commoners in Tokugawa Japan did not expect widows to remain celibate. In many of the cases recorded in the *Kankoku kōgiroku*, widows' neighbors and relatives urged them to remarry, pointing out that their lives would be easier if they could rely on a husband to help support the household. In fact, even when widows remained single, peasants tended to tolerate their illicit liaisons, perhaps because they believed that women who had already experienced intercourse within marriage were likely to become frustrated without a sexual outlet.³⁸ Widows' sexuality was a common topic of humorous verse, such as "when desiring a penis / widows visit / Yoshichō [a popular district for male prostitution]" or "with her finger / as if he were inside / the widow's orgasm."³⁹

In addition to suggesting licentiousness, the word *goke* also implied a certain degree of independence. Since there was no custom or law dictating that a peasant's widow should remain under the control of her husband's family, such women could choose whether to remain in the marital household, remarry, or return to their parents. In rare cases, they replaced their husbands as household heads and served on village councils.⁴⁰ For high-status women, too, widowhood could provide the freedom to travel and the opportunity for self-reinvention. Many took the tonsure to cement their new status. As Laura Nenzi points out, this step could entail "the complete redefinition of roles and identities, including the possibility of abandoning all family-related obligation."⁴¹ In the *goke*'s case, taking the tonsure would have been a terrible business decision, but the "abandonment of family-related obligation" was achievable. Unlike the *ukimi* on Teramachi, who were forced to relinquish their earnings to the "parents" (*oyakata*) who arranged their bookings, the *goke* kept their pay. They also charged more, which afforded them a measure of financial independence.⁴²

By allowing women to work as "widows," eschewing marriage to support their own livelihoods, Nagaoka officials had enabled them to survive—very visibly— outside the gendered order of the household. If not literally widowed, Niigata's *goke* were symbolically widowed, liberated from the household's requirements of sexual fidelity and productivity. Daughters answered to their parents, indentured prostitutes served their masters, and wives obeyed their husbands, but the *goke* were free agents. Their work in prostitution did not look like an expression of filial piety or confirmation of the feminine values of passivity and obedience. From an official perspective, these women, who were supposed to be subordinate and self-sacrificing, had allowed the cold calculations of profit and loss to supplant the bonds of obligation and protection that structured the household and the state. Yet Nagaoka domain, which was convinced that limiting prostitution would lead to economic collapse, remained silent.

FROM THE DOMAIN'S TROUBLED DAUGHTERS TO "SHAMELESS" SHOGUNAL SUBJECTS

The widows' challenge to the gendered order did not go unanswered for long. In 1842, after a major famine and several foreign incursions into Japanese waters, the shogunate's senior councilor Mizuno Tadakuni (1794–1851) inaugurated the Tenpō Reforms in an attempt to restore political stability. As chapter 2 has discussed briefly, the reform program included a campaign against clandestine prostitution that resulted in the closing or relocation of many Edo brothels. But the city of Niigata was more profoundly affected by one of Tadakuni's most controversial innovations: he demanded that the daimyō of strategically important areas cede their territory to the shogunate. The majority of these locations were in the immediate vicinity of Edo and Osaka, but Tadakuni also targeted Niigata, which was well situated for the defense of the Japan Sea coast. In Nagaoka, as in other areas marked for transfer, domain elders raised vociferous protests. But the daimyō was curiously passive. Perhaps he had come to an understanding with Tadakuni, who was convinced that this measure was necessary to protect the realm from a potential invasion from Britain, which had just crushed China in the first Opium War. Or perhaps it was politically impossible for him to resist, since the shogunate had just commissioned two reports indicating that the domain deliberately tolerated smuggling in Niigata. In any case, the daimyō barely protested when the shogunate took possession of his most prosperous city.[43]

The following year, a shogunal representative named Kawamura Nagataka arrived to assume control of the port. Kawamura was an ambitious man, whose talent had propelled him from his hereditary position as garden guard (*niwaban*), a middle-ranking office, in which he traversed the realm compiling secret reports for the shogun, to an appointment as distant province magistrate (*ongoku bugyō*). Some of his peers were allowed to perform their duties in Edo, but Kawamura was obliged to go to Niigata in person, taking along his wife, his children, and about eighty retainers. These numbers might have seemed excessive, since Nagaoka had administered the city with two magistrates and about a dozen men. But Kawamura, who had never assumed a position of such importance, must have been daunted by his new post. In Niigata, he would be responsible for preparing the naval defense of the northern Japan Sea coast, as well as controlling smuggling, stabilizing prices, bringing criminals to judgment, and, of course, rectifying the city's manners and customs.[44]

A lifelong Edoite, Kawamura was unfamiliar with Echigo. He had only traveled to the region once, on a mission to compile a secret report on smuggling in Niigata. Luckily, outgoing Nagaoka officials had prepared a document explaining various local customs. It detailed the several types of prostitution in Niigata, including the brothels in Teramachi and Furumachi, the geisha throughout town, the streetwalkers in back alleys, and the *goke*. Realizing the magistrate might not understand the significance of this last term, the domain authorities included an explanation:

> They are women who have returned from service in other provinces, or who were let out of service here, or who lost their husbands at an early age and fell upon hard times. These women, who have no relatives and no means of support, work clandestinely, so they dress and comport themselves much as non-professional women do, and they try not to attract attention when soliciting.[45]

This description, which minimized the *goke*'s activities, was likely intended to avoid creating the (accurate) impression that Nagaoka had failed to regulate the sex trade in its most important city. If the *goke* were really widows or otherwise without any means of support, then allowing them to solicit could be framed as an act of benevolence, rather than an abdication of responsibility.

Yet in the context of the Tenpō reforms, this extensive accounting of Niigata's prostitutes was alarming. If Kawamura wished to follow Mizuno Tadakuni's example and shut down clandestine prostitution, his task would be nearly impossible: by the shogunate's standards, every prostitute in Niigata was working illegally. Kawamura recognized the scope of the problem, and his diary of his first year in office notes several meetings with subordinates in which he discussed restricting the sex trade.[46] He even sent a letter to the harbor magistrate in Uraga, another shogunal port town, inquiring about his approach to the issue. The harbor magistrate described a situation much like the one Kawamura encountered in Niigata, explaining that in the era before his tenure, local officials had refused to regulate prostitution. Inspired by the reforms, however, the new magistrate required prostitutes to abide by strict sumptuary regulations and forced the brothels to limit the number of women they employed.[47] Kawamura might have followed his lead, but he faced a more complicated problem. According to the harbor magistrate's accounting, there had been only five brothels and eighty-eight prostitutes in Uraga before the reforms. Kawamura's own investigation had indicated that there were several times as many houses of prostitution in Niigata.[48]

Realizing that he needed advice tailored to his own jurisdiction, Kawamura asked one of his deputies to prepare a report detailing the opinions of the other staffers in his office.[49] They could not reach a consensus. One group insisted that all the brothels should be moved into an enclosed "pleasure quarter" like Yoshiwara in Edo, which would be constructed on an empty lot adjacent to Gansuiji, a temple at the northern edge of town. A second group disagreed with this suggestion, arguing that forcing prostitutes into an enclosed quarter would impose an undue financial burden on their masters. This, they warned, would not impress Niigata's townspeople with the compassion (*jihi*) of the new regime. Incongruously, considering the political environment, they recommended that Niigata follow the example of Edo *before* the Tenpō Reforms, when prostitution was allowed to flourish in areas outside Yoshiwara. This group believed that a few exhortations from the new magistrate would be enough to convince the city's brothel keepers to agree to abide by sumptuary regulations and refrain from encouraging irresponsible spending. The official in charge of compiling the document proposed a third solution. He suggested locating a new entertainment district on a landfill in the Shinano River, where it would be accessible to merchants and sailors. Unconsciously echoing Imamura Yodoshichi's argument decades earlier, he argued that the sex trade was an economic boon to the port. Since businesses benefiting from boat traffic understood this, they would happily contribute to the costs of construction. At the same time, the extra labor required to build the new landfill would provide gainful employment for indigent workers, highlighting the benevolence of the new administration.

Ultimately, Kawamura rejected the proposals to construct new entertainment districts, which would require significant outlays of cash. Instead, he followed the second group's advice, choosing to preserve the status quo by "confining" prostitution to the areas where it was already entrenched: Furumachi and Teramachi wards two through six, Bishamonjima, and Kumagaya kōji. But he did choose to reconcile Niigata's system with Edo's in one crucial respect: he created categories of legal prostitutes whose status designations distinguished them from other women. Prostitutes in the first two districts would be called "tea-serving girls" (*chakumi onna*) and their establishments would be named "teahouses" (*tomarijaya*); those in the second two districts would be called "laundry girls" (*sentaku onna*) and their establishments would be referred to as "boathouses" (*funayado*). ("Laundry girl" and "tea-serving girl" were common designations for prostitutes in shogunal territories: the former could be found at ports and the latter at teahouses in various jurisdictions.)[50] Technically, all other prostitutes were deemed illegal, but Kawamura never set out specific punishments for clandestine prostitution. When the newly recognized brothels in Teramachi and Furumachi took advantage of his new policy to push for restrictions on their competitors' activities, Kawamura directed his subordinates to look into the matter, but he never took action.[51]

In an ordinance the following year, Kawamura explained the reasoning behind his tolerant approach. He acknowledged that his policy, which allowed brothels to stand alongside other residences and businesses, was detrimental to "general manners and customs" (*ittai no fūzoku*). But he insisted that if he limited the sex trade to a designated area, "many would experience hardship and the poor would be displaced and dispersed."[52] His concern for the welfare of lower-class townspeople was not only a gesture toward the ideal of benevolent government, though Kawamura surely realized that publicizing this element of his policy would burnish his reputation as a wise magistrate. In fact, he likely had more immediate and practical concerns. As Fujita Satoru has argued, by the nineteenth century, many urban administrators had learned from experience that times of hardship could breed riots. For this reason, the Edo city magistrates bitterly opposed the excesses of the Tenpō Reforms, believing that overregulating manners and customs would only succeed in inciting unrest by depriving lower-class townspeople of their livelihoods.[53] Kawamura was not alone in viewing excessive reform as a threat to social stability.

But he continued to be preoccupied with Niigata's reputation in the realm, which was linked to his own political future. Like his predecessors in the domain administration, he was troubled by his subjects' willingness to indenture their daughters to brothels. In an exhortation to the townspeople, he complained that parents were not at all ashamed of sending their daughters to work as tea-serving girls and laundry girls; rather, parents and daughters alike viewed employment in prostitution as an achievement (*tegaradate*) and boasted of it to their neighbors. He insisted that this shamelessness was unique to the people of Niigata (though, as chapter 3 has argued, lower-class parents in Nagasaki espoused a similar attitude toward work in the sex trade). "Vulgar behavior such as child selling can be found anywhere," he conceded, "but the people here do not make clear distinctions [between what is vulgar and what is respectable]." According to Kawamura, "people of discernment" (*kokorozashi no aru monogara*) would not marry prostitutes, nor would they allow their daughters to work in brothels. Niigata's townspeople had long believed otherwise, but that was no excuse for continuing along their misguided path. "If we hesitate to reform something merely because it's popular among many people," he wrote, "then it's like an old phrase that says 'if you enter a stinking room, after awhile you no longer notice the smell.'"[54] In other words, the people of Niigata no longer recognized their own depravity, so outsiders such as Kawamura had a responsibility to bring it to their attention.

He placed the blame on selfish parents who treated their children as commodities: "If a man has no sense of shame about things like this [e.g., daughter selling], his covetous nature emerges, and his human feelings deteriorate to the point where he believes that even if he behaves immorally, it is worth it as long as he becomes wealthy. In the end, he becomes utterly depraved and unjust."[55] The implication that commoners indentured their daughters in order to "become wealthy" was intentional. Kawamura rejected the argument that only desperately poor families sent their girls to work in brothels, noting that "even parents who have no difficulty making a living" engaged in the practice. His observation may have been correct: although prostitutes' contracts often mentioned their parents' difficulty paying taxes or buying medicine, it is impossible to know whether dire poverty was the only factor motivating families to indenture their daughters. However, the ramifications of Kawamura's overall argument were clear: by insisting that parents relinquished their daughters by choice, not out of desperation, the magistrate attributed their behavior to moral deficiency. Like his predecessor Imamura Yodoshichi, Kawamura was reluctant to address the issue of uneven development, which had left peasants in Echigo worse off than their counterparts in other regions, while creating a national market through which they could exchange their daughters for cash.

Although large-scale economic problems might prove intractable, moral failings could be remedied with the help of an enlightened ruler. Kawamura was eager to assume this role. In the same proclamation in which he inveighed against daughter selling, he also chastised the *goke*, who corrupted the townspeople with their evil customs. He acknowledged that not everyone in Niigata was of the same mind, but he could not help perceiving a critical lack of shame among the city's women, which he attributed to the visibility of the widows' trade. Because they were able to make a living, he wrote, all women had begun to think that they could survive on their own if they saved enough money. Consequently, they were not ashamed to divorce their husbands. Instead, they thought it normal to flit from one man to another, and they failed to protect their chastity.[56] His proclamation implied that, for women at least, promiscuity and economic independence were inseparable. If women had any possible means of survival outside the household, he suggested, they eagerly freed themselves from the constraints of monogamy.

In reality, the *goke*'s "choice" to sell sex might not have been much of a choice at all. They may have resigned themselves to the best of a limited series of unappealing options, which might not even have included marriage. But Kawamura insisted that they were not driven by desperation; they did not work in prostitution "as a last resort" (*yondokoro naku*), he argued, but because they were shameless and greedy. In his proclamation, the domain officials' description of downtrodden women who "dressed modestly and tried not to attract attention while soliciting" was eclipsed by a new image of entrepreneurial women whose licentiousness was matched only by their lust for profit.

By consistently presenting the problem of prostitution as an issue of choice rather than poverty or exploitation, Kawamura's regime could reap the benefits of prosperity, which he and his advisors believed prostitution created, without taking responsibility for the victimization of the women who were indentured to brothels, or the transgressions of the widows who worked on their own. In that sense, Kawamura's policy was a continuation of Nagaoka domain's strategy of deliberate ignorance. What had changed, however, was how vigorously he condemned the women and families who supplied labor to the sex trade. When the port city belonged to the shogunate, and when the official in charge had a position in the central government's bureaucracy, challenges to the gendered order could no longer be overlooked.

But this did not mean that the magistrate had to take concrete steps to restrict prostitution. As long as Kawamura issued edicts chastising shameless women and greedy parents, he could rest assured that he had fulfilled his role as a moral ruler and protector of the household. Tellingly, Kawamura made no concerted effort to shut down the *goke*'s business. Instead, he made a gesture toward bringing them back within the realm of patriarchal authority by insisting that they reside with male guardians and requiring them to include their guardians' names on all documents submitted to the authorities.[57] He did not forbid them to engage in prostitution, however. Apparently, the idea of a woman having sex with multiple men was not a problem if she was not also living alone, making her own money, and signing her own petitions.

This policy suggested that limiting female promiscuity was not Kawamura's primary concern, even though he often invoked the concept of shame. Samurai stigmatized promiscuity among female members of their own status group, and this attitude was clearly indicated in Kawamura's admonitions to commoners who "made no distinctions between vulgar and respectable behavior" and "did not even feel ashamed" to indenture their daughters to brothels. In part, this use of language reflected a growing belief among samurai that commoners should adhere to the same standards of sexual morality as their social betters.[58] But in practice, officials like Kawamura were willing to overlook female commoners' sexual activities as long as they did not threaten the patriarchal household. When they perceived this possibility, the idea of "shame" provided the vocabulary in which they addressed the real issue at hand: the destruction of the gendered order.

Kawamura's half-hearted efforts at reform did not change the *goke*'s business model. Later sources such as the guidebook *Echigo miyage* (Echigo Souvenirs) stated that they lived and worked alone. In 1851, just five years after Kawamura's directive, Koikawa Shōzan, an Edo author and artist known for pornographic travel literature, offered a similar portrayal.[59] In his guide to sex on the road, which predictably praised Niigata for its beautiful white-skinned women, he described his encounter with a *goke*. He wrote that the proprietress of his inn escorted him to the *goke*'s gate and called inside to ask if she would accept a guest. The wary woman did not emerge from her rooms; instead, she called out: "Where's he from?" Only after the proprietress confirmed that the visitor was from Edo did the *goke* graciously accept him and entertain him for the night.[60] If she had a man living with her, he was not mentioned in Shōzan's account.

Nevertheless, Kawamura was convinced of his effectiveness as a social reformer. When he left his post in 1852, he boasted to his successor that he had done an excellent job rectifying manners and customs in Niigata.[61] An Edo merchant named Yohachi, who traveled to the port city in 1847, provided a more impartial assessment. He lauded the magistrate for building new administrative offices, hearing lawsuits, apprehending thieves, and rewarding the filial. But immediately after these words of praise, he launched into an account of how he actually spent his time in Niigata. He stayed at a famous brothel in Furumachi, where he was entertained by eight women and drank so much that he awoke the next morning with an incredible hangover. Nevertheless, he managed to take six of the women sightseeing (and drinking) the next day.[62] By coupling rigorous moral instruction with lax enforcement, Kawamura had created a city where men like Yohachi would come and spend money on prostitutes, then leave singing the wise magistrate's praises.

Carole Pateman has observed that the tendency to consider prostitution as a "problem about women" rather than a "problem about men" ensures that the women who supply sex are scrutinized while the men who demand it are overlooked.[63] This was certainly the case in Niigata, where samurai officials were quick to judge the women and families who supplied labor to brothels in their own city and distant provinces. While they focused on the supply side of prostitution, they ignored their role in tolerating, and even encouraging, the male demand for sexual services, which they viewed as a potential engine of growth. Moreover, as they enumerated the moral failings of their poorest subjects, they turned their attention from the region's stubborn economic and demographic problems, some of which were attributable to their own policy decisions.

Their discourse on the sex trade also reflected their anxiety about the destructive power of the market, which threatened to overtake the household and overturn the gendered hierarchies that structured the realm. This anxiety was not unique to Tokugawa Japan. As Amy Dru Stanley has explained, the prostitute was an ambiguous and disturbing symbol in the postbellum United States. She could be understood both as a vestige of slavery and as a representative of the horrors of the free labor market, in which even the most intimate relationships could be commodified. Moreover, by demonstrating that women could exchange sex for subsistence outside of marriage, she posed a threat to the unique status of the bond between husband and wife. In that sense, she was the embodiment of antebellum slaveholders' arguments that free labor markets destroyed domestic order. In the post-emancipation era, then, her trade "revealed not simply the corrosive aspects of free market relations but also the fragility of home life as their institutional and emotional counterweight."[64]

Tokugawa-era samurai were not sentimental about the emotional value of domestic life.[65] Indeed, as Imamura's "frank conversations" make clear, the brothel, not the household, was regarded as a refuge for merchants worn down by the daily grind of buying and selling. But samurai administrators valued the institutional importance of the family for a different reason. The patriarchal household, held together by the bonds between husband and wife and parent and child, was also the basic unit of political organization. It tied individuals to the state and served as a symbol of the realm. Women who traded sex for money and parents who sold their children revealed the weakness in this structure, and in the Tokugawa order itself, by raising the possibility that when ties of obligation were dissolved in the pursuit of profit, the household might disintegrate. The realm might thus be equally susceptible to collapse. While the visibility of widows supporting themselves by selling sex posed an obvious challenge to the institution of marriage, the noticeable increase in girls being trafficked outside the province made clear that the ideal of benevolent government was fragile. As members of families preyed upon by unscrupulous procurers and fractured by poverty, trafficked daughters and their parents exposed the vulnerability of poor peasants' households and the emptiness of their rulers' claim to protect them.

Samurai tended to express their anxiety about the triumph of the market over the household by blaming women and their families for their "choice" to engage with the sex trade. In contrast, American commentators who viewed prostitutes as lurid examples of the destructive force of the market tended to deemphasize the issue of volition and obscure prostitutes' free will, insisting that they had been victimized by economic circumstances beyond their control. To them, there was no clearer indication of the human degradation engendered by market relations than the spectacle of a woman reduced to selling her body.[66] But the Tokugawa-era samurai who raised similar concerns chose the opposite tactic: they emphasized the issue of choice, claiming that women who worked in prostitution were motivated by the pursuit of financial gain and not compelled by immiseration. In part, this approach was influenced by their position as rulers: conceding that their subjects were desperately poor was an admission of failure as governors. But it also stemmed from a different attitude toward the issue of autonomy in general. The men who ruled Niigata and its environs would not have celebrated the expansion of individual liberties. In their estimation, the fact that women behaved autonomously was in itself evidence of the breakdown of moral order. To them, there was no clearer indication of the harm caused by the expansion of the market economy than the spectacle of women who rejected marriage and family for the chance to wear gold hair ornaments.

Samurai officials pursued this line of argument because they knew that the growth of the sex trade, which they had played an important role in promoting, was undermining the vision of social order that they claimed to uphold. This did not necessarily damage their reputation among Niigata's townspeople. Limited evidence suggests that they welcomed prostitution, regarding their neighborhoods' "prostitutes, geisha, and hookers" as entrepreneurs who could do their part to aid the poor. But the residents of agricultural villages, where visiting brothels was becoming a more common pastime for peasants, often took a dimmer view of the authorities' reluctance to curtail the growing market for sexual services. Village headmen, who did not link their fortunes to the brothels' success, perceived the dangers of an unregulated and rapidly expanding sex trade, and they held their rulers responsible for failing to live up to their promises. Their disillusionment is the subject of the next chapter.

CHAPTER
FIVE

· Glittering Hair Ornaments
and Barren Fields

*Prostitution and the Crisis
of the Countryside*

In the foreground of Keisai Eisen's woodblock print of Fukaya station, issued in the late 1830s, an apron-clad maidservant holding a lantern leads two geisha on their way to an evening appointment. Recognizing a fellow geisha and her maidservant heading in the opposite direction, they pause briefly to exchange greetings. Meanwhile, in the brothel behind them, another maid is welcoming a group of clients in the entrance foyer and a few serving girls are sitting behind a lattice screen. They look out on the busy streets of the station, waiting for customers to arrive and request their services.

As Jilly Traganou has noted, images of post stations "overlaid material presence with cultural significance," evoking viewers' desire to travel and priming their expectations of what they might encounter on their journeys.[1] In this case, the audience for Eisen's print was invited to imagine Fukaya, the second-to-last stop along the Nakasendō Highway in northern Musashi province, as a bustling entertainment district. This would have seemed outlandish a hundred years earlier, when Fukaya was best known as a sleepy former castle town where, according to shogunal records, the major occupation was farming. But like other stations in the Kantō region, Fukaya had changed dramatically over the course of the late eighteenth and early nineteenth centuries as local people reoriented their businesses to take advantage of an increase in traffic along the highways. In Fukaya, the number of inns quadrupled: where there had been only twenty-two in the mid-eighteenth century, there were eighty in the 1830s. In a bid to lure pleasure-seeking travelers,

FIGURE 7.
Keisai Eisen, *Fukaya no eki* (Fukaya Station), no. 10 in the series *Kiso kaidō rokujū-kyū tsugi* (Sixty-nine Stations of the Kisokaidō Road), woodblock print, horizontal *Ōban*, 23.7 × 35.5 cm (c. 1835–38). A lively night out at Fukaya Station. Photograph © 2011 Museum of Fine Arts, Boston.

proprietors imported women from other areas to work as prostitutes. This recruiting effort changed the demographic composition of the station. At the turn of the nineteenth century, Fukaya had more male than female residents, but by 1842, this situation had reversed: while the male population held steady at just under 900, the female population increased from 835 to over a thousand.[2]

If a similar trend had occurred in a city such as Niigata or Edo, brothel keepers' neighbors might have celebrated their good fortune, reasoning that prostitution brought them prosperity by attracting customers to their businesses. But this was not the case in the villages surrounding the stations, where farmers worried that the stations' success had been achieved at their expense. In northern Kantō, rapid commercialization had led to uneven development. Production centers such as the silk-weaving town of Kiryū prospered—its population tripled between 1757 and 1855[3]—but many of the region's agricultural communities were in decline. Both village elites and members of the samurai class lamented the deterioration of the countryside, complaining that abandoned land (*arechi*) proliferated as small-scale cultivators abandoned their holdings, either compelled by poverty or attracted by new opportunities in domestic service and manufacturing. The villages they left were desperate for manpower, and peasants were forced to employ agricultural laborers from other provinces at high prices. In the 1830s, one village headman in Kōzuke complained that farmhands' wages had skyrocketed. In the Genroku period (1688–1704), he claimed, one or two gold *ryō* had paid for ten years' service, but now laborers were demanding an *annual* salary of five to seven gold *ryō*.[4] This was a dramatic increase, even accounting for inflation, and it imperiled the livelihood of wealthy peasants who farmed large tracts of land.[5] Although much of the Kantō was the shogun's own territory, by the last decades of the Tokugawa period, it was far from the agricultural utopia that the shogunate had intended to create. Disillusioned by an apparent failure of government, village headmen and shogunal officials alike were haunted by visions of barren fields.[6]

Rural elites worried about social decay as well as economic stagnation. While Tokugawa-era villages had never been harmonious or egalitarian, they had become particularly conflict-ridden by the early nineteenth century. Wealthy peasants' embrace of the market economy was partly responsible for this development. Their experiments with sericulture, soy-sauce brewing, and cotton weaving had raised the overall standard of living, but they had also heightened inequality. Those who had access to capital were able to invest wisely and profit, while smallholders, who were more subject to the vicissitudes of the market, were increasingly dependent on them for loans. Thus affluent peasants, a group that often included headmen, were able to exploit those who were less fortune, typically by becoming moneylenders and charging exorbitant interest rates. The socially corrosive effects of this trend were reflected in patterns of peasant contention: nineteenth-century protests often involved lower-class villagers united against their own putative leaders, rather than lower- and higher-class villagers protesting the abuses of their overlords.[7]

Involvement in the market economy also provoked generational conflict within peasant communities, though this was often muted and thus more difficult for outsiders to perceive. Young men and women who received cash wages for their labor in manufacturing were not necessarily enthralled by the prospect of inheriting land, and their earning potential empowered them to leave their native villages. With or without their parents' permission, they went off in search of economic opportunity. Some headed to production centers such as Kiryū. Others were attracted to the metropolis of Edo, where they could find work as domestics or shop hands.[8]

More ominously, bored and aimless youths fell in with roving bands of gangsters, gamblers, and masterless samurai. During the first decades of the century, village headmen received regular notices describing the features of suspected bandits, some of whom were their own sons and nephews.[9]

Headmen were reluctant to blame their overlords explicitly for their predicament, and they were loath to admit that changing economic relationships within the villages had affected community solidarity. Instead, they often concluded that outsiders were responsible for contaminating the villages with alien, market-driven values. In their view, the encroachment of the sex trade into rural areas was a perfect example of this. Most of the major players in this business—post-station innkeepers and serving girls who had migrated from other provinces—were not and never had been members of the village community, and they seemed to be profiting at the expense of peasants who had dutifully remained in their ancestors' fields. At the same time, by presenting the possibility that men could pay for sex, they had insinuated themselves into the realm of marriage and reproduction. This incursion threatened to destabilize the mechanisms through which villages were populated and households were perpetuated. If local youths could purchase sexual partners, and ultimately wives, from among the ranks of serving girls, then their unions would not necessarily proceed according to the dictates of custom and the guidance of their parents and elders.

As more peasants began to spend their money on commercial sex, it seemed that the same market forces that buffeted the prices of silk cocoons and bales of rice, which had pulled young men and women out of the countryside and raised the wages of temporary farmhands, would also undercut patriarchal authority in villages. Peasant leaders, who associated serving girls with willful destruction of long-held communal values, rather than with the idealized feminine behaviors of submission and sacrifice, believed that prostitution imperiled families. As more and more young women began to labor in post-station brothels, sometimes using their employment as a path toward social mobility, they found that they were viewed, not as dutiful daughters who contributed to their communities' prosperity, but as outsiders who posed a threat to the villages' existence.

A SHIFTING LANDSCAPE
CHANGE IN THE POST STATIONS

If Edo was Kantō's heart, the post roads were its veins and arteries. They brought merchants from the Japan Sea coast to urban centers along the Pacific, guided pilgrims to Nikkō, led traveling preachers and booksellers on their rounds, and hosted daimyō on their journeys to and from Edo. The stations along the highways benefited from the financial and cultural resources many of these travelers brought with them, and the proprietors of inns catering to daimyō were among the best-educated and most sophisticated people in the countryside. But post stations were also obligated to perform expensive official functions, such as providing horses, porters, and lodging to men on government business. These travelers paid only token amounts for the stations' services, and as their numbers increased throughout the period, station officials found themselves in a paradoxical situation: their jurisdictions seemed to be busy and prosperous, but their finances suffered.

The shogunate, which was concerned about the future of its transportation system, supported the stations through two policies, one aimed at short-term aid and the other at long-term development. First, it designated "assisting villages" (*sukegō*) and compelled them to provide horses and labor to the stations. The villages resented these appointments, since the associated obligations tore young men away from the fields during the growing season, when official traffic was particularly heavy. Protests against these corvée demands increased in frequency throughout the late eighteenth and early nineteenth centuries, contributing to contentious relationships between village headmen and post-station officials.[10] The second of the shogunate's strategies, which might have seemed more innocuous at the time, was to encourage the post stations' economic development, hoping that increased revenue from recreational travelers would supplement the stations' operating budgets and reduce the need for corvée labor. In 1718, as part of this approach, the shogunate amended its long-standing policy prohibiting prostitution in the post stations, allowing two serving girls per inn. Predictably, stations rushed to petition domain and shogunal officials for permission to employ prostitutes.[11]

As a strategy to promote economic growth, this policy was a success, just as it had been in underdeveloped neighborhoods in Osaka and Edo. Enticed by the erotic possibilities of sex on the road, male travelers (and some curious women) flocked to stations that were known for their brothel districts.[12] The period's most famous wayfarers, the fictional characters Yaji and Kita of Jippensha Ikku's *Shanks' Mare* (*Tōkaidōchū hizakurige*), decided where to stay based on the availability of attractive women.[13] Surely they were not alone. Such pleasure-seeking travelers were extremely profitable, not only for innkeepers but for station officials as well: levies on serving girls could account for as much as 10 percent of a station's operating budget.[14] Soon after the policy change allowing prostitution along the

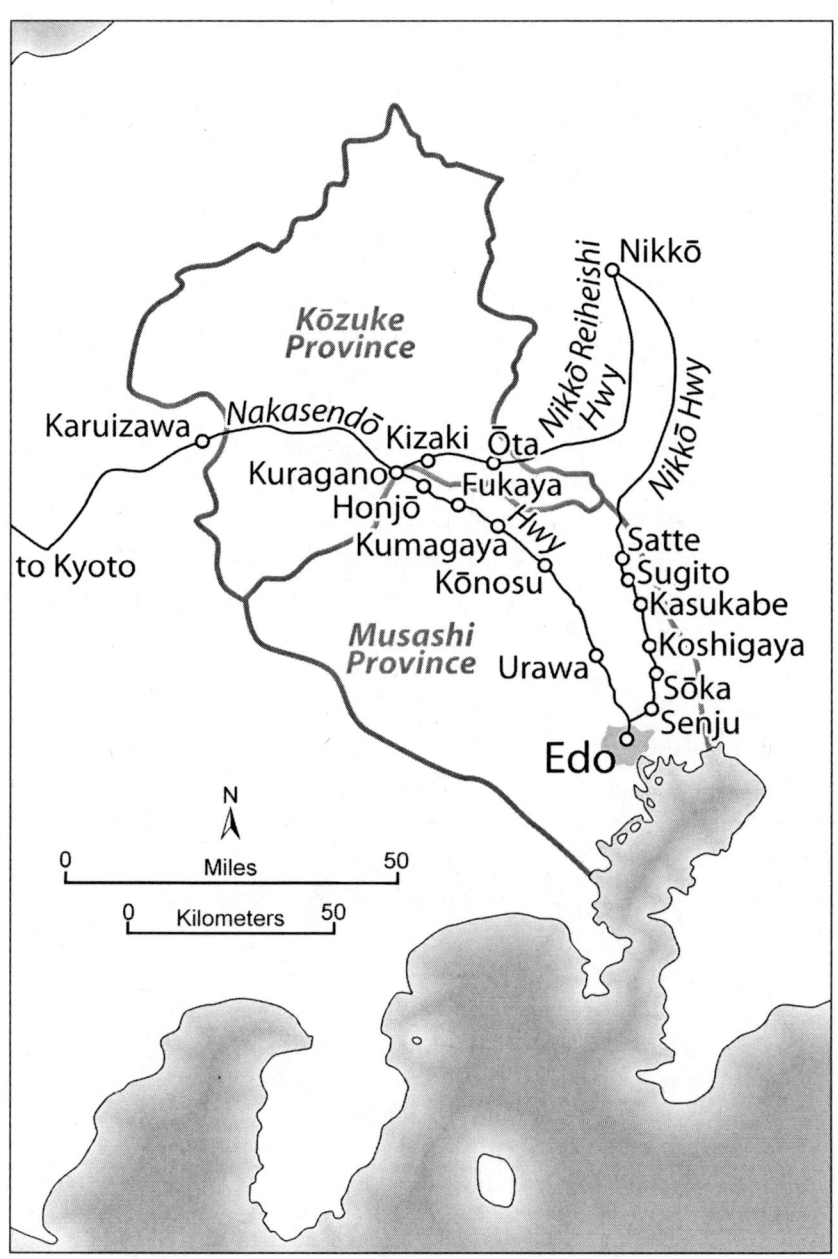

MAP 3.
Highways and major post stations in Musashi and Kōzuke provinces.

highways, its effect on the post stations' economies was obvious. In 1721, the headman at the Tōkaidō's Kawasaki station flatly declared, "There are stations that have these women [serving girls] and those that do not. Those with women prosper, while those without decline."[15]

Since stations were located in close proximity and travelers could pass through at least three of them in a good day of walking, competition between post towns was fierce. In many jurisdictions, serving girls lined up along roadways and literally dragged men to their establishments. This annoyed abstemious travelers, and certain fraternal organizations (*kō*) published guides informing their members about stations and inns where they would not be harassed by soliciting women.[16] But other travelers felt differently, and stations eager to maximize revenue employed more and more prostitutes as the decades passed, often exceeding the limit of two per establishment. Like urban "pleasure quarters," stations were touted in travel guides and ranked in gazetteers, and inns came to resemble brothels in both function and appearance.[17] Yaji and Kita described their visit to Fuchū on the Tōkaidō: "Turning off the main road you come to two big gates, where you must alight from your horse. Inside are rows of houses, from each of which comes a lively sound of music, meant to attract people to the house. In fact, it is much the same as in the Yoshiwara quarter of Edo."[18]

In most post stations, officials did not attempt to confine prostitutes and prostitution to separate spaces. Instead, brothels lined the highways running through the middle of the stations. These establishments were literally and symbolically central, and the women they employed were prominent local figures. In the late seventeenth century, Engelbert Kaempfer described his impression of serving girls crowding the streets of the stations:

> Discussing the crowds on the road, we cannot omit the prostitutes of large and small inns and roadside tea and food stalls in villages and towns on the large island of Nippon. As soon as they are dressed and made up, from around noon, they sit on verandas constantly eyeing approaching travelers; with amorous cries from here and there, they try to outdo each other calling him to their inn, the prattle ringing in the traveler's ears.[19]

In *Tōkaidō meishoki* (A Guide to Famous Places along the Tōkaidō), Asai Ryōi recorded their incessant cries: "Stop here! Stop here! The rooms are clean, not like at other inns. Come on, sir on the horse! Get off here! There aren't any more good inns after this one. Come on! Come on!"[20]

Technically, many of these women were clandestine prostitutes, but shogunal officials paid little attention. In Kaempfer's time, prostitution at post stations was still strictly prohibited, but no one protested when his procession passed by rows of soliciting serving girls. When the law changed to permit two women per inn, the regulation was regularly flouted. In the late eighteenth and early nineteenth centuries, the shogunate conducted sporadic raids of the post stations searching for "extra" women, but brothels soon returned to business as usual, often falsifying their records.[21] For example, in 1826, Kasukabe station on the Nikkō Highway informed the shogunate that it contained eleven serving-girl inns employing a total of twenty-two serving girls. This conformed perfectly to the stated limits. But a few months later, a document that innkeepers submitted to station officials indicated that there were ten such establishments employing fifty-five serving girls, an average of over five prostitutes per inn.[22] In nearby Koshigaya station, officials were merely reprimanded when they were found to have submitted inaccurate numbers.[23]

In reality, then, there was little to prevent inns from hiring as many prostitutes as they could profitably employ. Recruitment patterns were determined by the prices innkeepers were willing to pay for contracts and the type of women they preferred to offer their guests. Procurers tended to supply urban women to the stations on the outskirts of cities, where brothels attracted a more sophisticated clientele and charged higher prices. In Kanagawa and Kawasaki, two bustling stations just to the southwest of Edo, inns recruited serving girls from lower-class neighborhoods in the city.[24] Along the Nakasendō, however, where stations were more modest, innkeepers tended to employ women from poor rural regions in the northeast, particularly Echigo, where labor was cheap. Some women were signed into service by procurers from their home provinces, but others were brought to the station by post-station residents who traveled to Echigo on recruiting missions.[25]

Although women indentured to post-station brothels could usually be assured of the basic necessities of food and clothing, they worked in terrible conditions. They could not refuse customers, they had no days off, and they were not permitted to form romantic attachments with men who did not pay.[26] In addition, although prostitution was their main occupation, serving girls could also be required to perform all sorts of odd tasks, from light housework to heavy labor. Girls under the age of fifteen were considered too young to service customers, so they were employed as menial servants and drudges. Older, unpopular women were put to work in the fields, while those who were too ill or weak for farm labor looked after children.[27] Predictably, many half-starved and overworked women succumbed to disease. Most were buried in modest graveyards, which can still be found in former post-station towns.[28]

In one particularly wrenching account, a woman named Hatsu described her plight as a post-station prostitute at Kizaki station on the Nikkō Highway. The document she composed, awkwardly entitled "Hatsu's Testimony to the Lord" (*Kami-sama e Hatsu no kōjō*), was a desperate plea to be released from service.[29] In stark language, Hatsu recounted her personal history. She was born in Nishino-shinden village in Kanbara county, Echigo province, the oldest daughter of a peasant named Kishichi. Her parents, who were ill and deeply in debt, had indentured her to an inn called Moritaya in order to pay for medicine for themselves and Hatsu's younger sister. Hatsu worked day and night until she fell ill in the seventh month of 1841. "In the middle of the eighth month," she wrote, "I recovered a little, so I could return to work. At night I was sent out to see customers, and in the afternoon when there were no customers, I was sent to the mountains to gather firewood. Since I had no chance to rest during the day or at night, I could not recover from my illness. I would be viciously beaten if I begged my master to be allowed to rest even a little, so I endured and continued to work." After a few months, she took advantage of an opportunity to go buy medicine at a temple in a nearby village. There she realized that "even if I went back to my master and took some of that medicine, I would only be sent out to see customers again as soon as I recovered." She appealed to a peasant named Rinbei, who had been a friend of her father's, and he agreed to board her in the home of one of his relatives in Ryūmai village. He also lent her money to use during the period of her convalescence.

In the fourth month of the year, Hatsu finally recovered enough to return to the Moritaya, only to find that her master was enraged. As Hatsu explained, he was "extremely resentful," because even if she had been ill he could have sent her out to see customers in the afternoon and evening and made over one gold *bu* per encounter. He began to beat her viciously every day. Finally, she decided to appeal to her "lord" (it is unclear from the context whether she meant the shogunate's road magistrate or the samurai intendant who administered the area; it is very possible that she did not know whom she was addressing) asking for permission to return home to Echigo.

After relating this story, Hatsu attempted to explain away some of the stickier points of her situation. While she was staying in Ryūmai, an intermediary named Yoshibei had suggested a solution that would allow her to escape the brothel, while also permitting Rinbei to recover the money he had lent her. He wrote a letter to the Moritaya, falsely claiming that Hatsu (he called her by her working name, Some) had used the money she had borrowed from Rinbei to travel to Edo. He wrote that the Moritaya, which as her employer was responsible for any debt she had incurred, should repay Rinbei or allow him to indenture Hatsu elsewhere. Evidently, this strategy failed, because Hatsu did end up returning to the Moritaya in the fourth month of the year.[30] But when she did, she embellished the story of her visit to Edo and claimed to have received official protection. She explained her motives in her petition to be released from service: "One of Rinbei's acquaintances works for a retainer of the chief councilor Lord Mizuno [Tadakuni], so I thought if I lied and said I had received the protection of a retainer of Lord Mizuno, my master would fear the lord's authority and stop beating me." Realizing that this might be problematic for the officials she was addressing, she apologized preemptively: "I am sincerely sorry that I told such a lie to protect myself." In any case, the strategy was not effective. Her master was suspicious and continued to beat her.

Hatsu wrote plainly, using the kana alphabet interspersed with a few easy Chinese characters: she knew how to write her father's name and the name of her village; she could write "sick," "service," "money," various numbers, "month," and "day," among some other words. She did not use characters for Chinese-derived compounds such as "compassion" (*renbin*), "authority" (*ikō*), and "protection" (*kaihō*); instead, she spelled them out phonetically. (This was typical of even high-status women of her era, who wrote primarily in the kana script.)[31] Even if she had not mastered the complicated strokes necessary to imitate the style of the educated men who ordinarily composed petitions, she knew to use the vocabulary of benevolence and protection in her appeal.

Hatsu's problem was that she had to write at all. Alone in a distant province, she had to compose her own petition because no one else had the standing or the incentive to speak for her. Her father, who would ordinarily have assumed this role, was over a hundred miles and many jurisdictions away. She explained her predicament: "My father back in the province is so poor he had to sell me. He can't come and appeal for mercy here, and he has many other things to do, so he is unable to help me." No one would step forward on Hatsu's behalf—as a parent or a potential husband—to convince officials that she merited consideration or protection, so she painstakingly spelled out her own petition. Even though there are many surviving suits and petitions involving prostitutes, Hatsu's is the only example of a Tokugawa-era post-station prostitute writing about her own life.[32] Most of those who asked for official consideration did so indirectly through intermediaries. The rest did not bother petitioning at all. They were illiterate, they did not know which official to address, or they assumed that the attempt would be doomed to failure.

Hatsu certainly exercised agency, and feminist interpretations of this incident have emphasized her determination to resist the abuse she endured on a daily basis.[33] However, her brand of self-assertion was deeply problematic, because it did not provide a stable platform for a petition. Hatsu might have appealed as a daughter who had left the brothel to attend to sick or dying parents, playing the role of the filial daughter, but her parents had not called her home. To make matters worse, they were in Echigo and in no position to support her appeal. She had no choice but to speak as herself and *for* herself, writing as a woman named Hatsu, far from home, pleading for benevolence. But there is no evidence that this petition ever reached the appropriate authorities, and it is unlikely that she escaped from the Moritaya.[34]

Some of Hatsu's fellow migrants from Echigo found opportunities for social mobility in the Kantō region. As young women streamed into area post stations to work as serving girls, they created female-dominated islands in a predominantly male region. By the late eighteenth century, it was not unheard-of for men in Kōzuke villages to outnumber women by around 20 percent.[35] Sex-selective infanticide may have contributed to this imbalance: the lower the population dipped, the more male-heavy the sex ratio became, suggesting that peasants were intentionally limiting their families and favoring male babies.[36] Female out-migration also played a role, because the feminization of domestic labor in Edo provided more opportunities for peasant women to find work as maids in wealthy households.[37] This confluence of demographic trends meant that women who migrated to Kantō to work could often find husbands nearby if they managed to finish their terms of service; they did not need to return to their impoverished villages and desperate parents.

As in other places in Tokugawa Japan, a term of service in prostitution was not a significant barrier to matrimony. A good example of how serving girls fared in the marriage market comes from Kuragano station in Kōzuke. In 1803, the shogunate conducted a raid there, punishing innkeepers who employed more than two serving girls and temporarily detaining fifty-one women who had lost their jobs as a result of the raid. Suddenly "liberated" from service, forty-five of these women married, two were returned to their parents in Echigo, two others found other employment in the post station, one became a nun, and one was adopted. Of the forty-five who married, the vast majority wedded peasants from nearby villages.[38] Eleven years later, officials from Takasaki domain conducted another raid. This time, the sixteen "extra" prostitutes were asked where they wanted to go. One woman died before she could be placed, five returned to their parents, one was adopted as a daughter, one went to work as a maidservant in the station, and eight married local men (all of whom applied to the station officials for the privilege).[39]

Occasionally, authorities brokered marriages between Kantō men and serving girls as a matter of policy. During the Kansei Reforms in the late 1780s, the shogunate's chief councilor Matsudaira Sadanobu (1759–1829) decreed that if clandestine prostitutes were found in villages, they should be sent as brides to areas where women were scarce.[40] The road magistrates followed this precedent after their raid on Kasukabe station in the 1820s found forty-one clandestine prostitutes; all were sent to villages where there was abandoned land that the shogunate hoped to bring under cultivation. Presumably, they were meant to join established families as wives or servants.[41] During the same period, the headman of Ryūmai village made a habit of purchasing serving girls from nearby Yanada Station so that they could marry poor peasants in his jurisdiction. He explained that Ryūmai's population was declining and impoverished men were having a difficult time finding women with whom they could start families, so he obtained two or three serving girls from the station, trained them in farming, and gave them to local men as brides.[42]

More often, peasants married former serving girls on their own initiative. In 1846, a peasant named Isuke tried to negotiate with an innkeeper at Sōka station so that he could marry a serving girl named Masu. After a few unsuccessful attempts, he employed a go-between named Zennosuke, who eventually completed the transaction. Isuke's two older brothers wrote Zennosuke a thank-you note detailing Isuke's struggles and promising to bear full responsibility for Masu's future conduct.[43] If the two older brothers were willing to go through extended negotiations, retain a go-between, and pay off the remainder of Masu's contract, they probably approved of the match, and if Masu married into a family with enough disposable income to pay for her release, she probably entered a more stable situation than the one she left. Like many female migrants from Echigo, she had managed to parlay a term of service as a post-station prostitute into a future as a peasant woman in Kantō.

THE VIEW FROM THE VILLAGES

While post-station proprietors cultivated their relationships with nearby peasants, realizing that they were reliable clients, village leaders were wary. Even though some inns lowered rates significantly to accommodate local customers, prices were high by peasants' standards.[44] Headmen near Ōta station complained that charges and surcharges quickly added up. Youths might pay only two gold *shu* for a waitress and drinks, but proprietors charged them as much as a *bu* for a sexual encounter, and the services of geisha were even more expensive. When hapless young men could not afford to pay, their families were forced to take responsibility for their debts.[45]

For this reason, parents went to great lengths to try to control their sons' recreational activities. In Koguki village near Sugito station, a man named Shinpachi complained to the village headman that his twenty-four-year-old son Gonpachi often took his friends to Sugito and spent the night with serving girls. Shinpachi was not particularly troubled by his son's sexual misbehavior, but he was alarmed at the waste of money. Since his attempts to discipline his son had failed, he decided to send him to live with relatives in another village.[46] In 1858, a father from a farming community near Iwatsuki station took an even more desperate step: when he heard reports that his son had been visiting prostitutes while he was supposed to be in service, he asked to have the boy's name stricken from the family's entry in the temple register. Eventually, the young man was pardoned when he wrote the village headman a letter of apology and promised not to go near the station again.[47]

Presumably at the behest of their worried elders, village young men's associations (*wakamono nakama*) often included rules against visiting brothels in their regulations. Fifty young men from Kariyado village in Kōzuke signed a document that read, "Recently young people's conduct has been bad, and we have been wasting large sums of money going to see prostitutes [*yūjo*]. Some of us have had to pawn or sell the fields and homes we have received from our ancestors. This causes poverty within the village. If someone does this [i.e., visits a prostitute] for even one night, he will be excluded from the association."[48] Other associations agreed to less draconian terms. Thirty-two young men near Ōta station agreed that each of their members would pay a fine of three *kanmon* for each night he spent in the company of prostitutes.[49] This was an imperfect solution, however, since not every village youth belonged to a young men's association. In Makinishi village near Honjō, the entire community censured youths who visited prostitutes. A village agreement stated that any young man discovered to have patronized a brothel would have his head shaved, and his five-family group would be required to pay a fine of two *kanmon*.[50] Nevertheless, those who performed corvée labor obligations in the stations had many opportunities to defy their parents and their peers on this score.

The issue of young men patronizing post-station brothels was only one facet of a generational conflict dividing agricultural communities throughout the archipelago. Young men who received cash wages and tips for their labor were more inclined to spend their money drinking, gambling, whoring, or funding their own young men's associations than investing in their fathers' fields. Village elders often criticized this behavior, but they knew that young men were too important to alienate: their manpower was necessary to bring in the harvest, and they helped fulfill the villages' spiritual obligations by organizing festivals and officiating at weddings. Headmen worried that a crackdown might provoke even more antisocial behavior, and parents found it nearly impossible to curtail their sons' sexual escapades. Although older villagers repeatedly accused young men's associations of holding raucous drinking parties where members had illicit sex with widows and maidservants, they usually concluded that there was nothing anyone could do to stop them.[51]

The availability of commercial sex in post stations only exacerbated these problems. In theory, brothels provided an outlet for unruly sexual behavior that might otherwise have involved village daughters, maidservants, and widows, destabilizing families and distracting young women from their work. But opportunities to pay for sexual gratification did little to quell young men's destructive impulses. Serving girls were sexually accessible, but only to those who could pay, and the men who were most likely to be a serving girl's regular customers were among the least likely to be able to finance her release. Occasionally, their frustration could result in violent confrontations. Two related cases from Koshigaya station illustrate this. In 1818, an innkeeper named Chōhachi became infatuated with a serving girl named Nao who worked at an inn in Sōka station. Since he did not have the resources to pay off her contract, he stopped visiting for a few months while he raised money. While he was away, a man named Kihachi from Yoshikawa village bought out Nao's contract and married her. Furious, Chōhachi visited Kihachi in order to negotiate for Nao. When Kihachi would not consent to a deal, he tried to persuade Nao to run away with him, but she refused. Finally, Chōhachi rounded up a posse of young men from nearby villages and returned to kidnap her. Chōhachi's men ended up in a brawl with members of Kihachi's household, during which one houseguest was murdered and two servants were injured. Chōhachi escaped. In his absence, the local intendant sentenced him to exile (*chūtsuihō*) and confiscated his belongings.[52]

Later the same year, he became involved in a similar disturbance in Koshigaya station. This time, a serving girl named Man ran away from her inn to be with her lover, Saijirō, a young man from a nearby village. Saijirō was afraid that her master would come after them, so he brought Man to stay with his friend Chūemon in another village. Somehow, Chōhachi discovered their whereabouts and informed Man's master, Yahei. Yahei and Chōhachi charged into Chūemon's house brandishing weapons, injuring Chūemon's wife, who was trying to protect the couple.

Saijirō, who had been afraid this would happen in the first place, fled the scene. Yahei brought Man back to the station, and the incident was resolved by the local magistrate, who punished both Yahei and Saijirō by putting them in manacles.[53] As these incidents demonstrate, it was difficult for the villages to avoid the violence and disorder associated with post-station brothels.

Peasant elites perceived the danger of allowing the tumultuous culture of the entertainment districts to infiltrate their communities. During the last years of the eighteenth century, they began to complain to shogunal officials that prostitution in nearby post stations destabilized village society. In 1791, during the Kansei Reforms, a group of forty headmen near Kōnosu station wrote to the local intendant explaining their concerns and suggesting policies that would improve their lot. Along with a shortage of farm labor, the headmen listed post-station prostitution as an issue that required the shogunate's attention. They alleged that the station's inns employed too many prostitutes, that they were noisy, and that they held banquets with geisha and dancers. They complained that the post station had begun to resemble Yoshiwara, and they lamented that their young sons and farmhands went to Kōnosu, spent all their money, and refused to return to the villages.[54]

The remainder of the memorandum makes it clear that elites' anxiety encompassed many more issues than the familiar concern that young men were wasting money. The idea that older villagers were losing control over young men and women's sexual and reproductive behavior surfaces repeatedly. "Although men and women used to have an appropriate sense of shame about their sexual relationships," the headmen asserted, "they have forgotten their innate modesty."[55] The substance of this complaint is unclear. Were village men and women actually becoming more promiscuous, or were they merely flaunting their behavior in front of their disapproving elders? The headmen did not distinguish between these two issues. They insisted that the visibility of prostitution set a dangerous precedent: young men who saw their peers engaging in affairs with prostitutes began to feel entitled to recreational sex, and village women who observed serving girls' behavior began to realize that sex and reproduction could be separate endeavors.

The petitioners alleged that both trends had disastrous consequences. They complained that local men married former serving girls even though they knew that they were unlikely to produce healthy offspring (it is unclear here whether the headmen were referring to infertility caused by exposure to sexually transmitted diseases or to serving girls' familiarity with contraception and abortion). This had contributed to a sudden increase in childless marriages, which had previously been extremely rare. As a result, village women decided that they, too, wanted to limit the size of their families, and they induced miscarriages to control their fertility.[56] By linking prostitution to population decline, the headmen blamed serving girls who had migrated to their area for a problem endemic to the Kantō region. Since prostitutes working in urban "pleasure quarters" used contraception and abortion to avoid pregnancy and childbirth, it is plausible that former serving girls taught such techniques to women in Kantō villages. On the other hand, as chapter 4 has mentioned, the area was already notorious for infanticide, and abortion was widely practiced among peasant women across the archipelago. Commoner moralists and samurai officials derided this trend with increasing vehemence over the course of the late eighteenth century. As Susan Burns has argued, this new discourse on reproduction suggested that women could not be trusted to bear responsibility for the outcomes of their pregnancies; it called for the intervention of male officials and obstetricians in observing and regulating female bodies.[57] By connecting the issues of declining fertility and prostitution, then, village officials were able to blame their communities' problems on social contamination from outsiders at the same time as they provided a justification for asking officials to apply the same degree of scrutiny to prostitutes as they did to "ordinary" peasant women.

Moreover, by linking prostitution to the phenomenon of village women limiting their fertility, the headmen enlisted serving girls as representatives of a vaguely defined, but keenly felt, threat posed by female social and economic autonomy. As commercialization transformed agricultural villages in the Kantō region, peasant women had been presented with a wider array of opportunities to engage in paid labor. In many areas of northern Kantō, including Kōzuke province, wealthy families depended on income from sericulture, typically considered women's work, to supplement the proceeds from renting out land and lending money. As a result, women were responsible for a significant portion of the family economy, and many well-to-do matriarchs were empowered to spend money on cultural pursuits and recreational travel. The growth of the sericulture industry also provided lucrative, if temporary, employment for women from middling and lower-class families, who were hired in the late spring to help silkworm-producing households keep up with the taxing routine of tending to cocoons.[58] Even the poorest peasant women reaped the benefits of a changing village economy that provided more diverse and better-paying jobs for women. Although female farmhands typically earned less than their male counterparts, their pay steadily increased, both as a proportion of male wages and in absolute terms, over the course of the eighteenth and early nineteenth centuries.[59]

As village wives and daughters involved themselves in the market economy, headmen worried that they would attempt to resist their fathers' and husbands' authority in other arenas, possibly destroying the households that formed the basis of the village community. In the headmen's imagining, moving from one region to another for work, managing an independent source of income, laboring outside the household, exploiting one's sexuality, and limiting one's fertility were all related (and threatening) acts of female self-assertion. Yabuta Yutaka cites an example from a shogunal territory near the ancient capital of Nara. In 1842, a group of peasants complained to the official administering their jurisdiction that the women who migrated to their area to work in cotton weaving were painting their faces to look like prostitutes, then selling their bodies and using the proceeds to buy hair ornaments and other decorations. As a result, envious local women flocked to the profession of cotton weaving and abandoned agricultural labor, and both male and female peasants had become inclined toward immoral sexual behavior (which the petitioners defined as having sex without their parents' permission).[60]

The headmen were not attacking weaving women's promiscuity per se, but their autonomy. In fact, peasant leaders rarely attempted to prevent women from having sex with multiple partners, though they did try to exert some control over this behavior, so that it would not destroy marriages or ruin relationships between neighbors. Within the villages, groups of peasant youths managed lower-class young women's sexual liaisons by deciding among themselves which couplings they would tolerate and attacking youths from outside the village who made advances without their approval. Meanwhile, headmen settled adultery cases by brokering agreements between the aggrieved husband, the lover, and the adulteress's father.[61] As long as elders served as judges and referees, village patriarchs knew that promiscuity would not threaten the survival of their communities. But social autonomy—the power to disobey the head of household or the village elders and then ignore the consequences—had far more destructive potential, and this was the problem village headmen addressed when they complained about weaving women's immorality. In this, they were similar to the American reformers who lambasted the "low morals" of factory girls during the same era. As Christine Stansell has argued, "sexual freedom seems to have been the issue: not the fact of premarital sexual activity, but young women's freedom from parental control over their erotic ventures. Sexuality was both a consequence of social autonomy and its metaphor. The real sin of the factory girl lay not in premarital sex, but in advertising, with her fancy clothes and assertive ways, the possibilities of life outside the household."[62] The prospect that this advertising would be effective, leading other women to aspire to the same degree of personal freedom, was as great a concern in Tokugawa villages as it was in American cities.

Tokugawa-era village headmen connected the "possibilities of life outside the household" to control over reproductive as well as erotic endeavors. Ultimately, the point of the Nara peasants' petition was not to outlaw cottage industries such as weaving or even to request that sumptuary laws be reissued. Instead, the village elders asked samurai officials to repromulgate the laws forbidding abortion and infanticide. Peasant elites believed that women who labored outside the household, migrated between provinces, and sold sex were displaying a degree of autonomy that would inevitably lead to assertions of control in the realm of reproduction. According to this logic, serving girls—who engaged in all three activities, though not always of their own volition—could reasonably be blamed for population decline in agricultural villages.

Serving girls also challenged elite conceptions of village culture. Moving from one region to another along highways and through post stations, they embodied a pattern of cultural dispersion in which information and trends migrated from the countryside to the cities and back again.[63] But unlike the forms of cultural capital often highlighted by historians who address this exchange between rural and urban communities, prostitutes' brand of knowledge was neither mediated through the booksellers who visited prosperous households nor attached to the gifts of traveling samurai who visited the inns catering to daimyō. No one had to be literate or socially well connected to access it. It was available to even the most subordinate members of the village community: young girls. In the villages near Kōnosu, headmen made a poignant argument about the supposedly pernicious influence of serving girls on village daughters. They wrote:

> At the opening of memorial services or at religious festivals, young village girls between the ages of ten and thirteen or fourteen join hands and walk along singing songs from Niigata, Itako, and Jōshū, and they wear their hair in the style of apprentice prostitutes. . . . before, they sang planting songs and bean-pounding songs. But now they are jealous of the prostitutes' [*baijo*] beautiful clothing and their eye-catching style. Instead of being childlike, they merely imitate the women in service, and they lose the sincerity of youth, which can never be restored.[64]

This complaint addressed an inchoate fear that village culture would be overwhelmed by the influence of the more urbane, sophisticated post stations. Brothels and serving girls were emblematic of the post stations' urbanization (after all, the headmen had noted that the brothels reminded them of Yoshiwara, the ultimate symbol of urban decadence), and as such, they were blamed for broader social and cultural changes that elites could not control.

Headmen were correct to fear that village women would look to serving girls as paragons of style and sophistication. The ethnographer Segawa Kiyoko, who traveled through the countryside interviewing women in the Meiji period, described how famers' and fishermen's daughters would ask prostitutes to help them dress for festivals, since they were the only women in the vicinity who kept up with the latest fashions and hairstyles.[65] But for the same reasons, village women regarded serving girls as sexual competitors. Kusanagi Enseki (1817–68), a loyalist activist who grew up in a Shikoku village near the brothel districts in Konpira, wrote of his preference for serving girls over his neighbors' daughters. He explained, "Prostitutes are sophisticated and seductive, not at all like the village types."[66] If the stories of young men squandering their wages at post-station brothels are any indication, many in Kantō agreed.

When married men succumbed to the allure of commercial sex, they sometimes jeopardized their relationships with their spouses. In 1828, peasants near Kaneko station on the Mishima Highway in Kōzuke included "marital discord" (*fūfu fuwagō*) on a list of fifteen reasons they opposed prostitution.[67] A group of headmen near Ōta reported, "If young men [who visit serving girls] have wives and children, their households become fraught with conflict, and sometimes they end up getting divorced."[68] Some angry peasant wives might have been jealous, but others were probably more alarmed that their husbands were spending money that should have been apportioned for family expenses.

In a few instances, husbands risked further domestic discord by taking serving girls as concubines. Though legally permissible, it was rare for peasants to employ concubines, not only because they were expensive but also because wives and their families objected.[69] Moreover, concubinage was not an attractive option for women in villages where men outnumbered them and other labor opportunities were available. A peasant woman would have been reluctant to provoke the animosity of a local matron and her family in order to serve for a few years as a concubine. But serving girls desperate to leave prostitution were willing, and perhaps even eager, to agree to these conditions. A document from Ichinomiya station in Kōzuke records an agreement in which an innkeeper was paid eighty *ryō* (a staggering sum under the circumstances) to let a serving girl named Koyo out of service seven years early so that she could become a concubine to a local peasant's son. The deal specified that Koyo might be married to someone else or sent back to her mother in her home province if her new master was unsatisfied with her, but she could not be indentured elsewhere or returned to the inn.[70]

Unsurprisingly, some spurned wives and their families blamed serving girls for provoking domestic discord, and they were able to enlist other villagers' support in condemning prostitutes' erotic hold on local men. In 1776, a peasant from a village near Ōta complained that his wife's relatives were interfering in his divorce. They alleged that he planned to remarry a serving girl from the Nakasendō's Itahana station; apparently, they considered this a valid reason to obstruct his request for a separation. Village elders must have agreed, because when the husband was called to explain, he found it necessary to insist that he had no interest in marrying "that type of woman" (*migigara no onna*). By using this language, he was signaling his acceptance of community norms that cast serving girls as outsiders. This proved critical to his case: in the end, he was granted his divorce on the condition that he promised not to take a "wicked second wife" (*furachi naru gosai*).[71]

This perception of prostitutes as "wicked" women who destroyed families would have seemed painfully ironic to indentured serving girls. Within their native villages, they had been perceived as filial daughters who worked to preserve the integrity of the households they had left behind. But headmen in the Kantō region did not share this perspective. The social meanings commoners attached to prostitution varied across space even as they changed over time. In Kantō, Echigo's dutiful daughters were reframed as self-interested outsiders who corrupted peasant girls, shattered marriages, and bankrupted families.

THE FAILED PROMISE OF REFORM

Elite peasants who believed that the expansion of the sex trade was a threat to their communities also argued that allowing this trend to continue was antithetical to the exercise of benevolent government. In their opinion, officials should have been their natural allies in the attempt to preserve the patriarchal hierarchies that structured the villages; after all, shogunal authorities were constantly complaining about the deterioration of the countryside and the degradation of peasants' manners and customs. In the wake of the Kansei Reforms in 1789, which aimed to increase agricultural productivity and rehabilitate village communities after a catastrophic famine, the shogunate's memorials cited abandoned rice fields, declining populations, and unpaid taxes as critical issues demanding immediate attention.[72] In response, headmen argued that the availability of commercial sex in post-station brothels undermined social stability and agricultural production, contributing to the very problems the shogunate had identified. The abolition of prostitution, they argued, should be considered part of the reform agenda.

In 1799, a group of several dozen villages petitioned to outlaw the sex trade in Sugito, Kasukabe, and Satte:

> In the old days, there were no serving girls at Sugito, Kasukabe, and Satte stations, and even now, there are not any serving girls at the real inns. But in recent years, brothels have petitioned on the pretense that they are inns, and the magistrate has granted them permission to employ serving girls. They employ many women from distant provinces and of uncertain provenance, and they are supposed to provide services for travelers on the roads. But actually, these establishments are not inns at all—they are just plain brothels, and since they are only interested in immediate profit, they take in strangers, thieves, and drifters. Naturally, this has an effect on the manners and customs of people from nearby villages. Villagers who go to the post stations to fulfill their corvée labor obligations throw away their money on these prostitutes. Some run away with prostitutes and others abscond from their villages and get involved in incidents at brothels. They spend large sums of money, and they are distracted from their work as peasants. There are also many who contract foul diseases and remain invalids for the rest of their lives. If we do not send young, healthy men to the post stations to do corvée labor, it is difficult to fulfill our obligations. . . . elders and village leaders try to reason with these young men, but they are easily swayed, and they go to the brothels secretly.[73]

The villages were caught in a bind: corvée labor obligations forced them to send young men into the post stations, where they were enticed by new and exotic forms of entertainment. When they inevitably squandered their money on prostitution, villages lost not only their labor but their income, and often their health and fertility as well. If the most productive members of their communities were compromised, how could peasants be expected to clear abandoned fields, boost agricultural production, and pay their taxes?

The local intendant agreed to look into the villages' complaints, but the post stations responded with a detailed counterargument. They insisted that the serving girls they employed were waitresses and maids who did not exchange sex for payment. Turning the tables, they alleged that the petition had been motivated by the unreasonable hostility (*ikon*) of elements within the villages, and they complained that the headmen's appeal had inconvenienced the stations and distracted them from their official duties.[74] The intendant accepted their view of the situation, and he made no attempt to discipline the stations.

Although previous attempts to abolish prostitution had failed, headmen saw another window of opportunity in the wake of the Bunsei Reforms in 1827. Responding to reports of falling tax revenues and rising crime rates, the shogunate had sent village headmen memoranda exhorting peasants to return to rice agriculture as their primary occupation. They also announced an initiative to strengthen law enforcement in the countryside and a plan to rectify manners and customs in the villages by prohibiting plays, gambling, and even painting and flower-arranging clubs. They also temporarily disbanded young men's associations and cracked down on gambling, which was a favorite pastime of local youths.[75] Rural elites found certain aspects of this reform welcome. They were troubled by the bandits who plagued their villages, and they were eager to enlist shogunal officials' help in apprehending troublemakers.[76] Moreover, they sympathized with the reforms' emphasis on controlling the behavior of unruly young men.

The rhetoric of the Bunsei Reforms also confirmed a core principle that the village headmen had articulated in their complaints about prostitution: the countryside should remain untainted by urban decadence. When innkeepers agreed to abide by the provisions of the reforms, they were forced to reaffirm this vision of an ideal countryside in which peasants confined themselves to agricultural labor and were not distracted by frivolous pursuits. For example, in a letter confirming their compliance with the reforms, Kasukabe station officials and nearby village headmen agreed:

> After all, peasants are the foundation of the country, and they devote themselves to agriculture. But no matter how much they are exhorted to preserve their character, they fall into extravagant habits in the blink of an eye. They cast aside the vital work of tilling the fields. . . . they run off to work in Edo, and the fields are allowed to go fallow. This is a grave mistake.[77]

The peasants promised to support the villages that had been passed down from their ancestors, and in the next article, the post station promised to make sure that serving girls did not imitate the gaudy behavior of prostitutes in the cities. This rhetoric served as both a warning to the post stations and a reminder that the shogunate shared the headmen's concerns.

Attuned to the political environment, peasant leaders timed a series of petitions against prostitution to coincide with the first year of the reform, using language designed to remind the shogunal authorities of this convergence of interests. Near Ōta station, representatives from assisting villages complained that inns held raucous parties where serving girls wore *yūjo*'s makeup and Edo geisha played shamisen and drums. The peasants defined this as "extravagance that is unsuitable for peasant tenants [i.e., the innkeepers] and maidservants [i.e., serving girls]." They continued: "In the twenty years since the station has employed serving girls, it has prospered. Year after year, the station people have flourished. But in those same twenty years, the assisting villages have deteriorated." They described rice fields that had returned to wilderness and villages that contained only half as many households as they had thirty years earlier.[78] Mimicking the shogunate's reform edicts, their complaint linked status order to prosperity: if people would behave appropriately to their station, they insisted, dedicated peasants (and their tax-collecting overlords) would begin to reap the fruits of their labor in the fields.

In addition to appropriating the shogunate's language, village elites took advantage of the administrative structures created by the reforms. The shogunate had appointed inspectors (*torishimari shutsuyaku*), who visited each of the villages in the region to ensure that the regulations were enforced. Originally, the inspectors were intended to report to the shogunate on the villages' shortcomings, but eventually they came to serve as sounding boards for peasant complaints. In this capacity, they mediated between the headmen and station officials. When villagers had concerns about a certain local peasant who consorted with prostitutes, they could address them to the inspector.[79] This was an effective strategy, because the post stations had reason to be wary of the inspectors, who had taken over the shogunate's sporadic raids on inns employing "extra" serving girls.[80] Stations made sure their prostitutes did not attract attention during the inspectors' visits; for example, the Urawa innkeepers' association agreed that when the inspector stayed in the station, they should not send their women out to solicit travelers.[81] By addressing grievances related to prostitution to the inspector, even when he did not need to be informed, the villages called attention to a situation that the post stations would have preferred to keep quiet.

Villages also organized on the basis of their reform associations—groupings created by the shogunate and used to circulate official proclamations and share information on criminals—in order to negotiate with innkeepers. In 1833, villages belonging to the reform association based in Urawa station persuaded proprietors to agree not to accept local boys as customers, even if they disguised themselves as travelers.[82] Three years later, the union of Urawa innkeepers complained that when local youths were turned away, they threw rocks, shouted obscenities, and used stone stupas as battering rams to try to break down the gates. Still, they referenced their agreement with the reform association and reaffirmed their intention to abide by it.[83]

Although village elites often used the threat of shogunal intervention in order to pressure the post stations to govern themselves, they could not force samurai officials to make good on their promises. Authorities maintained a policy of sporadic and inconsistent enforcement, even in reform eras, and even in the face of the peasants' objections. In part, this was due to effective lobbying on the part of station officials, who vigorously protested any attempt to limit prostitution. In 1822, a zealous road magistrate tried to crack down on the post stations along the Nikkō Highway. At one point, inspectors apprehended nineteen "extra" women from Kasukabe and thirty-nine from Sugito; in another incident, four innkeepers from Koshigaya were arrested.[84] The innkeepers were not severely punished (they were briefly detained, fined, and put in manacles), but the incident troubled station officials, who attempted to protect their brothels. In Kasukabe, they supported the innkeepers' petitions disputing the claim that all nineteen women were clandestine prostitutes, and they argued each controversial case, protesting that some of the extra women were too young to work, others too ill, and others were only nominally employed while waiting for marriage arrangements to be finalized.[85] In Koshigaya, officials attempted to solve the problem of "extra" women retroactively by changing how they counted "plain" inns (*hira hatagoya*) and establishments that employed prostitutes (*meshimori hatagoya*). By calling all the inns *meshimori hatagoya*, they increased the base number of inns that were eligible to support prostitutes, and they reassigned serving girls so that there would be no more than two per inn.[86] Finally, after every raid, officials and innkeepers reiterated their economic argument. They explained that proprietors were having difficulty making a living without employing serving girls, blaming downturns in traffic, recent bad harvests, epidemics, or poorly attended town markets.[87] In any case, the implications were clear (and usually stated explicitly): if inns did not offer prostitution, they would go out of business and the stations would not be able to raise enough revenue to provide horses and labor to official travelers. This argument gained traction with officials worried about the stability of the transportation system. In Koshigaya, a sympathetic local intendant raised these concerns when he wrote to the road magistrate asking him to reconsider the effects of his raids.[88]

Since the stations' economic argument was powerful, village elders who opposed post-station prostitution learned to counter the station officials' claims at the same time that they employed the rhetoric of reform. In 1832, a union of 153 villages near Kumagaya station pursued this strategy in a uniquely successful mass protest. Kumagaya had never received permission to employ serving girls, and as a result its innkeepers lost business to brothels in the neighboring station of Fukaya.[89] Watanabe Kazan (1793–1841), a prominent artist and writer who traveled along the Nakasendō that year, explained their dilemma. According to his account, local merchants flocked to Kumagaya's market, which was held six times a month. But many of the young men who attended the market refused to stay over in Kumagaya, where they were unable to procure sex. Instead, they walked down the road to Fukaya and spent the night in brothels there.[90]

Recognizing the scope of the problem, Kumagaya officials submitted a secret petition to Oshi domain asking permission to employ prostitutes. When nearby village headmen caught wind of this request, they prepared a detailed counterargument. First, they claimed that Kumagaya's market was so profitable that the station did not need an additional economic stimulus. Although the station competed with Kōnosu and Fukaya, they wrote, the market attracted so many merchants that the station was ten times more prosperous than its neighbors. Second, they argued that prostitution caused social disorder in nearby villages. When serving girls had been employed on a trial basis in the 1780s, they said, young people held gambling parties in the station, squandered their money, and were disinherited by their parents. Third, they contended that the post station's stated goal of increasing the number of post stations was suspect, since there were already more than enough inns to accommodate travelers. Finally, they attacked the post station's continued dependence on assisting villages to provide horses and labor. They claimed that the stations should be able to run without serving girls and also without excessive demands on the assisting villages.[91]

In this case, the peasants were able to portray themselves as opponents of change and defenders of an older, more familiar order, appealing to the shogunate's conservatism in the wake of the Bunsei Reforms. By arguing that further development was not necessary to support the transportation system, they neutralized the post-station officials' claims, while simultaneously employing the rhetoric of the reforms, contrasting upright and honorable villages with depraved and corrupt post stations. They supported the status quo—a post station without prostitution—and they were successful in their petition. Oshi domain and shogunal officials declined the post station's request.

This success was short-lived, however. Kumagaya officials attempted the same petition three years later, again arguing that prostitution was necessary to revitalize the post station's finances. They tried to keep this maneuver quiet, but their strategy backfired when village headmen heard about the request from a domain official at the Oshi daimyō's residence. The news so alarmed the Oshi peasants' representative (*sōbyakushō daihyō*) Saburōzaemon that he convened an emergency meeting a few days later. The headmen went to Kumagaya to speak to the post-station official, who cited the station's financial difficulty in his refusal to withdraw the request. In the following weeks, the increasingly worried headmen visited a domain official to present their counterpetition, then set off for Edo to deliver their request to the road magistrates.[92]

Surprisingly, Saburōzaemon was able to enlist the support of parties within the station, including the master of the largest and most important inn (*honjin*) and representatives of the residents of the station. In their petition, which the village headmen carried with them to Edo, the people of the station raised familiar concerns about the behavior of their own young people, which were remarkably similar to those expressed by peasants in the 1832 petition. They explained that when serving girls had been employed on a trial basis in the 1780s, they were popular with youths from both the station and surrounding villages. These youths then neglected their work to feast with serving girls day and night, and many who had spent too much money on prostitution ran away, leaving their masters or families to pay back their loans. Others were disinherited, and still others turned to gambling, drank heavily, fought, stole, and became homeless drifters.[93]

At the same time, the arguments of the post station's residents reveal the multitude of related issues that could get caught up in an argument about prostitution. The petition restated the villages' contention that the station should be able to finance itself without serving girls, but it also added a new allegation: the station official was corrupt, hoping to profit personally from the employment of serving girls by embezzling tax money and taking bribes from innkeepers.[94] (This was a typical complaint: when villagers near Ōta organized to protest prostitution in that station, they claimed that one of the post-station officials was making a fortune renting futons to the inns employing serving girls "whether they really needed them or not.")[95] It is also possible that in Kumagaya, as in other stations, competition for customers motivated residents of less urbanized districts to protest against the employment of serving girls in the center of town. In Fuchū, poor residents used this type of protest in order to force proprietors in prosperous areas to contribute more money to the station's operating budget.[96]

Ultimately, Saburōzaemon's counterpetition succeeded, and the road magistrates again declined the post station's request. But the lessons of this incident were not encouraging to headmen who wished to follow his example. The Kumagaya-area peasants' victory was limited. They had only managed to preserve the status quo, and they were left with the unpleasant task of having to defend it every time the post-station officials decided to submit a new petition. (In 1868, peasants mobilized yet again in response to the same issue, and the headman they chose as their representative was so irritated that he included in his own records a detailed account of how annoyed he was to be taking on that responsibility.)[97] Notably, shogunal inspectors made no attempt to curtail prostitution in nearby Fukaya station, which the peasant movement's leaders had pilloried as a prime example of the ill effects of prostitution. In stations where brothels had already been established by the 1830s, there was no prospect of change. Officials offered little support beyond moral exhortations and sporadic raids, and the shogunate never abolished prostitution in any post station where it had previously been sanctioned.

From the perspective of samurai administrators, this was a necessary and familiar trade-off: they had sacrificed a rigid ideal of social order in order to promote prosperity, which would ultimately do far more than showy moral reform to ensure that their institutions could continue to function. To them, this was a strategy toward promoting stability: without adequate funding, the entire transportation system would collapse, and the alternate attendance system would disintegrate. This arrangement of priorities could also be understood as a manifestation of benevolence. Permitting prostitution allowed innkeepers to make a living and generated tax revenue that enabled post stations to operate without imposing undue financial hardship on their own residents or the peasants who lived in assisting villages. But understandings of the government's obligation to its subjects conflicted when they were articulated at different scales of the polity. To peasant leaders, who believed in the urgency of moral reform, samurai authorities had proved that they were more concerned with filling their own coffers than preventing social disintegration. They had prioritized decadent, commercialized post stations at the expense of virtuous, hardworking villages. In that sense, they had failed to deliver on the promise of benevolence.

Just as serving girls established a presence in village life, elite peasants were experiencing the loss of patriarchal control in several arenas: they could not prevent young men from squandering their money, peasant wives from limiting their fertility, or children from trying out new fashions. For these anxious village elders, the increasing popularity of prostitution was not only the ultimate symbol of the insidious influence of urban culture, it was also a powerful illustration of the deleterious effects of commercialization. The exchange of sex for money was a disturbing example of how cash had come to mediate relationships and activities that had customarily proceeded under the supervision of local patriarchs. When peasant elites complained about the sex trade, they were lamenting how financial exchanges had come to dominate village social life, how women and younger sons were gaining power at the expense of their husbands and fathers, and how headmen were losing their ability to harness peasants' labor.

Like samurai administrators in Echigo, these peasant elites viewed prostitution as a threat to the gendered order that linked the household, the village, and the state. But they expressed their apprehension in a different vocabulary. Occasionally, they invoked the concept of "shame," but they rarely held serving girls responsible for their own fate. Instead, they contributed to the stigmatization of prostitutes in more subtle ways, primarily by invoking narratives that constructed a dichotomy between willful women who worked in the sex trade and dutiful peasant wives and daughters who remained in the household. Since headmen had no reason to believe that prostitution could coexist with and reinforce patriarchal hierarchies (in fact, they had seen many examples to the contrary), they did not consider prostitutes to be plausible representatives of the feminine ideals of submission and sacrifice. Rather than invoking the pitiful image of the exploited daughter, then, they portrayed serving girls as working women who inspired others to reject the obligations of family in favor of the immediate rewards of wage labor and the fleeting pleasures of consumption. Paradoxically, women who had no control over the conditions of their employment, and whose salaries were paid directly to their parents, came to serve as lurid examples of how engagement with the market economy could destabilize households by freeing women to exert control over their labor, their spending, and their bodies.

Although peasant elites could not reverse the incursion of the sex trade into the countryside, their perception of the role of prostitutes and prostitution went uncontested. When village headmen complained that the sex trade was destroying their communities, post-station officials and magistrates responded with economic arguments, insisting that brothels were necessary to attract paying customers to the stations. They never suggested that prostitution affirmed the patriarchal order they exalted in their proclamations. While magistrates in urban districts suggested that allowing the sex trade to flourish was an act of benevolence, since it allowed daughters to sacrifice themselves so that poor families might survive, shogunal authorities posted in rural areas never pursued this line of argument. Perhaps they realized that this explanation would fall on deaf ears: after all, the families that serving girls supported were almost always residents of distant provinces. Still, this silence must have suggested to villagers that shogunal representatives, like post-station officials, were more concerned with development and prosperity than preserving the integrity of rural communities. Meanwhile, post-station prostitutes were left without anyone—parents, commoner officials, or magistrates—who would speak on their behalf, represent their interests, or defend them as filial daughters.

CHAPTER SIX · **Tora and the "Rules of the Pleasure Quarter"**

Tora was born in 1851, and she spent her childhood in the town of Takehara in Hiroshima domain. A port on the Inland Sea, Takehara was a popular destination for boats of almost every variety: large ships transporting bales of tax rice to central brokers in Osaka, smaller vessels carrying handicrafts and marine products to local markets, and dinghies ferrying passengers back and forth across the water. Takehara's wholesalers (*ton'ya*) served as distribution centers for the commercial vessels' cargo, and its boat lodges (*funayado*) provided sailors with foodstuffs and other necessities. The town's businesses also catered to recreational travelers, whose numbers had increased markedly during the first decades of the nineteenth century. Takehara's inns and teahouses offered lodging and entertainment for the wayfarers who flocked to religious destinations such as Konpira and Zentsūji in Sanuki province, the shrine at Itsukushima, the sacred sites of Saikoku, and the eighty-eight temples comprising the Shikoku pilgrimage circuit.

Tora's world was literally a floating world. Her parents and neighbors crossed the water in order to find work, attend parties, visit relatives, and recruit employees. Unlike the elite peasants of the Kantō region, whose social lives and livelihoods were tied to the land, the commoners who lived in Inland Sea port towns were more attuned to the cycles of the tides than the rhythms of the harvest. They also experienced political authority more indirectly than peasants, who were reminded of their obligations to their rulers every time they brought in the harvest or sent their sons to labor in post stations. Inland Sea townspeople watched daimyō processions come to port, received edicts from magistrates, and paid special levies and guild association fees, but they were never assigned to groups of assisting villages or reform associations. Nor were they subject to constant reminders of their duty to dress plainly, eschew wasteful spending, and devote themselves to productive labor. Since commercially minded domain officials realized that the port towns' economies depended on attracting tourists and sailors, they were reluctant to hector their residents with exhortations to modesty and frugality. In Hiroshima's Onomichi, for example, the town magistrate reacted to a brief downturn in 1817 by reminding the townspeople to repair their salt-stained and wind-battered storefronts and "make them splendid." "Now more than ever," he wrote, "the good opinion of the passenger boats [*kyakusen*] is the basis of our prosperity."[1]

Tora's neighbors did not count their fortunes in bales of rice or reels of silk; instead, they tallied the number of boats registered in harbor logs and the quantity of amulets sold at temples and shrines. To entice sailors and pilgrims, they offered an array of diversions, including markets, festivals, sumo bouts, plays, lotteries, and many varieties of prostitution. Realizing that the sex trade was an important moneymaking endeavor, samurai administrators variously tolerated and encouraged it. In Tora's domain, Hiroshima, brothels were allowed to operate in ports such as Takehara and Onomichi, at least as long as the officials in those areas did not bring the matter to the authorities' attention. In Shikoku's Takamatsu domain, the daimyō prohibited prostitution in most places, but he permitted and even promoted it within areas administered by religious institutions such as the shrine and temple complex Konpira.[2] Taking advantage of lax government oversight, proprietors and procurers recruited women from across the Inland Sea, using pilgrimage and trade circuits to transport them between their natal homes and places of work or between brothels based in different towns.

In 1862, Tora became one of these women when her parents indentured her to a brothel on the island of Mitarai. Three years later, she returned to Takehara, setting off a protracted custody dispute between her parents and her master. The record of this episode forms the basis of this chapter, a microhistory that explores the dynamics of the Inland Sea's sex trade at the close of the Tokugawa era. This was no ordinary episode of contention. The feuding parties were so obstinate, and so eager to submit petitions and testimony to the authorities, that town elders in both jurisdictions were forced to reconcile at least three plausible stories about what had happened and why. These accounts, rich in detail and rife with unsubstantiated accusations, illuminate an otherwise obscure social world, one populated by struggling brothel keepers, small-time traveling merchants, itinerant prostitutes, and minor gangsters.³ While this case is uniquely convoluted, and thus unrepresentative of most conflicts between prostitutes' parents and employers, its details are revealing. They suggest how families reacted to the proliferation of labor opportunities in the sex trade and how proprietors attempted to retain control of their employees and stabilize the market.

As chapters 2 and 3 have argued, brothel keepers in Edo and Nagasaki's designated "pleasure quarters," who sought to eliminate competition and to justify the legality of their business, embraced the trope casting prostitutes as filial daughters. But proprietors in the Inland Sea, who did not enjoy similar state protection from upstart competitors, had no reason to be invested in the gendered order or its ideological underpinnings. The idea that prostitutes were daughters and subjects, entitled to a degree of official protection, was only a hindrance to brothel keepers in this region, who often hired employees without asking questions about their backgrounds and moved them between jurisdictions with impunity. Their interest was not in justifying their trade, but in insulating the workings of their labor market from the moral claims of the household and the intervention of paternalistic rulers.

In this context, the quarrel between Tora's parents and her employer, ostensibly about the fate of one teenager, became a clash between two visions of the market. One was the older conception of a moral economy, which assumed that the sex trade functioned in support of the gendered order. The other was a newer understanding espoused by proprietors and commoner officials who relied on brothels for revenue. They envisioned a market governed by the "rules of teahouses," in which the pursuit of profit, not the integrity of the patriarchal household or the stability of the realm, was the primary objective. Moreover, they had no expectation that their profits be distributed according to status hierarchy, and they generally distrusted domain officials. Arguing that the contractual relationship between employer and employee should be understood on its own terms, and not as analogous to the bonds between parent and child or ruler and subject, they worked to undermine the tropes that cast Tora as a passive, filial daughter.

This reenvisioning of the market—and prostitutes' role in it—was a product of both its time and its place. It was made possible by economic developments that had begun to change the character of the Inland Sea region in the middle of the eighteenth century (before this period, the town of Mitarai did not even exist) and accelerated in the early 1800s, when the "travel boom" produced the type of traffic that sustained brothel keepers' businesses and made entire communities dependent on their trade. Because this trend was uncontested by samurai officials, who played no role in settling this dispute, Tora's case fits into the narrative of change over time detailed in earlier chapters, in which provincial authorities eschewed regulation and capitulated, uneasily, to the "logic of the market." At the same time, the dynamics of this particular market were specific to the Inland Sea, a maritime region where people led fairly itinerant lives and informal commercial exchanges among strangers were common. Tora's story is not, then, meant as an example of a larger process in which proprietors across the realm wrote their own rules and began to contest an officially sponsored understanding of the prostitute as a filial daughter. Instead, it is one of many examples of how economic change led people of various social statuses to reinterpret the meaning of work in the sex trade, often in ways that stigmatized prostitutes and their families.

A SEA OF WOMEN

In the late summer of 1862, the Mitarai brothel keeper Sadaemon paid Tora's parents ten *ryō* in gold in exchange for ten years of her labor. This was not a large sum for a prostitute's contract; in Kanagawa and Kawasaki stations along the Tōkaidō Highway, brothel proprietors were paying up to fifty *ryō* for contracts of shorter duration.[4] But their counterparts in Mitarai could not afford to pay as much, since their district was in the midst of an economic downturn. Decades earlier, the island's merchants had maintained a thriving business unloading rice, cotton, sake, oil, salt, and a variety of other products from eastbound ships and selling them to vendors in other domains. Their prosperity was evident in the imposing architecture of their warehouses and in the famous names adorning the lanterns at the town's shrine: the donors of these decorations were the wholesalers' business associates, a group that included the wealthiest merchant houses in Osaka.[5] But by Tora's time, the island had begun to suffer from a change in the economic complexion of the region as a whole. As ship captains began to take charge of buying and selling as well as transporting goods, they started to bypass the middlemen in intermediate distribution centers such as Mitarai, preferring to stop in places like Onomichi, where they could purchase directly from producers based in the surrounding countryside.[6] Meanwhile, the many domestic and international crises of the 1860s, while they did not curtail commercial traffic, contributed to an atmosphere of apprehension in the region.[7] On Mitarai, new gun batteries stood ready to repel foreign invaders and Japanese enemies of Hiroshima domain, signaling to traders that the calm waters of the Inland Sea might soon be roiled by violence.

Mitarai's businesses catering to recreational travelers had been suffering for several decades as competition between port towns intensified and other jurisdictions began to feature plays, lotteries, and teahouses of their own.[8] By the middle of the nineteenth century, Mitarai's four brothels—Sakaiya, Wakaebisuya, Tomitaya, and Ebiya—were shadows of their former glory. In the mid-eighteenth century, their indentured women had comprised about 20 percent of the town's total population of 543, but this proportion had fallen steadily in the ensuing decades.[9] The Wakaebisuya, a grand establishment that had employed almost a hundred women in its heyday, retained only a few dozen by the 1860s. Meanwhile, its neighbor, the Ebiya, was barely surviving after its proprietor absconded in an attempt to outrun his debts.[10] Tora's brothel, the Tomitaya, employed roughly a dozen women and it, too, was on the brink of failure. Sadaemon, who was running the operation for a landlord who held rights to the business (*kabu*), constantly complained that he was having trouble making ends meet.

Tora, who was thirteen by the Japanese count, was a good investment for Sadaemon, who had little cash on hand. If she had been older, her parents, Isaburō and Matsu, might have demanded a larger sum of money for a shorter term of service. But they thought she was still too young to have sex with clients, and they made Sadaemon promise that he would wait four years before requiring her to do so. During that time, he would pay for her room and board while she worked as a maidservant and trained in the arts (*geidō*). This meant that she would not generate much revenue for the brothel, so her parents could not expect to receive a large initial payment. As it turned out, Sadaemon wasted no time breaking his word. The record of Tora's case makes clear that he waited only eight months before compelling her to service customers sexually. This may have been part of his overall strategy. By hiring a young girl, and then putting her to work as soon as possible, Sadaemon received the maximum return on a paltry initial investment.

Soon after Tora's parents agreed to her contract, she became one of thousands of girls who crossed the water to work in the Inland Sea's sex trade. Like Tora, most indentured prostitutes in the region's small ports were provincial girls who had been acquired relatively cheaply from other coastal towns and villages. Hishiya Heishichi, an Owari textile merchant who traveled through the Inland Sea in 1802, recorded many encounters with women who spoke with pronounced local accents. In a dilapidated brothel in the town of Muro, he found *yūjo* in their twenties whose rough speech and clothing plainly revealed their lower-class, provincial upbringing.[11] This anecdotal evidence is corroborated by other sources. In his extensive

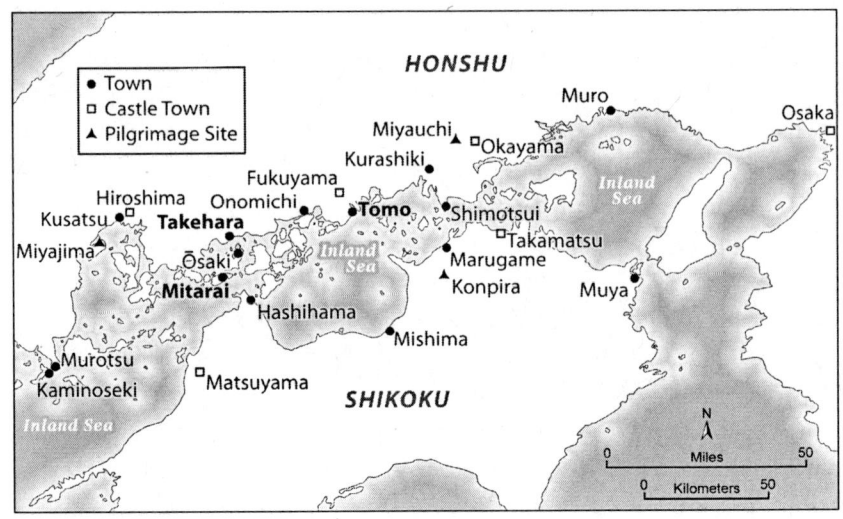

MAP 4.
The eastern Inland Sea region, with Takehara, Mitarai, and Tomo in boldface type.

study of the Inland Sea's traffic in women, Maki Hidemasa cites cases in which women traveled from Muya to Shimotsui, from Ryōtsu (Sanuki) to Miyauchi (Bizen), from Tomo to Miyauchi, from Takehara to Mitarai, from Kusatsu (Aki) to Murotsu (Suō), and from Onomichi to Konpira.[12]

Other women, particularly highly trained geisha, came from the great cities of Kansai. They were concentrated in the hubs of the tourist trade, including neighborhoods such as Uchimachi and Kinzanji in Konpira, which attracted sophisticated men who appreciated the erotic charge of a lilting Kansai accent.[13] Brothel and teahouse proprietors in these locales might recruit waitresses from nearby villages, but they imported geisha and higher-priced prostitutes from cities with an established tradition of training entertainers. When Hishiya visited Konpira, he encountered a chubby waitress who prattled on in her provincial accent, telling him of the *yūjo* and *geiko* from Osaka who entertained tourists in Kinzanji. He noted that the town's teahouses were built in the fashion of some of the smaller establishments in Kyoto, confirming his impression that the town's nightlife owed its sophistication to the influence of men and women from Kansai.[14] This was also the case in provincial castle towns. As Sone Hiromi has observed, women working in Miyazu's "pleasure quarter" were differentiated by both occupation and place of origin: women from surrounding villages worked as low-level prostitutes, while those from Kyoto were "drink-serving girls" (*shakutori onna*) who offered music and dance performances and commanded higher hourly rates.[15]

Prostitutes of both varieties maintained ambiguous relationships with the law. In some towns they were recorded in population records as *yūjo*, indicating that their occupation was legally recognized, but in most Inland Sea jurisdictions, they were referred to as maidservants (*gejo*) or indentured women (*kakae onna*), euphemisms suggesting that the domain administration had never recognized their employers or sanctioned their activities.[16] In Mitarai, the commoners who served as town officials instructed brothel keepers to record their employees in the population registers as maidservants with "ordinary" (*jōtai*) women's names. In their own records, however, they used the term *yūjo* and referred to women by professional names.[17] In fact, local officials had strong incentives to protect the brothel keepers' business. At pilgrimage sites like Konpira, authorities were eager to encourage pleasure-seeking visitors. As Sarah Thal has explained, "performances, prostitution, and gambling proved as integral to the growth of the site as amulets and worship."[18] Meanwhile, in small port towns, officials were reluctant to inhibit the growth of any business that attracted sailors, and they were wary of penalizing employers whose taxes supported the towns' operating budgets. In Mitarai, where brothel keepers paid the most lucrative of all the levies assessed on the town's establishments, officials made special exceptions for the proprietors of these businesses. For example, when a fire started at Wakaebisuya and caused widespread damage, the town elders agreed to shut down the brothel, but only for two days. Moreover, since they feared that even such a brief closure would adversely affect the town's economy, they determined that the brothel could admit customers through its backdoor during this period.[19]

Samurai officials were certainly aware that so-called "maidservants" and "indentured women" were being used as prostitutes, but they were content to go along with the fiction that they were "ordinary" women. As a result, the Inland Sea's indentured prostitutes were difficult to place within the matrix of status and geography that structured the sex trade in the shogunate's cities. Officially, these women had set places of residence, but in reality they moved frequently. Provisions in their contracts allowed their masters to transfer them to any other brothel for any reason at any time without procuring their or their parents' consent. This type of clause was standard in the contracts of geisha and prostitutes all over Japan, but in the highly mobile and economically volatile Inland Sea region, where it was difficult for a proprietor to estimate the number of women he would require from season to season, the master's right to move a woman was absolute; he did not have to send her back through the go-between who had brought her to the brothel.[20] In order to deal with fluctuations in the market, brothels in Mitarai traded women to teahouses, geisha houses, and bathhouses as far as Osaka, Matsuyama, and Kaminoseki.[21] They also exchanged indentured women to settle debts. When a Kaminoseki teahouse master fell behind on his payments to a Mitarai clothing dealer in 1753, he repaid the loan by giving him the rights to thirty-one geisha. The clothing dealer had no use for them, so he sold them to a Kaminoseki bathhouse and recouped his investment.[22]

As these indentured women moved back and forth across the Inland Sea, they were joined by a significant population of itinerant prostitutes who had no stable places of residence. They did not belong within the political purview of local officials or under the contractual authority of brothel keepers. Instead, they moved from town to town looking for employment wherever they could find it. Like streetwalkers in Edo and "widows" in Niigata, they rarely conformed to patterns of labor expected of legal prostitutes. Some worked independently, selling sex as a side occupation. For example, port town residents complained about the activities of so-called "vegetable-selling women" (*yasai uri fujin*), rough-hewn peasants who arrived on market days to solicit customers. Brothel keepers in Mitarai worried that the upstarts were poaching their clients, and town officials attempted to curtail their activities by reminding them that peasant women should limit themselves to selling produce. This warning proved ineffective, however, and eventually domain authorities from Hiroshima were summoned to arrest the defiant women.[23]

Commoner officials who attempted to penalize these itinerant prostitutes usually found their options limited. They could not punish them by sending them to a "pleasure quarter": their towns and villages did not feature designated spaces set aside for prostitution, and local authorities were reluctant to interfere with subjects of other domains. The usual course of action, then, was to expel the offenders, which did nothing to disrupt the plans of people who were already accustomed to drifting across jurisdictions. For example, an 1811 raid on the Honshu port town and shogunal intendant's headquarters Kurashiki resulted in the brief detention of eleven women ranging in age from eleven to twenty-three, none of whom was a resident of that district. A nineteen-year-old named Koma provided the most information to her interrogators. Born in the Shikoku port town of Marugame, she had married a man named Kanzō at the astonishingly early age of eleven. Kanzō, who came from the mercantile city of Hakata in Kyushu, was a peripatetic type who worked on the periphery of the theatre world. He manned ticket gates and recruited security guards for performances, while Koma sewed costumes for the players. When money ran short, she also sold sex. She explained that she had intended to accompany Kanzō on a "pilgrimage" to Konpira, but she fell ill along the way, so he had left her behind.[24] Officials apprehended Kanzō and then expelled the couple from Kurashiki; they probably continued on their way to Konpira.

The other women detained in the same raid were also accustomed to moving between jurisdictions. They traveled with biological parents or grandparents who served as their masters (*kakaenushi*), taking advantage of family connections that spanned the Inland Sea. Fourteen-year-old Kumayoshi, who had arrived in Kurashiki in the company of her grandmother, explained that her grandfather's acquaintance, a local innkeeper, had invited her to teach dance lessons to local children.[25] Unlike Koma, who was clearly an amateur, she had assumed a working name and identified herself as a geisha. Fifteen-year-old Imayoshi, another geisha, had arrived from Osaka with her mother. By the time of the raid she had already been transferred to the custody of a man from Miyauchi, a popular pilgrimage site in Okayama.[26]

Itinerant prostitutes' pattern of labor had a significant advantage over traditional brothel prostitution: they could move to find customers instead of waiting for men to arrive at their door. This allowed them to capitalize on seasonal patterns of pilgrimage by seeking out places where there was likely to be a temporary market for their services. As the Inland Sea's tourist trade expanded in the late eighteenth century, brothels began to imitate this model. Proprietors in Mitarai sent their indentured women to festivals in Miyauchi, and they brought geisha to Miyajima, Mishima (in northern Kyushu), and Hashihama (in Shikoku) to work on market days.[27] Even in summer, when the Kansai-bound tax rice boats came to port, Ebiya sent women across the water to Fukuyama to work.[28] To facilitate these excursions, the Mitarai brothels formed professional connections that spanned the Inland Sea. For example, in 1785, Ebiya's proprietor brought fifteen women to Tomo, where they spent twenty days working out of a local brothel during the popular Gion festival.[29] This worked out well for both establishments: one drew more customers and enhanced its reputation during a period when many tourists visited, while the other generated income during a slow season.

In the town of Konpira, which could count on a steadier flow of tourists headed to the temple and shrine complex, the seasonal problem that plagued Mitarai's brothel keepers was reversed. Konpira's proprietors often suffered from a shortage of women during the triennial Eshiki, a series of religious lectures and ceremonies that incorporated a kabuki performance known as the Great Play (*Ōshibai*). Brothel keepers complained to authorities at Konkōin, the administrative temple responsible for the religious institution and its environs, that guests were inconvenienced when there were insufficient women to attend to their needs.[30] The brothel keepers' solution was to hire temporary employees known as "day-laboring women" (*hiyatoi onna*), a group that included itinerant as well as indentured prostitutes from other domains.[31] In 1843, they received Konkōin's permission to establish a clearinghouse for male and female servants (including prostitutes), which they used to trade laborers between establishments and to hire people from outside the territory for half-year or one-month terms.[32]

By the mid-nineteenth century, then, brothel keepers in various areas of the Inland Sea had greatly expanded the scope of their business, extending their geographical reach and enlarging the pool of women from which they recruited. In the brothel keepers' view, potential employees were differentiated from one another by their value to prospective employers and clients, not necessarily by their relationships to political authorities, family ties, or places of origin (although the latter could affect their perceived value in the region-wide market). Proprietors did not attempt to contain their operations within jurisdictional boundaries, and they did not pay attention to status distinctions between prostitutes and "ordinary" women. They regarded their women as investment properties, not as daughters or subjects. It was this vision of the sex trade, as primarily a profit-seeking operation and not as a partner in upholding samurai authorities' ideals of order, that would determine how Sadaemon perceived his newest employee—and how he responded to her parents' challenge to his authority.

TORA'S "ABDUCTION"

On the morning of the fifth day of the fifth month of 1865, Tora's older sister Risa, who worked as a prostitute in Takehara, stopped at the Tomitaya after accompanying one of her clients on his way home to the nearby town of Ōsaki.[33] Apparently, it was not unusual for Tora's family to visit her in Mitarai. According to Sadaemon, both Risa and her mother often dropped by the brothel to check on Tora and socialize with his wife, Jū. Sadaemon did not comment on whether he found this atypical, but there are few other references to this type of relationship in the Mitarai town record. Like their counterparts in Nagasaki, brothel keepers in Mitarai encouraged women to maintain ties with their families. When a woman became too ill to work, it was common practice for her master to send word to her parents, hoping that they would take her home and foot the bill for her care.[34] However, as the previous two chapters have also argued, the everyday familial interactions that characterized prostitutes' lives in places like Nagasaki, where most women working in brothels were natives of surrounding neighborhoods, were more difficult to maintain when girls entered service farther away. While Nagasaki parents took custody of their indentured daughters' children, for example, Mitarai prostitutes tended to raise their children at the brothels. Wakaebisuya kept a death register (*kakochō*) containing entries for several babies and toddlers who had passed away while their mothers were in service. They were buried in Mitarai's graveyard, alongside prostitutes who had died during their terms of indenture.[35]

Tora, whose family often came to visit the brothel, initially might have considered herself more fortunate than her peers. But on that morning in 1865, Risa delivered disturbing news: their mother, Matsu, was desperately ill, and she was asking to see Tora one more time before she died. Jū, the brothel keeper's wife, gave Tora a temporary leave to visit her mother's deathbed. She dressed her in a good kimono and hairpins before sending her home to Takehara with a get-well gift. Tora promised to return soon, and Jū probably assumed she would be back the next day. The journey from Mitarai to Takehara did not take long, and small boats made the trip regularly.

When Tora had not returned after a few days, Sadaemon and Jū sent a messenger to retrieve her. In the meantime, the brothel received a letter from a Takehara boat captain. They had not yet opened it when their messenger returned complaining that he had not been able to find Tora. More ominously, he reported that Takehara officials had refused to help him. Sadaemon and Jū hurried to read the letter, which explained that Isaburō would return the money Sadaemon had paid for Tora's contract, with the interest it would have accrued over the past three years, if Sadaemon would allow Tora to remain in Takehara with her parents. This was a clear violation of Tora's contract: she had been indentured to the brothel for ten years, and she had worked for less than three.

In response, Sadaemon sent Jū to Takehara to negotiate with Matsu. Since the two had enjoyed a cordial relationship, he might have expected that they could resolve the matter quickly. However, when Jū arrived in Takehara, no one would tell her where she could find Tora. Instead, she was directed to a man she called an *oyabun*; the word indicates that he was a local man of influence, who may or may not have had underworld connections. She refused to speak to him and returned to her boat to spend the night. The next morning, she was approached by two Takehara residents—a monk and a local shopkeeper—who claimed to represent Tora's stepfather, Isaburō. They made a point of saying that they were reluctant to negotiate with a woman, but they also suggested that they could help her case if she paid them a bribe. Jū returned home in disgust, and Sadaemon decided to take over the negotiations, only to find that Tora's parents had changed their terms: they insisted on receiving fifty *ryō* and a new, shorter contract for Tora. This was a ridiculous demand, and it was a clear sign that Matsu and Isaburō had no intention of sending their daughter back to Mitarai. Even the Takehara-based intermediaries thought these terms were preposterous, and negotiations broke down.

Unwilling to relinquish his claim to Tora, and under pressure from his landlord Fujiya Gensuke, who refused to accept Isaburō's initial offer to pay back Tora's indenture money, Sadaemon informed the head of Mitarai's teahouse association (*chaya nakama*) that his employee had been abducted. He procured a copy of Tora's original contract (the association kept such documents in its central headquarters) and brought it to Takehara, where he read it aloud to Matsu, who had miraculously recovered from her mysterious illness. However, she refused to believe that it was the same document she had signed three years earlier: "The document from back then was only one sheet of paper," she protested. "It wasn't really long like this one" (*sono setsu no shomon to mōsu wa ichimai no kami nite, sayō naganagashiki koto ni wa gozana/ku sōrō/*). Apparently, Matsu had decided to use her illiteracy as a negotiating tactic, which was a daring move, considering that the ability to read documents was more often wielded as a weapon *against* lower-class women who dared to question the status quo.[36]

Stunned by Matsu's intransigence, Sadaemon petitioned the commoners who served as town officials (*machi yakunin*) in Mitarai, explaining that Tora (he insisted on calling her by her working name, Koeda) had absconded. Since they depended on the brothels' business, the Mitarai authorities were favorably disposed to Sadaemon's complaint, and they dutifully contacted their counterparts in Takehara, explaining that the indentured girl should be returned. But when Takehara officials questioned Tora's parents, they heard a very different story.[37] Isaburō maintained that he could not send his daughter back to the Tomitaya because Sadaemon's second son Sōbei had been making inappropriate sexual advances to her. She had tried to refuse, but he continued harassing her until she had no choice but to give in. At the same time, Sadaemon was forcing her to see customers, and when Matsu visited, she noticed that Tora looked ill and exhausted. Isaburō claimed that he was "truly shocked and extremely disturbed that she would be forced to do such things when she is still so young" (*makoto o motte oodoroki, imada wakaki no toshi no mono kore made mo aisemari sōrō gi hanahada fubin ni zonji tatematsuri sōrō*). Since illicit sex with a woman in service would be against the rules at any teahouse, whatever the province (*subete meshikakae no onna to mittsū tsukamatsuri sōrō gi wa chaya uchi daiichi no seikin nite dōkoku mo dōyō*), Isaburō argued that he was under no obligation to return his daughter. He had made a more than fair offer to pay back ten *ryō* with interest, and it was not his fault that Sadaemon and Jū had refused it. (Isaburō neglected to mention his subsequent demand for fifty *ryō* and a shorter contract.)

Throughout his testimony, Isaburō made an effort to portray himself as a caring parent. Significantly, he never mentioned that he was actually Tora's stepfather (*keifu*), rather than her biological father; perhaps he realized that the laws of the realm tended to favor blood relatives' claims over those of stepparents. His version of events seems designed to convey the impression that his major concern was Tora's well-being, not the potential profit from her labor. At the beginning of his account, he explained that he had sent Tora and Risa into service because he was being hounded by bill collectors; in other words, he confirmed that he had indentured his stepdaughters as a last resort, not because he was trying to avoid paying for their upbringing. Moreover, he established that he was willing to take a financial loss in order to protect his children. In spite of his avowed poverty, he insisted that he was not willing to accept a cash settlement if it meant returning Tora to an abusive master. Isaburō alleged that Sadaemon and Jū had offered his family "get-well money" for Matsu if they would send Tora back to the brothel, but he had refused. By repeating at several points that he was concerned about Tora's welfare rather than his own financial gain, he was invoking the power of a conventional narrative about benevolent parents and filial daughters. Initially, it seemed that this strategy would succeed: Takehara officials accepted his story, and they petitioned their superiors in the Kamo county office (*Kamo-gun yakusho*) to resolve the case, noting that there were extenuating circumstances.

But Sadaemon was ready to counter this version of events. He never denied that his son was involved with Tora, but he took issue with other portions of Isaburō's account. Several months later, the brothel keeper wrote another petition to the Mitarai town elders in which he explained that the Takehara townsman had more than his daughter's best interests at heart. The source of this information was a gossipy Mitarai merchant who just happened to be one of Tora's sister Risa's clients. He said that Risa had told him that Isaburō had entered negotiations to send Tora into service at a brothel in the port town of Tomo in Fukuyama domain. Other reports suggested that while Isaburō was finalizing this arrangement, he was sending Tora to entertain the Takehara officials at boating parties, where she was serving tea and singing.[38]

This was particularly galling to Sadaemon, who had paid for the rights to Tora's body and her labor for the next seven years. In addition, the brothel keeper had invested his time and money in Tora's care (*yōiku*), which included artistic training that undoubtedly increased her value on the market. Since Tora, now older and more experienced, could begin working immediately, her next contract would command a much higher price. In other words, if Isaburō succeeded in indenturing sixteen-year-old Tora to a brothel in Tomo, he would make a tidy profit even if he repaid Sadaemon his original ten *ryō* and interest. To make matters worse, officials in Takehara had absolutely no interest in resolving the situation in Sadaemon's favor, since Isaburō was bribing them by sending Tora to their parties to entertain.

If Isaburō succeeded in sending Tora to work at a brothel in Tomo, it would become nearly impossible for Sadaemon to pursue his case through official channels. In this regard, Isaburō was at a distinct advantage: there were labor opportunities for women at many ports and pilgrimage sites across the Inland Sea, all of which belonged to different jurisdictions. Because towns competed viciously for boat traffic, Tomo officials would be reluctant to intervene on behalf of a brothel keeper from a rival port unless they were compelled to do so. Moreover, Sadaemon would have a difficult time persuading the Hiroshima authorities to enforce his contractual rights in another domain. Before he could get them to take up his case, he would have to forward his petition through a complicated hierarchy. First, he would have to convince the Mitarai town elders to petition Toyota county officials to hear his grievance. If they agreed, they would have to bring the case to domain officials in the castle town, who might be unwilling to address the problems of a small-town brothel keeper whose legal status was uncertain. Even if they did deign to investigate the matter, securing Tora's return would require them to open talks with their counterparts in Fukuyama, which administered the port of Tomo. They would have to undertake their own investigation, which would likely involve dispatching deputies to interview Tomo's town elders. There was no guarantee that this process would proceed in a timely manner, and negotiations could break down at any level.

Luckily, Sadaemon could pursue a different strategy, one that took advantage of his professional connections and leveraged the Inland Sea brothel keepers' common assumptions about how the regional market should operate.

THE FLOATING UNDERWORLD

Like many Inland Sea brothel keepers, Sadaemon boasted professional ties that reached far beyond his own jurisdiction, past the realm of officialdom, and into the underworld. This domain was populated by a diverse group of outlaws (*kyōkaku*) who ranged from hardened criminals to aimless drifters and petty thieves. The most familiar type, often referenced in popular culture, was the gambler (*bakuto*) who traveled the countryside. He sponsored card and dice games, provided "protection" for local shopkeepers, and occasionally stole from prosperous peasants. Some men of his ilk were self-styled folk heroes: they used their ill-gotten gains to aid poor peasants and drew on their nefarious connections to threaten corrupt officials. The outlaw's most important attribute, however, was not his abiding concern for the downtrodden, but his ability and willingness to use violence.[39]

In the Inland Sea region, outlaws were closely associated with troupes of entertainers who traveled through a familiar circuit of port towns and pilgrimage sites. For example, bands of sumo wrestlers offered assistance to people looking to settle disputes through extralegal means. Kanda Yutsuki has described how local brothel proprietors and shopkeepers relied on sumo wrestlers to move trafficked women and apprehend debtors. In 1804, an Osaka teahouse proprietor named Kichibei complained to one of that city's magistrates that he was on his way home from a pilgrimage to Usa Hachimangū in Kyushu with his daughter and two indentured women when three sumo wrestlers seized the women and sold them to a brothel. Although this seemed to be a straightforward case of kidnapping, the investigation revealed that Kichibei had a troubled history. On a similar trip to Kyushu market towns two years earlier, he had incurred the wrath of a man named Heishirō, who specialized in providing lodging for itinerant prostitutes and their masters, by neglecting to make payment on a loan. When Heishirō heard that Kichibei had returned to the area, he arranged to have the women abducted. The sumo wrestlers who were hired for the job explained that they had taken the women as "human collateral" (*hitoshichi*). They sold them to a brothel keeper of their acquaintance and forwarded the proceeds to Heishirō as payment on Kichibei's loan.[40]

Although they skirted the margins of respectability, outlaws were not necessarily anti-establishment figures. As chapter 2 has mentioned, the shogunate and domain governments often recruited the most influential among them to act as informers (*meakashi* or *toorimono*) and report on other criminals' activities. Informers were particularly useful to the authorities because they maintained ties to underground organizations that crossed political boundaries. If a criminal escaped into a neighboring domain, for example, an informer could leverage his connections with the underworld figures who controlled that territory in order to apprehend him. The domain's initial failure to capture the offender would never become common knowledge, and the domain's official representatives would not be faulted for overreaching their jurisdiction. For their part, outlaws prized appointments as *meakashi* or *toorimono* as markers of status within their own communities. A man who possessed one of these titles had been confirmed as a leader of his organization, and he could use his official connections to benefit his followers. Usually, he did this by facilitating their requests for permission to put on plays, which were always lucrative endeavors.[41]

Officials at Inland Sea port towns and pilgrimage sites, which were magnets for criminal activity, were in desperate need of outlaws' services. Mitarai town elders hired *meakashi* to prevent drifters from burglarizing the town's wholesalers and boat lodges. In 1784, nearby villagers complained that these newly appointed informers were troublesome (*futodoki*) (apparently one of them had even been apprehended by the domain authorities and exiled). They urged the Mitarai elders to consider hiring a man from their own village, a local person who would be more knowledgeable about the area and presumably better behaved. They did not, however, contest the necessity of employing such men.[42]

Across the water in Konpira, underworld figures became mediators who negotiated between authorities at Konkōin and brothel keepers in the lively neighborhood of Kinzanji. The brothels played an important role in facilitating the Great Play: they paid a levy called *hanegin* that subsidized actors' fees and even took up a special collection to fund the construction of a new theater in 1833. But the clerics on Mt. Zōzu, who for the sake of propriety had exempted themselves from collecting "dirty money" (*fujōkin*), could not intervene in their petty squabbles or compel them to contribute on an orderly schedule.[43] As a result, drifters from Kansai, who were involved in the related businesses of sumo wrestling, plays, and prostitution, took over responsibility for collecting "dirty money," as well as soliciting so-called contributions from local shops. One of them, a man named Yamatoya Gen'emon, had committed murder in Osaka and fled the area to settle in Konpira, where he helped resolve violent disputes and collected money from teahouses to support sumo tournaments and the Great Play.[44] Like the peasants in the village neighboring Mitarai, the residents of nearby shogunal territories objected to the outlaws' unruly behavior: representatives from Noda, Ennai, and Gojō villages complained to Konkōin that Kinzanji fundraisers did things that were "dishonest and unjust" (*fuhō fujitsu gamashiki koto*), including luring village youths into brothels and harassing local residents by demanding contributions.[45]

Occasionally, underworld figures turned against brothel keepers and acted as advocates for poor families. As chapter 3 has mentioned, Nagasaki proprietors complained that prostitutes' parents hired local "helpers" (*sukedan no mono*) and "bosses" (*kaoyaku*) to help them convince brothel keepers that runaway girls were dead.[46] In

Tora's case, however, the ability to call on the assistance of underworld figures as intermediaries was a crucial advantage for the proprietor Sadaemon. Tora's parents had employed a local monk and a pair of shopkeepers to argue on their behalf; although one was referred to as an *oyabun,* suggesting that he might have been able to bring some pressure to bear on Sadaemon, all three had quit at the first sign of trouble. The brothel keeper had more intimidating, and much more effective, connections. He made contact with a pair of bosses from Tomo, the port town where Isaburō was rumored to be sending Tora into service, and charged them with a simple task: explaining to Tora's parents and the Takehara town officials that the "rules of the pleasure quarter" (*kuruwa no kisoku*) prohibited their behavior.

The "rules of the pleasure quarter" were vague and flexible; no one involved in the dispute listed their tenets or explained who had drafted them. It is likely that they were never written down. However, the existence of a commonly agreed-upon set of principles was crucial to the functioning of the Inland Sea's sex trade, which relied on a certain degree of trust and cooperation between proprietors in various port towns who traded women back and forth across the water. In order for this labor market to work, there had to be safeguards that would keep brothels from poaching each other's employees. If officials in different jurisdictions could not be counted on to force the brothels to honor their various commitments (and if Tora's case is any indication, they could not), then the proprietors themselves had to have rules in place to protect their business.

In fact, "the rules of the pleasure quarter" had already been referenced in the dispute over Tora. When the teahouses in Mitarai organized on Sadaemon's behalf, they wrote in their petition to Mitarai officials that teahouse operators followed specific rules (*kisoku*) and carefully considered how their conduct would affect business conditions. According to these rules, they wrote, they were bound to protest Isaburō's behavior.[47] Isaburō, too, had attempted to use a version of this concept to his advantage, arguing that Sōbei's conduct toward his daughter would be against the rules at any teahouse in any province. But even the Takehara town officials acknowledged that it was Isaburō's case that was untenable according to the rules of teahouses (*chaya uchi no kisoku*); after all, these regulations had been set up to protect the financial interests of brothel keepers, not to shield young women from exploitation or defend fathers who had failed to maximize the terms of indenture contracts.[48] When the Tomo gangsters met with Isaburō, they were probably very insistent on this point.

Nevertheless, Isaburō refused to yield to their pressure. Although the option of sending Tora into service in Tomo had been precluded by the Tomo bosses' appearance in Takehara, he proceeded with his plan to send his daughter away. When the Takehara headman (*shōya*) Tomojirō offered to employ Tora and Matsu as maidservants and take them on a trip to attend his younger sister's wedding in the castle town of Fukuyama, Isaburō seized the opportunity. Although Matsu was still too "ill" to work as a maidservant, she agreed to go as far as Onomichi to see her daughter off, indicating that perhaps Tora's trip to Fukuyama was intended to be more permanent than Tomojirō's offer had suggested. However, when bad weather forced the wedding party to dock at Tomo unexpectedly on the twelfth day of the first month of 1866, they found that the local bosses had called in reinforcements to block Tora's violation of "the rules of the pleasure quarter." Her boat was surrounded by a band of roughly fifteen outcasts (*kawata*) from Mitarai, who forcibly removed her from Tomojirō's custody. They delivered her to the Tomo bosses, who eventually sent her back to Mitarai.[49]

THE SETTLEMENT

Six weeks later, the Mitarai and Takehara town officials agreed to a meeting to negotiate a settlement. Both sides realized that it would not be to their benefit to allow the dispute to reach the domain level, where they would likely be criticized for their various forms of misconduct. Isaburō alone refused to attend: "Even if you piled up boxes full of a thousand *ryō*," he said, "I'd never give in" (*tatoe senryōbako tsumorikasane sōrōtemo ryōken itasazu yoshi mōshiide sōrō*). Obstinate to the very end, he demanded to see his stepdaughter. Even in the face of mounting evidence that he was seeking to profit from Tora's labor, he refused to abandon his role as the protective patriarch. But the other interested parties proceeded with plans for talks, and they had Tora questioned by two neutral officials from a Hiroshima domain village.

A torn scrap of paper included among the documents of the Mitarai wholesaler Takeharaya describes the interview, which is never mentioned in any of the official town records.[50] According to the anonymous observer from Mitarai who composed this account, Tora (whom he referred to as Koeda) seemed quite small in comparison to the men in the room. He marveled at her "little head," which she tilted to the side while considering her answers. The content of her testimony was surprising. When Tora was asked why she had gone back to work at the brothel (as if she had a choice in the matter after she was abducted by gangsters from Tomo), she replied that she had returned out of a desire to be filial to her parents and fulfill her obligations to Sadaemon. The interrogators asked whether it was true that she had encountered some trouble at the Tomitaya, and she conceded that she had on several occasions asked her parents to bring her home. At one point, she had even told them she would rather die than stay in Mitarai. When asked why she had made such a strong statement, she explained that she had borrowed money and had no idea how to repay it. If she threatened to commit suicide, she thought, her parents would take her complaints seriously and welcome her back to Takehara.

Of course, this was not the story that the investigators had heard from Isaburō, so they proceeded to question Tora about the nature of her relationship with the brothel keeper's son Sōbei. She hesitated, but eventually answered that she had pursued him whenever she had a break from seeing clients. Subsequently, the interrogators asked whether she had also been having sex with his older brother (a charge that never appears in any of the other records of the case), but she denied it. She also denied that Sōbei had forced himself on her: "It's all my fault," she said, "Sōbei is blameless" (*nanigoto mo watakushi no tsumi, Sōbei no tsumi ni wa kore naku*). When asked about her future, Tora suggested that she might return to the Tomitaya and work there for a few more years, at least long enough to dispatch her obligations to her parents, Sadaemon, and also Sōbei. The investigators wondered why she thought she was indebted to Sōbei, and she replied that she had caused him trouble by "bothering" (*tedasu*) him. According to her version of events, he had not been able to refuse her advances.

Tora's testimony is difficult to reconcile with any of the other participants' accounts of this incident. The idea that prostitutes ran away in order to escape debts, rather than abuse, was a trope brothel keepers often employed to explain why their employees had absconded. Curiously, however, Sadaemon never mentioned that Tora owed money, even though this detail might have bolstered his case against Isaburō and Matsu. Moreover, Tora's insistence that returning to the Tomitaya would be an act of filial piety is surprising, given that Isaburō and Matsu had on several occasions expressed their opposition to such an outcome. It seems likely that the Tomo bosses (who, after all, specialized in violence) had influenced Tora's testimony, convincing her to present her story in terms that were preapproved by Sadaemon and his allies in Mitarai. In fact, the observer from Takeharaya noted at the end of his account that he had written a letter to Mitarai informing officials there that Tora had done a good job with her statement. They responded that they had been worried that she would not acquit herself well, but they were relieved to read his description of her interview.

In fact, Tora's recollection of the incident served the brothel keeper's interests in several respects. It recast the terms of the dispute by calling into question Isaburō and Matsu's story that they were protecting their daughter from abuse, overturning the narrative about filial daughters and desperate parents that Isaburō had crafted so carefully in his own testimony. Tora never denied her obligations to her parents, but she balanced every mention of this responsibility with an assertion that she was also indebted to the brothel keeper. This placed the relationship between parent and child, which had occupied a privileged place in the gendered order, on equal footing with the contractual relationship between employer and employee. At the same time, by insisting that she had been the sexual aggressor in her relationship with Sōbei, Tora described herself as a temptress, a role that was completely at odds with the impression her stepfather had hoped to create. Isaburō had depicted her as a filial daughter whose sacrifice supported her family, but she portrayed herself as an outsider who had damaged Sadaemon's household through her reckless pursuit of pleasure. When her interrogators castigated her, pointing out that her lust was to blame for the entire dispute, she remained silent. Finally, they indicated that they were leaning toward arranging a marriage for her, which would keep her out of trouble. But they made sure she heard their conclusion that she was a "bad sort" (*koitsu ikenu yatsu*).

A few weeks after this interview, Sadaemon and Isaburō finally reached an agreement: Tora would marry Sōbei. When she returned to the Tomitaya, she would be considered a chaste wife (*teijo*), and Sadaemon would no longer require her to work as a prostitute. (Oddly, however, the record of the agreement calls her by her working name, Koeda, and since Sadaemon had already proven himself willing to abandon his promises, one wonders at the sincerity of this statement.) This was the solution that had been tentatively proposed by the neutral village representatives at Tora's interview. If the Mitarai response to Takeharaya's letter is any indication, it was an acceptable solution to the brothel keeper. Isaburō's initial reaction does not appear in the documentary record. In any case, he pressed his seal to the agreement, in which all the parties agreed that they would bear no grudges. Only Tora and Sōbei's seals are absent from the contract that determined their future.[51]

Since the parties involved in this dispute created constant doubt about their adversaries' motives and agendas, it is not clear who would have been most satisfied with this settlement. If Isaburō was motivated by concern for his stepdaughter, if his bitterness toward Sadaemon's entire family was genuine, and if he was correct in his characterization of Tora and Sōbei's relationship as a series of unwanted advances that a teenage indentured servant was powerless to resist, then this was likely not a happy ending for either Tora or her parents. Even if Sōbei's suit had been welcome, Tora had married into a household in which her in-laws resented her, which was a difficult position for any young bride. A brief entry from the

Mitarai population register might confirm the interpretation that Tora's marriage was unstable: five years later, Sōbei left Mitarai to become an adopted son of a shopkeeper in Osaka, and the record of his departure makes no mention of his wife.[52] Perhaps she had died in the interim. Or perhaps, like so many other women of her era, she simply disappeared from the documentary record as soon as she stopped causing problems for the men around her.

On the other hand, although Tora's version of her own story was likely shaped by pressure from the brothel keeper, the Tomo outlaws, and Mitarai officials, it is also possible that she was telling the truth when she insisted that her affair with Sōbei was consensual. In that case, Tora won the dispute and the brothel keeper suffered a loss, because he could no longer send her out to see customers.[53] Even so, it seems unlikely that rewarding Tora was the village officials' intention, since they had concluded in no uncertain terms that she was a "bad sort" and the incident was her fault. It is more plausible that they decided legitimating Tora and Sōbei's relationship was the only way to reconcile the parties to the dispute while upholding the so-called rules of teahouses. Once the two were married, Isaburō could not break Tora's contract and squander Sadaemon's investment by sending her into service elsewhere, and Sadaemon could not continue to violate the "rules in any teahouse in any province" by tolerating an illicit relationship between his son and his employee. Neither party would be a clear victor, but the principle that the "rules of teahouses" should prevail (an argument closely linked to Sadaemon's interests) would be maintained.

Indeed, according to the "rules of teahouses," Sadaemon was the winner in one important respect: he did not have to watch as a woman he had trained was sent to work in a rival brothel. According to the same logic, Isaburō was the loser: he lost the opportunity to profit from his daughter's labor by sending her into service in Tomo. While the authorities in Takehara and Mitarai sent memoranda back and forth and quarreled over the times and places for meetings, Sadaemon had found a more efficient method of protecting his investment in his employee. No matter how much support he might receive from the local authorities, no one knew better than an Inland Sea brothel keeper that there were many ways of doing business, and going through official channels was not always the most productive. Although the large market for women in the Inland Sea might have worked to Isaburō's advantage when he was looking for potential employers for his daughter, Sadaemon could use professional connections forged within that market against him. Those connections were embodied by the Tomo bosses, who took the decisive action that brought this case to its resolution. In the end, Sadaemon understood that the dispute could only be solved by taking advantage of his position in a cartel that self-regulated the businesses of the "pleasure quarter" according to a commonly agreed-upon set of rules. These were not articulated in the measured edicts of officialdom, but in the rough justice of outlaws. If the incident was not resolved precisely as he had hoped, at least he could be content knowing that neither Isaburō nor another Inland Sea brothel keeper would reap the dividends from his investment.

In the middle of the nineteenth century, the geography of prostitution in the Inland Sea did not conform to maps of counties and domains, which carved the region into stable political jurisdictions. A brothel keeper in Mitarai might exchange women with a counterpart in Fukuyama, an itinerant prostitute from Hakata might journey to Konpira to work during the Great Play, and an indentured *yūjo* from Takehara might accompany a customer on a pilgrimage to Itsukushima. To some extent, this disregard for jurisdiction was a function of the setting, a maritime region where circuits had long been more relevant than boundaries. But it was also a product of a steady rise in travel—initially commercial and then recreational—throughout the late eighteenth and early nineteenth centuries. There was more traffic overall, which meant a greater potential to profit, but travelers had to be enticed to stop, and they were fickle, choosing different ports depending on the season or the time of the month. Adjusting their business model to fit this climate, brothel keepers formed relationships with counterparts in other domains so that they could unload women when traffic decreased or acquire them quickly when demand spiked. The concept of the "rules of the pleasure quarter" emerged from these connections and made it easier for proprietors to form new ties. Although the "rules" were not concrete or undisputed, the idea that they existed was important. It established a baseline level of trust in the market, which allowed brothel keepers to be confident that rivals in other domains would not poach their women. It also created a loose set of principles for resolving conflict when samurai officials could not reach across jurisdictional boundaries to arbitrate disputes.

The tension between brothel keepers' ideas of how their business should function and the ideal of gendered order is evident in Sadaemon's effort to assert his authority over Tora. He used the brothel keepers' association and his contacts in the underworld to attack the premise of Isaburō's case for custody, which was expressed in the familiar vocabulary of benevolence and protection. To this end, Sadaemon made two claims. First, he argued that Tora and her parents had a moral obligation to ensure that he could recoup his investment in Tora's body. This assertion put the contractual relationship between master and servant on equal footing with the bond between parent and child. He also insisted that Tora could make her own choices: she had *chosen* to pursue Sōbei and make trouble for her employers, and she could *choose* to remedy the situation by returning to the brothel.

Sadaemon's insistence on Tora's capacity for independent choice and action—or, to put it another way, his assertion of her agency—was an awkward fit with the narrative that portrayed prostitutes as filial daughters who worked to serve their parents' and masters' interests. Isaburō's story had portrayed Tora as a victim: she conformed to the model of the dutiful daughter who was incapable of performing any role other than sacrificing on behalf of her family. But Tora's testimony, of which the Mitarai brothel keepers and officials heartily approved, and indeed, probably dictated, depicted a completely different person. This version of Tora was a manipulative girl who lied and schemed to get what she wanted. Her story asked the interrogators to believe that a fifteen-year-old indentured prostitute, who had been sent into service in a brothel at the age of thirteen and kidnapped by a group of outcasts at the age of sixteen, was fully capable of taking responsibility for her actions, but Sōbei was a powerless victim of female lust. In reality, Sadaemon and his allies had severely limited Tora's options; after all, the Tomo bosses had kidnapped her from Fukuyama and sent her straight back to the brothel. Yet when she was asked why she had "chosen" to return to work, she claimed to have acted on her own initiative.

Whether or not Tora was telling the truth, the Mitarai brothel keeper and his allies approved of this narrative for a simple reason: if Tora asserted agency, then the blame for the entire incident could be placed on her small shoulders. This was an effective strategy, and the neutral village officials concluded that she was a "bad sort." This was not because she was a prostitute who had sexual relations with many men, or even because she had run away from the brothel at her parents' request. Instead, they determined that she was culpable because (according to her testimony, at least) she had used her sexuality for her own gain, endeavoring to entrap the brothel keeper's son. They condemned her for her "desire" (*yokujō*); as a prostitute, she could be the receptacle for others' desires, but she was not entitled to her own. By claiming to be a sexual aggressor, she had discredited herself in the eyes of her interrogators and also undercut her stepfather's appeal to officials' sensibilities: a dutiful daughter was a figure to be praised and admired, but a lustful woman did not deserve the same kind of consideration. Her stepfather's attempt to shield her from the consequences of her own choices would be misguided at best, and at worst a cynical ploy to take advantage of the situation by sending her into service while she was already under contract.

This invocation of autonomy was hardly empowering, and it was applied to a girl who in reality had very few choices. But this was typical of the broader discourse about female agency that flourished during the nineteenth century as people across Japan grappled with women's engagement in the market economy. By the end of the Tokugawa period, when Tora entered service, women's labor outside the household had become commonplace, and the economic impact of their work was obvious. Prostitution, in particular, was an enormous industry, which had reached almost every corner of the archipelago and played a major role in supporting poor families and sustaining entire communities. It had even become possible for commoner officials in provincial towns to form credible arguments that the overregulation of this business posed a threat to their economic survival. But poor women did not necessarily benefit from these changes. In some cases, the chance to work in a faraway province could be a path to social mobility, but for the women in Tora's situation, who were moved around to serve everyone's interests but their own, mobility and autonomy were inversely correlated.

Yet this did not prevent some from blaming women like Tora for choices that they had never made. In part, the idea that prostitutes were free agents was a reaction to a changed economic landscape that presented women with more options to work in all kinds of environments. Because they labored outside the household and moved across jurisdictions, prostitutes represented a larger group of women whose engagement with the market had allowed them to distance themselves (both figuratively and literally) from the authority of their husbands, fathers, village elders, and governors. At the same time, prostitutes' trade presented its own, particular challenge to patriarchal hierarchies. The rapid expansion of a business that separated women from their families and marketed sex raised the alarming possibility that all social relations might be subsumed by market relations. In this scenario, women might emerge as autonomous actors who sold their bodies and their labor to the highest bidder, oblivious to their obligations to their husbands and fathers. Regardless of their individual situations, prostitutes were harbingers of this dystopian future. As such, they were anxiously examined for signs that they were benefitting, either materially or socially, from their work. Even indentured teenage girls were scrutinized and derided at the slightest indication that they did not conform to social norms that demanded female passivity and self-sacrifice.

Meanwhile, women who worked in the sex trade, particularly those whose migration patterns had separated them from their families, often found that they had no effective means of countering these allegations. Because officials celebrated female passivity as a virtue, prostitutes could not advocate for their own interests without proving that they were morally compromised, and thus undermining their own appeals. If they could not rely on their parents to speak for them, they could not petition for protection as dutiful daughters or loyal subjects. Moreover, both samurai officials and commoner elites were increasingly invested in the idea that prostitutes and their families were morally suspect, or, at the very least, that the women who worked in the sex trade were likely to be more selfish than those who remained safely contained within the bonds of marriage and family. Samurai used this line of argument to absolve themselves of responsibility for creating the conditions that had allowed the sex trade to thrive, while peasant elites pursued these ideas in order to blame prostitutes and prostitution for economic and cultural changes that had undermined village patriarchs' authority. For many indentured women, including those who survived their terms of service without needing to call on parents or officials for assistance, these changes in the social meanings attached to work in the sex trade might have been barely perceptible. But for women like Tora, who asked her parents to help her escape the brothel—for whatever reason—they could be devastating.

CONCLUSION

As the chapters of this book have moved from the mountains of Akita to the islands of the Inland Sea, they have also traced the development of a vast market for sexual services. In the seventeenth century, prostitution was primarily an urban phenomenon, fueled by the demographic movement of unattached young men to recently opened mines and newly constructed cities. But by the eighteenth and the nineteenth centuries, the locus of growth had shifted to smaller provincial towns, where it was powered by the expansion of commercial agriculture and the emergence of a culture of travel. By the close of the era, the sex trade had spread its tentacles into every corner of the archipelago, from Niigata to Nagasaki, from the great metropolis of Edo to the small port of Mitarai.

Although the expansion of the sex trade was a product of broader economic trends, it also generated growth on its own terms. Urban neighborhoods thrived when they became the sites of *okabasho*, post stations employing "serving girls" prospered, and ports that featured prostitution attracted free-spending sailors. A reputation for sexually available women was a boon to any district that relied on the patronage of travelers; as even the most unsophisticated merchants were aware, men who came to spend money drinking and carousing in brothels would also buy souvenirs and trinkets in nearby shops. Meanwhile, in stagnating agricultural areas, the income earned from daughters' service in prostitution was a lifeline for desperate peasant households. If a quick injection of ten or twenty *ryō* for a brothel contract was more often applied to loan interest and tax bills than invested in fields and fertilizer, at least it could forestall ruin for another year. In that sense, prostitution enabled tax collectors and wealthy commoners to continue to extract revenue from overburdened cultivators who might otherwise have absconded or defaulted. Prostitution, like the service sector more generally, had become a crucial component of Tokugawa Japan's economy.

But as it expanded, the sex trade undermined the political ideal of the patriarchal household. Samurai envisioned a realm in which husbands and fathers wielded benevolent authority over their wives, children, and other dependents, and in which every commoner household reflected the shogun or daimyō's dominion over his subjects. Initially, magistrates in the shogun's great cities imagined that the market for female bodies to provide sexual services could be managed in ways that supported this gendered order, which structured both the household and the state and strengthened both institutions through their association with each other. By the late eighteenth century, however, it was clear that the market had begun to follow its own, destructive course. Parents sold their daughters to faraway provinces, young men in the countryside defied their elders to spend money in brothels, single women in port towns supported themselves by selling sex, and rural prostitutes in glittering hair ornaments advertised the material compensations of work outside the household.

The gendered order of the realm had fallen victim to the creative and destructive energies of entrepreneurial commoners—post-station innkeepers, parents who hired their daughters out as geisha or indentured them to brothels, and "selling women" of all kinds. But it would be too simplistic to frame this as a case in which outmatched samurai authorities yielded to economic pressure from those lower on the social scale. If the growth of the sex trade represented the triumph of the market over the rigid Tokugawa-supported hierarchy, then it was a victory that many samurai officials had actively abetted. Magistrates in shogunal cities such as Edo and Nagasaki worked to maintain the logic of the household, continuing to insist that the only recognized prostitutes would be those whose work served their parents. But their counterparts along the highways and in provincial towns, where the expansion of the sex trade had been most dramatic, found that they could not disaggregate their interests in social order and economic development; they depended on the revenue generated by prostitution to fund their administrations and to stabilize communities of poor peasants and townspeople who otherwise would have been deprived of their livelihoods. Given a choice between preserving the abstract ideal of the household and nurturing the sex trade, they followed the latter course in nearly every circumstance, even as they issued edict after edict suggesting otherwise. In fact, shogunal officials in the countryside considered the growth of the business to be central to so many of their political interests—including raising tax receipts and subsidizing the transportation system—that by the nineteenth century, they were even willing to ignore peasants' protests that the lure of commercial sex was disturbing young men's investment in the most ideologically freighted of all productive endeavors: growing rice.

Meanwhile, for village elites, the threatened collapse of the Tokugawa social order was not a welcome development. They were heavily invested in at least some aspects of the social and legal framework of the status system, particularly those that preserved the patriarchal household. As elders and heads of household themselves, they looked to the state for assistance as they lost control over the sexual habits and spending patterns of their dependents. Thus even if they patronized brothels in their spare time, they could not wholeheartedly support policies that prioritized economic development over correct "manners and customs." In their view, it was the government's responsibility to protect hierarchical modes of authority from the destructive force of the market.

For other men, the triumph of the market might have been freeing. Commoners' creation of a thriving "culture of play," which prioritized pleasure and profit over the officially propagated values of diligence and submission, is often recognized as one of the great achievements of the Tokugawa era. According to this interpretation, ordinary people's embrace of travel, pilgrimage, and prostitution was a form of emancipation from the stultifying concerns of everyday life as well as the confines of a rigid social and political hierarchy. For example, H. D. Harootunian has described a "sense of liberation" in the late Tokugawa period, which "demanded freedom from fixed positions as a condition for endless movement" and "authorize[d] crossing established geographical and social boundaries." He extends this language of emancipation to apply to men's celebration of commodified sex, portraying their indulgence in "the joys of the flesh" as "concern for autonomy of the body."[1]

Yet this new freedom for some was oppressive for others. Men pursued "autonomy of the body" by commodifying women's bodies; as a result, commoners' "culture of play" had the unfortunate side effect of transforming tens of thousands of poor women into products. By the nineteenth century, they were circulating within a rapidly expanding market that had broken free of official constraints but was no less constraining for them. This market was more sophisticated and differentiated than the free-for-all of buying and selling that had prevailed in a place like early seventeenth-century Innai, but for the women caught up in this system of exchange, the end result was much the same: they were valued primarily for the amount men would pay for access to their bodies, and they were unable to appeal for official consideration as filial daughters and loyal subjects, much less as human beings with individual rights.

There was no question that the Tokugawa authorities' vision of status order had been confining for women: it subordinated them to male household heads and emphasized the values of obedience and submission. Indeed, some must have welcomed the opportunity to step outside their narrowly defined roles as wives and daughters. The financially independent "widows" of Niigata, like the Kansai cotton-weaving women who used their newfound purchasing power to defy scandalized village elders, were among those who exploited the possibilities created by the market economy's challenge to the status quo. But for the vast majority of women who worked in the sex trade, the crisis of the gendered order, and the disintegration of the limited protection it offered, was hardly a form of liberation.

Ironically, a newfound recognition of prostitutes' agency was a product of the same developments that turned so many into products. As the second half of this book has argued, by the nineteenth century, some samurai and elite commoners began to perceive women who worked in the sex trade as autonomous economic actors rather than daughters embedded in families and communities. This new idea could be construed as empowering for women, since it recognized that they were capable of acting in their own interests. But the attention paid to prostitutes' volition—the repeated assertions that they chose or welcomed their work, or that they were motivated by the prospect of wearing gold hair ornaments—had exactly the opposite effect. Prostitutes were often most empowered when they were *not* asserting agency: they were far more capable of influencing authorities to act in their interests when they were able to play the role of passive daughters, and when their parents were able to speak for them. To them, recognition as individuals was not as valuable as consideration as dutiful daughters, and they lost an important means of appeal when they were perceived as dangerously autonomous rather than inherently submissive.

Many of these trends in the late Tokugawa period persisted into the Meiji era (1868–1912), ensuring that prostitution would continue to play an outsized role in modern Japan's economy. To borrow Morisaki Kazue's provocative phrase, the archipelago became a "kingdom of whoring" (*baishun ōkoku*).[2] As railroads were constructed along the old highways, more young men began to leave their villages. They congregated in big cities and provincial towns, which were home to factories, garrisons, naval bases, and shipyards. As in the Tokugawa period, this heightened mobility contributed to a steadily growing demand for sexual services, and supply increased accordingly. Between 1884 and 1916, the number of registered brothel prostitutes (*shōgi*) nearly doubled—from 28,432 to 54,049—while the total Japanese population grew by only 50 percent. This total did not account for 79,348 geisha and 48,291 registered barmaids, most of whom provided sexual services. According to Sheldon Garon's estimate, by the early Taishō period, the sex trade, even excluding streetwalkers, unlicensed prostitutes, and those in brothels overseas, employed about 1 out of 31 young Japanese women. Unsurprisingly, most were from poor families, and a disproportionate number came from villages in the northeast.[3] The same people who had supplied labor to provincial brothels in the eighteenth and nineteenth centuries—desperate farmers defaulting on loans—continued to do so in the modern era.

Like the Tokugawa shogunate, the Meiji state depended on prostitutes' labor to achieve its political ends. Income from brothels proved particularly important to the development of infrastructure. In some cases, brothel keepers and prostitutes made voluntary contributions to building projects, hoping to cement their eroding status within their communities. Whereas in the Tokugawa period they might have geared their donations toward the construction of playhouses, in the late nineteenth century they helped finance local elementary schools.[4] At the same time, taxes on brothels, euphemistically called "installment payments," poured into local administrators' coffers, where they were used to fund a variety of projects, from police investigations to public health initiatives. In some prefectures, they were even used to pay for the violent suppression of the Freedom and People's Rights Movement.[5] Although Meiji statesmen would never have listed the growth of prostitution as one of their goals, many of their interests lay with the expansion of the sex trade. In this, they resembled their predecessors in the shogunate, who claimed to be limiting prostitution even as they deliberately allowed it to thrive.

Meanwhile, the old arguments that the sex trade destabilized the household continued unabated in the new era. Rather than meeting in villages and submitting petitions to samurai magistrates, however, local elites met in prefectural assemblies and issued petitions to prefectural governors. During the first Gunma Prefectural Assembly in 1879, for example, representatives composed a proposal to ban prostitution, arguing that the business encouraged reckless spending and caused the deterioration of the family.[6] In the first years of the period, at least, there is evidence that local skirmishes over prostitution were being fought on familiar ground: elite men were still appealing to the state to protect a vision of social order that subordinated women and young men to paternalistic heads of household. The primary anxiety attached to prostitution in the Tokugawa period—that youths might use their newfound earning and purchasing power to assert control over their own sexual and reproductive behavior—remained potent.

Ultimately, however, new currents of thought and changes in the law would alter the social context of work in the sex trade and inspire a new national discourse on prostitution. In 1872, responding to domestic and foreign critics of Japan's sex trade, the new government issued the "Edict for the Liberation of Geisha and Prostitutes" (*Geishōgi kaihōrei*), which required brothels and geisha houses to release their employees from the terms of their indenture contracts.[7] Newspapers were full of reports of young women streaming out of the former "pleasure quarters," but in fact, the new law did little to change the status quo for women who worked in the business. Many found that they had nowhere to go and no other way to make a living, and when brothels reopened as "room rental establishments" (*kashizashiki-gyō*), they agreed to new contracts with similar terms. In 1875, the government reconfirmed the legality of indenture agreements for prostitution.[8] But the edict did have one important and lasting effect: it introduced the ideal of liberation into public discourse on the sex trade.[9]

This new emphasis on freedom (at least in theory if not in practice) was an awkward fit with the older moral justification of prostitution as an expression of filial piety. Meiji-era officials did not wish to "free" women to sell sex for their own personal profit or gratification. At the turn of the century, bureaucrats still commended daughters who sacrificed themselves for their parents and contrasted them with selfish women who entered the business to pursue promiscuous sex and easy money.[10] But in the post-emancipation era, it was difficult to distinguish these groups and nearly impossible for prostitutes to present themselves as passive, and therefore moral, daughters. After all, they had rendered their consent, affirming that they had freely chosen their profession. This made them increasingly vulnerable to the claim that they were self-interested and also to some degree absolved the state from responsibility for their plight.[11]

Meanwhile, Meiji intellectuals, many of whom were influenced by European and American sexual mores, disparaged prostitutes—and all promiscuous women—as impure. Proponents of "civilization and enlightenment" (*bunmei kaika*), such as Fukuzawa Yukichi (1835–1901) and Mori Arinori (1847–89), promoted the idea that monogamous marriage was the only moral form of sexual interaction between men and women. They differed in their tolerance of men's extramarital exploits (Fukuzawa excused them as an unfortunate consequence of natural urges, while Mori was less forgiving), but they agreed that women were irrevocably tainted by promiscuity. In a series of essays in 1885, Fukuzawa repeatedly described work in the sex trade as "degrading," invoking images of filth and mud.[12] The Christian activists who began to take up the cause of abolition in the 1890s employed similar vocabulary. Their national organization, formed in 1911, was named the "Purity Society" (*Kakuseikai*), and its publications described prostitutes as "bad elements" and "outcastes who should be managed in filthy brothels and slums."[13]

The association of female promiscuity with filth, which had never been a prominent component of early modern criticisms of the sex trade, was likely related to new concerns about venereal disease. Like the idealization of "pure," monogamous marriage, anxiety about contagion was influenced by foreign—specifically European—ideas about sexuality and the body. During the last years of the Tokugawa era, foreigners residing in treaty ports entreated the shogunate to adopt a system of testing prostitutes for syphilis. The officials in charge of these areas complied, requiring regular examinations for prostitutes serving foreign (typically white) clients. Eventually, Meiji officials, who wished to safeguard the health of male army recruits and factory workers, began to see the wisdom of implementing a testing system for prostitutes serving the domestic market as well.[14] By the 1880s, women across the archipelago were subject to regular examinations, and the notion of contagion had become central to both the state's efforts to manage prostitution and activists' efforts to abolish it. This marked a clear change from the recent past. Tokugawa-era peasants had occasionally raised the issue of disease in their petitions against prostitution, but it had never been their chief concern. Where Tokugawa-era commoners and samurai had seen the dangers of prostitution in economic terms, perceiving the potential of the vast market for sexual services to alter the hierarchical structures of the household and the state, Meiji-era commentators—both regulationists and abolitionists—focused their anxiety on the physical bodies of Japanese citizens. As a result, sex, rather than money, finally became the dominant issue in the reformist discourses and regulatory practices surrounding prostitution.

At the same time, the lingering memory of the early modern period created new, and increasingly unattainable, standards for the moral behavior of prostitutes. Whether intellectuals indulged in nostalgia for a bygone age or congratulated themselves on the achievements of civilization and enlightenment (or did both at once), they used the Tokugawa era as a foil for the modern.[15] But in doing so, they invoked a fictionalized version of the recent past. Elite men did not look back to the Tokugawa period and see "serving girls," streetwalkers, and *goke;* they saw only the *yūjo* who were the heroines of tragic plays and stories. Their rhetoric created the impression that those working as prostitutes and barmaids in the present were neither as culturally accomplished nor as virtuous as their early modern counterparts. It also implied that prostitutes in the present were far more fortunate than their predecessors and thus less entitled to complain about their fate. After all, they were theoretically free to leave the profession at any time. Of course, this line of argument did not acknowledge that many women were still bound by filial obligations that made it impossible for them to terminate their contracts without betraying their families and forsaking any future claims to economic or emotional support.

Long after the Meiji era came to a close, elite men continued to insist that prostitutes in the past had sacrificed on behalf of their families, whereas prostitutes in the present were selfish and spoiled. This type of discourse tended to reach a fever pitch during eras when the earning and purchasing power of young women became visible, and older men were perceived to be in crisis. During the Occupation period, for example, Japanese intellectuals argued that prostitutes in the prewar era had been motivated by filial piety, whereas the *panpan* girls who catered to American servicemen were frivolous and greedy.[16] The same anxieties about self-interest and acquisitiveness replacing duty and sacrifice also surfaced in media discussions of the "compensated dating" (*enjo kōsai*) phenomenon in the 1990s, just as salarymen seemed to be losing their place at the top of Japan's social hierarchy.[17] This discussion, which focused on the supposedly voluntary exploits of middle-class Japanese students who solicited older men in return for expensive gifts, formed a counterpoint to a more wrenching public debate about the state's obligation to the mostly poor, non-Japanese "comfort women" who had been forced to service Japanese soldiers at military brothels during the Pacific War.[18] At a time when feminist activists drew parallels between the suffering of comfort women, young girls indentured to brothels in the prewar era, and women trafficked from other Asian nations to work in the contemporary Japanese sex industry, conservative politicians and media commentators turned their attention to a familiar, titillating narrative about "shameless" girls eagerly exchanging sex for money.

The idea that young women's greed is responsible for the undesirable commercialization of sex and the family has resurfaced continually since the mid-nineteenth century. But the recurrence of this discourse is subject to an odd type of historical amnesia: prostitutes' selfishness and acquisitiveness is always viewed as a new and frighteningly modern or postmodern problem that never existed in the idealized past. This approach to the issue obscures the late Tokugawa debate about women's engagement with the sex trade and the burgeoning market economy. In its place, it constructs a comforting vision of a bygone era in which women were always passive and therefore beyond reproach. Ironically, this dichotomy—between the self-sacrificing prostitutes of the past and the self-interested harlots of the present—is itself a legacy of the early modern period.

But perhaps the persistence of this trope should not be surprising. In many ways, the postmodern era is closer to the early modern past than we realize. After all, female promiscuity is tolerated, if not celebrated; women's labor patterns and spending habits are portrayed as a threat to the traditional family; and young women's fertility is the subject of constant official scrutiny. At the same time, with prostitutes taking advantage of new technologies to market themselves directly to their clients, the sex trade has once again become highly visible. Now, as then, social commentators express their anxiety at the extent to which sex has become commoditized by scrutinizing prostitutes' motivations, often overlooking those who are compelled by poverty—or forcibly trafficked—in order to focus on those who seem to be motivated by greed. The text-messaging high school student carrying a Louis Vuitton handbag has replaced the serving girl wearing gold hair ornaments as the figure who captures the popular imagination by exhibiting the material compensations of work in the sex trade, presenting the uncomfortable, unlikely, but nonetheless tantalizing possibility that prostitution can be a path toward social mobility and individual economic empowerment.

NOTES

FOREWORD

1. Scott, "Gender: A Useful Category."
2. One is reminded of Wolf's description in *Women and the Family in Rural Taiwan*, chap. 13, of "filial daughters" in mid-twentieth century Taiwan who were similarly indentured into prostitution in order to support their parents. In Taiwan, too, the term "filial" was used without irony.
3. Sommer, *Sex, Law, and Society*.
4. In the late 1920s, when Shanghai's total female industrial labor force numbered just over 173,000 (of whom about 84,000 worked in cotton-spinning mills), there were an estimated 120,000 prostitutes in the city, totaling nearly 10 percent of its women (Hershatter, *Dangerous Pleasures*, 39–40, 422; and see also Henriot, *Prostitution and Sexuality in Shanghai*).

INTRODUCTION

1. See the difficulties mentioned in Walkowitz, *Prostitution and Victorian Society*, 14–15; Hershatter, *Dangerous Pleasures*, 38–39; Rosen, *Lost Sisterhood*, 75; and Gilfoyle, *City of Eros*, 57–58.
2. These counts were made immediately following the Tenpō Reforms (1842), when there were proportionally more *yūjo* in Yoshiwara because 2,000 clandestine prostitutes from other districts had been relocated there. My estimate is compiled from information on Shin-Yoshiwara's population of *yūjo* in 1844–46 in Heibonsha chihō shiryō sentā, ed., *Tōkyō-to no chimei*, 633; the number of "serving girls" the shogunate

permitted to work in Shinagawa, Itabashi, Senju, and Naitō Shinjuku listed in Usami, *Shukuba to meshimori onna*, 19; and Seigle, *Yoshiwara*, 210. On the problems of delineating Edo's boundaries, see Katō, "Governing Edo," in *Edo and Paris*, ed. McClain et al., 43–45.

3. Griffis, *Mikado's Empire*, 2: 555.

4. See Allison, "Memoirs of the Orient."

5. Christine Overall summarizes this debate in "What's Wrong with Prostitution?" Also see the essays in Spector, ed., *Prostitution and Pornography*. Because this debate has been so influential, historians have often framed their discussions about prostitution around the question "Did they choose this profession, and if so, why?" See, e.g., Stansell, *City of Women*, 171–92.

6. On the connection between religion and sexuality in Tokugawa Japan and the diversity of beliefs and practices surrounding sex, see Hur, *Prayer and Play in Late Tokugawa Japan;* Lindsey, *Fertility and Pleasure;* and Sawada, "Sexual Relations as Religious Practice in the Late Tokugawa Period."

7. See Fuess, *Divorce in Japan*, 18–74; Walthall, "Life Cycle of Farm Women"; and Amy Stanley, "Adultery, Punishment, and Reconciliation."

8. Lie, "Transformation of Sexual Work," 312; Deuchler, "Propagating Female Virtues."

9. Traganou, *Tōkaidō Road*, 81.

10. See Ropp, "Ambiguous Images."

11. Sommer, *Sex, Law, and Society*, 272–75.

12. See Theiss, *Disgraceful Matters*.

13. Fass, "Cultural/Social History," describes prostitution as an issue of "sexuality on the margins," for example, and Karras writes: "Very few if any societies have treated prostitution neutrally as work; it has always had implications for the status of the women involved which derive from its sexual nature" (*Common Women*, 9). Studies that consider modern regulationists' and abolitionists' attempts to reform the sexual practices of populations they deemed undisciplined include Walkowitz, *Prostitution and Victorian Society*, and Levine, *Prostitution, Race, and Politics*. A notable exception to this approach is White, *Comforts of Home*. For a useful overview of the state of the field as of 1999, see Gilfoyle, "Prostitutes in History."

14. My argument here is inspired by a similar discussion in Johnson, *Soul by Soul*, 17.

15. A more nuanced take on this issue can be found in Howell, *Geographies of Identity*.

16. Scott, *Gender and the Politics of History*, 46. Thanks to Melissa Macauley for pointing this out.

17. There are brief discussions of the relationship between gender and status in Howell, *Geographies of Identity*, 27, and Botsman, *Punishment and Power*, 73–74. Botsman writes that women were a "trans-status" category, while Howell maintains that

women were relatively "unmarked" by status. For an argument that gendered difference often proved less relevant than status difference, see Anderson, *Place in Public*, 19–27.

18. See Nagano, "Bakuhan hō to josei"; Mega, *Hankachō no naka no onnatachi*.

19. See, e.g., Wigen, *Making of a Japanese Periphery*, and Howell, *Capitalism from Within*.

20. The phrase "culture of play" is from Harootunian, "Late Tokugawa Culture and Thought." In a different vein, Eiko Ikegami argues in *Bonds of Civility* that the floating world, which prioritized sensual experience and aesthetic expression, allowed for "categorical protest" against the rigidly hierarchical Tokugawa state.

21. This is a common argument of feminist social historians in Japan. See Sone, *Shōfu to kinsei shakai*, and Usami, *Shukuba to meshimori onna*. The cultural historian Kurachi Katsunao makes a similar point in *Sei to karada no kinseishi*, 80–81.

22. Kobayashi, "Kōshōsei no seiritsu to tenkai," in *Nihon joseishi*, 3: 128–29; 148.

23. Sone, *Shōfu to kinsei shakai*, 26–29.

24. I translate *onna* as "girl" in these instances because the word "girl," more than "woman," seems to capture both the sexualized nature of their work (e.g., "call girl," "bar girl," "dancing girl") and the low regard in which they were held.

25. In contrast, Hershatter found that the working conditions and material situations of streetwalkers and courtesans in modern Shanghai diverged so radically that there was no meaningful similarity between them other than occupation (*Dangerous Pleasures*, 19).

26. See Pflugfelder, *Cartographies of Desire*, and Hanasaki, *Edo no kagemajaya*.

27. Pflugfelder, *Cartographies of Desire*, 93–95.

28. Ibid., 156.

29. Hershatter, *Dangerous Pleasures*, 4.

1. ADULTEROUS PROSTITUTES, PAWNED WIVES, AND PURCHASED WOMEN

1. Umezu, *Umezu Masakage nikki* (cited below as UMN), 2: 121. *Umezu Masakage nikki* is notoriously difficult to interpret. The glosses in Satō, *Akita-ken yūri shi*, 17–34, are helpful in this regard. When I have relied on another scholar's interpretation, I have cited that scholar along with the original source.

2. Hasegawa, "Keichō Genna-ki ni okeru Dewa kuni no shakai jōkyō," in *"Tōhoku" no seiritsu to tenkai*, ed. Numata, 18.

3. Yamaguchi, *Sakoku to kaikoku*, 4–5.

4. On the significance of public display in Tokugawa-era punishment, particularly the visual impact of severed heads, see Botsman, *Punishment and Power*, 26–27.

5. See, e.g., Jansen, "Tosa in the Sixteenth Century," and Katsumata and Colcutt, "Development of Sengoku Law."

6. On Hideyoshi's many political innovations, see Berry, *Hideyoshi*, 99–146, and "Public Peace and Private Attachment."

7. See Vaporis, *Tour of Duty*.

8. See Hall, "Rule by Status in Tokugawa Japan."

9. Howell, *Geographies of Identity*, 20–29; Botsman, *Punishment and Power*, 59–61.

10. On the cadastral surveys, see Brown, *Central Authority and Local Autonomy*. On villages, see Ooms, *Tokugawa Village Practice*, 72.

11. Mines such as the one in Innai technically belonged to the shogun. Domains were supposed to pay taxes (*unjōkin*) on their output, but beginning in 1617, the shogun returned these fees as a "gift" to Satake Yoshinobu, who had fought on his side in the battles of Osaka in 1615. On the early history of Innai, see Akita-ken, ed., *Akita kenshi*, vol. 2: *Kinsei jō* (1964), 301–28. On the importance of mining to domain revenues and development, see Yoon, "Domain and Bakufu."

12. This was roughly equal to the number of commoners in the castle town Kubota. Yamaguchi, "Kinsei shoki ni Akita han ni okeru kōzan machi," 210.

13. "Ugo no kuni Senboku Ogachi-gun Innai ginzanki" (cited below as "Innai ginzanki"), 505.

14. Yamaguchi, "Kinsei shoki ni Akita han ni okeru kōzan machi," 197–89, 201.

15. Hasegawa, "Keichō Genna-ki ni okeru Dewa kuni no shakai jōkyō."

16. Ooms, *Tokugawa Village Practice*.

17. "Innai ginzanki," 505.

18. Ooms, *Tokugawa Village Practice*, 110.

19. See Yamaguchi Keiji, "Umezu Masakage."

20. This drive was evident in the masses of edicts issued during the first half of the seventeenth century. See Nakai and McClain, "Commercial Change and Urban Growth."

21. Nelson, "Slavery in Medieval Japan."

22. Conlan, *State of War*, 204. Shinran's wife, the nun Eshinni (1182–1268?), bequeathed to her daughter seven servants, lamenting that she could not also give her a three-year-old boy, because his father belonged to another household. "Overall," she wrote, "it is a most unfortunate situation when a servant in my house enters into a liaison with a servant of another person" (Dobbins, *Letters of the Nun Eshinni*, 22; 51–52).

23. Tonomura, "Sexual Violence against Women," in *Women and Class in Japanese History*, ed. id. et al., 140–41.

24. Goodwin, *Selling Songs and Smiles*, 27–40.

25. Ibid., 34–35; Wakita, "Medieval Household and Gender Roles," in *Women and Class in Japanese History*, ed. id. et al., 91.

26. Tonomura, "Re-envisioning Women," in *Origins of Japan's Medieval World*, ed. Mass, 160–61.

27. On the traffic in people in late sixteenth century Japan, see Maki, *Jinshin baibai*, and Nelson, "Slavery in Medieval Japan." This pattern of trading and holding people

in bondage had parallels elsewhere in the world. Like systems of slavery in Africa and the American borderlands, it involved "wars of capture, the mediating role of kinship, the predominance of women and children as slaves, the relative absence of plantation or industrial organization, the muted role of racial as opposed to ethnic differentiations, and finally, the agency of a 'conquest' state in suppressing traditional practices" (Brooks, *Captives & Cousins*, 35).

28. Nelson, "Slavery in Medieval Japan," 463.

29. Keinen, *Chōsen nichinichiki* (1600), translated and quoted in Elisonas, "Inseparable Trinity," in *Cambridge History of Japan*, vol. 4: *Early Modern Japan*, 293.

30. Nelson, "Slavery in Medieval Japan," 465–67; Maki, *Kinsei Nihon no jinshin baibai no keifu*, 29–33.

31. Maki, *Jinshin baibai*, 86–87; Botsman, *Punishment and Power*, 74. A notable exception is the use of unfree male Ainu labor in Ezochi fisheries. See Howell, *Capitalism from Within*. This feminization of trafficking had parallels in other societies. See Robertson and Robinson, "Re-modeling Slavery," in *Women and Slavery*, vol. 2: *Modern Atlantic*, ed. Campbell et al., 253–83.

32. Yamaguchi, "Kinsei shoki ni Akita han ni okeru kōzan machi," 201–3. Yoon, "Domain and Bakufu," 86.

33. Watanabe Keiichi, "*Umezu Masakage nikki*" *tokuhon*, 143. The characters for *baijo* ("bought women") are not the same as those used for the *baijo* ("selling women") referred to in later shogunal documents as clandestine prostitutes. Nevertheless, the similarity in terminology is suggestive. Most prostitutes were "bought women" before they were "selling women."

34. UMN, 1: 91.

35. Kobata, *Nihon kōzanshi no kenkyū*, 532.

36. Yamaguchi, "Kinsei shoki ni Akita han ni okeru kōzan machi," 200.

37. UMN, 1: 81–82.

38. UMN, 3: 206–7.

39. UMN, 1: 28.

40. UMN, 3: 54.

41. UMN, 1: 98.

42. Satō, *Akita-ken yūri shi*, 28; UMN, 2: 73–74.

43. UMN, 1: 107.

44. Watanabe Keiichi, "*Umezu Masakage nikki*" *tokuhon*, 144–45; UMN, 8: 31–32.

45. UMN, 1: 6.

46. "Innai ginzanki," 506.

47. Ibid.

48. The revenue from these monopolies exceeded the revenue from taxes on all the businesses in the mining towns combined. Kobata, *Nihon kōzanshi no kenkyū*, 533.

49. Satō, *Akita yūrishi*, 13.

50. UMN, 2: 243; Watanabe Kenji, *Edo yūri seisuiki*, 155. Here the reference is probably to female kabuki actors, who were active in the early seventeenth century. In 1629, they were permanently banned from the stage because they inspired men to fight over their favors. Masakage is referring to ineffective earlier attempts to contain their business. On the shogunate's regulation of *yūjo* kabuki in seventeenth-century Edo, see Takano, *Yūjo kabuki*, and Donald Shively, "Popular Culture," 749–51.

51. UMN, 2: 37. Akita-ken, ed., *Akita kenshi*, vol. 2: *Kinsei jō*, 309–10. There was a similar abortive (and perhaps half-hearted) attempt at occupational segregation among artisans in sixteenth-century Kanazawa. McClain, *Kanazawa*, 40–41.

52. For example, when Masakage set rates for the brothel levy, he told his underlings to inform brothel keepers in Yokobori. UMN, 1: 160.

53. UMN, 3: 81.

54. Tsukada, "Kinsei no keibatsu," in *Saiban to kihan*, ed. Asao, 92.

55. Kobata, *Nihon kōzanshi no kenkyū*, 529–30.

56. Ibid., 582.

57. UMN, 7: 251.

58. Satō, *Akita-ken yūri shi*, 20–21; UMN, 1: 85.

59. Satō, *Akita-ken yūri shi*, 20; UMN, 1: 61.

60. UMN, 1: 70.

61. UMN, 1: 70–71.

62. UMN, 1: 79.

63. UMN, 1: 91.

64. UMN, 1: 111.

65. *Maotoko* appears in medieval law codes as a term for an adulterous lover, but husbands were usually called *otto*. See Goodwin, *Selling Songs and Smiles*, 73–74, and Tonomura, "Black Hair and Red Trousers," 136. The phrase *moto no otoko* could also be read *hon no otoko* and interpreted as meaning "true" or "real" man. Both meanings are probably present here.

66. UMN, 1: 203.

67. UMN, 2: 191; 4: 175. Later in the Tokugawa period, both domain and shogunal authorities specifically avoided creating a spectacle by applying punishments involving nudity to female criminals. Sone, "Josei to keibatsu," in *Mibun no naka no josei*, ed. Yabuta and Yanagiya, 77.

68. UMN, 5: 134; 9: 211.

69. UMN, 1: 226–27, 229.

70. UMN, 2: 163, 226.

71. UMN, 2: 228–29. In this instance, her master had issued the reward for her return.

72. Sakuzō did finally return, and he later became involved in another dispute over a woman, this time because a middleman had appropriated a prostitute belonging to him as compensation for his landlord's unpaid debt. UMN, 2: 154.

73. Watanabe Keiichi, "*Umezu Masakage nikki* tokuhon," 143–44; UMN, 7: 171–72.

74. UMN, 5: 352.

75. Shimojū, "Miuri hōkō to josei," in *Mibun no naka no josei*, ed. Yabuta and Yanagiya, 110–11.

76. On travel, see Nenzi, *Excursions in Identity*, and Shiba, *Kinsei onna tabi nikki*; on education and literacy, Tocco, "Made in Japan," and Yabuta, "Moji to josei"; on peasant families, Walthall, "Life Cycle of Farm Women."

2. CREATING "PROSTITUTES"

1. Seigle, *Yoshiwara*, 20–24.

2. Ono, *Yoshiwara, Shimabara*, 35. In the medieval period, brothel keepers in Kyoto had been recognized and paid taxes to various warrior families. Tonomura, "Re-envisioning Women," 161.

3. Seigle, *Yoshiwara*, 23–24.

4. Eventually there would be five streets—the fifth was added in 1626. Sone, "Prostitution and Public Authority," 171.

5. Seigle, *Yoshiwara*, 30.

6. Ooms, *Tokugawa Ideology*, 66–69.

7. On the reciprocal aspects of benevolence, see Botsman, *Punishment and Power*, 41–50; Vlastos, *Peasant Protests and Uprisings*, 21–41; Makihara, *Kyakubun to kokumin no aida*, 43–68.

8. See the discussion of female household heads in Anderson, *Place in Public*, 23–31.

9. This how Bennett, *History Matters*, 55–56, defines "domestic" patriarchy.

10. Sone, "Kinsei baibaishun no kōzō: kōshōsei no shūen," in *Ajia joseishi*, ed. Hayashi and Yanagida , 388–89.

11. Pflugfelder, *Cartographies of Desire*, 105.

12. Shively, "Bakufu versus Kabuki," 329.

13. Tsukada, *Kinsei mibunsei to shūen shakai*, 165–66.

14. Miyachi, *Bakumatsu ishinki no bunka to jōhō*, 42. The restrictions on prostitutes' comings and goings were relaxed over the course of the period. See Sone, "Prostitution and Public Authority," 171.

15. Seigle, *Yoshiwara*, 49–50. The following year, the Meireki fire destroyed the old quarter, and the brothels were temporarily relocated for several months while the new quarter was constructed.

16. Ishii, ed., *Kinsei hōsei shiryō sōsho*, vol. 1: *Oshioki saikyochō, Genshōshū, Genroku gohōshiki*, 249–50.

17. Morinaga, ed., *Hankachō*, 1: 186–87.

18. Ishii, ed., *Tokugawa kinrei kō goshū*, 3 (1960): 63.

19. Miyachi, *Bakumatsu ishinki no bunka to jōhō*, 44–61; 68.

20. On Kanazawa, see Miyamoto, "Kanazawa no kuruwa," in *Ronshū kinsei joseishi*, ed. Kinsei joseishi kenkyūkai, 293–344; on Shimonoseki, Shimonoseki-shi shishi henshū iinkai, ed., *Shimonoseki shishi minzoku hen*, 579–604; on Fukuoka, Yokota Takeko, "Bakumatsu Hakata Yanagimachi yūjoya Toraya."

21. Jippensha, *Shanks' Mare*, trans. Satchell, 81.

22. Yonemoto, *Mapping Early Modern Japan*, 129–72.

23. Ikegami, *Bonds of Civility*, 270–71, makes a similar point.

24. The only anomaly was that during the first half of the period the district headmen were usually also the heads of the brothel keepers' association. See Tsukada, *Mibunsei shakai to shimin shakai*, 106.

25. Using evidence from Edo's flourishing popular culture, many scholars have argued that men drew sharp distinctions between their sexual activities inside and outside the district, using their wives for reproduction and the quarter's prostitutes for pleasure. See, e.g., Keene, *World within Walls*, 161; Hibbet, *Floating World in Japanese Fiction*, 29. Lindsey, *Fertility and Pleasure*, 8, takes a slightly different view, arguing that "segregated institutions of play separated [the wife's] roles of mother and household manager from her role as her husband's sexual satisfier, leaving the latter function to be shared with the courtesan."

26. Lindsey, *Fertility and Pleasure*, 79.

27. Maki, *Jinshin baibai*, 81.

28. Ishii, ed., *Kinsei hōsei shiryō sōsho*, vol. 2: *Gotōke reijō, ritsuryō yōryaku*, 207–8; vol 3: *Buke genseiroku, genseidan*, 108–9.

29. Shimojū, "Miuriteki hōkō to zegen ni tsuite."

30. Nagano, "Bakuhan hō to josei."

31. Amy Stanley, "Adultery, Punishment and Reconciliation," argues similarly.

32. Ōhashi, ed., "Go Taiheiki shiroishi banashi."

33. The various penalties imposed in the seventeenth century are listed in Ishii, ed., *Kinsei hōsei shiryō sōsho*, 1: 458.

34. Tsukada, *Kinsei mibunsei to shūen shakai*, 163.

35. Ibid., 164.

36. Ishii, *Zoku Edo jidai manpitsu*, 91–93.

37. Sawayama, *Edo no sutegotachi*, 31.

38. Ishii, ed., *Kinsei hōsei shiryō sōsho*, 1: 202; Tsukada, *Kinsei mibunsei to shūen shakai*, 163. Later, the term was set at three years of uncompensated labor in Yoshiwara for a wife who consented to prostitute herself with her husband's permission, and a life term for a woman who did so without her husband's knowledge. Maki, *Jinshin baibai*, 96.

39. Ishii, ed., *Kinsei hōsei shiryō sōsho*, 1: 215–16.

40. Amy Stanley, "Adultery, Punishment and Reconciliation," 323.

41. Maki, *Kinsei Nihon no jinshin baibai no keifu*, 209–10, reproducing "Yūjo hōkōnin ukejō no koto" (1803).

42. Maki indicates that Hisa and her mother used seals, but in most cases women in this situation would have used the imprints of their fingernails. See Rubinger, *Popular Literacy in Early Modern Japan*, 57.

43. Usami, *Shukuba to meshimori onna*, 133–43

44. See discussion in Leupp, *Servants, Shophands, and Laborers*, 100–101.

45. Most Tokugawa-era contracts for prostitution followed a pattern in which a woman served for set length of time regardless of her earnings, but toward the end of the period there were some variations. Yokota, "Bakamatsu Hakata Yanagimachi yūjoya Toraya," a study of *bakumatsu*-era Yanagimachi, the "pleasure quarter" in Hakata, includes examples of contracts that made it possible for the indentured woman to earn her way out of service (282). These types of arrangements were predominant in the modern period. See Ramseyer, *Odd Markets in Japanese History*, 122–23.

46. Maki, *Jinshin baibai*, 159–62; and Shimojū, "Miuri hōkō to josei," 122–24. Strikingly, these distinctive provisions are also included in a contract for a 15-year-old *yakusha deshi*, who likely worked as a male prostitute, in 1865. Maki, *Kinsei nihon no jinshin baibai no keifu*, 259–60.

47. Tsukada, *Kinsei mibunsei to shūen shakai*, 160.

48. Seigle, *Yoshiwara*, 183–84.

49. Ihara, *Life of an Amorous Woman*, 192–203.

50. Sone, *Shōfu to kinsei shakai*, 41–44.

51. *Keichō kenbunroku* (1614) quoted in Konno, *Edo no furo*, 15–18.

52. Konno, *Edo no furo*, 97–98.

53. Ibid., 103–4.

54. Ishii, ed., *Kinsei hōsei shiryō sōsho*, 1: 211–15.

55. Seigle, *Yoshiwara*, 211.

56. Kita, *Edo no geisha*, 5; Hur, *Prayer and Play*, 138.

57. Usami, *Shukuba to meshimori onna*, 12–19. At the time, Naitō Shinjuku had been temporarily shut down, but it was reopened later the same year. Edo's post stations were particularly insolvent because they failed to attract overnight guests. Serving girls were thus considered necessary to attract day-trippers. See Yoshida, *Mibunteki shūen to shakai*, 448.

58. Maki, *Kinsei Nihon no jinshin baibai no keifu*, 385–89; Tsukada, "Kinsei Osaka no keisei machi to chaya."

59. For discussion of standard *meshimori onna* contracts and some examples, see Ishii, ed., *Nihon dantai hōshi*, 429–68, and Usami, *Shukuba to meshimori onna*, 105–30.

60. Miyachi, *Bakumatsu ishinki no bunka to jōhō*, 65.

61. Tsukada, *Mibunsei shakai to shimin shakai*, 132–33.

62. Botsman, *Punishment and Power*, 93–94; Abe, *Meakashi Kinjūrō no shōgai*, 6–13.

63. Tsukada, *Mibunsei shakai to shimin shakai*, 135.

64. Tsukada, *Kinsei mibunsei to shūen shakai*, 170–75.

65. Yoshida, "Yūkaku shakai," in *Toshi no shūen ni ikiru*, ed. Tsukada, 19–21.

66. Yoshida, *Mibunteki shūen to shakai*, 462.

67. Fujita, *Toyama Kinshirō no jidai*.

68. Yoshida, "Yūkaku shakai," 22–30.

69. Ishii, ed., *Oshioki reiruishū kōruishū*, 4: 174, 176–77. The principle underlying both cases was that a prostitute did not qualify as a wife; therefore she could not be guilty of adultery.

70. Ibid., 120.

71. Sone, "Prostitution and Public Authority," 174.

72. There is some disagreement about the origin of female geisha. They were *odoriko* who were hired out to perform at banquets for high-ranking samurai, according to Kishii, *Onna geisha no jidai*, 2–7, whereas Kita, *Edo no geisha*, 19–22, says they were originally shamisen players in the Fukagawa *okabasho*. On *haori*, see Seigle, *Yoshiwara*, 172. A later regulation discouraged women from wearing *haori* jackets to follow trends, stating that this fashion was only permitted if the woman in question was actually cold. Kishii, *Onna geisha no jidai*, 15.

73. Seigle, *Yoshiwara*, 170–72.

74. Kishii, *Onna geisha no jidai*, 138.

75. Maki, *Kinsei Nihon no jinshin baibai no keifu*, 253–57.

76. Kobayashi, "Kōshōsei no seiritsu to tenkai," 154

77. Tokyo daigaku shiryō hensanjo, ed., *Shichū torishimari ruishū*, vol. 2: *Shichū torishimari no bu 2*, 84.

78. Ibid., 84–115.

79. Ishii, ed., *Tokugawa kinreikō zenshū*, 5 (1959): 460.

80. Lindsey, *Fertility and Pleasure*, 47–48.

3. NEGOTIATING THE GENDERED ORDER

1. See the images in Nagasaki-shi Dejima shiseki seibi shingikai, ed., *Dejima-zu*, 187–231. On the pornographic prints, see Screech, *Sex and the Floating World*, 282–87.

2. Nenzi, *Excursions in Identity*, 170–71.

3. See, e.g., Koga, *Maruyama yūjo to tō kōmōjin*, Leupp, *Interracial Intimacy in Japan*, and Shiraishi, *Nagasaki Dejima no yūjo*.

4. White, *Comforts of Home*, 2, 9.

5. Miyamoto, "Maruyama yūjo no seikatsu."

6. Scheiner, "Benevolent Lords and Honorable Peasants"; Vlastos, *Peasant Protests and Uprisings*, 21–41; Makihara, *Kyakubun to kokumin no aida*, 43–68.

7. Walthall, "Devoted Wives / Unruly Women."

8. Lindsey, *Fertility and Pleasure*, 47, addresses this as an "ethical paradox" in moralizing discourse: "Is a woman a daughter loyally serving her parents or a courtesan loyally serving her bordello by satisfying the sexual needs of its clients?"

9. Blussé, *Bitter Bonds*, 6.

10. Ibid., 32–33.
11. Wang, "Merchants without Empire," in *Rise of Merchant Empires*, ed. Tracy, 416–19.
12. Leupp, *Interracial Intimacy*, 56–58.
13. For a discussion of why *kaikin* is a better description of Tokugawa Japan's foreign policy than the more traditional *sakoku* ("closed country"), see Toby, *State and Diplomacy in Early Modern Japan*.
14. Kaempfer, *Kaempfer's Japan*, 189.
15. Koga, *Maruyama yūjo zenpen*, 714–25, estimates 1645 as the most likely date.
16. Kaempfer, *Kaempfer's Japan*, 232.
17. Koga, *Maruyama yūjo zenpen*, 593. The relationship between a Chinese trader and a Nagasaki townsman's daughter that may have precipitated this statement is mentioned in Nagasaki shiyakusho, ed., *Nagasaki shishi fūzoku hen*, 43–45. Koreans used the same justification for confining Japanese to a specially designated Japan House in 16th century Pusan. Lewis, *Frontier Contact*, 192–97.
18. Koga, *Maruyama yūjo zenpen*, 598–608.
19. Thunberg, *Travels in Europe, Africa, and Asia*, 3: 75. Occasionally, Dutchmen were permitted to venture out to Maruyama and Yoriai for assignations with their favorite women, but this was unusual. Leupp, *Interracial Intimacy*, 109–10.
20. Miyamoto, "Maruyama yūjo no seikatsu," 20.
21. Chaiklin, *Cultural Commerce and Dutch Commercial Culture*, 15–16. Chaiklin observes that *yūjo* smuggled goods out of the Chinese wards much more often than from Dejima (28).
22. Morinaga, ed., *Hankachō*, 3: 25.
23. Etchū, ed., "Yoriaichō shoji kakiage hikaechō zoku" (cited below as YSKHz), in *Nihon toshi seikatsu shiryō shūsei*, vol. 7, ed. Harada, 85, 97, 99, 103, and 110.
24. This was the ruling in an unusual case in which a retired prostitute lodged a complaint against her former master for confiscating her gift from a Chinese trader. Morinaga, ed., *Hankachō*, 1: 338–39; Fukuyama, "Hankachō no yūjotachi."
25. Leupp, *Servants, Shophands, and Laborers*, 59–64.
26. Yabuta, "Kinsei josei no raifu saikuru," in *Nihon josei seikatsu shi*, 3: 255–64; Walthall, "Family Ideology," 472, and "Life Cycle of Farm Women," 49–50. On service in the harem, see Hata, "Servants of the Inner Quarters."
27. Utagawa Toyokuni III, *Onna kyōkun shusse sugoroku* (1840s or 1850s) reproduced in Salter, *Japanese Popular Prints*, 173.
28. Yokota, "Imagining Working Women," 159–63.
29. Miyamoto, "Maruyama yūjo no seikatsu," 29–31; Nagasaki shiyakusho, ed., *Nagasaki shishi fūzoku hen*, 26–27. There were rumors that such women were working again in 1760, but they were quieted after the Nagasaki magistrate threatened to punish the Maruyama and Yoriai ward elders (ibid., 30–31).

30. YSKHz, 58–63; Nishimura, "Tokugawa-ki ni okeru toshi to minshū shakai," 212.

31. Shiraishi, *Nagasaki Dejima no yūjo*, 75–76.

32. Morinaga, ed., *Hankachō*, 10: 95–96. Miyamoto, "Maruyama yūjo no seikatsu," 23–25, also mentions several of the cases that appear in this section.

33. Morinaga, ed., *Hankachō*, 2: 29.

34. Miyamoto, "Yūri no seiritsu to taishūka," in *Nihon no kinsei*, ed. Takeuchi, 14: 210–11.

35. Hidemura and Harada, eds., *Hakata-tsu yōroku*, 2: 591.

36. Etchū, ed., "Yoriaichō shoji kakiage hikaechō" (cited below as YSKH), in *Nihon toshi seikatsu shiryō shūsei*, vol. 6, ed. Harada, 339.

37. See the examples in YSKHz: 410.

38. Ibid., 64.

39. YSKH, 339. Maki, *Kinsei nihon no jinshin baibai no keifu*, 471.

40. Sugano, "State Indoctrination of Filial Piety in Tokugawa Japan," in *Women and Confucian Cultures*, ed. Ko, 171.

41. Sugano, *Edo jidai no kōkōmono*, 184–89.

42. Walthall, "Devoted Wives / Unruly Women," 117.

43. YSKH, 321.

44. Morinaga, ed., *Hankachō*, 4: 338, 346; 5: 83.

45. See, e.g., YSKHz, 70.

46. Nishimura, "Tokugawa-ki ni okeru toshi to minshū shakai," 203.

47. Morinaga, ed., *Hankachō*, 1: 317.

48. Miyamoto, "Maruyama yūjo no seikatsu," 39–42; Morinaga, ed., *Hankachō*, 2: 149. A similar case appears in *Hankachō*, 4: 223.

49. YSKH, 428.

50. Morinaga, ed., *Hankachō*, 2: 202.

51. Ibid., 107–8.

52. Lindsey, *Fertility and Pleasure*, 137–48.

53. Sone, *Shōfu to kinsei shakai*, 54–56.

54. Of course, some women used these practices in cynical ploys to "prove" their love to well-paying clients. See Rogers, "She Loves Me."

55. In one other (seemingly one-sided) case of mutilation-as-protest, a frustrated lover forcibly cut a *yūjo*'s hair after hearing that she was pregnant with another man's child. YSKHz: 53–54, Morinaga, ed., *Hankachō*, 2: 94–95.

56. Kaempfer, *Kaempfer's Japan*, 143.

57. Koga, *Maruyama yūjo zenpen*, 378.

58. Chikamatsu Monzaemon, *Hara-kiri of a Woman at Nagamachi* (c. 1712), trans. Paul Atkins http://ceas.uchicago.edu/japanese/Sibley_Translation_Project.shtml (accessed October 17, 2011).

59. YSKH, 428.
60. Ibid., 318–19.
61. Ibid., 320.
62. Leupp, *Servants, Shophands and Laborers*, 74, mentions that employers often considered themselves to be *in loco parentis*.
63. Quoted in Goodman, *Japan and the Dutch*, 22.
64. Siebold, *Manners and Customs*, 27.
65. Koga, *Maruyama yūjo zenpen*, 622–23.
66. YSKH, 402–3. Also see a similar case in Morinaga, ed., *Hankachō*, 10: 71.
67. Koga, *Maruyama yūjo kōhen*, 482–84.
68. YSKHz, 179–80.
69. YSKH, 401.
70. Morinaga, ed., *Hankachō*, 10: 223. Since 1708, it had been illegal for *yūjo* to give Chinese traders gifts. Nagasaki shiyakusho, ed., *Nagasaki shishi fūzoku hen*, 19.
71. Sone, "Prostitution and Public Authority," 179. Lindsey, *Fertility and Pleasure*, 101–3, largely agrees with Sone's observation that maternity was denied to Edo's prostitutes, but mentions the example of Minowa, a residence where *yūjo* could give birth and recover from illness.
72. Miyamoto, "Maruyama yūjo no seikatsu," 33–35.
73. Leupp, *Interracial Intimacy*, 121–24.
74. For examples, see YSKH, 386–89.
75. This stipulation was written into at least one woman's contract. Maki, *Kinsei nihon no jinshin baibai no keifu*, 471.
76. YSKH, 350–89.
77. YSKHz, 48.
78. YSKH, 399, 413.
79. YSKHz, 115–16, 123; Koga, *Maruyama yūjo*, 111–13.
80. Leupp, *Interracial Intimacy*, 121; Siebold, *Manners and Customs of the Japanese*, 28. Thunberg, *Travels in Europe Asia and Africa*, 76–77, mentions seeing a six-year-old child, who much resembled her European father, residing on Dejima.
81. The famous seventeenth-century *yūjo* Takao paraded through Yoshiwara with her wet nurse, but this was an exceptional case (Lindsey, *Fertility and Pleasure*, 101).
82. YSKH, 446–47, 452; Nagasaki shiyakusho, ed., *Nagasaki shishi fūzoku hen*, 83.
83. Morinaga, ed., *Hankachō*, 7: 164–65; Morinaga, *Hankachō: Nagasaki bugyō no kiroku*, 142–43.

PART II. PROLOGUE

1. Watanabe Kenji, *Edo yūri seisuki*, 29–31.
2. Buyō Inshi, *Seji kenmonroku*, 239–41.

3. On commercialization and protoindustrialization, see Smith, *Native Sources*, Howell, *Capitalism from Within*, Wigen, *Making of a Japanese Periphery*, and Pratt, *Japan's Protoindustrial Elite*.

4. See Walthall, "Peripheries"; Ikegami, *Bonds of Civility*, and Rubinger, *Popular Literacy*.

5. On the travel boom, see Vaporis, *Breaking Barriers*, Nenzi, *Excursions in Identity*, and Traganou, *Tōkaidō Road*.

6. Nenzi, *Excursions in Identity*, 165–77.

7. Wigen, *Making of a Japanese Periphery*, 75.

8. On domains' strategies to increase revenue by promoting some forms of commercial development, see Ravina, *Land and Lordship*, Roberts, *Mercantilism in a Japanese Domain;* and Pratt, *Japan's Protoindustrial Elite*, 16–27.

4. FROM HOUSEHOLD TO MARKET

1. Satō, "Keizai yōroku" (1827), in *Nihon keizai taiten*, 18: 434. This passage is available in translation in *Sources of Japanese Tradition*, ed. de Bary et al., vol. 2, pt. 1: 512–13.

2. Niigata-shi hensan kinseishi bukai, ed., *Niigata shishi tsūshi hen* [cited below as NSSt], vol. 2: *Kinsei ge-kan* (1997), 36–44.

3. Ibid., 390–92.

4. Itō, "Bakumatsu, ishin-ki no Niigata machi ni kurasu hitobito."

5. NSSt, 2: 398.

6. Ibid., 207–8.

7. Ibid., 62–64; Pratt, *Japan's Protoindustrial Elite*, 23–24.

8. In 1751, shogunal villages reassigned to Nagaoka domain protested, citing exactly these issues. NSSt, 2: 191–93.

9. Drixler, "Infanticide and Fertility in Eastern Japan," 151–56, 307–12.

10. Ōtsuka, *Aizu-han josei o meguru hankachō*, 55–56.

11. "Oboe" Kyōhō 15.11 in Niigata-shi kyōdo shiryōkan, ed., *Niigata machi kaisho monjo I*, 41; *Niigata shishi shiryō hen* [cited below as NSSs] vol. 2: Kinsei 1 (1990), 63–64.

12. Drixler, "Infanticide and Fertility," 168.

13. "Kanbara-gun yori Hitachi Shimōsa e onna hōkōnin ikken tomechō," Kansei 4.2, in *Niigata kenshi shiryō hen* vol. 7: Kinsei 2 (1981), 899.

14. Yabuta, *Joseishi to shite no kinsei*, 163–64.

15. Odajima, *Echigo yashi, gekan*, 464.

16. Igarashi, *Meshimori onna*, 131; Drixler, "Infanticide and Fertility," 303–7.

17. NSSt, 2: 229.

18. Murata Ryūmin, "Shichiron" (1791), quoted in Drixler, "Infanticide and Fertility," 304.

19. Buyō, *Seji kenmonroku*, 234–35.
20. Imamura, *Shinbo jōwa*.
21. Ibid., 22.
22. Ibid., 23.
23. Quoted in Burns, "Body as Text," 210.
24. Quoted in Ropp, "Ambiguous Images," 32.
25. NSSt, 2: 89, and Nagaoka-shi, ed., *Nagaoka shishi tsūshi hen*, vol. 1 (1996), 670.
26. Niigata-shi, ed., *Niigata shishi* vol. 1 (1934), 636.
27. Itō, "Kinsei chūki Niigata-machi ni okeru baibaishun," in *Bakumatsu ishin to minshū shakai*, ed. Aoki and Abe, 162.
28. Imamura, *Shinbo jōwa*, 27–28.
29. Itō, "Kinsei chūki Niigata-machi ni okeru baibaishun," 175.
30. Howell, *Geographies of Identity*, 16.
31. Itō, "Kinsei chūki Niigata-machi ni okeru babaishun," 175.
32. "Habakarinagara kuchitashi no oboe," Bunsei 13.n.d., in Kazama, *Niigata yūjo kō*, 22–23. Linking their own interests to the domain's economic success was a common ploy for commoners who wished to influence policy. See Roberts, *Mercantilism*, 134–53.
33. Odajima, *Echigo yashi*, 46.
34. Fujiwara, "Fude makase," in *Nihon shomin seikatsu shiryō shūsei*, 3: 663. Parts of this diary are translated in Plutschow, *A Reader in Edo Period Travel*, 261–81. For more on Fujiwara Morohide (also known as Tomimoto Shigetayū), see Oda, *Edo no gokuraku tonbo*.
35. These women were called *shingintori* (new money takers). Morikuri, "Karayuki-san and Shingintori," in *Gender and Japanese History*, vol. 1, ed. Wakita et al., 333–34.
36. Solt, "Willow Leaftips," in *Imaging/Reading Eros*, ed. Jones, 132.
37. Sugano, *Edo jidai no kōkōmono*, 56–58, 174–78.
38. Walthall, "Masturbation and Discourse," 4, and ibid., "Life Cycle of Farm Women," 63, discussing a scandal in Suzuki Bokushi's (Echigo) village. In rural areas, the association of widows and promiscuity survived into the twentieth century. In a classic anthropological study based on fieldwork undertaken in 1935, Ella Embree describes a village widow who took lovers in exchange for cash. One village woman is quoted as saying that it must be nice to be a widow, "for then you can have any number of lovers" (Smith and Wiswell, *Women of Suye-Mura*, 187–89).
39. Solt, "Willow Leaftips," 132–33.
40. Walthall, "Life Cycle of Farm Women," 63, 68.
41. Nenzi, *Excursions in Identity*, 81.
42. Fujiwara, "Fude makase," 663–64, notes that the usual fee for a night with a prostitute was 300 *mon*, while the *goke* he visited charged 400 *mon*, plus 100 *mon* for the room rental.

43. Bolitho, "Tempo Crisis," in *Cambridge History of Japan*, 5: 153–54. For two different accounts of the daimyō's response, see Komatsu, *Bakumatsu ongoku bugyō no nikki*, 54–55, and NSSt, 2: 392–93.

44. Komatsu, *Bakumatsu ongoku bugyō*, 53–54.

45. "Shichū fūzokugaki," Tenpō 14.12, in *NSSs*, 2: 598–99.

46. "Zaikin nikki," Tenpō 14, in Niigata-shi kyōdo shiryōkan, ed., *Shodai Niigata bugyō Kawamura Nagataka monjo*, 1 (1978).

47. Untitled letter, Tenpō 14.5, in Niigata-shi kyōdo shiryōkan, ed., *Shodai Niigata bugyō Kawamura Nagataka monjo*, 2 (1978), 96–97.

48. Komatsu, *Bakumatsu ongoku bugyō*, 150.

49. "Niigata-machi baijo no gi ni tsuki mōshiage sōrō kakitsuke," Tenpō 14.12, in Niigata-shi kyōdo shiryōkan, ed., *Shodai Niigata bugyō Kawamura Nagataka monjo*, 8 (1985), 68–70.

50. "Kendan toshiyori sono amari no machi yakunin made e mōshikikase sōrō oboe," Kōka 2.1, in *NSSs*, 2: 285.

51. Niigata-shi kyōdo shiryōkan, ed., *Shodai Niigata bugyō Kawamura Nagataka monjo*, 8: 12.

52. "Kendan toshiyori sono amari," in *NSSs*, 2: 285.

53. Fujita, *Toyama Kinshirō no jidai*.

54. "Kendan toshiyori sono amari," in *NSSs*, 2: 285.

55. Ibid.

56. Ibid., 286.

57. "Shichū ofure #49," Kōka 3.i5, in *NSSs*, 2: 289.

58. See Amy Stanley, "Adultery, Punishment, and Reconciliation," 317–19.

59. On some of Koikawa Shōzan's other works, see Screech, *Sex and the Floating World*, 272.

60. Koikawa, "Kōshoku shugyō shokoku monogatari," in *Kōshoku shugyō shokoku monogatari*, ed. Yagi, 16–17.

61. Niigata-shi kyōdo shiryōkan, ed., *Shodai Niigata bugyō Kawamura Nagataka monjo*, 9 (1986): 12.

62. Niigata-shi shishi hensanka, "Edo shōnin no Niigata kenbutsu," 65–67.

63. Pateman, *Sexual Contract*, 193.

64. Amy Dru Stanley, *From Bondage to Contract*, 219.

65. See the brief discussion in Sand, *House and Home*, 22.

66. Amy Dru Stanley, *From Bondage to Contract*, 227–30.

5. GLITTERING HAIR ORNAMENTS AND BARREN FIELDS

1. Traganou, *Tōkaidō Road*, 163

2. "Fukaya-shuku," in Heibonsha chihō shiryō sentā, ed., *Saitama-ken no chimei*, 818–19. In contrast, in Kumagaya, the next station up the road from Fukaya, where inns

were not allowed to employ serving girls, the 1842 population registers listed 1,706 men and 1,557 women. Saitama-ken, ed., *Shinpen Saitama kenshi tsūshi hen*, vol. 4: *Kinsei* 2 (1989), 550.

3. Smith, *Native Sources*, 29.

4. "Akatsuma-gun ka sesō no hensen kakitome," Tenpō (no date), in Gunma-kenshi hensan iinkai, ed., *Gunma kenshi shiryō hen*, 11 (1980), 929.

5. Howell, "Hard Times in the Kanto," cites the example of Nojiri in Shimōsa, where over 10 percent of the native population was in service elsewhere, but servants working in the village were almost all recruited from outside (355–56).

6. As Howell observes, "contemporary observers could see only a rural society in decay, rather than a growing and dynamic economy" (ibid., 350).

7. For an explanation of this process as it played out in the advanced protoindustrial region of Shindatsu, see Vlastos, *Peasant Protests and Uprisings*, 73–91.

8. Migration to cities increased over the last century of the period. Since mortality was higher in urban centers, many who had intended to leave for short terms of service never returned to their rural hometowns. See Leupp, *Servants, Shophands, and Laborers*, 62; Drixler, "Infanticide and Fertility," 157–58; and Hayami, *Historical Demography*, 52–53.

9. Ōguchi, "Mura no hanzai to Kantō torishimari shutsuyaku."

10. Vaporis, *Breaking Barriers*, 87–97.

11. Usami, *Shukuba to meshimori onna*, 12–23.

12. Nenzi, *Excursions in Identity*, 168–77.

13. Jippensha, *Shanks' Mare*, 119.

14. Taxes on serving girls constituted roughly 10 percent of Fuchū station's revenue in 1861 (Sugano, *Mura to kaikaku*, 258). Taxes on *meshimori hatagoya* formed almost 10 percent of revenue in Odawara in 1843, but Usami, *Shukuba to meshimori onna*, 28–29, sees this as less significant than the women's role in attracting paying customers to the station.

15. Tanaka, "Minkan seiyō," in *Nihon keizai taiten*, 5: 358.

16. Mitsuyo, "Tōkaidō Futagawa-shuku ni okeru hatagoya to meshimori onna," 46

17. Ibid., 48.

18. Jippensha, *Shanks' Mare*, 81.

19. Kaempfer, *Kaempfer's Japan*, 279.

20. Asai Ryōi, *Tōkaidō meishoki* (c. 1665) quoted in Kondō, *Kinsei no kōtsū to chihō bunka*, 80.

21. Igarashi, *Meshimori onna*, 54–72.

22. Nihei, "Nikkō dōchū Kasukabe-shuku no meshimori onna ni tsuite."

23. Koshigaya-shi kyōiku iinkai shakai kyōikuka, ed., *Koshigaya shishi*, vol. 1: *Tsūshi-hen jō* (1980), 883.

24. Usami, *Shukuba to meshimori onna*, 130–32.

25. In 1834, for example, a man from Koshigaya station journeyed to Echigo and returned with five women to indenture as serving girls. Koshigaya-shi kyōiku iinkai shakai kyōikuka, ed., *Koshigaya shishi*, 1: 883–84.

26. Igarashi, *Meshimori onna*, 144–85.

27. Examples are cited in a case where shogunal inspectors apprehended "extra" women and their employers insisted that they were actually not working as prostitutes for various reasons of youth, ill health, etc. "Meshiuri onna omeshitorae ikken narabi ni hira-hatagoya meshiuri-hatagoya kakiage," Bunsei 5.11, in Kasukabe-shi kyōiku iinkai, ed., *Kasukabe shishi*, vol. 3: *Kinsei shiryō hen*, bk. 1 (1982), 218–20.

28. For an evocative description of an old post station graveyard, see Minakami, *Ryōkan o aruku*, 32–42. On serving girls and venereal diseases, see Igarashi, *Meshimori onna*, 166–70.

29. "Kizaki-shuku hatagoya meshikakae onna Hatsu kikyō ōsewatashikata ni tsuki kōjōsho," Tenpō 13, in *Ōta shishi shiryō hen: Kinsei* 2 (1979), 433–34. Also see the discussions of this document in Rubinger, *Popular Literacy*, 159–60; Usami, *Shukuba to meshimori onna*, 143–50; Igarashi, *Meshimori onna*, 168–70; and Minakami, *Ryōkan o aruku*, 28–32.

30. At that point, Rinbei and the Moritaya inn settled the matter of the borrowed money. "Kizaki-shuku hatagoya shakuzai no kado ni yori meshikae onna Ushizawa-mura nanushi sashitome ikken sumikuchi shōmon," in *Ōta shishi shiryō hen: Kinsei* 2, 432.

31. Yabuta, "Moji to josei," 246–47.

32. Even records by high-class prostitutes are extremely rare. Nenzi, *Excursions in Identity*, 84–85, mentions an entertainer named Takejo who wrote a travel diary.

33. Usami, *Shukuba to meshimori onna*, 149–50.

34. This petition's rough format, as well the location where it was discovered—among the papers of a private individual in Ushizawa village, where Hatsu's half-hearted protector Rinbei lived—make it unlikely that this version could have been submitted. If there was another, more polished version, it has never surfaced.

35. Pratt, *Japan's Protoindustrial Elite*, 110.

36. Saitama-ken, ed., *Shinpen Saitama kenshi tsūshi hen*, vol. 4: *Kinsei* 2, 482.

37. Leupp, *Servants, Shophands, and Laborers*, 62.

38. Igarashi, *Meshimori onna*, 88–93. "Kuragano-shuku hatagoya meshiuri onna teire ikken kakitsuke," Kyōwa 3.12 to Bunka 1.3, in Takasaki shishi hensan iinkai, ed., *Shinpen Takasaki shishi shiryō hen*, vol. 6: *Kinsei* 2 (1997), 527–33.

39. "Kuragano-shuku gejo hōkōnin masu ninzū no mono hikitori ni tsuki uke-shochō," Bunka 11.6, in Takasaki shishi hensan iinkai, ed., *Shinpen Takasaki shishi shiryō hen*, vol. 8: *Kinsei* 4 (2002), 237–41.

40. Ishii, ed. *Tokugawa kinreikō goshū*, 1: 237.

41. "Meshiuri onna onmeshitorae ikken narabi ni hira-hatagoya meshiuri-hatagoya kakiage," Bunsei 5.11, in Kasukabe-shi kyōiku iinkai, ed., *Kasukabe shishi*, vol. 3: *Kinsei shiryō hen*, bk. 1 (1982), 212–23.

42. "Ryūmai-mura yakunin meshimori onna hikiwatasu goshui ni tsuki ryōsannin hikiwatashikata negai," Bunsei 12.10, in *Ōta shishi shiryō hen: Kinsei* 2, 430. Years earlier, the same headman had bought a troublesome serving girl named Maki from Yanada. "Koizumi-mura Tomikichi Yanada-shuku meshimori onna to kakeochi ikken shimatsu ni tsuki issatsu," ibid., 429–30.

43. "Meshiuri onna miuke kakeai tanomu issatsu," Kōka 3.2, in Sōka shishi hensan iinkai, ed., *Sōka shishi shiryō hen*, 5 (1996), 536–37.

44. Usami, "Meshimori onna deiri ikken," in *Edo jidai no joseitachi*, 209–10.

45. "Meshimori onna sashiokazaru yō ōsetsukekata sukegō muramura negaiagesho," Bunsei 10 (no date), in *Ōta shishi shiryō hen: Kinsei* 3 (1983), 601.

46. "Irioku mōsu issatsu no koto" (no date), Onikubo-ke monjo, #1415, and "Gonpachi mibun hikiukeru issatsu" (no date), Onikubo-ke monjo, #1427, Saitama Prefectural Archive.

47. "Fumimochi wabisho," Ansei 5.5, in Iwatsuki-shi, ed., *Iwatsuki shishi kinsei shiryō hen*, vol. 4, bk. 2: *Chihō shiryō gekan* (1982), 96.

48. "Okazuma-gun Kariyado-mura wakamono-gumi gitei renpanjō," Tenpō (no date), in *Gunma kenshi shiryō hen*, 11: 929.

49. "Gōdo-mura wakamono fūgi ni tsuki torikime issatsu," Kaiei 2.1, in *Ōta shishi shiryō hen: Kinsei* 2, 742.

50. Igarashi, *Meshimori onna*, 204.

51. Nagano, "Nihon kinsei nōson ni okeru masukyuriniti no kōchiku to jendā," in *Jendā de yomitoku Edo jidai*, ed. Sakurai et al., 200–204.

52. "Hatagoya Chōhachi ikken saikyo ukesho," Bunsei 1.8, in Sōka shishi hensan iinkai, ed., *Sōka shishi shiryō hen*, 2 (1989), 492–94.

53. Koshigaya-shi kyōiku iinkai shakai kyōikuka, ed., *Koshigaya shishi*, 1: 884–86; "Hatagoya Yabei ikken saikyo ukesho," Bunsei 1.10, in *Sōka shishi shiryō hen*, 2: 494–97.

54. "Ōma-mura nado yonjūkason shoshoku takane teamarichi zōdai nado ni tsuki sogan kakitome," Kansei 3.7, in Kōnosu-shi, ed., *Kōnosu shishi shiryō hen*, vol. 3: *Kinsei* 1 (1993), 804–5.

55. Ibid., 805.

56. Ibid.

57. Burns, "Body as Text."

58. On women and sericulture, see Walthall, *Weak Body*, 93–99; Partner, *Mayor of Aihara*, 13–17, 43–44.

59. Sugano, "Nōson josei no rōdō to seikatsu," in *Nihon joseishi*, 3: 63.

60. Yabuta, "Josei no raifusaikuru," 265.

61. On unmarried women, see Mega, "Wakamono renchū to mura no musume," and Nagano, "Nihon kinsei nōson ni okeru masukyuriniti no kōchiku to jendā." On adultery, see Amy Stanley, "Adultery, Punishment, and Reconciliation."

62. Stansell, *City of Women*, 127.

63. Vaporis, *Tour of Duty*, 205–36; Nishiyama, *Edo Culture*.

64. "Ōma-mura nado yonjūkason shoshoku takane teamarichi zōdai nado ni tsuki sogan kakitome,"Kansei 3.7 in Kōnosu-shi, ed., *Kōnosu shishi shiryō hen*, vol. 3: *kinsei* 1, 813.

65. Segawa, *Mura no onnatachi*, 212.

66. Aihara, *Kusanagi Enseki kenkyū*, 2: 63–64.

67. Igarashi, *Meshimori onna*, 202.

68. "Meshimori onna sashiokazaru yō ōsetsukekata sukegō muramura negaiagechō," Bunsei 10 (no date), in *Ōta shishi shiryō hen: Kinsei* 3, 600.

69. Fuess, *Divorce in Japan*, 55–56.

70. "Kanra-gun Ichinomiya-mura meshimori gejo rakuseki shōmon," Kansei 7.11, in *Gunma kenshi shiryō hen*, 9: 831.

71. "Nakajimayama-mura Yogozaemon musume rien sashisawari deiri sumikuchi shōmon," An'ei 5.6, in *Ōta shishi shiryō hen: Kinsei* 3, 789.

72. On the Kansei Reforms, see Tsuji, "Politics in the Eighteenth Century," in *Cambridge History of Japan*, 4: 425–77. On their architect, Matsudaira Sadanobu, see Ooms, *Charismatic Bureaucrat*.

73. "Sugito-shuku hoka futajuku meshimori onna sashitome gansho," Kansei 11.6, in Sugito chōshi hensanshitsu, ed., *Sugito chōshi kinsei shiryō hen*, 149.

74. "Meshiuri onna sashitsukawasu gi otadashi ni tsuki ren'in kōjōsho sashiage," Kansei 11.7, in *Kasukabe shishi*, vol. 3: *Kinsei shiryō hen*, bk. 1, 27–28.

75. For a discussion of how the reforms affected Musashi, see Saitama-ken, ed., *Shinpen Saitama kenshi tsūshi hen*, vol. 4: *Kinsei* 2, 660–71.

76. For an analysis of how village elites turned to the inspectors established by the reforms for support in apprehending criminals, see Ōguchi, "Mura no hanzai."

77. "Nakayama Sei'ichirō-sama yori otorishimari suji mōshiwatasare," Tenpō 13.5, in Kasukabe-shi kyōiku iinkai, ed., *Kasukabe shishi*, vol. 3: *Kinsei shiryō hen*, bk. 1 (1978), 249.

78. "Meshimori onna sashiokazaru yō ōshitsukekata sukegō muramura negaiagesho," Bunsei 10 (no date), in *Ōta shishi shiryō hen: Kinsei* 3, 601–2. This case is discussed in detail in Usami, *Shukuba to meshimori onna*, 93–104.

79. See, e.g., "Otorishimarikata Shinjuku shinden Fukuzō narabi ni Shōbei gejo Fumi tangan," Kōka 2.7, in *Kasukabe shishi*, vol. 3: *Kinsei shiryō hen*, bk. 1: 724–25.

80. For example, the *torishimari shutsuyaku* arrested four innkeepers in Koshigaya in 1841. Saitama-ken, ed. *Shinpen Saitama kenshi tsūshi hen*, vol. 4: *Kinsei* 2, 542.

81. "Shokuuri hatagoya nakama gitei ren'inchō," Tenpō 7.8, in Urawa-shi sōmubu shishi hensanshitsu, ed. *Urawa shishi*, vol. 3: *Kinsei shiryō hen*, 3 (1984), 543.

82. "Urawa-shuku torishimari fuyukitodoki ni tsuki todoki," Tenpō 4.12, in Urawa-shi sōmubu shishi hensanshitsu, ed. *Urawa shishi*, vol. 3: *Kinsei shiryō hen*, 2 (1985), 272.

83. Ibid., 547.

84. Nihei, "Nikkō dōchū Kasukabe-shuku no meshimori onna ni tsuite," 84; *Koshigaya shishi*, 1: 882–83.

85. "Meshiuri onna omeshitorae ikken narabi ni hira-hatagoya meshiuri-hatagoya kakiage," in Kasukabe-shi kyōiku iinkai, ed., *Kasukabe shishi*, vol. 3: *Kinsei shiryō hen*, bk. 1, 218–20.

86. Koshigaya-shi kyōiku iinkai shakai kyōikuka, ed., *Koshigaya shishi*, 1: 882–83.

87. "Meshiuri onna omeshitorae ikken narabi ni hira-hatagoya meshiuri-hatagoya kakiage," in Kasukabe-shi kyōiku iinkai, ed., *Kasukabe shishi*, vol. 3: *Kinsei shiryō hen*, bk. 1, 217; "Gejo meshikakae hatagoya meshitorae ikken ni tsuki," Tenpō 12.10, in Sugito chōshi hensanshitsu, ed., *Sugito chōshi kinsei shiryō hen*, 152.

88. Koshigaya-shi kyōiku iinkai shakai kyōikuka, ed., *Koshigaya shishi*, 1: 880–81.

89. Villagers had successfully countered an earlier petition in 1824 (Usami, "Meshimori onna deiri ikken," 206–9).

90. Watanabe, "Hōchōroku," in Saitama-ken, ed., *Shinpen Saitama kenshi shiryō hen*, vol. 10: *Kinsei* 1, 751.

91. "Kumagaya-shuku shinki meshimori onna sashioki ni tsuki naisho," Tenpō 3.1 through Tenpō 5.7, in Saitama-ken, ed., *Shinpen Saitama kenshi shiryō hen*, vol. 15: *Kinsei* 6 (1984), 228–29. Peasants near Ōta made a similar point ("Meshimori onna sashiokazaru yō oshitsukekata sukegō muramura negaiagechō," Bunsei 10 (no date), in *Ōta shishi shiryō hen: kinsei* 3, 602.

92. Usami, "Meshimori onna deiri ikken," 192–93.

93. Ibid., 194; "Kumagaya-shuku shinki meshimori onna sashioki ni tsuki naisho" (cited n. 91 above), 231.

94. Ibid., 233.

95. "Meshimori onna sashiokazaru yō oshitsukekata sukegō muramura negaiagechō," Bunka 10 (no date), in *Ōta shishi shiryō hen: kinsei* 3, 603.

96. Sugano, *Mura to kaikaku*, 259–61. In Hirakata, too, the employment of *meshimori onna* intensified the competition between inns and restaurants, leading to conflict within the station. Yahisa, "Kinsei kōki Hirakata-shuku no hatagoya to meshimori onna."

97. "Kumagaya-shuku hatagoya nado mitsudan no ue jōge rinjuku dōyō joroya tosei negaiage sōrō omomuki ni tsuki Oshi onyakusho e tangansho sashidashi sōrō hikae narabi ni kono ichijō nikki," Keiō 4.8, Kubo-ke monjo, #731, Saitama Prefectural Archive.

6. TORA AND THE "RULES OF THE PLEASURE QUARTER"

1. "Onomichi machihamasuji no han'eisaku ni kansuru furegaki," Bunsei 14.9, in Hiroshima-ken, ed., *Hiroshima kenshi kinsei shiryō hen, 4* (1975), 197–98.
2. Kotohira chōshi henshū iinkai, ed., *Chōshi Kotohira,* 3 (1998), 199.
3. See the discussions of "episodic microhistory" in Gregory, "Is Small Beautiful?" 102; and Brewer, "Microhistory," 91.
4. Usami, *Shukuba to meshimori onna,* 139–40.
5. Yutaka-chō kyōiku iinkai, ed., *Yutaka chōshi honbun hen,* 390–97; Kawai, *Seto naikai no rekishi,* 220–21.
6. Fukuyama-shi Tomo-no-ura rekishi minzoku shiryōkan, ed., *Kitamaebune to sono jidai,* 94.
7. Makino, *Kitamaebune no jidai,* 159.
8. Yutaka-chō kyōiku iinkai, ed., *Yutaka chōshi honbun hen,* 397–98.
9. "Mitarai-machi," in Heibonsha chihō shiryō sentā, ed., *Hiroshima-ken no chimei,* 482–83.
10. "Chaya Ebiya Shōemon shuppon ni tsuki torihakarai ikken," Bunsei 12.10, in Gotō, *Setochi Mitarai-kō no rekishi,* 447–48.
11. Hishiya, "Tsukushi kikō," in *Nihon shomin seikatsu shiryō shūsei,* 20: 164. Also see Plutschow, *A Reader in Edo Period Travel,* 249. On references to Muro's prostitutes in classical literature, see Kawashima, *Writing Margins,* 57–66. Kawashima notes that stories about the "prostitute at Muro" tended to emphasize the woman's sinfulness and need of male intervention to achieve salvation; perhaps Hishiya had these ideas in mind when he portrayed the pathetic women he met there.
12. Maki, *Kinsei Nihon no jinshin baibai no keifu,* 440–65. In addition, Mitarai officials recorded cases where girls born in their jurisdiction entered service across the water in Onomichi and Miyajima.
13. On the development of these neighborhoods, see Kotohira chōshi henshū iinkai, ed., *Chōshi kotohira,* 3: 154–55, and Thal, *Rearranging the Landscape,* 74–76.
14. Hishiya, "Tsukushi kikō," in *Nihon shomin seikatsu shiryō shūsei,* 20: 166, and Plutschow, *A Reader in Edo Period Travel,* 250.
15. Sone, "Conceptions of Geisha."
16. Maki, *Kinsei Nihon no jinshin baibai no keifu,* 440.
17. Gotō, *Setochi Mitarai-kō no rekishi,* 408.
18. Thal, *Rearranging the Landscape,* 74.
19. Yutaka-machi kyōiku iinkai, ed., *Yutaka chōshi honbun hen,* 400, 412.
20. Maki, *Jinshin baibai,* 450.
21. Gotō, *Setochi Mitarai-kō no rekishi,* 446.
22. Yutaka-chō kyōiku iinkai, ed., *Yutaka chōshi honbun hen,* 409.
23. "Wazawaza mōshi tsukawasu," Bunsei 10.4, in "Shoji kakitsuke hikae—Ochō-mura." A transcription of this document appears in Kataoka, "Mitarai-machi yūjo

kankei shiryō" (a series of documents related to prostitution in Mitarai compiled by the Yutaka-chō archivist Kataoka Satoshi; cited below as MYKS), 12.

24. "Kakushi baijo sashioki sōrō ikken shorui," Bunsei 8.11, in Kurashiki shishi kenkyūkai, ed., *Shinshū Kurashiki shishi*, 10: 253; ibid., 6: 724.

25. Ibid., 10: 252.

26. Ibid, 248.

27. On Mitarai prostitutes' excursions to a festival in Miyauchi, see Fukuyama shishi hensankai, ed., *Fukuyama shishi chūkan* (1968), 760. On market days, see Yūtaka-machi kyōiku iinkai, ed., *Yutaka chōshi honbun hen*, 411. On an expedition to solicit customers in a Fukuyama fishing village, see Gōtō, *Setouchi Mitarai-kō no rekishi*, 369, and *Fukuyama shishi chūkan*, 760.

28. Yutaka-machi kyōiku iinkai, ed., *Yutaka chōshi honbun hen*, 411.

29. Gōtō, *Setouchi Mitarai-kō no rekishi*, 411.

30. "Zenkyoku gonainai mōshiage tatematsuru kōjō," Tenpō 14.9 in Kotohiragū, ed., "Kotohiragū shiryō," vol. 77.

31. "Shakutori onna yatoiire chaya dōshuku ichidō e mōshiwatasu narabi ni ukesho katsu dōnen jūgatsu tsuigan koikomi," Bunsei 7.3, in Kotohira chōshi henshū iinkai, ed., *Chōshi kotohira*, 2 (1997), 312–18. Before prostitution was legal in Konpira, prostitutes would come in from villages in Ikegoryō, a shogunal domain adjacent to the religious complex's territory (ibid., 3: 196); Hayashi, "Kinsei Konpira no yūjo," 50.

32. "Zenkyoku gonainai mōshiage tatematsuru kōjō," in Kotohiragū, ed., "Kotohiragū shiryō," vol. 77. The servants were paid prorated salaries based on the number of half-days they worked

33. These and subsequent details from Sadaemon's rendition of Tora's disappearance are related in "Onegai mōshiage tatematsuru kōjōsho," in "Sho kakitsuke hikae," Genji 2.7. This document is also reproduced in Gōtō, *Setochi Mitarai-kō no rekishi*, 534–35.

34. For an example of a brothel keeper in Miyajima sending a desperately ill girl home to her mother in Mitarai, see Yutaka-chō kyōiku iinkai, ed., *Yutaka chōshi honbun hen*, 446.

35. Gōtō, *Mitarai-kō no rekishi*, 178–79, 610–24. On average, about two or three of the Wakaebisuya's prostitutes died every year; curiously, the number did not change drastically between the mid-eighteenth century, when the brothel counted nearly a hundred prostitutes in its service, and the late nineteenth, when it employed around half that number.

36. See Oom's discussion in *Tokugawa Village Practice*, 11–70, of the illiterate peasant woman Ken's lawsuit against village authorities; and Walthall's account in "Devoted Wives, Unruly Women," 127–28, of another illiterate peasant woman, Fumi, who was tricked into stamping her husband's seal on a document she did not understand.

37. This side of the story is related in "Tōchō Nishizawaya Isaburō no musume Tora gi ni tsuki mōshiageru kakitsuke," Keiō 1.10, in Tada-ke monjo, #369; MYKS, 2–3.

38. "Tōchō Sadaemon kakae onna Koeda gi, Takehara-machi oyamoto e hikitori tsukamatsuri sōrō ikken, kore made kakebiki omomuki mōshiage tatematsuri sōrō kakitsuke," in "Sho kakitsuke hikae Genji 1," Keiō 2.4.

39. Siniawer, *Ruffians, Yakuza, Nationalists*, 20–25.

40. Kanda, *Kinsei no geinō kōgyō to chiiki shakai*, 230–35.

41. Botsman, *Punishment and Power*, 94; Abe, *Meakashi Kinjūrō no shōgai*, 6–13.

42. "Meakashi oki mōshitaku narabi ni sukedekigin no uchi nite tsukawashitaku gi negai," Tenmei 4.10, in Gōtō, *Setochi Mitarai-kō no rekishi*, 410.

43. *Chōshi Kotohira*, 2: 312–18; Kanda, *Kinsei no geinō kōgyō*, 83; Thal, *Rearranging the Landscape*, 104.

44. Kanda, *Kinsei geinō kōgyō*, 51, 84–88, recounts the dubious histories of these characters.

45. "Konkōin nitchō," Tenpō 13.9, Kotohiragū toshokan.

46. YSKH, 428.

47. "Saisan onegaiage tatematsuru kōjōsho," Keiō 1.12, Tada-ke monjo #369; MKYS, 3.

48. "Tōchō Nishizawaya Isaburō no musume Tora gi ni tsuki mōshiageru kakitsuke," Keiō 1.10 in MYKS, 3.

49. "Tōchō Isaburō musume Tora Toyota-gun Mitarai-machi kakariau gi ni tsuki on-ukagai mōshiageru kakitsuke," Keiō 2.1 (excerpted from "Takehara-machi oboegaki Keiō 2") in MYKS, 7–8.

50. Untitled (no date), Tada-ke monjo, #1555; MYKS, 1.

51. "Torikawashigaki," Keiō 2.3 (excerpted from "Takehara-machi oboegaki Keiō 2") in MKYS, 7.

52. "Ninbetsu okuri tegata no kobun," in "Chōyō kakubetsu-chō," Meiji 3.2.

53. This is the judgment of the Yutaka-chō archivist Kataoka Satoshi, who suggests that this case did have an (ambiguously) happy ending for Tora. Yutaka-chō kyōiku iinkai, ed., *Yutaka chōshi honbun hen*, 447–48.

CONCLUSION

1. Harootunian, "Late Tokugawa Culture and Thought," 173.

2. Morisaki, *Baishun ōkoku no onnatachi*.

3. Garon, *Molding Japanese Minds*, 94.

4. Such instances were often recorded in newspapers. See, e.g., *Yomiuri shinbun*, 23 February 1875, 23 December 1875, and 2 May 1882.

5. Fujime, "Licensed Prostitution System," 141–145.

6. Ishihara, "Kōshōsei to haishō undō," 51–52.

7. On the "Liberation Edict" and its relationship to the international judicial case resulting from the Maria Luz incident, see Morita, *Kaikoku to chigai hōken*, 246–63.

8. Hayakawa, *Kindai tennōsei kokka to jendā*, 188–206; Sanders, "Prostitution in Postwar Japan," 22–25; Ramseyer, *Odd Markets*, 97–98.

9. Thanks to Dani Botsman for pointing this out.

10. Garon, *Molding Japanese Minds*, 102.

11. Fujime, "Licensed Prostitution System," 140–41, makes a similar point.

12. Fukuzawa, "On Morality" (*Hinkōron*), in *Fukuzawa Yukichi on Japanese Women*, 70–102.

13. Fujime, "Licensed Prostitution System," 154–55.

14. Ibid., 138–39; Burns, "Bodies and Borders."

15. For a mid-Meiji example of the same type of thinking, see Fukuzawa's discussion in "On Morality," 96–98. On a similar discourse about café waitresses in the 1920s, see Garon, *Molding Japanese Minds*, 107.

16. Kovner, "Base Cultures," 785.

17. Iida, "Between the Technique," 431–34.

18. On this discussion, see Hein, "Savage Irony."

BIBLIOGRAPHY

ARCHIVAL SOURCES

"Chōyō kakubetsu-chō." Meiji 3. Yutaka-chō kyōiku iinkai, Hiroshima-ken, Yutaka-chō.

Kataoka Satoshi, ed. "Mitarai-machi yūjo kankei shiryō." Yutaka-chō kyōiku iinkai, Hiroshima-ken, Yutaka-chō.

"Konkōin nitchō." Kotohiragū toshokan. Kagawa-ken, Kotohira-chō.

Kotohiragū, ed. "Kotohiragū shiryō." 90 vols. Kotohiragū toshokan. Kagawa-ken, Kotohira-chō. 1911–44.

Kubo-ke monjo. Saitama Prefectural Archive. Saitama-ken, Saitama-shi.

"Machi oboechō." Bunsei 12. Yutaka-chō kyōiku iinkai. Hiroshima-ken, Yutaka-chō.

Onikubo-ke monjo. Saitama Prefectural Archive. Saitama-ken, Saitama-shi.

"Sho kakitsuke hikae Genji 1." Yutaka-machi kyōiku iinkai. Hiroshima-ken, Yutaka-chō.

"Sho kakitsuke hikae Genji 2." Yutaka-chō kyōiku iinkai. Hiroshima-ken, Yutaka-chō.

"Shoji kakitsuke hikae: Ochō-mura" Bunsei 3 through 13. Yutaka-chō kyōiku iinkai. Hiroshima-ken, Yutaka-chō.

Tada-ke monjo. Yutaka-chō kyōiku iinkai. Hiroshima-ken, Yutaka-chō.

PUBLISHED SOURCES

Abe Yoshio. *Meakashi Kinjūrō no shōgai: Edo jidai shomin seikatsu no jitsuzō*. Tokyo: Chūō Kōronsha, 1981.

Aihara Kotosaburō. *Kusanagi Enseki kenkyū*. 2 vols. Tokyo: Aihara Kotosaburō, 1967.

Akita-ken, ed., *Akita kenshi*. 13 vols. Akita-ken: Akita-ken, 1961–66.

Allison, Anne. "Memoirs of the Orient." *Journal of Japanese Studies* 27, no. 2 (2001): 381–98.

Anderson, Marnie. *A Place in Public: Women's Rights in Meiji Japan*. Cambridge, MA: Harvard University Press, 2010.

Bennett, Judith. *History Matters: Patriarchy and the Challenge of Feminism*. Philadelphia: University of Pennsylvania Press, 2006.

Berry, Mary Elizabeth. *Hideyoshi*. Cambridge, MA: Harvard University Press, 1982.

———. "Public Peace and Private Attachment: The Goals and Conduct of Power in Early Modern Japan." *Journal of Japanese Studies* 12, no. 2 (1986): 237–71.

Blussé, Leonard. *Bitter Bonds: A Colonial Divorce Drama of the Seventeenth Century*. Translated by Diane Webb. Princeton, NJ: Markus Weiner, 2002.

Bolitho, Harold. "The Tempo Crisis." In *The Cambridge History of Japan*, vol. 5: *The Nineteenth Century*, ed. Marius Jansen, 116–67. New York: Cambridge University Press, 1989.

Botsman, Daniel. *Punishment and Power in the Making of Modern Japan*. Princeton, NJ: Princeton University Press, 2005.

Braisted, William, trans. and ed. *Meiroku Zasshi: Journal of the Japanese Enlightenment*. Cambridge, MA: Harvard University Press, 1976.

Brewer, John. "Microhistory and the Histories of Everyday Life." *Cultural and Social History* 7, no. 1 (2010): 87–109.

Brooks, James. *Captives & Cousins: Slavery, Kinship, and Community in the Southwest Borderlands*. Chapel Hill: University of North Carolina Press, 2002.

Brown, Philip. *Central Authority and Local Autonomy in Early Modern Japan: The Case of Kaga Domain*. Stanford, CA: Stanford University Press, 1993.

Burns, Susan. "Bodies and Borders: Syphilis, Prostitution, and Nation in Nineteenth-Century Japan." *U.S.–Japan Women's Journal*, no. 15 (1998): 8–20.

———. "The Body as Text: Confucianism, Reproduction, and Gender in Tokugawa Japan." In *Rethinking Confucianism: Past and Present in China, Japan, Korea, and Vietnam*, ed. Benjamin Elman, John Duncan, and Herman Ooms, 178–219. Los Angeles: UCLA Asian Pacific Monograph Series, 2002.

Buyō Inshi. *Seji kenmonroku*. 1816. Edited by Honjō Ejirō. Tokyo: Kaizōsha, 1930.

Chaiklin, Martha. *Cultural Commerce and Dutch Commercial Culture: The Influence of European Material Culture on Japan, 1700–1850*. Leiden: Leiden University, 2003.

Chikamatsu Monzaemon. *Hara-kiri of a Woman at Nagamachi* (c. 1712). Translated by Paul Atkins. http://ceas.uchicago.edu/japanese/P.Atkins.Harakiri.pdf (accessed October 21, 2011).

Chizu de yomu Edo jidai. Edited by Yamashita Kazumasa. Tokyo: Kashiwa Shobō, 1998.

Conlan, Thomas. *State of War: The Violent Order of Fourteenth-Century Japan*. Ann Arbor: Center for Japanese Studies, University of Michigan, 2003.

Dejima zu: sono keikan to hensen. Edited by Nagasaki-shi Dejima shiseki seibi shingikai. Nagasaki-shi: Nagasaki-shi, 1987.

Deuchler, Martina. "Propagating Female Virtues in Chosŏn Korea." In *Women and Confucian Cultures in Premodern China, Korea, and Japan*, ed. Dorothy Ko, JaHyun Kim Haboush, and Joan Piggott, 142–69. Berkeley: University of California Press, 2003.

Dobbins, James C. *Letters of the Nun Eshinni: Images of Pure Land Buddhism in Medieval Japan*. Honolulu: University of Hawai'i Press, 2004.

Drixler, Fabian. "Infanticide and Fertility in Eastern Japan: Discourse and Demography, 1660–1880." Ph.D. diss., Harvard University, 2008.

Elisonas, Jurgis. "The Inseparable Trinity: Japan's Relations with China and Korea." In *The Cambridge History of Japan*, vol. 4: *Early Modern Japan*, ed. John Hall, 235–300. New York: Cambridge University Press, 1991.

Etchū Tetsuya, ed. "Yoriaichō shoji kakiage hikaechō." In *Nihon toshi seikatsu shiryō shūsei*, vol. 6, ed. Harada Tomohiko, 280–459. Tokyo: Gakushū Kenkyūsha, 1975.

———. "Yoriaichō shoji kakiage hikaechō: zoku." In *Nihon toshi seikatsu shiryō shūsei*, vol. 7, ed. Harada Tomohiko, 42–233. Tokyo: Gakushū Kenkyūsha, 1976.

Fass, Paula. "Cultural/Social History: Some Reflections on a Continuing Dialogue—The Cultural Turn and Beyond." *Journal of Social History* 37, no. 1 (2003): 37–46.

Fuess, Harald. *Divorce in Japan: Family, Gender, and the State, 1600–2000*. Stanford, CA: Stanford University Press, 2004.

Fujime Yuki. "The Licensed Prostitution System and the Prostitution Abolition Movement in Modern Japan." *Positions* 5, no. 1 (1997): 135–70.

Fujimoto Kizan. *Shinpan shikidō ōkagami*. 1678. Edited by Shinpan shikidō ōkagami kankōkai. Tokyo: Yagi shoten, 2006.

Fujimura Makoto. "Niigata ni okeru kagai no hensen." *Shishi Niigata* 14 (1994): 4–22.

Fujita Satoru. *Toyama Kinshirō no jidai*. Tokyo: Azekura shobō, 1992.

Fujiwara Morohide. "Fude makase." C. 1842. In *Nihon shomin seikatsu shiryō shūsei*, vol. 3, ed. Takeuchi Toshimi, Mori Kahei, and Miyamoto Tsune'ichi, 595–708. Tokyo: San'ichi Shobō, 1969.

Fukuyama shishi hensankai, ed. *Fukuyama shishi*. 3 vols. Fukuyama-shi: Fukuyama Shishi Hensankai, 1963–78.

Fukuyama-shi Tomo-no-ura rekishi minzoku shiryōkan, ed. *Kitamaebune to sono jidai: Tomo-no-tsu no nigiwai tokubetsuten*. Fukuyama-shi: Fukuyama-shi Tomo-no-ura rekishi minzoku shiryōkan, 2004.

Fukuyama Yasuko. "Hankachō no yūjotachi." *Edo-ki onna kō* 8 (1993): 178–83.

Fukuzawa Yukichi. *Fukuzawa Yukichi on Japanese Women: Selected Works*. Translated by Eiichi Kiyooka. Tokyo: University of Tokyo Press, 1988.

Garon, Sheldon. *Molding Japanese Minds: The State in Everyday Life*. Princeton, NJ: Princeton University Press, 1997.

Gilfoyle, Timothy. *City of Eros: New York City, Prostitution, and the Commercialization of Sex*. New York: Norton, 1992.

———. "Prostitutes in History: From Parables of Pornography to Metaphors of Modernity." *American Historical Review* 104, no. 1 (1999): 117–41.

Goodman, Grant. *Japan and the Dutch, 1600–1853*. Richmond, UK: Curzon, 2000.

Goodwin, Janet. *Selling Songs and Smiles: The Sex Trade in Heian and Kamakura Japan*. Honolulu: University of Hawai'i Press, 2007.

Gotō Yōichi. *Setochi Mitarai-kō no rekishi*. Hiroshima-ken, Yutaka-chō: Mitarai-shi Hensan Iinkai, 1962.

Gregory, Brad. "Is Small Beautiful? Microhistory and the History of Everyday Life." *History and Theory* 38, no. 1 (1999): 100–110.

Griffis, William Elliot. *The Mikado's Empire*. 1895. 2 vols. Reprint of the 8th ed. Wilmington, DE: Scholarly Resources, 1973.

Gunma kenshi hensan iinkai, ed. *Gunma kenshi shiryō hen*. 27 vols. Maebashi-shi: Gunma-ken, 1977–.

———. *Gunma kenshi tsūshi hen*. 10 vols. Maebashi-shi: Gunma-ken, 1989–92.

Hall, John W. "Rule by Status in Tokugawa Japan." *Journal of Japanese Studies* 1, no. 1 (1974): 39–49.

Hanasaki Kazuo. *Edo no kagemajaya*. Tokyo: Miki Shobō, 1992.

Harootunian, H. D. "Late Tokugawa Culture and Thought." In *The Cambridge History of Japan*, vol. 5: *The Nineteenth Century*, ed. Marius Jansen, 168–258. New York: Cambridge University Press, 1989.

Hasegawa Seiichi. "Keichō Genna-ki ni okeru Dewa kuni no shakai jōkyō." In *"Tōhoku" no seiritsu to tenkai: Kinsei, kingendai no chiiki keisei to shakai*, ed. Numata Satoshi, 15–36. Tokyo: Iwata Shoin, 2002.

Hata Hisako. "Servants of the Inner Quarters: The Women of the Shogun's Great Interior." Translated by Anne Walthall. In *Servants of the Dynasty: Palace Women in World History*, ed. Anne Walthall, 172–90. Berkeley: University of California Press, 2008.

Hayakawa Noriyo. *Kindai tennōsei kokka to jendā: seiritsuki no hitotsu no rogikku*. Tokyo: Aoki Shoten, 1998.

Hayami Akira. *The Historical Demography of Pre-modern Japan*. Tokyo: Tokyo University Press, 2001.

Hayashi Megumi. "Kinsei Konpira no yūjo." *Kagawa shigaku* 28 (2001): 48–75.

Heibonsha chihō shiryō sentā, ed. *Hiroshima-ken no chimei*. Vol. 35 of *Nihon rekishi chimei taikei*. Tokyo: Heibonsha, 1982.

———. *Tōkyō-to no chimei*. Vol. 13 of *Nihon rekishi chimei taikei*. Tokyo: Heibonsha, 2002.

———. *Saitama-ken no chimei*. Vol. 11 of *Nihon rekishi chimei taikei*. Tokyo: Heibonsha, 1993.

Hein, Laura. "Savage Irony: The Imaginative Power of 'Military Comfort Women' in the 1990's." *Gender and History* 11, no. 2 (1999): 336–72.

Henriot, Christian. *Prostitution and Sexuality in Shanghai: A Social History*. New York: Cambridge University Press, 2001.

Hershatter, Gail. *Dangerous Pleasures: Prostitution and Modernity in Twentieth-Century Shanghai*. Berkeley: University of California Press, 1997.

Hibbet, Howard. *The Floating World in Japanese Fiction*. New York: Oxford University Press, 1959.

Hidemura Senzō and Harada Yasunobu, eds. *Hakatatsu yōroku*. 3 vols. Fukuoka: Nishinihon bunka kyōkai, 1975–78.

Hiroshima-ken, ed. *Hiroshima kenshi kinsei shiryō hen*. 6 vols. Hiroshima-shi: Hiroshima-ken, 1973–79.

———. *Hiroshima kenshi tsūshi*. 7 vols. Hiroshima-shi: Hiroshima-ken, 1980–84.

Hishiya Heishichi. "Tsukushi kikō." In *Nihon shomin seikatsu shiryō shūsei*, vol. 20, ed. Takeuchi Toshimi. 155–262. Tokyo: San'ichi Shobō, 1972.

Howell, David. *Capitalism from Within: Economy, Society, and the State in a Japanese Fishery*. Berkeley: University of California Press, 1995.

———. *Geographies of Identity in Nineteenth-Century Japan*. Berkeley: University of California Press, 2005.

———. "Hard Times in the Kanto: Economic Change and Village Life in Tokugawa Japan." *Modern Asian Studies* 23, no. 2 (1989): 349–71.

Hur, Nam-Lin. *Prayer and Play in Late Tokugawa Japan: Asakusa Sensōji and Edo Society*. Cambridge, MA: Harvard University Press, 2000.

Igarashi Tomio. *Meshimori onna: shukuba no shōfutachi*. Tokyo: Shin jinbutsu ōraisha, 1981.

Ihara Saikaku. *The Life of an Amorous Man*. Translated by Kengi Hamada. Rutland, VT: Charles Tuttle, 1964.

———. *The Life of an Amorous Woman and Other Writings*. Translated by Ivan Morris. New York: New Directions Books, 1963.

Iida, Yumiko. "Between the Technique of Living an Endless Routine and the Madness of Absolute Degree Zero: Japanese Identity and the Crisis of Modernity in the 1990s." *positions: east asia cultures critique* 8, no. 2 (2000): 423–64.

Ikegami, Eiko. *Bonds of Civility: Aesthetic Networks and the Political Origins of Japanese Culture*. New York: Cambridge University Press, 2005.

Imamura Yodoshichi. *Shinbo jōwa*. C. 1795. Niigata: Taishōdō Shoten, 1937.

Ishihara Yukiaki. "Kōshōsei to haishō undō: Gunma-ken o jirei to shite." *Rekishi hyōron* 540 (1995): 48–61.

Ishii Ryōsuke. *Nihon dantai hōshi*. Tokyo: Sōbunsha, 1978.

———. *Yoshiwara: Edo yūkaku no jittai*. Tokyo: Chūō Kōronsha, 1967.

———. *Zoku Edo jidai manpitsu: Edo no yūjo sono ta*. Tokyo: Sōbunsha, 1961.

Ishii Ryōsuke, ed. *Kinsei hōsei shiryō sōsho*. 3 vols. Tokyo: Sōbunsha, 1959.

———. *Oshioki reiruishū*. 16 vols. Tokyo: Meicho shuppan, 1971.

———. *Tokugawa kinreikō goshū*. 4 vols. and 1 appendix vol. Tokyo: Sōbunsha, 1959–61.

———. *Tokugawa kinreikō zenshū*. 6 vols. Tokyo: Sōbunsha, 1959–61.

Itō Yūshi. "Bakumatsu, ishin-ki no Niigata-machi ni kurasu hitobito." *Shishi Niigata* 18 (1996): 4–23.

———. "Kinsei chūki Niigata machi ni okeru baibaishun." In *Bakumatsu ishin to minshū shakai*, ed. Aoki Michiko and Abe Tsunehisa, 156–79. Tokyo: Koshi Shoin, 1998.

Iwai Denjū. *Karuizawa sanshuku to meshimori onna*. Nagano-ken, Saku-shi: Ichii, 1987.

Iwatsuki-shi, ed. *Iwatsuki shishi kinsei shiryō hen*. 4 vols. Iwatsuki: Iwatsuki-shi, 1980–82.

Jansen, Marius. "Tosa in the Sixteenth Century: The 100 Article Code of Chōsokabe Motochika." In *Studies in the Institutional History of Early Modern Japan*, ed. John W. Hall and Marius B. Jansen, 89–114. Princeton, NJ: Princeton University Press, 1968.

Jippensha Ikku. *Shanks' Mare*. Translated by Thomas Satchell. Tokyo: C. E. Tuttle, 1960.

Johnson, Walter. *Soul by Soul: Life Inside the Antebellum Slave Market*. Cambridge, MA: Harvard University Press, 1999.

Kaempfer, Engelbert. *Kaempfer's Japan: Tokugawa Culture Observed*. Edited and translated by Beatrice Bodart-Bailey. Honolulu: University of Hawai'i Press, 1999.

Kanda Yutsuki. *Kinsei no geinō kōgyō to chiiki shakai*. Tokyo: Tōkyō Daigaku Shuppankai, 1999.

Karras, Ruth Mazo. *Common Women: Prostitution and Sexuality in Medieval England*. London: Oxford University Press, 1996.

Kasukabe-shi kyōiku iinkai, ed. *Kasukabe shishi*. 14 vols. and 1 appendix vol. Kasukabe: Kasukabe-shi, 1978–2002.

Katō Takashi. "Governing Edo." In *Edo and Paris: Urban Life and the State in the Early Modern Era*, ed. James McClain, John Merriman, and Ugawa Kaoru, 41–67. Ithaca, NY: Cornell University Press, 1994.

Katsumata, Shizuo, and Martin Colcutt. "The Development of Sengoku Law." In *Japan before Tokugawa: Political Consolidation and Economic Growth, 1500–1650*, ed. John Hall, Nagahara Keiji, and Kōzō Yamamura, 101–24. Princeton, NJ: Princeton University Press, 1981.

Kawai Masaharu. *Seto naikai no rekishi*. Tokyo: Shibundō, 1967.

Kawashima, Terry. *Writing Margins: The Textual Construction of Gender in Heian and Kamakura Japan*. Cambridge, MA: Harvard University Press, 2001.

Kazama Shōtarō. *Niigata yūjo kō*. Tokyo: Koshi Shoin, 1999.

Keene, Donald. *World within Walls: Japanese Literature of the Pre-modern Era, 1600–1867*. New York: Holt, Rinehart and Winston, 1976.

Kino Okiyuki. *Echigo miyage*. 1864. Edited by Nakazawa Kenrō. Sanjō-shi: Yashima Shuppan, 1972.

Kishii Yoshie. *Onna geisha no jidai*. Tokyo: Seiabō, 1974.

Kita Sōichirō. *Edo no geisha*. Tokyo: Chūō Kōronsha, 1989.

Kitagawa Morisada. *Morisada mankō zuhan shūsei*. Edited by Takahashi Masao. Tokyo: Yūzankaku, 2002.

Kobata Atsushi. *Nihon kōzanshi no kenkyū*. Tokyo: Iwanami Shoten, 1968.

Kobayashi Masako. "Kōshōsei no seiritsu to tenkai." In *Nihon joseishi*, vol. 3, ed. Hayashi Reiko, 127–63. Tokyo: Tokyo Daigaku Shuppansha, 1982.

Kodera Heikichi. *Hokkaidō yūrishi kō*. Sapporo: Kita Shobō, 1974.

Koga Jūjirō. *Maruyama yūjo to tōkōmōjin*. 2 vols. Nagasaki-shi: Nagasaki Bunkensha, 1968–69.

Koikawa Shōzan. "Kōshoku shugyō shokoku monogatari." 1851. In *Kōshoku shugyō shokoku monogatari*, ed. Yagi Keiichi. Tokyo: Taihei Shoya, 1982.

Komatsu Shigeo. *Bakumatsu ongoku bugyō no nikki: oniwaban Kawamura Nagataka no shōgai*. Tokyo: Chūō Kōronsha, 1989.

"Konpirasan meishozue." In *Kagawa sōsho*, vol. 3, ed. Kagawa-ken. Takamatsu-shi: Kagawa-ken, 1943.

Kondō Tsuneji. *Kinsei no kōtsū to chihō bunka*. Tokyo: Meichō Shuppan, 1986.

Konno Nobuo. *Edo no furo*. Tokyo: Shinchōsha, 1989.

Kōnosu-shi, ed. *Kōnosu shishi shiryō hen*. 7 vols. Kōnosu: Kōnosu-shi, 1989–2004.

Koshigaya-shi kyōiku iinkai shakai kyōikuka, ed. *Koshigaya shishi*. 9 vols. Koshigaya: Koshigaya-shi, 1971–82.

Kotohira chōshi henshū iinkai, ed. *Chōshi Kotohira*. 5 vols. Kotohira: Kotohira-chō, 1995–98.

Kovner, Sarah. "Base Cultures: Sex Workers and Servicemen in Occupied Japan." *Journal of Asian Studies* 68, no. 3 (2009): 777–804.

Kurachi Katsunao. *Sei to karada no kinseishi*. Tokyo: Tokyo Daigaku Shuppankai, 1998.

Kurashiki shishi kenkyūkai, ed. *Shinshū Kurashiki shishi*. 13 vols. Okayama-shi: San'yō Shimbunsha, 1994–2005.

Leupp, Gary. *Interracial Intimacy in Japan: Western Men and Japanese Women, 1543–1900*. New York: Continuum, 2003.

———. *Servants, Shophands, and Laborers in the Cities of Tokugawa Japan*. Princeton, NJ: Princeton University Press, 1995.

Levine, Philippa. *Prostitution, Race, and Politics: Policing Venereal Disease in the British Empire*. New York: Routledge, 2003.

Lewis, James Bryant. *Frontier Contact between Choson Korea and Tokugawa Japan*. London: RoutledgeCurzon, 2003.

Lie, John. "The Transformation of Sexual Work in 20th-Century Korea." *Gender and Society* 9, no. 3 (1995): 310–27.

Lindsey, William. *Fertility and Pleasure: Ritual and Sexual Values in Tokugawa Japan*. Honolulu: University of Hawai'i Press, 2007

Maki Hidemasa. *Jinshin baibai*. Tokyo: Iwanami Shoten, 1971.

———. *Kinsei Nihon no jinshin baibai no keifu*. Tokyo: Sōbunsha, 1970.

Makihara Norio. *Kyakubun to kokumin no aida: kindai minshū no seiji ishiki*. Tokyo: Yoshikawa Kōbunkan, 1998.

Makino Ryūshin. *Kitamaebune no jidai: Kinsei igo no Nihonkai kaiunshi*. Tokyo: Kyōikusha, 1979.

Maruo Hiroshi. "Kinsei Konpira monzenmachi no hattatsu ni tsuite." *Kagawa shigaku*, no. 26 (1999): 59–83.

McClain, James. *Kanazawa: A Seventeenth-Century Castle Town*. New Haven, CT: Yale University Press, 1982.

Mega Atsuko. *Hankachō no naka no onnatachi: Okayama-han no kiroku kara*. Tokyo: Heibonsha, 1995.

———. "Wakamono renchū to mura no musume." *Nihonshi kenkyū* 376 (1993): 37–60.

Minakami Tsutomu. *Ryōkan o aruku*. Tokyo: Shūeisha Bunko, 1990.

Mitsuyo Yoshinori. "Tōkaidō Futagawa-shuku ni okeru hatagoya to meshimori onna." *Toyohashi bijutsukan kenkyū kiyō* 9 (2000): 27–60.

Miyachi Masato. *Bakumatsu ishinki no bunka to jōhō*. Tokyo: Meicho Kankōkai, 1994.

Miyamoto Yukiko. "Kanzawa no kuruwa." In *Ronshū kinsei joseishi*, ed. Kinsei joseishi kenkyūkai, 193–244. Tokyo: Yoshikawa Kōbunkan. 1986.

———. "Maruyama yūjo no seikatsu: 'Nagasaki bugyōsho hanketsu kiroku hankachō' no bunseki o chūshin to shite." *Komazawa shigaku* 31 (1984): 19–46.

———. "Yūri no seiritsu to taishūka." In *Bunka no taishūka*, vol. 14 of *Nihon no kinsei*, ed. Takeuchi Makoto, 169–218. Tokyo: Chūō Kōronsha, 1993.

Mori Yasuhiko. "Kinsei shukuba joseishi kenkyū: Hokkoku ōkan Shinshū Shimo-Togura shuku no 'meshimori onna.'" In *Nihon chiikishi kenkyū*, ed. Murakami Tadashi, 397–440. Tokyo: Bunken Shuppan, 1986.

Morikuri Shigekazu. "Karayuki-san and Shingintori: Prostitution and the Industrial Economy in Amakusa at the End of the Edo Period." Translated by Llewelyn Hughes. In *Gender and Japanese History*, vol 1, ed. Wakita Haruko, Anne Bouchy, and Ueno Chizuko, 327–43. Osaka: Osaka University Press, 1999.

Morinaga Taneo. *Hankachō: Nagasaki bugyō no kiroku*. Tokyo: Iwanami Shoten, 1962.

———, ed. *Hankachō: Nagasaki bugyōsho hanketsu kiroku*. 11 vols. Nagasaki-shi: Hankachō Kankōkai, 1958–61.

Morisaki Kazue. *Baishun ōkoku no onnatachi: shōfu to sanpu ni yoru kindaishi*. Tokyo: Hōtōsha, 1993.

Morita Tomoko. *Kaikoku to chigai hōken: ryōji saiban seido no un'yō to Maria Rusu-gō jiken*. Tokyo: Yoshikawa Kōbunkan, 2005.

Nagano Hiroko. "Bakuhan hō to josei." In *Nihon joseishi*, vol. 3, ed. Joseishi Sōgō Kenkyūkai, 163–91. Tokyo: Tōkyō Daigaku Shuppankai, 1982.

———. "Kinsei kōki joshi rōdō no hensen to tokushitsu." In *Ronshū kinsei joseishi*, ed. Kinsei joseishi kenkyūkai, 103–37. Tokyo: Yoshikawa Kōbunkan, 1986.

———. "Nihon kinsei nōson ni okeru masukyuriniti no kōchiku to jendā." In *Jendā de yomitoku Edo jidai*, ed. Sakurai Yuki, Sugano Noriko, and Nagano Hiroko, 173–212. Tokyo: Sanseido, 2001.

Nagaoka-shi, ed. *Nagaoka shishi shiryō hen*. 5 vols. Nagaoka: Nagaoka-shi, 1992–94.

———. *Nagaoka shishi tsūshi hen*. 2 vols. Nagaoka: Nagaoka-shi, 1995–96.

Nagasaki shishi fūzoku hen. Edited by Nagasaki shiyakusho. Nagasaki-shi: Nagasaki-shi, 1929.

Nakai Nobuhiko and James McClain. "Commercial Change and Urban Growth in Early Modern Japan." In *The Cambridge History of Japan*, vol 4: *Early Modern Japan*, ed. John Hall, 519–95. New York: Cambridge University Press, 1991.

Nelson, Thomas. "Slavery in Medieval Japan." *Monumenta Nipponica* 59, no. 4 (2004): 463–92.

Nenzi, Laura. *Excursions in Identity: Travel and the Intersection of Place, Gender, and Status in Edo Japan*. Honolulu: University of Hawai'i Press, 2008.

Nihei Sachiko. "Nikkō dōchū Kasukabe shuku no meshimori onna ni tsuite." *Komazawa shigaku* 60 (2003): 57–58.

Niigata-ken, ed. *Niigata kenshi shiryō hen*. 24 vols. Niigata: Niigata-ken, 1980–86.

———. *Niigata kenshi tsūshi hen*. 9 vols. Niigata: Niigata-ken, 1986–88.

Niigata-shi, ed. *Niigata shishi*. 2 vols. Niigata: Niigata-shi, 1934.

Niigata-shi hensan kinseishi bukai, ed. *Niigata shishi shiryō hen*. 12 vols. Niigata: Niigata-shi, 1990–94.

———. *Niigata shishi tsūshi hen*. 5 vols. Niigata: Niigata-shi, 1995–97.

Niigata-shi kyōdo shiryōkan, ed. *Niigata machikaisho monjo*. Vol. 1 of *Niigata-shi kyōdo shiryōkan chōsa nenpō*. Niigata: Niigata-shi Kyōdo Shiryōkan, 1977.

———. *Shodai Niigata bugyō Kawamura Nagataka monjo*. 15 vols. Vols. 2–16 of *Niigata-shi kyōdo shiryōkan chosa nenpō*. Niigata: Niigata-shi Kyōdo Shiryōkan, 1978–92.

Niigata-shi shishi hensanka. "Edo shōnin no Niigata kenbutsu: *Kōsei dōchūki* no shōkai." *Shishi Niigata* 16 (1995): 56–86.

Niigata-shi, ed. *Niigata shishi*. 2 vols. Niigata: Niigata-shi, 1934.

Nishimura Keiko. "Tokugawa-ki ni okeru toshi to minshū shakai: Nagasaki Maruyama Yoriaichō o tōshite." *Nihon joshi daigaku bungaku-bu kiyō* 44 (1994): 183–233.

Nishiyama Matsunosuke. *Edo Culture: Daily Life and Diversions in Urban Japan, 1600–1868*. Translated and edited by Gerald Groemer. Honolulu: University of Hawai'i Press, 1997.

Nolte, Sharon H., and Sally Ann Hastings. "The Meiji State's Policy toward Women, 1890–1910." In *Recreating Japanese Women*, ed. Gail Lee Bernstein, 151–74. Berkeley: University of California Press, 1991.

Nussbaum, Martha. "'Whether from Reason or Prejudice: Taking Money for Bodily Services." In *Prostitution and Pornography: Philosophical Debate about the Sex Industry*, ed. Jessica Spector. 175–208. Stanford, CA: Stanford University Press, 2006.

Oda Hisashi, *Edo no gokuraku tonbo: "Fude makase" no aru tabigeinin no kiroku*. Akitashi: Mumyōsha Shuppan, 1997.

Odajima Masatake. *Echigo yashi, gekan*. Niigata: Echigo Yashi Kankōkai, 1936.

Ogi Shinichirō. *Kinsei kōzan shakaishi no kenkyū*. Tokyo: Shibunkaku Shuppan, 1996.

Ōguchi Yūjirō. "Mura no hanzai to Kantō torishimari shutsuyaku." In *Kinsei no mura to machi*, ed. Kawamura Masaru sensei kanreki kinenkai, 81–101. Tokyo: Yoshikawa Kōbunkan, 1988.

Ōhashi Tadayoshi, ed. "Go-Taiheiki shiroishi banashi." In *Shinpen Nihon koten bungaku zenshū*, vol. 77: *Jōruishū*, ed. Torigoe Bunzō et al., 460–669. Tokyo: Shogakkan, 2002.

Ōi-machi shi hensan iinkai, ed. *Ōi-machi shiryō*. 37 vols. Ōi-machi, Saitama-ken: Ōi-machi Kyōiku Iinkai, 1978–82.

Ono Takeo. *Yoshiwara, Shimabara*. Higashimurayama: Kyōikusha, 1978.

Ooms, Herman. *Charismatic Bureaucrat: A Political Biography of Matsudaira Sadanobu, 1758–1829*. Chicago: University of Chicago Press, 1975.

———. *Tokugawa Ideology: Early Constructs, 1570–1680*. Princeton, NJ: Princeton University Press, 1985.

———. *Tokugawa Village Practice: Class, Status, Power, Law*. Berkeley: University of California Press, 1996.

Ōta-shi, ed. *Ōta shishi shiryō hen*. 5 vols. Ōta-shi: Ōta-shi, 1978–87.

———. *Ōta shishi tsūshi hen*. 8 vols. Ōta-shi: Ōta-shi, 1984–97.

Ōtsuka Minoru. *Aizu-han josei o meguru hankachō*. Aizuwakamatsu-shi: Rekishi Shunjū Shuppan, 1998.

Overall, Christine. "What's Wrong with Prostitution? Evaluating Sex Work." *Signs* 17, no. 4 (1992): 705–24.

Partner, Simon. *The Mayor of Aihara: A Japanese Villager and His Community, 1865–1925*. Berkeley: University of California Press, 2009.

Pateman, Carole. *The Sexual Contract*. Stanford, CA: Stanford University Press, 1988.

Pflugfelder, Gregory. *Cartographies of Desire: Male-Male Sexuality in Japanese Discourse, 1600–1950*. Berkeley: University of California Press, 1999.

Plutschow, Herbert. *A Reader in Edo Period Travel*. Folkstone, Kent, UK: Global Oriental, 2006.

Pratt, Edward. *Japan's Protoindustrial Elite: The Economic Foundations of the Gōnō*. Cambridge, MA: Harvard University Press, 1999.

Ramseyer, Mark. *Odd Markets in Japanese History: Law and Economic Growth*. New York: Cambridge University Press, 1996.

Ravina, Mark. *Land and Lordship in Early Modern Japan*. Stanford, CA: Stanford University Press, 1999.

Roberts, Luke. *Mercantilism in a Japanese Domain: The Merchant Origins of Economic Nationalism in 18th-Century Tosa*. New York: Cambridge University Press, 1998.

Robertson, Claire, and Marsha Robinson. "Re-modeling Slavery As If Women Mattered." In *Women and Slavery*, vol. 2: *The Modern Atlantic*, ed. Gwyn Campbell, Suzanne Miers, and Joseph C. Miller, 253–83. Athens: Ohio University Press, 2007.

Rogers, Lawrence. "She Loves Me, She Loves Me Not: Shinjū and *Shikidō Ōkagami.*" *Monumenta Nipponica* 49, no. 1 (Spring 1994): 31–60.

Ropp, Paul S. "Ambiguous Images of Courtesan Culture in Late Imperial China." In *Writing Women in Late Imperial China*, ed. Ellen Widmer and Kang-i Sun Chang, 17–45. Stanford, CA: Stanford University Press, 1997.

Rosen, Ruth, *The Lost Sisterhood: Prostitution in America, 1900–1918*. Baltimore: Johns Hopkins University Press, 1982.

Rubinger, Richard. *Popular Literacy in Early Modern Japan.* Honolulu: University of Hawai'i Press, 2007.

Saitama-ken, ed. *Shinpen Saitama kenshi shiryō hen.* 26 vols. Urawa: Saitama-ken, 1979–91.

———. *Shinpen Saitama kenshi tsūshi hen.* 7 vols. Urawa: Saitama-ken, 1987–91.

Sakamoto Tadahisa. "Osaka ni okeru 'Tenpō kaikaku' seisaku no ritsuan to sono rongi—kinsei kōki no toshi seisaku no kadai." *Chiba daigaku hōgaku ronshū* 16, no. 3 (2001): 33–66.

Salter, Rebecca. *Japanese Popular Prints: From Votive Slips to Playing Cards.* Honolulu: University of Hawai'i Press, 2006.

Sand, Jordan. *House and Home in Modern Japan: Architecture, Domestic Space, and Bourgeois Culture, 1880–1930.* Cambridge, MA: Harvard University Press, 2003.

Sanders, Holly Vincele. "Prostitution in Postwar Japan: Debt and Labor." Ph.D. diss., Princeton University, 2005.

"Sanuki no kuni meishozue." In *Shikoku no kan*, vol. 14 of *Nihon meisho fūzoku zue*, ed. Matsubara Hideaki. Tokyo: Kadokawa Shoten, 1981.

Satō Nobuhiro. "Keizai yōroku." 1827. In *Nihon keizai taiten*, vol. 18, ed. Takimoto Sei'ichi. Tokyo: Hōbunshokan, 1992.

Satō Seiichirō. *Akita-ken yūri shi.* Akita: Mumyōsha Shuppan, 1983.

Sawada, Janine Anderson. "Sexual Relations as Religious Practice in the Late Tokugawa Period: Fujidō." *Journal of Japanese Studies* 32, no. 2 (2006): 341–66.

Sawayama Mikako. *Edo no sutegotachi: sono shōzō.* Tokyo: Yoshikawa Kōbunkan, 2008.

Scheiner, Irwin. "Benevolent Lords and Honorable Peasants: Rebellion and Peasant Consciousness in Tokugawa Japan." In *Japanese Thought in the Tokugawa Period, 1600–1868*, ed. Tetsuo Najita and Irwin Scheiner, 39–62. Chicago: University of Chicago Press, 1978.

Scott, Joan Wallach. *Gender and the Politics of History.* New York: Columbia University Press, 1988.

———. "Gender: A Useful Category of Historical Analysis." *American Historical Review* 91, no. 5 (1986): 1053–75.

Screech, Timon. *Sex and the Floating World: Erotic Images in Japan, 1700–1820*. Honolulu: University of Hawai'i Press, 1999.

Segawa Kiyoko. *Mura no onnatachi*. Tokyo: Miraisha, 1970.

Seigle, Cecilia Segawa. *Yoshiwara: The Glittering World of the Japanese Courtesan*. Honolulu: University of Hawai'i Press, 1993.

Shichū torishimari no bu 2. Edited by Tokyo daigaku shiryō hensanjo. Vol. 2 of *Shichū torishimari ruishū*, vol. 6 of *Dai nihon kinsei shiryō*. Tokyo: Tōkyō Daigaku Shuppankai, 1960.

Shiba Keiko. *Kinsei onna tabi nikki*. Tokyo: Yoshikawa Kōbunkan, 1997.

Shimojū Kiyoshi. "Miuri hōkō to josei." In *Mibun no naka no josei*, ed. Yabuta Yutaka and Yanagiya Keiko, 100–131. Tokyo: Yoshikawa Kōbunkan, 2010.

———."Miuriteki hōkō to zegen ni tsuite." *Minshūshi kenkyū* 34 (1987): 34–46.

Shimonoseki shishi minzoku hen. edited by Shimonoseki-shi shishi henshū iinkai. Shimonoseki-shi: Shimonoseki-shi, 1992.

Shiraishi, Hiroko. *Nagasaki Dejima no yūjo: Kinsei e no mado o hiraita onnatachi*. Tokyo: Bensei Shuppan, 2005.

Shively, Donald. "Bakufu versus Kabuki." *Harvard Journal of Asiatic Studies* 18, nos. 3–4 (1955): 326–56.

———. "Popular Culture." In *The Cambridge History of Japan*, vol. 4: *Early Modern Japan*, ed. John Hall, 706–70. New York: Cambridge University Press, 1991.

Siebold, Philipp von. *Manners and Customs of the Japanese in the Nineteenth Century*. New York: Harper & Brothers, 1855.

Siniawer, Eiko Maruko. *Ruffians, Yakuza, Nationalists: The Violent Politics of Modern Japan, 1860–1960*. Ithaca, NY: Cornell University Press, 2008.

Smith, Robert John, and Ella Lury Wiswell. *The Women of Suye-Mura*. Chicago: University of Chicago Press, 1982.

Smith, Thomas C. *The Agrarian Origins of Modern Japan*. Stanford, CA: Stanford University Press, 1959.

———. *Native Sources of Japanese Industrialization, 1750–1920*. Berkeley: University of California Press, 1988.

Sōka shishi hensan iinkai, ed. *Sōka shishi shiryō hen*. 4 vols. Sōka-shi: Sōka-shi, 1985–92.

———. *Sōka shishi tsūshi hen*. 2 vols. Sōka-shi: Sōka-shi, 1997–2001.

Solt, John. "Willow Leaftips." In *Imaging/Reading Eros: Proceedings for the Conference Sexuality and Edo Culture, 1750–1850*, ed. Sumie Jones, 129–34. Bloomington: East Asian Studies Center, Indiana University, 1995.

Sommer, Matthew H. *Sex, Law, and Society in Late Imperial China*. Stanford, CA: Stanford University Press, 2000.

Sone Hiromi. "Conceptions of Geisha: A Case Study of the City of Miyazu." In *Gender and Japanese History*, vol. 1, ed. Wakita Haruko, Anne Bouchy, and Ueno Chizuko, 213–33. Osaka: Osaka University Press, 1999.

———. "Josei to keibatsu." In *Mibun no naka no josei*, ed. Yutaka Yabuta and Yanagiya Keiko, 67–98. Tokyo: Yoshikawa Kōbunkan, 2010.

———. "Kinsei baibaishun no kōzō: kōshōsei no shūen." In *Ajia joseishi: hikaku shi no kokoromi*, ed. Hayashi Reiko and Yanagita Setsuko, 387–93. Tokyo: Meiseki Shoten, 1997.

———. "Prostitution and Public Authority in Early Modern Japan." In *Women and Class in Japanese History*, ed. Hitomi Tonomura, Anne Walthall, and Wakita Haruko, 169–85. Ann Arbor: University of Michigan Press, 1999.

———. *Shōfu to kinsei shakai*. Tokyo: Yoshikawa Kōbunkan, 2003.

Sources of Japanese Tradition. Vol. 2: *1600 to 2000*. Edited by Wm. Theodore de Bary, Carol Gluck, and Arthur E. Tiedemann. 2nd ed. New York: Columbia University Press, 2006.

Spector, Jessica, ed. *Prostitution and Pornography: Philosophical Debate about the Sex Industry*. Stanford, CA: Stanford University Press, 2006.

Stanley, Amy. "Adultery, Punishment, and Reconciliation in Tokugawa Japan." *Journal of Japanese Studies* 33, no. 2 (2007): 309–35.

Stanley, Amy Dru. *From Bondage to Contract: Wage Labor, Marriage, and the Market in the Age of Slave Emancipation*. New York: Cambridge University Press, 1998.

Stansell, Christine. *City of Women: Sex and Class in New York, 1789–1860*. Urbana: University of Illinois Press, 1987.

Sugahara Kenji. "Kinsei Kyōto no chō to sutego." *Rekishi hyōron* 422 (1985): 34–60.

Sugano Noriko. *Edo jidai no kōkōmono: kōgiroku no sekai*. Tokyo: Yoshikawa Kōbunkan, 1999.

———. "Meshiuri hatagoya to meshiuri onna." *Nihon rekishi* 471 (1987): 53–66.

———. *Mura to kaikaku: Kinsei sonraku shi, joseishi kenkyū*. Tokyo: Sanseidō, 1992.

———. "Nōson josei no rōdō to seikatsu." In *Nihon joseishi*, vol. 3, ed. Sōgō joseishi kenkyūkai, 63–94. Tokyo: Tōkyō Daigaku Shuppankai, 1982.

———. "State Indoctrination of Filial Piety in Tokugawa Japan: Sons and Daughters in *The Official Records of Filial Piety*." In *Women and Confucian Cultures in Premodern China, Korea, and Japan*, ed. Dorothy Ko, 170–89. Berkeley: University of California Press, 2003.

Sugito chōshi hensanshitsu, ed. *Sugito chōshi kinsei shiryō hen*. Sugito: Sugito chōshi hensanshitsu, 2004.

Suzuki Bokushi. *Snow Country Tales: Life in the Other Japan.* Translated by Jeffrey Hunter and Rose Lesser. New York: Weatherhill, 1986.

Takano Toshio. *Yūjo kabuki.* Tokyo: Kawade Shobō Shinsa, 2005.

Takasaki shishi hensan iinkai, ed. *Shinpen Takasaki shishi shiryō hen.* 13 vols. Takasaki-shi: Takasaki-shi, 1994–2002.

Tanaka Kyūgu. "Minkan seiyō." 1721. Reprinted in *Nihon keizai taiten,* vol. 5, ed. Takimoto Seiichi. Tokyo: Shishi Shuppansha, 1928.

Thal, Sarah. *Rearranging the Landscape of the Gods: The Politics of a Pilgrimage Site in Japan, 1573–1912.* Chicago: University of Chicago Press, 2005.

Theiss, Janet. *Disgraceful Matters: The Politics of Chastity in Eighteenth-Century China.* Berkeley: University of California Press, 2004.

Thunberg, Carl Peter. *Travels in Europe, Africa, and Asia, Made between the Years 1770 and 1779.* 2nd ed. Vol. 3. London, 1795.

Toby, Ronald. *State and Diplomacy in Early Modern Japan: Asia in the Development of the Tokugawa Bakufu.* Princeton, NJ: Princeton University Press, 1984.

Tocco, Martha. "Made in Japan: Meiji Women's Education." In *Gendering Modern Japanese History,* ed. Barbara Molony and Kathleen Uno, 36–60. Cambridge, MA: Harvard University Asia Center, 2005.

Tonomura, Hitomi. "Black Hair and Red Trousers: Gendering the Flesh in Medieval Japan." *American Historical Review* 99, no. 1 (1994): 129–54.

———. "Re-envisioning Women in the Post-Kamakura Age." In *The Origins of Japan's Medieval World: Courtiers, Clerics, Warriors and Peasants in the Fourteenth Century,* ed. Jeffrey Mass, 138–69. Stanford, CA: Stanford University Press, 2002.

———. "Sexual Violence against Women: Legal and Extralegal Treatment in Premodern Warrior Societies." In *Women and Class in Japanese History,* ed. Hitomi Tonomura, Anne Walthall, and Wakita Haruko, 135–52. Ann Arbor: Center for Japanese Studies, University of Michigan, 1999.

Traganou, Jilly. *The Tōkaidō Road: Traveling and Representation in Edo and Meiji Japan.* London: RoutledgeCurzon, 2004.

Tsuji Tatsuya. "Politics in the Eighteenth Century." Translated by Harold Bolitho. In *Early Modern Japan,* vol. 4 of *The Cambridge History of Japan,* ed. John Whitney Hall, 425–77. New York: Cambridge University Press, 1991.

Tsukada Takashi. "Kinsei no keibatsu." In *Saiban to kihan,* ed. Asao Naohiro. Tokyo: Iwanami shoten, 1987.

———. "Kinsei Osaka no keiseimachi to chaya." *Rekishi hyōron* 540 (1995): 31–47.

———. *Kinsei mibunsei to shūen shakai.* Tokyo: Tōkyō Daigaku Shuppankai, 1997.

———. *Mibunsei shakai to shimin shakai: Kinsei Nihon no shakai to hō*. Tokyo: Kashiwa Shobō, 1992.

"Ugo no kuni Senboku Ogachi-gun Akita Innai ginzanki" C. 1640. Reprinted in *Nihon shomin seikatsu shiryō shūsei*, vol. 10, ed. Miyamoto Tsuneichi, Haraguchi Torao, and Tanigawa Ken'ichi, 499–543. Tokyo: San'ichi Shobō, 1970.

Umezu Masakage. *Umezu Masakage nikki*. 1612–33. 9 vols. Vols. 3–11 of *Dai nihon kokiroku*, ed. Tokyo daigaku shiryō hensanjo. Tokyo: Iwanami Shoten, 1953–66.

Urawa-shi sōmubu shishi hensanshitsu, ed. *Urawa shishi*. 19 vols. Urawa: Urawa-shi, 1974–2001.

Usami Misako. "Meshimori onna deiri ikken: Kumagaya-shuku meshimori onna setchi o megutte." In *Edo jidai no joseitachi*, ed. Kinsei joseishi kenkyūkai, 185–217. Tokyo: Yoshikawa Kōbunkan, 1990.

———. *Shukuba to meshimori onna*. Tokyo: Doseisha, 2000.

Vaporis, Constantine Nomikos. *Breaking Barriers: Travel and the State in Early Modern Japan*. Cambridge, MA: Council on East Asian Studies, Harvard University, 1994.

———. *Tour of Duty: Samurai, Military Service in Edo, and the Culture of Early Modern Japan*. Honolulu: University of Hawai'i Press, 2008.

Vlastos, Stephen. *Peasant Protests and Uprisings in Tokugawa Japan*. Berkeley: University of California Press, 1986.

Wakita Haruko. "The Medieval Household and Gender Roles within the Imperial Family, Merchants, Nobility, and Commoners." Translated by Gary Leupp. In *Women and Class in Japanese History*, ed. Hitomi Tonomura, Anne Walthall, and Wakita Haruko, 99–118. Ann Arbor: University of Michigan Press, 1999.

Walker, Brett. *The Conquest of Ainu Lands: Ecology and Culture in Japanese Expansion, 1590–1800*. Berkeley: University of California Press, 2001.

Walkowitz, Judith. *Prostitution and Victorian Society: Women, Class, and the State*. New York: Cambridge University Press, 1980.

Walthall, Anne. "Devoted Wives / Unruly Women: Invisible Presence in the History of Japanese Social Protest." *Signs* 20, no. 1 (1994): 106–36.

———. "The Family Ideology of Rural Entrepreneurs in Nineteenth-Century Japan." *Journal of Social History* 23, no. 3 (1990): 463–83.

———. "The Life Cycle of Farm Women in Tokugawa Japan." In *Recreating Japanese Women, 1600–1945*, ed. Gail Lee Bernstein, 42–70. Berkeley: University of California Press, 1991.

———. "Masturbation and Discourse on Female Sexual Practices in Early Modern Japan." *Gender and History* 21, no. 1 (2009): 1–18.

———. "Peripheries: Rural Culture in Tokugawa Japan." *Monumenta Nipponica* 39, no 4 (1984): 371–392.

———. *The Weak Body of a Useless Woman: Matsuo Taseko and the Meiji Restoration*. Chicago: University of Chicago Press, 1998.

Wang, Gungwu. "Merchants without Empire: The Hokkien Soujourning Communities." In *The Rise of Merchant Empires: Long-Distance Trade in the Early Modern World*, ed. James D. Tracy, 400–22. New York: Cambridge University Press, 1990.

Watanabe Kazan. "Hōchōroku." C. 1832. Reprinted in *Shinpen Saitama kenshi shiryō hen*, vol. 10: *Kinsei* 1, ed. Saitama-ken, 727–66. Urawa: Saitama-ken, 1979.

Watanabe Keiichi. "*Umezu Masakage nikki*" *tokuhon: Akita-han karō no nikki o yomu*. Akita-shi: Mumyōsha Shuppan, 1992.

Watanabe Kenji. *Edo yūri seisuiki*. Tokyo: Kōdansha, 1994.

White, Luise. *The Comforts of Home: Prostitution in Colonial Nairobi*. Chicago: University of Chicago Press, 1990.

Wigen, Kären. *The Making of a Japanese Periphery, 1750–1920*. Berkeley: University of California Press, 1995.

Wolf, Margery. *Women and the Family in Rural Taiwan*. Stanford, CA: Stanford University Press, 1972.

Yabuta Yutaka. *Joseishi to shite no kinsei*. Tokyo: Azekura Shobō, 1996.

———. "Kinsei josei no raifu saikuru." In *Nihon josei seikatsu shi*, vol. 3: *Kinsei*, ed. Joseishi sōgō kenkyūkai, 237–71. Tokyo: Tōkyō Daigaku Shuppankai, 1990.

———. "Moji to josei." In *Nihon tsūshi*, vol. 15: *Kinsei* 5, ed. Asao Naohiro et al., 225–54. Tokyo: Iwanami Shoten, 1995.

Yagi Keiichi, ed. *Kōshoku shugyō shokoku monogatari*. Tokyo: Taihei Shoya, 1982.

Yahisa Kenji. "Kinsei kōki Hirakata-shuku no hatagoya to meshimori onna." *Nenpō toshishi kenkyū* 7 (1999): 117–32.

Yamaguchi Keiji. "Kinsei shoki ni Akita-han ni okeru kōzan machi: Innai ginzan o chūshin ni." In *Kokumin seikatsushi kenkyū*, vol. 2: *Seikatsu to shakai keizai*, ed. Itō Tasaburō, 189–224. Tokyo: Yoshikawa Kōbunko, 1959.

———. *Sakoku to kaikoku*. Tokyo: Iwanami Shoten, 1993.

———. "Umezu Masakage: Akita-han kensetsu o ninatta mono." In *Nihon jinbutsu shi taikei*, vol. 3, ed. Kitajima Masamoto, 174–209. Tokyo: Asakura Shoten, 1959.

Yokota Fuyuhiko, "Imagining Working Women in Early Modern Japan." In *Women and Class in Japanese History*, ed. Hitomi Tonomura, Anne Walthall, and Wakita Haruko, 153–67. Ann Arbor: University of Michigan Press, 1999.

Yokota Takeko. "Bakamatsu Hakata Yanagimachi yūjoya Toraya: Hinichijō no sekai o nichijō ni ikita musumetachi." *Sainan chiikishi kenkyū* 11 (1996): 269–305.

Yonemoto, Marcia. *Mapping Early Modern Japan: Space, Place, and Culture in the Tokugawa Period*. Berkeley: University of California Press, 2003.

Yoon, Byung Nam. "Domain and Bakufu in Tokugawa Japan: The Copper Trade and Development of Akita Domain Mines." PhD diss., Princeton University, 1995.

Yoshida Nobuyuki. *Mibunteki shūen to shakai: bunka kōzō*. Kyoto: Buraku Mondai Kenkyūjo, 2003.

———. "Yūkaku shakai." In *Toshi no shūen ni ikiru*, vol. 4 of *Mibunteki shūen to kinsei shakai*., ed. Tsukada Takashi, 13–52. Tokyo: Yoshikawa Kōbunkan, 2006.

Yoshida Yuriko. "Gaikokujin yūsansho to Yokosuka." *Shishi kenkyū Yokosuka* 1 (2002): 52–88.

Yutaka-chō kyōiku iinkai, ed. *Yutaka chōshi honbun hen*. Takehara-shi: Yutaka-chō Kyōiku Iinkai, 2000.

———. *Yutaka chōshi shiryō hen*. Takehara-shi: Yutaka-chō Kyōiku Iinkai, 1993.

INDEX

Italic page numbers refer to illustrations.

abortion, 94, 148–49, 151
accounts of official business (*goyōdome*), 19
actors, 178
"actors," as male prostitutes, 16
actresses, 49
Adams, William, 77
adoption, 55, 68
adultery, 4–5, 39, 41, 54; as capital offense, 50; as "illicit sex," 68; prostitutes acquitted for, 65, 208n69; as treason, 9
agency, female, xi, xiii, 4, 144, 150; anxiety surrounding, 7; empowerment and, 192; market economy and, 186; prostitutes' desires, 185
agriculture, commercial, xiv, 6, 105, 113, 149, 189
Akita domain, 23–24, 27, 54
"alternate attendance" (*sankin kōtai*), 26, 160
Asai Ryōi, 140
asobi (medieval sexual entertainers), 30

"assisting villages" (*sukegō*), 138, 156, 160, 164

banzuke, 103
barmaids, 193
bathhouses, 11, 36, 50, 60–61, 62
bathing girls (*yuna*), 60, 61
benevolent government ideal, 54, 63, 65, 70, 160; filial daughters and, 98; fragility of, 132; market economy as strain on, 120; petitions to officials and, 76
blood feuds, 30
board games, 81
boathouses (*funayado*), 127, 163
"body-selling" (*miuri*), 4
"bosses" (*kaoyaku*), 178
Botsman, Daniel, 32
"bought women" (*baijo*), 33, 42, 43, 203n33
Britain, in Opium War, 125
brothel keepers, 2, 6, 7; abusive, 10; "benevolent" governors and, 48; broken

243

brothel keepers (*continued*)
contracts and, 90, 91; children of *yūjo* and, 96; expansion of sex trade and, 18; filial ties of prostitutes and, 86, 87–88; indenture contracts and, 58, 59; in Inland Sea region, 164, 165, 166, 169, 176, 183; in Innai Ginzan, 35; magistrates and, 69, 84, 94; in Mitarai, 172, 173, 184, 185; in Nagasaki, 83; petitions to shogunate for recognition, 45; pleasure quarters as invention of, 48; profitability of prostitution and, 44; resistance to authority of, 17, 99; "rules of the pleasure quarter" and, 184; selective enforcement against clandestine prostitutes, 63–66, 70; shogunate and, 14, 17, 49; as spies and informers, 49; in temples, 61; underworld connections of, 176–80; women as, 90–92; women victimized by, 11, 86; in Yoshiwara, 49, 63; *yūjo* as dutiful daughters and, 76

brothels, 2, 11, 33; Chikugoya (Yoriai, Nagasaki), 90; children raised in, 95; geisha houses and, 67; Hikitaya (Yoriai, Nagasaki), 93; in "hill places" *okabasho*, 66; Kyō-no-shio-ya, 33; as "laundries," 37; levies paid to the state, 36–37, 44; in Meiji era, 193; of Mitarai, 167, 171; Nagasaki-ya (Fushimi), 37; in Niigata, 127, 128; in port towns, 164; prostitutes indentured to, 4, 12; provincial, 12; recruitment networks, 106; runaways from, 89; taxes on, 193; Tomitaya (Mitarai), 167, 172–74, 180–82; transfer between (*sumikae*), 58; urbanization and, 12–14, 151–52

Buddhism, 26, 31, 46, 115
Bunsei era (1818–29), 67
Bunsei Reforms (1827), 155, 158
Burns, Susan, 149
Buyō Inshi, 117, 119

castle towns, 2, 13, 28, 120, *168*; of Inland Sea region, *168*; magistrates' headquarters in, 25; samurai in, 8
celibacy, xiii, 4, 124
chastity, female, xv, 5, 63; Confucian texts on, 4; of widows, 123–24, 129
Chikamatsu Monzaemon, 90
childbirth, 94–95, 211n71
children, 3, 7, 190; adoption of, 55; benevolent government ideal and, 47; child attendants (*kamuro*), 50, 83; dutiful, 17; exploited by parents, 8; indentured as prostitutes, 4; as possessions, 30, 33; sale of, 18; sold to meet tax obligations, 43; of *yūjo*, 95–96
China, xv–xvi, 119–20; defeated by Britain in Opium War, 125; Qing dynasty, 5, 120, 123; Republican era, xvi
Chinese traders, 72, 75, 79, 84, 209n17; children with Japanese women, 95; "marriages" with *yūjo*, 93, 94, 211n70
Christianity, 3, 57, 77, 93
Chūshingura [A Treasury of Loyal Retainers] (play), 71
cities, 32, 44, 151; city wards (*chō*), 26; demographic profiles of, 2; migration to, 136, 192, 215n8; samurai in, 28; sex trade as urban phenomenon, 12–14
civil wars, 31
clandestine prostitutes (*kakushi baijo*), 16, 66, 98, 125, 203n33; geisha and, 68; in Niigata, 122–23; number of women employed as, 105; in post stations, 141; targeted enforcement against, 63–66; Yoshiwara monopoly and, 59–63
cohabitation, 4, 93
"comfort women," in Pacific War, 196
commoners, xv, 2, 48, 99, 124, 190; assigned occupations of, 8–9; expansion of sex trade and, 108; female promiscuity viewed by, 4; marriage as bondage, 47; in Niigata, 114; sex as commodity sold to, 31; sex trade

growth and prosperity of, 10; violent quarrels among, 25
"compensated dating" (*enjo kōsai*), 196
concubines, 5, 31, 56, 77, 152–53
Confucianism, 4, 5, 6, 47, 118, 119
consumer culture, xii, xiv, 11, 13
"containers," of status order, 26, 29, 54, 92, 97
contraception, 94, 148–49
contract system, 53–59, 66, 67, 70, 76. *See also* indenture contracts
corvée labor, 26, 138, 146, 154
courtesans, 5, 45, 201n25, 206n25
Coxinga (Zheng Chenggong), 77
crime/criminals, 8, 27, 29, 98, 156; crisis of countryside and, 155; female criminals, 39, 41–42, 50, 204n67; informers among, 177–78; in Innai Ginzan, 35; streetwalkers employed by, 60; traffic in "Echigo women," 115
criminal registers (*hankachō*), 19, 75
culture of play, 10, 191, 201n20
currency, xxi–xxii, 57

daimyō, 25–26, 81, 116, 138; as "benevolent rulers," 47; cities controlled by, 52; foreign trade and, 77; human trafficking and, 32; tax revenues of, 120; Tenpō Reforms and, 125
dancers (*odoriko*), 66, 208n72
daughters, xii, 42, 53, 114; "families" of sexual entertainers, 31; of free commoner status, xv; geisha, 67, 68; indentured to brothels, 12; obedience to parents, 54; part-time sexual labor for foreign men, 82–83; prostitutes as dutiful daughters, 9; social/economic autonomy for, 6; traffic in, 17, 29. *See also* filial daughters
"day-laboring women" (*hiyatoi onna*), 172
debts, 86, 88, 98; debt peonage, 32; incurred by local youths, 146; indenture contracts on, 57; as obstacle to marriage for *yūjo*, 90; petitions for forgiveness of, 33; samurai indebted to merchants, 107; wives pawned for, 34
Dejima, island of, 77–83, 93; children of *yūjo* on, 96, 97, 211n80; map, *78*
diaries (*nikki*), 19, 24, 29, 201n1
"dirty money" (*fujōkin*), 178
disease, venereal, 63, 98, 148, 154, 195
divorce, 4, 50, 91
drink-pouring girls (*shakutori onna*), 15, 169
Drixler, Fabian, 115
Dutch East India Company, 77
Dutch traders, 72, *74*, 75, 80, 209n19; children with Japanese women, 95, 96; "marriages" with *yūjo*, 93

Echigo miyage (Echigo Souvenirs), 131
Echigo province, 12, 18, 114, 142; daughter selling in, 114–20; women as "famous products" of, 111, 113
Echigo yashi (Echigo Field journal), 117, 123
"Edict for the Liberation of Geisha and Prostitutes" (*Geishōgi kaihōrei*), 194
Edo (Tokyo), city of, 2, 14, 99, 125, 189; actresses in, 49; "alternate attendance" policy and, 26; entertainment districts, 108; magistrates of, 55, 60, 62; post stations leading out of, 61; sex trade reshaped by status order, 47–48; Shinagawa district, 103; as thriving urban center, 8; undeveloped neighborhoods, 138. *See also* Fukagawa district; Yoshiwara "pleasure quarter"
entertainment districts, 2, 108
eternal term of service (*eidai hōkō*), 53, 63, 116

families/family ties, 4, 11, 71, 137; balance of power within, 2; in conflict with brothel keepers, 172–76; daughters in distant service, 172–73; "good

families/family ties (*continued*)
families," 10, 45; pregnant *yūjo* assisted by, 95–96; prostitutes as threat to, 153; prostitution as family labor, 74–75; prostitution as vital income for, xv, 7, 19, 69; sex workers free from, xiv, xv. *See also* parents
"famous products" (*meibutsu*), 18, 108, 111, 113
feminists, xi, xiii, 9, 144, 196; interpretations of Tokugawa law, 43; on sex work as choice, 4
festivals, prostitutes at, 171
fiction, popular, 6
filial daughters, xii, xiv, 19, 113, 162, 199n2 (Foreword); female agency and, 144; market economy and, 192; in Nagasaki, 83–89; prostitutes as, 70; replaced by "shameless women," 18, 125–33; sacrificial support for family, 182; serving girls of Echigo province, 153
filial piety, 7, 10, 71, 92, 124, 196; in conflict with sex trade, 118; precedence over master–servant relationship, 85–86
floating world (*ukiyo*), 11, 108, 163, 201n20
foreigners. *See* Chinese traders; Dutch traders
Freedom and People's Rights Movement, 193
Fujimoto Kizan, 103
Fujita Satoru, 128
Fujiwara Morohide, 123
Fukagawa district (Edo), 60, 65, 123; "hill places" (*okabasho*), 64, 67, 69, 208n72; temples and shrines, 61
Fukaya no eki [*Fukaya Station*] (Keisai Eisen), 134, *135*
Fukaya station, 134–35, 158
Fukuoka, city and domain of, 52, 84
Fukuzawa Yukichi, 194–95
funerals, attendance at, 85

gamblers/gambling, 60, 137, 155, 177
gangsters, 60, 137, 165, 179
Garon, Sheldon, 193
geisha, 2, 66–71, 98, 190, 208n72; from Kansai region, 168; in Nagasaki, 99; in Niigata, 122, 126, 133; number of women employed as, 105, 193; in post-station inns, 156; "selfish," 100; in woodblock prints, 134, *135*
gendered order, 62, 70, 75; contract system and, 69; disintegration of, "192; employer–employee relationship and, 182, 184–85; establishment of, 14; hierarchy of, 10; Inland Sea brothel keepers and, 165; magistrates and, 47–48; politics and, 9; promotion of sex trade and, 99; prostitutes' self-determination and, 97; status order and, 9, 200–201n17; widows' challenge to, 124–25. *See also* status order
Genroku period (1688–1704), 136
gifts, from lovers and clients, 4, 30, 80–81, 94, 97, 211n70
"girl," as translation for *onna*, 15, 201n24
girls: age of majority, 58; from "good families," 45; kidnapped, 49; postmodern high school girls, 197; runaway, 34–35
Golden, Arthur, 3–4
Goodwin, Janet, 30
"gourd sellers" (*kawauri*), 111
grandparents, 85–86, 95–96, 171
graves, visiting of, 85
Griffis, William Elliot, 3

Hall, John, 26
Hara-kiri of a Woman at Nagamachi [*Nagamachi onna harakiri*] (Chikamatsu), 90
Harootunian, H. D., 191
"helpers" (*sukedan no mono*), 178
Hershatter, Gail, 19

high school students, in postmodern era, 197
"hill places"(*okabasho*), 62, 65, 66, 69, 189; benevolent government ideal and, 63; geisha in, 67; number of, 61
Hirado, port of, 77, 78, 82
Hiroshima domain, 163, 164, 166, 170, 180
Hishiya Heishichi, 72
Hitomi Tonomura, 30
household, 7, 98, 109, 190; boundaries with marketplace, 3; of free commoner status, xv; integrity of, 6, 69, 98, 99, 153, 165; men's and women's roles in, 16; status order and, 26, 47, 92; sustained by sex trade, 97; Tokugawa state-building and, 54; women in profit-making enterprises outside, 6. *See also* patriarchal order
household, male head of, 9, 43, 47, 193; biological parents and, 55, 56; shogunal laws and, 54–55; widow as replacement for, 124. *See also* husbands
Howell, David, 121–22
husbands, 7, 23; diminished power of, 161; fishermen lost at sea, 123; husband as "original man," 39; as pimps, 63, 65, 70; power over wives' bodies, 17, 39; property rights, 30; wives' bodies pawned or "employed" by, 33–35, 41; wives hired out as prostitutes, 23, 24, 69. *See also* household, male head of

Ihara Saikaku, 60
Imamura Yodoshichi, 118, 119, 120, 121, 127, 129; on brothel as refuge for merchants, 132; prostitution in inns opposed by, 122
indenture contracts, 15, 53, 56–58, 62, 70, 179; length of service, 57, 207n45; Meiji liberation edict and, 194; parents' authority versus, 92; signing of, 58, 207n42. *See also* contract system

indentured prostitutes, 7, 88, 94, 119, 124; contract system and, 66; "day-laboring women" (*hiyatoi onna*), 172; of Inland Sea region, 169; permitted reasons to leave brothels, 84–85
indentured women (*kakae onna*), 67–68, 91, 109, 169, 171; of Mitarai brothels, 167; of *yūjo* status group, 75
infanticide, 115, 144, 149
infertility, 148
Inland Sea region, 14, 114, 165; "logic of the market" in, 166; outlaws, 176–80; pilgrimage routes/sites, 12, 19; port towns, 19, 163; "servant girls" (*gejo*) in, 15; townspeople of, 163–64
Innai Ginzan, city of, 14, 16–17, 42–44, 191; founding of, 27; isolation in mountains, 26; as mining town, 23, 29, 202n11; sex trade in, 35–38; traffic in women, 29, 35
innkeepers, 2, 62, 141, 147; corruption and, 159; prostitution as vital income for, 160; village reform associations and, 156–57
inns (*hatagoya*), 2, 59, 61, 134, 140; "plain," 157; serving girls allowed in, 138, 141
inspectors, shogunal, 67–68, 156, 157, 160, 216n27
"islands" (*shima*), 62

Japan: early modernization, xii; geography of sex trade, 11–14, *13*; as "kingdom of whoring," 192; Orientalist stereotypes of, 3–4; urban–rural differences, 6. *See also* Meiji era; Tokugawa era; *specific cities and regions*
Jippensha Ikku, 52, 138

kabuki theater, 36, 55, 204n50; Great Play (*Ōshibai*), 171, 178, 184; peasants and, 105; tragic heroines of, 1

Kaempfer, Engelbert, 89, 140, 141
Kamakura period (1185–1333), 30
Kanazawa, city of, 52
Kanda Yutsuki, 177
Kankoku kōgiroku (Official Records of Filial Piety), 85, 123–24
Kansai region, xxii, 27, 37, 56, 168
Kansei Reforms, 145, 148, 153
Kantō region, 14, 116, 117, 144, 163; commercialized agriculture in, 149; post roads of, 18, 137, *139*; uneven development in, 135; village headmen of, 153
karayuki (going to the Chinese), 79–80
Kasukabe station, 141, 155, 157
Kawahara Keiga, 74
Kawamura Nagataka, 125–31
Keichō kenbunroku (Things Seen and Heard in the Keichō Era), 60
Keisai Eisen, 134, 135
kidnapping, 49, 53, 54, 177, 185
kinship, 30, 203n27
kisaeng (Korean legal prostitutes), 5
Kitagawa Morisada, 103, 104
Koikawa Shōzan, 131
Konpira, 16, 152, 163, 164; in ranked list of brothel districts, 104; temple-shrine complex at, 15, 171; underworld figures and, 178
Korea, 5, 31, 209n17
Koshigaya station, 141, 147, 157
Kōzuke province, 14, *139*, 144, 149, 152
Kubota, town of, 27, 28–29, 33, 36, 202n12
kugutsu (medieval sexual entertainers), 30
Kumagaya station, *139*, 158, 159, 214–15n2
Kusanagi Enseki, 152
Kusumoto Taki, 93–94. See also Sonogi
Kyoto, city of, 6, 35, 41, 168; actresses in, 49; brothel keepers in, 46, 205n2; as emperor's capital, 46; number of prostitutes in, 103, 105; rules for brothels in, 54; as thriving urban center, 8. See also Shimabara "pleasure quarter"

laborers, 26, 29, 32, 36, 105, 115
laundry girls (*sentaku onna*), 15, 127–28
licensing fees (*myōgakin*), 122
Life of an Amorous Woman, The [*Kōshoku ichidai onna*] (Saikaku), 60
Lindsey, William, 53, 88, 206n25
literacy and illiteracy, 19, 174, 221n36
literati, Confucian, 5
lover/"in-between man" (*maotoko*), 39, 204n65

"madame person of a narrow alley" (*zushigimi*), 31
"madame stander" (*tachigimi*), 31
magistrates, 7, 60, 66; brothel keepers and, 69, 84, 94; distant province magistrate (*ongoku bugyō*), 125; geisha and, 69; gendered order and, 47–48, 190; mine, 24, 27, 28, 40; in Nagasaki, 79, 81, 86, 87, 88, 190; in Niigata, 122, 126–27; in Osaka, 62; "pleasure quarters" and, 49, 50; profit-seeking parents and, 75; prostitutes' appeals to, 12; road magistrates (*dōchū bugyō*), 61, 62, 107, 159; in Sengoku era, 25; sex trade viewed as benevolence, 161–62; temple and shrine magistrates (*jisha bugyō*), 61; traffic in women and, 17
maidservants (*gejo*), 39, 42, 81, 87, 147; contracts of, 58; as debt collateral, 33; in Inland Sea region, 169; traffic in, 17, 29; in woodblock prints, 134, *135*
Maki Hidemasa, 32, 168
male prostitution, 15–16, 61, 124
market economy, xv, 108, 150, 196; established orders threatened by, 10, 18; female agency and, 186; gendered order undermined by, 190; rural development and, 8; samurai anxiety over, 132–33
marriage, 4, 38, 42, 51, 137, 187; as bondage, 47; Confucian ideals of, 5; definition of, 43; of "extra" prostitutes,

145; monogamous marriage promoted in Meiji era, 194–95; prostitution as threat to, 132, 153; prostitution prior to, xiii, 76, 81, 89–98; trafficking separated from, 59; widows and, 124, 132; Yoshiwara rituals as parody of, 53; *yūjo*'s paths toward, 89–98

Maruyama "pleasure quarter" (Nagasaki), 72, *73*, 75, *78*, 93; Dutch traders in, 209n19; in ranked list of brothel districts, 104; ward elders, 86

"masterless samurai" (*rōnin*), 28, 46, 48, 137

Matsudaira Sadanobu, 145

medieval period, 29–31, 205n2

Meiji era (1868–1912), 152, 192–96

Meijlan, G. F., 93

Meireki fire (1657), 60–61, 205n15

Memoirs of a Geisha (Golden), 4

men: as clients of male prostitutes, 15; control over women's bodies limited by Tokugawa state, 9; as geisha, 66; as household heads, 26; laborers, 32–33; prostitution as "problem about men," 131; transient population, 11

merchants, 12, 27, 29; apprentices of, 45; brothels as necessary amenity for, 121; in human trafficking, 31, 32; Nagasaki foreign trade and, 80; of Niigata, 115; samurai in debt to, 107; traveling, 164

microhistory, 164, 220n3

Mikado's Empire, The (Griffis), 3

mines/mining operations, 12, 26, 28–29, 42, 189, 202n11; prostitution and, 36; sex ratio in mining towns, 32; silver boom, 27

Mitarai, town of, 164, 165, 189; brothels of, 167, 171; commoners as town officials, 174; gun batteries of, 166; map, *168*; outlaw informers in, 178; population registers, 169, 183

Miyamoto Yukiko, 75

Mizuno Tadakuni, 125, 126

monogamy, xii, 5, 40, 130; as entitlement and obligation for wives, 9, 41, 56; with foreign partners, 93; monogamous marriage promoted in Meiji era, 194–95; suicide or mutilation as expression of desire for, 89, 210n54

Mori Arinori, 194

Morisaki Kazue, 192

motherhood, 76, 89, 95–97

Murata Ryūmin, 117, 118

Musashi province, 14, 134, *139*

musical instruments, 35

Nagano Hiroko, 54

Nagaoka domain, 18, 113, 125, 126; daughter selling in, 114–20; prostitution "ignored" by authorities, 120–25

Nagasaki, city of, 14, 17, 97, 98, 119, 189; brothel district, 50; Chinese ward, 79–80, 85, 94; foreign trade and, 76–80; map of, *78*; marriage of former prostitutes in, 89. See also Maruyama "pleasure quarter"; Yoriai ward

Nagasaki Maruyama no kei [*View of Maruyama in Nagasaki*] (Utagawa), *73*

Nakasendō Highway, 134, 141, 153, 158

naval bases, 192

Nenzi, Laura, 124

Niigata, city of, 15, 18, 104, 189; domestic sea trade and, 114; Furumachi district, 111, 126, 127; map of, *112*; prostitution "ignored" by officials in, 120–25; smuggling in, 125; Tenpō Reforms and, 125–31; Teramachi, 111, 126, 127

Nijenroode, Cornelis van, 77

Nikkō Highway, 117, 141, 142, 157

noh theater, 105

obstetricians, male, 149

Occupation period, 196

odoriko (dancers), 66, 208n72

Oine, 93

oiran, 14

One Hundred Articles, 50, 56, 61, 69
Onna isshō michi shirube (A Woman's Map through Life), 81, *82*
Ooms, Herman, 27, 28
Opium War, first, 125
orandayuki (going to the Dutch), 80
Orientalist stereotypes, 3–4
Osaka, battle of (1615), 202n11
Osaka, city of, 6, 105, 108, 125, 168; Shinmachi licensed "pleasure quarter," 48, 49, 56, 61–62; as thriving urban center, 8; undeveloped neighborhoods, 138
Oshioki saikyochō (Collection of Punishments and Precedents), 49, 56, 65
outcasts, 8, 26
outlaws (*kyōkaku*), 176–80, 183
Overall, Christine, 200n5

panpan girls, 196
parents, 7, 9, 70, 100, 187; adoptive, 68; attitudes toward prostitution, 55–56, 128; children exploited by, 8, 97; in conflict with brothel keepers, 19, 86–88, 165, 178, 184–85; illness of prostitute daughters and, 84, 172; marriage of prostitute daughters and, 90; prostitutes' salaries paid to, 4, 161; protective, 17, 75, 76; sex without permission of, 150; "shamelessness" of, 128–29, 131; shogunal laws on guardianship and, 55; supported by prostitute daughters, 71; Tokugawa rulers analogous to, 75. *See also* families/family ties
passivity, as feminine virtue, 124, 186
Pateman, Carole, 131
patriarchal order, xii, 7, 66; benign patriarchal authority, 86; contract system and, 70; filial daughters and political stability, 85; household and, 54; market economy as threat to, 161; Neo-Confucian "benevolent ruler" ideal and, 47; patriarchs as child sellers, 8; prostitutes as threat to, xiv–xv, 187; shogunal laws and, 54–55; threatened by social/economic changes, xiii, 6; Tokugawa rulers and, 9, 47, 48; "widows" (*goke*) and, 130; *yūjo* as dutiful daughters and, 76
peasants, xiv, 3, 71, 107, 163, 190; "broken peasants," 116; crisis of countryside and, 136; daughter selling of, 115–18, 129; disarming of, 25; discretionary income of, 13; expansion of sex trade and, 18–19; failed promise of reforms and, 153–60; girls recruited from peasant class, 12; petitions for tax relief, 75–76; rebellions of, 86; sold into slavery, 31–32; in status order, 26; tax revenues extracted from, 8; travel culture and, 113; wealthy, 105, 136. *See also* villages
"perisexual" behavior, 49, 69
petitions (*gansho, sojō*), 19
Pflugfelder, Gregory, 16, 49
pilgrimage sites, 2, 14, 107, 108, 163; geography of sex trade and, 11, 12; of Inland Sea region, 19, *168*, 176
pimps, 6, 31, 60; husbands as, 63, 65, 70; punished for "illicit sexual intercourse," 5
playwrights, 71
"pleasure quarters" (*kuruwa, yūkaku*), 1, 10, 48–53, *52*, 107; in Inland Sea region, 169; licensed and unlicensed women in, 14; Meiji era closing of, 194; post-station inns compared with, 140, 149; ranked list of, 103, *104*; service in, as punishment, 61
port towns, 10, 107, 169; competition between, 167; of Inland Sea, 19, 163; prostitutes' prices in, xxii; serving girls in, 15; "vegetable-selling women" in, 170
Portuguese traders, 31, 32, 77
postmodern era, 197

post roads, 12, 18, 137
post stations, xiv, 10, 14, 64–65, 99; brothels outside, 69; change in, 137–38, 140–45; failed promise of reforms and, 153–60; "hill places," 61; map of, *139*; number of prostitutes in, 105; peasant youths and, 145–47; serving girls in, 2; status order and, 62; on Tōkaidō Highway, 103; village headmen in conflict with, 154–55
poverty, 119, 129, 130
pregnancies, 94–95, 96, 149
prices, xxi–xxii, 68, 87; charged by "widows" (*goke*), 124, 213n42; in post stations, 145–46;
procurers, 12, 23, 117
promiscuity, female, xiv, 5–6, 150, 197; adultery and, 4–5; Meiji-era intellectuals' view of, 194–95; stigma attached to, xiii, 4, 7, 130; of "widows" (*goke*), 124, 213n38
property rights, 30, 37
prostitutes: abuse of, 86–88, 97, 98, 143–44, 181; age of, 123; boundary with "ordinary" women, 15; clothes, 50, *74*, 122, 150, 151–52; death of, 57, 58, 141–42, 173, 221n35; as embodiment of consumerist values, xiv; as "famous products" (*meibutsu*), 18, 108, 111, 113; foreign clients of, 72; hair styles and ornaments of, 72, *74*, 152, 190, 197; indentured to brothels as children, 4; itinerant, 164, 171, 177, 184; market values represented by, 109; married, 41, 47; in medieval period, 31; in Meiji era, 195, 196; names for, 14–15; number of women employed as, 1–2, 103, 105, 193; obligations to parents and employers, 72, 208n8; paternalistic status system and, xi; paternal state as protector of, xii; prostitute as iconic figure, 1; resistance to brothel keepers' authority, 17, 99; scapegoating of, xv, xvi; status categories for, 44; stigmatization of, xiii, 166; travelers and, 106; venereal disease testing for, 195; voices and stories of, 19; in Yoshiwara, 53. *See also* clandestine prostitutes; geisha; indentured prostitutes; serving girls; *yūjo*
prostitution: as business, 6; in China, xv, 5; criminalization of, xv; economic impact of, 1, 158–59, 189–90; female agency and, xi, xiii, 4; households destroyed by, 10; "ignored" by officials, 120–25; legality of, xii, 5, 14–15; male, 15–16, 61, 124; market economy and, 108; proposed abolition of, 154, 155, 160, 193; as secondary occupation, 66; ten-year limit of service, 53, 59, 62; as threat to social order, 99–100; transition to marriage and motherhood, 89–98; vital economic role of, xv. *See also* male prostitution; sex trade
Purity Society (*Kakuseikai*), 195

Qing dynasty (China), 120, 123

railroads, 192
Ransen nyūkō no zu [*Arrival of a Dutch Ship*] (Kawahara), *74*
rape, 30, 93
rice cultivation, 28, 36, 122, 164, 166; as assigned occupation, 8–9; Bunsei Reforms and, 155; crisis of countryside and, 153, 156; in Echigo province, 115; expansion of sex trade and, 105; market economy and, 137; taxes and, 8, 106, 114, 163, 171
"river sellers," 111
roads, 12, 105, 154
"room rental establishments" (*kashizashiki-gyō*), 194
rules of teahouses, xiii, 19, 165, 179, 183. *See also* teahouses
"rules of the pleasure quarter" (*kuruwa no kisoku*), 179, 180, 184

INDEX · 251

sailors, 11, 13, 77, 107, 189; brothels as necessary amenity for, 121; diversions for enticement of, 164; revenue stream of sex trade and, 113, 169

samurai, xiii, 6, 17, 19, 71; anxiety about market economy, 132–33; benevolent government ideal and, 160, 190; control of sex trade, 106; cultural activities and, 105; economic problems of, 106–7; female promiscuity viewed by, 130–31; forced to abandon countryside, 25; Inland Sea officials, 169; lament over decline of countryside, 136; magistrates and, 12, 99; masterless (*rōnin*), 27, 46, 48, 137; profitability of prostitution and, 44; prostitutes criticized by, 7, 149, 187; prostitutes seen as autonomous economic actors, 192; rebellion against shogunate, 9; responsibilities delegated to, 8; sex trade seen as destabilizing force, 10; violent pacification of domains, 27

Satake Yoshinobu, 27, 28, 202n11

Satō Nobuhiro, 111, 118

Scott, Joan, xi, 9

Segawa Kiyoko, 152

Sekigahara, battle of (1600), 27, 30, 48

"selling women" (*baijo, baita*), 2, 6, 14, 190, 203n33

Sengoku era (1467–1568), xi, 23, 25

servants, hereditary (*fudai genin*), 30, 202n22

serving girls (*meshimori onna*), 2, 15, 61, 62, 161, 215n14, 219n96; absent from Meiji-era nostalgia, 195; as concubines, 152–53; as daughters working on behalf of families, 63; elite village culture challenged by, 151–52; families supported by, 162; fertility control practiced by, 149; marriage of, 145; in post stations, 61, 117, 137, 141, 157, 189, 207n57; urban prostitutes as models for, 155, 156; village youths and, 159

sex: exchanged for payment, 7, 161; extramarital, xv, 56, 93, 194; "illicit sex" (*mittsū*), 5, 68, 79; premarital, 5, 150; religious beliefs and practices concerning, 4; reproduction separated from, 148–49; unruly sexual behavior, 51–52

sex ratios, 32, 116, 144

sex trade, 48, 76, 187; confined to designated space, 49; cultural production surrounding, 1; deregulation of, xii; disregard for jurisdictional distinctions, 106; as economic benefit, 127; filial piety and, 88, 118–19; geography of, xiv, 11–14, *13*; in Inland Sea region, 164, 167; in Innai Ginzan, 35–38; in late medieval period, 31; marketization of, xii–xiii; Meiji era laws and, 194; organization of, 12–16; Orientalist stereotypes of, 3–4; part-time and temporary sex work, xiii, 2; postmodern visibility of, 197; proposed abolition of, 154; sex work as free choice, xiii, xiv, 4; stigma and female agency, xi; studies based on history of sexuality and the body, 5, 200n13; tax revenues and, 122; Tokugawa history and, 8–11. *See also* prostitution

sex trade, expansion of, xii, 3, 6, 10, 17; deterioration of social order and, 121; market revolution and, 105; Meiji state and, 193; patriarchal household undermined by, 190; in rural areas, 137, 161; social order improved by, 69; turn away from regulation and, 107–8

sexual pleasure guide literature, 16

shamisen, skill in playing, 35, 60, 68, 81, 156

Shanghai, prostitution in, xv, 19, 120, 199n4 (Foreword), 201n25

Shanks' Mare [*Tōkaidōchū hizakurige*] (Jippensha Ikku), 52, 138

Shikidō Ōkagami [*The Great Mirror of Love*] (Fujimoto), 103

Shimabara "pleasure quarter" (Kyoto), 48, 49, 56, 62, 71
Shimojū Kiyoshi, 43
Shimonoseki, city of, 52
Shinbo Jōwa [Frank Conversations from the Port of Niigata] (Imamura), 118, 121
shingintori (new money takers), 213n35
Shinkoku Hizen Nagasaki zu (New Edition of Nagasaki in Hizen), *78*
shipyards, 192
shogunate, 16, 43, 98, 120–21; benevolent government ideal of, 54, 63, 65; brothel keepers and, 45; collapse of, 9; filial piety promoted by, 85; informers and spies for, 177; law codes of, 30; pacification of Japanese archipelago, 8; policy shifts, 59–63, 69; post-station inns and, 141, 155, 160; prostitution promoted by, 69–70; reform edicts, 156; status order of, xi, 26, 46, 47; strategic territories acquired by, 125; surveillance of prostitutes, 14; transportation system, 138; wary of rebellion in early period, 48; *yūjo* of Nagasaki and, 75. *See also* inspectors, shogunal; Tokugawa era
Shokoku yūsho kurabe (A Ranking of Pleasure Districts in the Various Provinces), *104*
shopkeepers, 26, 177
short stories, 16
Siebold, Phillip Franz von, 93–94, 96
slavery/slave trade, 31–32, 202–3n27; enslavement as punishment for female offenders, 32; in United States, 132
smuggling, 80, 84, 97, 99, 125, 209n21
Sone Hiromi, 14, 168–69
Sonogi, 93, 96. *See also* Kusumoto Taki
Stanley, Amy Dru, 132
Stansell, Christine, 150
status order, 11, 26, 62, 88, 165; market economy and, 192; petitions to officials and, 75–76; prostitutes' self-determination and, 97; village elites and, 191. *See also* "containers," of status order; gendered political order
stigma, xiii–xiv, 4, 6, 7, 109; economic change and, 166; female agency and, xi; female promiscuity and, 130; legal prostitutes' immunity to, 98; peasant elites and, 161
streetwalkers, 2, 14–15, 59–60, 66; absent from Meiji-era nostalgia, 195; labor patterns of, 63; in Niigata, 126; in Shanghai, 201n25; as threat to ideal of benevolent government, 70
Sugano Noriko, 85
suicides, 39, 67, 89
sumo wrestlers/wrestling, 36, 60, 103, 114, 164, 177
sumptuary regulations, 46, 127

Taiheki shiroishi banashi [*The Tale of Shiroishi and the Taihei Chronicles*] (kabuki play), 55
Taishō period, 193
Takehara, town of, 163, *168*, 173, 179, 180
taxes, xii, 8, 12, 47, 119; "alternate attendance" policy as form of taxation, 26; collection of, 17; credit and, 107; daughter selling and, 120; evasion of, 2; "installment payments," 193; land taxes as primary source of Tokugawa revenue, 106; on maritime commerce, 113; parents' difficulty paying, 129; petitions for tax relief, 76; prostitute levy (*keisei yaku*), 35–36; prostitution and increased revenues, 48, 215n14; unpaid, 153; violent extortion of, 28; women sold to meet tax obligations, 43
tayū, 14
teahouses (*chaya, kagemajaya, tomarijaya*), 16, 59, 61, 62; geisha in, 68; in Inland Sea region, 170, 179; in

teahouses (*continued*)
  Niigata, 127; in Takehara, 163. *See also* rules of teahouses
tea-serving girls (*chakumi onna*), 127, 128
tea-steeping girls (*chatate onna*), 15, 62
technologies, postmodern sex trade and, 197
temples, 12, 57, 62, 111; Eitaiji, 61; Ekōin, 61; Kannōji, 61; Konpira complex, 15, 163, 164; Sensō ji, 50
Tenpō Reforms (1842), 65, 66, 126, 199n2 (Introduction); as attempt to restore political stability, 125; Edo magistrates' opposition to, 128; prostitutes forbidden to leave "pleasure quarter," 84, 127
Thal, Sarah, 169
Tōkaidō Highway, 103, 140, 166
Tōkaidō meishoki [*A Guide to Famous Places along the Tōkaidō*] (Asai), 140
Tokugawa era (1600–1868), xv, 1, 2, 69, 136; close of, 164, 195; cultural dynamism of, 10; culture of play, 191; economic problems, 106–7; history of sex trade, 8–11; Nagasaki's foreign trade, 76–80; as "regime of conquest" in early period, 27–28; shoguns, 25–26; stigmatization of prostitutes, xiii, xiv. *See also* shogunate
Tokugawa Ieyasu, xi–xii, 25, 77
townspeople, 3, 33, 92, 190; daughters indentured to brothels, 12; geisha and, 67; of Inland Sea, 163–64; monopolies on daily necessities of, 36, 203n48; Nagasaki *yūjo* and, 83; of Niigata, 115, 127, 128–29, 133; sexual practices, 4; in status order, 26; travel culture and, 113
Toyotomi Hideyoshi, 25–26, 31, 32, 53, 103
trafficking, human, 29, 31–32, 42; in Echigo province, 115–20; proclamations outlawing, 32; shogunal laws against, 53

Traganou, Jilly, 134
transportation routes/system, 12, 13, 113, 160, 191
travelers, 13, 105–6; in Fukaya, 134–35; post-station prostitution and, 138; sexual services provided to, 18; in *Shanks' Mare*, 52; village youths disguised as, 156–57
trousseau, bridal, xiii, 77
Tsukada Takashi, 49, 63–64

Umezu Masakage, 14, 24–25, 28–29; conflicting roles and identities of women and, 39–42; kabuki performances allowed by, 36, 204n50; as procurer of women, 32–33; prostitution in Innai Ginzan and, 36–38; women viewed as property assets by, 34–35, 42, 44
Umezu Noritada, 28
United States: images of Japanese prostitution, 3–4; slavery and prostitution in, 132, 133
Usami Misako, 14
Utagawa Hiroshige II, 73

"vegetable-selling women" (*yasai uri fujin*), 170
village headmen and elders, 7, 16, 109, 136, 137, 138; post-station prostitution and, 146, 148, 161; serving girls' challenge to authority of, 151–52, 153
villages, xiv, 12, 16, 106; "assisting villages" (*sukegō*), 138, 156, 160, 164; consumer culture in, 13; crisis of countryside and, 136, 145–53; destroyed in civil wars, 31; failed promise of reforms and, 153–60; hierarchical relationships in, 18; population density, 11; saved by prostitution, 7; in status order, 26; tax burden on peasants, 8. *See also* peasants

waitresses, 66, 154, 168

Walthall, Anne, 76, 85
warlords, 25
Warring States era. *See* Sengoku era
Watanabe Kazan, 158
Watanabe Kenji, 14
wet nurses, 96, 211n81
White, Luise, 74
"whores" (*baita*), 6, 15, 60
widows, 5, 147; geography of sex trade and, 11; promiscuity associated with, 124, 213n38; remarriage of, 4; war widows, 31
"widows" (*goke*), 15, 111, 123–25, 126, 131; absent from Meiji-era nostalgia, 195; "choice" of selling sex, 130; Kawamura's criticism of, 129–30
Wigen, Kären, 106
wives, 33–35, 42, 53, 59, 114, 206n25; chastity ideal and, 5; as debt collateral, 33–34; fertility control practiced by, 160–61; of fishermen, 123; of free commoner status, xv; husbands' authority over, xii, 24, 25; pawned, 41, 43, 47; prohibition of traffic in wives, 43; property rights and, 38; punished for prostitution with husbands' permission, 56, 206n38; runaway, 23–25, 34, 41; serving girls resented by peasant wives, 152–53; social/economic autonomy for, 6; traffic in, 17, 29
women: adulterous, 39; in agricultural labor, 150; American views of Japanese women, 3–4; as autonomous economic actors, 7; as clients of male prostitutes, 15; as commodities, xvi, 10; Confucian moral views of, 5; divided into wives and prostitutes, 9–10, 24, 29, 43, 53; household and, 54; magistrates and, 29; "ordinary," 79, 169, 172; place within families, 3; poor women caught up in sex trade, 18; as property, 17, 30; reproductive autonomy of, 148–49, 151; "shameless," 18, 109; status transformation under Tokugawa order, xi, xii, 9, 47; subjugation of, 1; working-class, xv
woodblock prints, 1, 72, 134

Yabuta Yutaka, 116, 150
Yonemoto, Marcia, 52
Yonezawa domain, 43
Yongzheng era (China, 1723–35), xv
Yoriai ward (Nagasaki), 75, 78–79, *78*, 80; births in, 95; brothel keepers' association, 84, 87; conflicts over broken contracts, 90–91; Dutch traders in, 209n19; in ranked list of brothel districts, 104; *yūjo*'s relationships with foreigners, 94
Yoshida Nobuyuki, 64
Yoshiwara "pleasure quarter" (Edo), 2, 48, 55, 140; establishment of, 46, 69; as fantastic, separate world, 52; geisha in, 67; Great Gate, 49, *51*, 52; headman and elders of, 53; "hill places" (*okabasho*) and, 65; intelligence-gathering function of, 51–52; masterless samurai in, 48; as model for Niigata, 127; monopoly on prostitution, 50, 60, 61, 63, 69; number of prostitutes in, 105; rank of prostitute types, 14; Shin-Yoshiwara (New Yoshiwara), 50, *51*, 104, 199n2 (Introduction); as site of punishment for women, 50; term of service in, 62
yotaka (night hawk), 14
youths, local, 16, 18, 137, 145–47, 150; disguised as travelers, 156–57; family wealth squandered on prostitutes, 107, 145–46, 154, 160; rice cultivation and, 191; seduced from their duties, xiv, 159
yūjo, 1, 59, 76, 146, 184; in artworks, *74*; barriers to marriage for, 89; bathing girls compared with, 60; as cultural or sexual mediators, 74; definition of, 14–15; families of, 74–75, 95, 97; filial

yūjo (continued)
ties in Nagasaki, 83–89; foreigners as clients of, 78–83, 92–94; indenture contracts of, 56–58; in Inland Sea region, 167, 169; literacy training of, 19; magistrates and, 99; Meiji-era nostalgia and, 195; number of women employed as, 2, 199n2 (Introduction); of Osaka, 62, 168; part-time or "nominal," 83; in "pleasure quarters," 14; "serving girls" compared with, 15, 156; short leaves granted to, 85; transition to marriage and motherhood, 89–98; wet nurses in temporary role as, 96; in Yoshiwara, 46, 72, 79, 84

Yūjo daigaku (The Greater Learning for Prostitutes), 71

Zheng Zhilong, 77

Text:	10.25/14 Fournier
Display:	Fournier
Compositor:	BookComp, Inc.
Printer and binder:	IBT Global